'Dark, compelling, and illuminating. Bennetts meets priests,
lawmakers, spin-doctors, ordinary Russians, left-wing
agitators, and riot cops in this vivid first-hand portrait.'
Luke Harding, *Guardian* correspondent and author of *Mafia State:
How One Reporter Became an Enemy of the Brutal New Russia*

'A lively, sardonic account of Putin's reign and those opposed to it.'
Metro

'Electrifying.'
Booklist

'An engagingly grim, frequently absurdist portrait of
Vladimir Putin and the popular protests against him.'
Kirkus Reviews

'This book gives a fascinating peek at the shifting political
landscape in one of the world's most opaque nations.'
Press Association

'[An] entertaining book… The huge variety of his interviews, through
which he elicits a pleasing selection of anecdotes, as well as accusations of
being a foreign spy, shows his familiarity with the country and its people.'
We Love This Book

'Colourful and authoritative. The best account of Russia's
protest movement and Putin's ferocious crackdown.'
Angus Roxburgh, author of *The Strongman: Vladimir Putin and the Struggle for Russia*

'Vivid and insightful. Bennetts captures a transitional moment in
Russian history. Years from now, when researchers are seeking to explain
the second Putin era, they would do well to use this reportage.'
Daniel Kalder, author of *Lost Cosmonaut*

'Bennetts has done an excellent job of drawing together
the scattered beads of a sobering story.'
Susan Richards, author of *Lost and Found in Russia: Encounters in a Deep Heartland*

ABOUT THE AUTHOR

Marc Bennetts is a British journalist based in Moscow, where he has lived for the past fifteen years. He has reported from Russia, Iran, and North Korea for the *Guardian*, *The Times*, the *Observer, Politico* and the *New York Times*, among other publications.

www.marcbennetts.com
@marcbennetts1

Marc Bennetts

I'M GOING TO RUIN THEIR LIVES

ONEWORLD

A Oneworld Book

Originally published as *Kicking the Kremlin*
by Oneworld Publications, 2014
This extended edition published 2016

Copyright © Marc Bennetts 2014, 2016

ISBN 978-1-78074-524-4
eISBN 978-1-78074-432-2

Printed and bound in Great Britain by Clays Ltd, St Ives plc

Oneworld Publications
10 Bloomsbury Street
London WC1B 3SR
England

Stay up to date with the latest books,
special offers, and exclusive content from
Oneworld with our monthly newsletter

Sign up on our website
www.oneworld-publications.com

CONTENTS

To Daniil Kharms, Viktor Tsoi,
and the mountains of the Altai

PROLOGUE

ONE DAY IN DECEMBER

'*Rossiya bez Putina!*' came the chant. Then again, louder now, as if the tens of thousands of protesters had convinced themselves the first time around that such a thing might actually be attainable. 'Russia without Putin! Russia without Putin!'

The words floated high into the Russian capital's frigid winter skies. The slogan would, a speaker promised as demonstrators stamped their feet to keep warm, be audible in the nearby Kremlin. Especially if the protesters turned towards its elaborate towers, still topped by Soviet-era ruby-red stars, and shouted the rallying cry once more.

Up until that exact moment, the possibility of a Russia without Vladimir Putin in charge had appeared about as probable as a Moscow winter without snow. Or, perhaps, a Russia without the engrained, high-level corruption that had seen the country slide to the very lower reaches of Transparency International's global corruption index, sharing 143rd place out of 182 nations with Nigeria.[1]

But, on 10 December 2011, at Moscow's Bolotnaya Square, less than a week after what had looked like a blatant case of mass vote-rigging to secure Putin's United Russia party an unlikely parliamentary majority, nothing was unthinkable anymore. Moscow's richest and most educated residents – the so-called 'creative class' – were suddenly out on the streets in an unprecedented show of discontent. Even rank-and-file riot police looked taken aback at the size of the crowd. I spotted a group of officers taking snapshots of protesters, including a bride still in her white wedding dress, on mobile phones. (This could, of course, quite easily have been for surveillance purposes.)

'To fight for your rights is easy and pleasant. There is nothing to be afraid of,' said Alexei Navalny, the opposition's de facto leader, in a message passed out of a Moscow detention facility. 'Every one of us has the most powerful and only weapon we need – a sense of our own worthiness.'[2]

Could Putin hear them? I wondered. Could he hear the disparate gathering of liberals, nationalists and leftists? The humiliated and the insulted? And, if he could, what did he feel? Fear? Shock? Or, perhaps, scorn? While large-scale dissent was a new thing for modern Russia, Putin could still boast of approval ratings that were the envy of any Western leader. He also possessed an incomparable control over national television channels, the main source of news for the vast majority of Russians.

I looked around the square at the families, the pensioners, the young men and women flush with the excitement of participation in a genuinely historic moment. 'I never thought I'd see this,' a veteran activist told me, the words pouring from her. 'In the past, a few hundred people turned up to protest rallies, but just look at how many there are here now. A lot of people have come to a demonstration for the first time – and not the last.'

✱

The mass anti-Putin protests that began in Moscow that afternoon confounded analysts and inspired Kremlin critics, both of whom had believed that the ex-KGB officer's long stranglehold over political life meant such a thing was all but impossible. As crowds wearing the white ribbons that quickly became the symbol of the protest movement filled the streets of the Russian capital, Putin's foes could have been forgiven for believing that their arch-nemesis's days were numbered. The Kremlin seemed initially uncertain how to respond to the mass protests, alternately threatening and making half-hearted proposals on political reform. 'It appeared back then to many people that victory was just around the corner,' recalled Sergei Udaltsov, the fiery, shaven-headed leftist who 'symbolically' tore up a Putin portrait to ecstatic applause at a February 2012 Moscow rally.[3]

It would not be quite so easy to get rid of the man himself. 'Do we love Russia?' Putin yelled at a rare presidential election campaign rally in south Moscow in the spring of 2012, jabbing his finger into the driving sleet. 'Of course we do,' he continued, after the cries of '*da*' had faded away. 'And there are tens of millions of people like us all across Russia.

'The battle for Russia goes on!' Putin told the crowd, many of them bussed in en masse from the country's conservative heartland, as his speech came to an end, his hand reaching up then swiftly down as if to snatch victory from the chill Moscow air. 'And we will triumph!'[4]

Inevitably, within weeks of Putin's controversial return to the Kremlin in May 2012, the long-expected clampdown began. 'They ruined my big day,' Putin was reported to have said of the protesters who had marred his inauguration for a third presidential term. 'Now I'm going to ruin their lives.'[5]

First, a series of laws designed to make open dissent harder and more dangerous was fast-tracked through a compliant parliament. Next, Putin and his allies in the increasingly powerful Investigative Committee – an FBI-style law-enforcement agency answerable only to the president – systematically set about neutralizing the protest leaders and their most vocal supporters through a combination of smear campaigns, politically motivated criminal charges and darkly absurd show trials.

'No 1937!' chanted protesters, a reference to the year that saw the peak of Soviet dictator Joseph Stalin's Great Terror, as the first opposition figures were jailed or charged. For many, the analogy was insulting to the millions of victims of Stalin's purges: after all, for now at least, no one was being shot in the back of the head or sent to the frozen north to be worked to death. But for Russia's modern-day dissidents, as they languished in grimy pre-trial detention centres or served time in remote penal colonies, there could be little doubt that the Kremlin had regained a taste for political repression.

It was an appetite that swelled to new, monstrous proportions when neighbouring Ukraine erupted with revolutionary fervour, and an unlikely combination of liberals, nationalists and leftists, as well as hundreds of thousands of 'ordinary' people, united to drive the country's pro-Moscow president, Viktor Yanukovych, from power. Fearful that this passion for protest could spread to Russia, Putin escalated his war on dissent.

In the aftermath of Russia's annexation of Crimea in March 2014, Putin lashed out at his detractors, denouncing them as a 'fifth column' and 'national traitors', the latter insult a term he had borrowed from Adolf Hitler. Once-marginal nationalist groups gained a new prominence. Less than a week after tens of thousands of Kremlin supporters had marched through central Moscow calling for the 'destruction' of the opposition, Boris Nemtsov, one of the anti-Putin movement's most recognizable figures, was gunned down in front of the Kremlin walls. For many in the opposition who had seen out the first wave of Putin's fightback, Nemtsov's murder was the signal to flee Russia, while they still could.

However, even the very real dangers associated with opposing the Kremlin would be unable to extinguish the protest movement entirely. 'Wake up Russia!' read a flyer handed out at a Moscow demonstration, and, for many, the protests were life-changing events, transforming thousands of once apathetic Russians into active opponents of Putin's rule. Backing down when the going got tough was simply not an option.

✳

For this book, I have explored Russia's beleaguered protest movement in all its bewildering diversity, from the radical left-wingers seeking to set the country once more on the path to communism to the iPad-toting hipsters who, as one young activist put it, wish to 'live in Europe, without leaving Russia'. I sought out not only its high-profile leaders and the lesser-known activists who have formed the backbone of the movement, but also its opponents, from pro-Kremlin officials to church leaders. Like the protest movement itself, my investigations are focused largely, but not exclusively, on Moscow. Discontent may be widespread in the provinces, but it is in the Russian capital that history has always been made.

Over fifteen years after he first addressed Russians as their new president, it is hard to recall a time when the 'national leader' of the largest country on Earth was a virtual unknown, a faceless politician who was expected to be little more than a footnote in post-Soviet Russia's short history. But Putin proved the sceptics wrong, first consolidating and then strengthening his unlikely grip on power. He shows few signs of wanting to let go.

1

PUTIN'S PACT

President Boris Yeltsin had earned a reputation for the sensational and the unpredictable during his two terms in the Kremlin, from ordering tanks to shell an unruly Russian parliament, to playing the spoons on the bald head of Askar Akayev, the president of ex-Soviet Kyrgyzstan. And, on 31 December 1999, with the world fretting over the potential menace to global security posed by the Y2K millennium computer bug, Yeltsin captured the headlines again.

'I am leaving. I have done all I could,' modern Russia's first president said as he addressed the nation for the final time, his words slurred by a combination of ill health and a well-documented alcohol problem. Bloated and sickly, Yeltsin bore little resemblance to the energetic and charismatic politician who in 1991 had defied Communist hardliners seeking to overturn Soviet leader Mikhail Gorbachev's reforms.

The timing of Yeltsin's departure half a year ahead of the scheduled presidential elections was surprising, but his decision was welcomed by the overwhelming majority of Russians, who had grown weary of the poverty and lawlessness that their country had slid into following the sudden break-up of the Soviet Union.

'Many of our dreams failed to come true,' Yeltsin continued, with typical bluntness, as millions watched his televised speech. 'Things we thought would be easy turned out to be painfully hard. I am sorry that I did not live up to the hopes of people who believed that we could, with a single effort, a single strong push, jump out of our grey, stagnant, totalitarian past and into a bright, wealthy, civilized future.

'A new generation is coming,' he went on. 'They can do more, and better.'[1]

As the Kremlin clock ticked down to the new millennium, a grimfaced representative of that 'new generation' addressed Russia as acting president for the first time.

'Like you, I intended this evening to listen to the New Year greetings of President Boris Yeltsin,' said Vladimir Putin, the little-known, former security-services chief Yeltsin had recently appointed as Russia's third prime minister in less than a year. 'But things turned out otherwise.'

As if sensing his fellow citizens' yearning for a strong hand, the new president spoke firmly and deliberately. The contrast with the almost incoherent Yeltsin was striking.

'I want to warn that any attempt to exceed the limits of Russia's law and the Russian constitution will be decisively crushed,' Putin said. Then, without missing a beat, he made a pledge that his opponents would later accuse him of breaking, time and time again.

'The freedom of speech, the freedom of conscience, the freedom of the media and property rights, these fundamental principles of a civilized society will be protected by the state,' he declared, a Russian flag to his right.

Putin paused. This was the head of state's annual New Year's Eve address; even an acting president in the job for less than a day would be expected to offer a holiday toast.

'Let's raise a glass for a new century for Russia,' he said, his tone and expression unchanged. 'And for love and peace in every one of our homes.'[2] The camera faded out.

Putin had not smiled once during his more than three-minute speech. Watching in the company of Russian friends, I was not alone in noting he had also declined to drink to his own toast.

That night, as Russians saw in the New Year at parties across their vast country, when the talk turned to the new man in the Kremlin, it was inevitably positive. After years of Yeltsin's drunken antics, the teetotal, German-speaking Putin found strong initial support among young people, residents of Moscow and the highly educated. Ironically, these very same social groups would later form the core of the opposition to his rule.

'I really liked Putin when he first came to power,' recalled Yevgenia Chirikova, a bitter Kremlin critic who by her own admission was a 'political dunce' throughout most of Putin's first two terms. 'I remember how I used to cringe whenever they showed Yeltsin meeting foreign politicians. I'd think, "Oh no, he's going to embarrass us again." But Putin didn't drink, and that was important. He was young and he seemed very capable.'[3]

✱

I had arrived in Moscow for the first time in the spring of 1997, early on in Yeltsin's second term. Life back then in Russia was exhilarating, but also grotesque, as a people cast adrift from the safety nets of the Soviet system floundered in the rough waters of the free market. The ideologies that had dominated political and public life for most of the previous century had been unceremoniously tossed on to history's garbage dump, leaving a nation accustomed to a frequently dreary, predictable life centred on a lip-service to Marxism and Leninism to adapt to this strange new beast called capitalism. It was a task many were simply not up to: suicide rose, mental-health problems mushroomed and crime rocketed. Contract killings became almost an accepted mode of business negotiation. All over the country, fearful householders fitted steel doors.

Yeltsin and his government had wasted no time in introducing the 'shock therapy' economic reforms championed by their US advisers, and millions were quickly plunged into poverty. As ideological and economic uncertainties ravaged Russia, a centuries-old belief in the supernatural and the occult re-emerged to fill the gap left by the sudden collapse of the

Soviet system. Russians had once relied on Communist Party officials to organize their lives for them; in the 1990s they turned en masse to wild-eyed 'psychic healers' and urban 'wizards' to resolve their problems. A people unused to the complexities of capitalism were likewise easy game for financial conmen: millions suffered when a massive Ponzi scheme collapsed in 1994. In a sign of the widespread desperation, liberals began discussing the need for a 'Russian Pinochet' – the Chilean dictator who brought his homeland both terror and eventual economic prosperity.

Russia was a dead empire, rotting fast. It was a world where the weak suffered terrible indignities and the rich had no inhibitions about flaunting their newfound fortunes. For me, the chaos of the Yeltsin years was perhaps best summed up by the bribe of $20 that a group of brand-new and very drunk Muscovite friends gave a bus driver late one snowy night to persuade him to alter his scheduled route drastically and drop us off at their doorway. The driver hadn't even haggled, so eager was he to get his hands on the cash.

The break-up of the Soviet Union meant Russians were freer than they had ever been, but at what cost? Soviet propaganda had depicted life in the West as unrelenting misery for all but the very richest, and the 1990s seemed to prove the Communists had been right. 'Everything our leaders told us about communism was false. But it turns out that everything they told us about capitalism was true,' Russians joked bitterly.

Sights that had been almost unthinkable under the Soviet authorities became the norm in the newly independent Russia. Pensioners selling their household possessions piece by piece in filthy underpasses to buy their daily bread. Gangs of homeless children scavenging for food. Crippled soldiers back from Chechnya begging for money to drink away the day. Highly educated people – professors, lawyers, physicists – forced to moonlight as taxi drivers to supplement their meagre, or often non-existent, official salaries. The former superpower was visited by a host of humiliations.

On one evening in my first long, hazy winter in Moscow, I found myself drinking with strangers on a patch of snowy wasteland. 'We used to be a great country, you know? We could have fucked anyone over,' an unshaven, off-duty police officer muttered half to himself, half to me, before pouring another shot of vodka into the plastic cups that had appeared from nowhere.

Less than a year later, in August 1998, Russia defaulted on its debt, the rouble was devalued and millions lost their life savings – again.

In the euphoric aftermath of the largely peaceful collapse of the Soviet state, the well-known literary critic Yury Karyakin had declared: 'For the first time in this century, God has smiled on Russia.' As the 1990s dragged to an end, the Almighty, went the whispers, had turned His face away from Mother Russia. 'Russia is cursed,' a friend wailed late one night just after the default. 'The sooner I get out of here the better.'

'PUTIN SAVED RUSSIA'

Putin knew what his fellow citizens wanted and he intended to deliver. 'Russians have had no sense of stability for the past ten years,' he told state television in a wide-ranging interview less than two months after taking over from Yeltsin. 'We hope to return this feeling.'[4] And over the next eight years, he set about doing just that. By May 2008, towards the end of Putin's second term in office, Russia, on the surface at least, had been transformed. Its major cities, from the Pacific Coast to its European borders, were almost unrecognizable. On the bare spot of land where I had listened to the vodka-guzzling cop, a bright, three-storey shopping centre had sprung up. Salaries were not only being paid on time, but they were also higher than ever before. The disastrous war in Chechnya was as good as over and the devastated republic's capital, Grozny, was being reconstructed from scratch. Its central thoroughfare would soon be renamed 'Putin Avenue'. The Kremlin strongman may have ridden roughshod over post-Soviet democratic reforms and been aided immensely by rocketing prices for oil – Russia's main export and the lynchpin of its economy – but there was no denying that Russians had never had it so good.

Flush with oil dollars, the streets of Russia's major cities suddenly began to fill with advertisements for easy loans, or *kredit*, and a people long accustomed to thrift suddenly found they could afford foreign holidays, new cars and plasma-screen TVs. Although political freedoms were being curtailed and high-level corruption was soaring, it seemed churlish to complain about such things when you could spend two weeks a year sunning yourself at a Turkish Black Sea resort and then come back to your newly installed home entertainment centre. And the TV programmes Russians could now watch were not the comforting lies of Soviet-era broadcasting, where everything had been – as the Siberian punk rocker Yegor Letov once screeched caustically – 'going to plan'. The Kremlin's new spin doctors – 'political technologists' – were sharper than that. Modern Russian TV was not shy about the country's many problems. But the underlying message was this: 'If you think things are bad now, just remember what they were like under Yeltsin.'

And so Russians stayed, for the large part, silent as the independent media was strangled, the courts and parliament tamed, and money that should have been used to build up vital infrastructure was often siphoned out of the country. Yes, public health services were dangerously unfit for purpose, but at least you could choose from a dozen types of pizza – or cheaper and more available than ever vodka – at the new hypermarket. For the majority, it was simply a case of making the best of a bad deal; opinion polls regularly indicated that the vast majority of Russians felt they could have no influence on political developments. So why not take the sweeteners Putin was offering? A 13% flat income-tax rate introduced early on in Putin's first term did nothing to dissuade the tiny middle class that this unspoken agreement with the Kremlin was one worth sticking to.

'People agreed on a pact with the devil,' said Oleg Orlov, the veteran head of Memorial, Russia's oldest human-rights organization. 'They said, "We will stay out of the social and political process and concentrate on our private lives – just don't touch us and leave us a small slice of the profits from your oil booty."'[5]

It was, as the Russians like to say, a simple case of 'sausages in exchange for freedom'. Sausages, predictably, won out. 'What good is freedom of speech if my fridge is empty?' an elderly woman asked me in the central Russian city of Voronezh, midway through Putin's second term.

I wasn't sure what to reply, so I mumbled something about how, in an ideal world, she would have both. My answer didn't impress her.

'Both?' she retorted incredulously. 'Who is going to give me both?'

Putin also set about restoring national pride, which had been battered by the loss of Moscow's superpower status. For a people who had been brought up on stirring patriotic songs that proclaimed 'The Red Army is the strongest',[6] Russia's near impotence on the international arena throughout the 1990s was an unheralded disgrace. Under Yeltsin, a toothless Kremlin was powerless even to prevent NATO from bombing Serbia, Russia's Orthodox Christian ally, in 1999.

Much of what Putin did was cosmetic, such as the resumption of flights by strategic bombers over the Arctic, Atlantic and Pacific oceans in August 2007, but there was also a bite to the president's bark. In August 2008, Russian forces defeated the former Soviet republic of Georgia – and its US military advisers – in a five-day war over the breakaway republic of South Ossetia. 'Putin's Plan for Russia is Victory!' had read the propaganda posters in the months before fighting broke out, and, for many, the destruction of the Georgian military in the South Caucasus was mere confirmation that the 'national leader' was a man who delivered on his promises. In the immediate aftermath of the conflict, Putin's approval ratings soared to over 80%. Earlier the same year, in a sign of the Kremlin's growing confidence, Russia had displayed its intercontinental ballistic missile launchers on Red Square for the first time since the collapse of the Soviet Union. High-profile sporting triumphs and – bizarrely – a Russian victory at the Eurovision Song Contest were also hyped by state-run media as indications that the country was on the verge of regaining its superpower status.

It was around this time that the sale of Putin memorabilia went overboard – shops were suddenly full of clocks, mugs and even wall rugs bearing his image. 'Who buys a Putin wall rug?' I asked a shop assistant at a market near Moscow, unable to contain my curiosity.

'Usually office workers, for their bosses,' she told me, after a moment of hesitation while she considered whether to answer.

Putin's successes earned him praise from unlikely quarters. 'Putin inherited a ransacked and bewildered country, with a poor and demoralized people,' said Alexander Solzhenitsyn, the Nobel Prize-winning chronicler of Soviet gulags. 'And he started to do what was possible – a slow and gradual restoration. These efforts were not noticed, nor appreciated, immediately.'[7]

Solzhenitsyn was not the only fan. 'I want a man like Putin, full of strength / I want a man like Putin, who doesn't drink / I want a man like Putin, who won't offend me / I want a man like Putin, who won't run away,' went the lyrics to an infectious hit by a female pop duo.[8]

A few weeks after Russia had flashed its big guns at the world, I spent the afternoon wandering the streets of Tobolsk, a small, partially ramshackle town in west Siberia. I hadn't come to Tobolsk because of politics – I was on a travel-writing assignment – but everywhere I looked there seemed to be images of Putin. Eventually, tired by my explorations and weary of the sight of the ex-KGB man, I ended up at a local arts centre, where I made the acquaintance of Minsalim, a friendly, self-proclaimed shaman with unruly white hair and an obsession with Britain. Minsalim, it turned out, made a living by carving ornaments from the mammoth bone preserved in the region's permafrost soil, and he was eager to show off his work to me: 'Her Majesty's representative!' The centrepiece of his collection was a tiny figure that the shaman had somehow managed to invest with a startling resemblance to Russia's steely-eyed leader. 'Putin saved Russia – like a Siberian hero of old,' Minsalim intoned. He may have been a shaman, but I half expected him to cross himself.

In less than a decade, the little-known prime minister that Yeltsin had told to 'take care of Russia' had transformed himself into a modern-day tsar in the Kremlin, eliminating all but the most stubborn opposition to his rule. But who was he, this cocksure, diminutive man who emerged from the shadows of the security services to rule the largest country on Earth? What forces had shaped him, and how had he risen so far, so fast?

2

PUTIN AND HIS 'SOVEREIGN DEMOCRACY'

Born in 1952 in the Soviet Union's northern port city of Leningrad (now St Petersburg), Putin was – as he himself has admitted – a childhood 'hooligan'[1] who took up martial arts at school to 'assert my position in the pack'.[2] But his aggression was not limited to the judo mat, with Russia's future leader frequently scrapping it out on the streets of his hometown. His childhood fights, both his victories and his defeats, instilled in Putin a credo that would come to define his long rule as president and prime minister: 'I realized that in every situation – whether I was right or wrong – I had to be strong. I had to be able to answer back,' he would later say.[3]

Less than a year old when Joseph Stalin died in March 1953, Putin's early childhood coincided with 'the thaw' in political and cultural life ushered in by the dictator's successor as Soviet leader, Nikita Khrushchev. But his teenage years were spent in a Soviet Union ruled over by Leonid Brezhnev, the bushy-eyebrowed Communist Party leader who clamped down on Khrushchev's tentative and modest attempts at liberalization.

In 1966, just two years after Brezhnev had come to power, the Soviet Union witnessed its first show trials since the Stalin era, when the dissident writers Andrei Sinyavsky and Yuli Daniel were jailed for seven and five years, respectively, for publishing 'anti-Soviet agitation and propaganda' under pseudonyms abroad.

After university, Putin joined the KGB, an ambition born of Soviet-era films and books that glorified the secret police, but made no mention of the millions they had murdered during Stalin's Great Terror. 'I was a pure and utterly successful product of Soviet patriotic education,' he later reminisced.[4] But Putin was no Soviet super spy; he rose no higher than lieutenant colonel during his sixteen years in the KGB, and performed what he called 'ordinary intelligence' work in Dresden, East Germany – his only foreign posting. There is little reliable information on Putin's work in Dresden; one possibility is that he was tasked with entrapping and recruiting foreigners who were studying or working in the city. Soviet neighbours in Dresden remember a man who was able to 'put on a good spread'.[5]

Putin served just five years in East Germany, but this period coincided with the heady era back home of Gorbachev's perestroika and glasnost. As a result, Russia's future leader failed to experience at first hand the many dramatic changes taking place in Soviet society. He did not witness his fellow citizens' new willingness to denounce Stalin's crimes, nor the sudden passion for all things Western. As Gorbachev's reforms took hold, previously banned books and films flooded into bookshops and cinemas; people were now free to discuss subjects that would have once seen them jailed. It was a period of intense national soul-searching. 'Rarely, if ever, in its 1,000-year history was Russia as honest with herself' is how the Russian–American scholar Leon Aron describes these years.[6]

Putin's occasional trips home from East Germany appear to have overwhelmed him. It was, he later recalled, difficult to 'get used to reality' as he walked the streets of perestroika-era Leningrad, where everything seemed to be 'in a state of decay'.[7] And no wonder. East Germany in the late 1980s was a hardline Communist state, whose leader, Erich Honecker, was deeply hostile to the changes taking place in Moscow. He even banned 'subversive' Soviet magazines that championed perestroika. Those living in East Berlin and other East German cities may have been able to tune into Western TV broadcasts, but this was not the case in Dresden. Even Western radio stations were hard to pick up, had Putin wished to do so. Not for nothing was the city known by East Germans as 'the valley of the clueless'.[8] Having been isolated from the startling changes in his homeland, it is hard to imagine what must have gone through Putin's mind back in Leningrad when he switched on his TV set. Soviet television had once fed its viewers a steady diet of party congresses, rhythmic gymnastics and agricultural news; now there were mocking intellectuals discussing the possibility that 'Lenin was a mushroom'[9] and bizarre state-approved psychics pledging to cure the nation of its ills.

In January 1990, shortly after the collapse of the Berlin Wall, Putin left East Germany for the final time and returned to Leningrad. In a sign of the changes sweeping the Soviet Union, the city would soon revert to its pre-revolutionary name of St Petersburg. Unable or unwilling to find anything more exciting for the new arrival, Putin's KGB bosses appointed him assistant to the rector at Leningrad University, although his real job would be to spy on foreign students.[10] Soon after Putin took up his new post, one of the university's leading professors, Anatoly Sobchak, an enthusiastic advocate of Mikhail Gorbachev's reforms, was named head of the city government. Short on staff, Sobchak looked to his old university for personnel. A member of the law faculty recommended Putin, and Sobchak offered him a job as head of the city's foreign-relations department.

As Putin tells it, when he went for the job interview, he revealed to the unsuspecting Sobchak that he was a KGB officer, to which the startled democrat replied, 'Well, screw it,' and repeated his offer of work.[11] Impressed by this no-nonsense approach, Putin accepted. When Sobchak was elected city mayor in the summer of 1991, he took Putin with him to City Hall. Less than a year later, he appointed Putin his deputy.

That, at least, is Putin's version of events. Many Russian investigative journalists believe it was impossible for Sobchak not to have known Putin was in the KGB. It also remains unclear when exactly Putin resigned from the Soviet spy agency. He says he handed in his notice around a year before the botched 1991 takeover by Communist hardliners seeking to revive the Soviet Union, but that his letter was misplaced. This may or may not be true; in any event, he was still a KGB officer when the coup began.

✱

As post-Soviet chaos gripped St Petersburg, which quickly gained the moniker of 'Russia's crime capital', many Russians looked back wistfully to the certainties of the Communist era. Putin was among them. But, publicly at least, he remained committed to his homeland's break with its past. 'It sometimes seem to us – and I won't hide it, I sometimes think like this, too – that, if we had a firm hand to bring about order, then we would all live better, more comfortably, and in safety,' he said in a 1996 TV interview. 'But, in fact,' Putin went on, after a pause, 'this comfort would be very short-lived. This firm hand would quickly begin to strangle us all.'[12]

Was Putin genuine in his insistence in this interview that Russia needed a 'democratic system', and not a return to authoritarianism? Or was he merely parroting Sobchak's words for the cameras? The answer may be a little of both. However, it is important to understand that Putin had no real reason to want the return of autocratic Soviet rule. After all, he hadn't exactly flourished under communism. And, like the majority of Russians in the 1970s and 1980s, he was no fervent believer in the ideas of Marx and Lenin. Under Brezhnev, the Soviet Union's 'march to communism' ground to a halt in favour of 'developed socialism'. In other words, maintaining the status quo and the power of the elite. Yes, Putin later famously described the break-up of the Soviet Union as the 'greatest geopolitical catastrophe of the century', but his regret over the chaos and suffering that accompanied the disintegration of the superpower was misunderstood by Western commentators, often wilfully.

And democracy had been good to Putin. Sobchak may have liked to think of himself as a great democrat, but his rule was notoriously corrupt. There would have been ample opportunity for Putin to enrich himself. Indeed, his tenure as deputy mayor was marred by allegations of massive embezzlement, when he was accused of siphoning off millions of dollars in a food imports scheme. The official who investigated the allegations, Marina Salye, would estimate that some $100 million worth of goods had been sent abroad, but that the impoverished city had received almost no food in return. Suspecting that Putin had profited, Salye demanded his dismissal, but Sobchak protected his protégé. Putin denied the charges and claimed they were revenge for his KGB past.[13]

In 1996, after Sobchak was voted out of office, Putin moved to Moscow to take up the position of deputy head of the Kremlin's property-management department, later rising to deputy chief of the presidential administration. 'The injection of new blood is always beneficial,' Putin said before leaving for the Russian capital. 'And when that new blood is healthy, it is doubly advantageous.'[14]

In Moscow, Putin was taken under the wing of Yeltsin and his 'Family', the Kremlin's inner circle comprising of presidential administration officials, his influential daughter, Tatyana, and Boris Berezovsky, one of the powerful, so-called oligarchs: the men who had taken advantage of the post-Soviet chaos to carve up the country's resources among themselves.

With Yeltsin's approval ratings close to absolute zero, and the threat of international criminal investigations into suspected corruption looming, the president and his entourage needed someone they could trust to ensure their future safety. Putin was chosen because he was a relative newcomer to Moscow and had no serious connections among the capital's security and political elite. This KGB specialist in 'mingling with people',[15] as Putin once described himself, was seen as someone malleable, a yes-man who could be relied on to do as he was instructed.

Just two years on from his move to the Russian capital, in July 1998, Putin made a return to the world of the secret police, when Yeltsin named him head of the Federal Security Service (FSB), the KGB's successor. His welcome was reportedly frosty. He hadn't exactly enjoyed a glittering career in the KGB, and one of his reported duties as Yeltsin's deputy chief of staff had been to 'control the security services'.[16] As FSB head, Putin impressed the Family by blocking criminal investigations that threatened members of Yeltsin's entourage, including by approving the release of a sex-tape that discredited the country's top prosecutor. Just a year later, in August 1999, Yeltsin promoted Putin to prime minister, the second in the series of rapid appointments that would soon take the former childhood 'hooligan' all the way to the presidency.

TAKING THE KREMLIN

Yeltsin had named Putin his 'heir for the year 2000' when he appointed him prime minister, but, as the sixth politician to hold the post in eight years, there was little to suggest the prediction was anything but wishful thinking on the ailing president's part.

'Do you see Putin as president?' the respected broadsheet *Kommersant* asked a range of political figures just days after Putin took office. Not a single respondent said yes.

'Why on earth would anyone?' replied Alexei Mitrofanov, chairman of the Russian parliament's committee on geopolitics.

'I believe even Vladimir Putin does not see himself in this role,' said lawmaker Oleg Morozov, a future member of Putin's United Russia party.[17]

Not only would the rookie prime minister be up against rivals such as veteran statesman Yevgeny Primakov at the presidential polls, but he was also tainted by his association with the deeply unpopular Yeltsin.

As a result of Yeltsin's actions, Putin was faced with a growing crisis in Chechnya, the tiny, mainly Muslim republic in Russia's south that had been ravaged by a brutal separatist war. In 1996, as part of a ceasefire deal, Russia had granted the breakaway republic a de facto autonomy, delaying the issue of its future status. But Chechnya's president, Aslan Maskhadov, had proved unable or unwilling to clamp down on warlords who controlled much of the republic. Kidnapping raids into neighbouring Russian regions were growing more frequent and Islamic extremism had also taken hold, with amputations and public executions broadcast on live television. Chechnya had become a black hole on the map of Russia.

In August 1999, Chechen 'field commander' Shamil Basayev and the Jordanian-born Islamist Khattab – believed to have been an ally of Osama bin Laden – launched what they dubbed a 'liberation crusade' into the neighbouring republic of Dagestan. The Russian army was sent in, and eventually managed to drive the militants back into Chechnya. At the height of the fighting, Yeltsin fired Prime Minister Sergei Stepashin – a relative dove on Chechnya – and appointed Putin. The new head of the government wasted no time. According to Yeltsin, in his *Midnight Diaries* memoirs, Putin immediately requested 'absolute power' over Russia's security structures.

The request granted, Putin began sending troops to Chechnya's borders, ostensibly to ensure security in the region. With Russian forces poised, blasts tore through four apartment blocks in Moscow and the southern cities of Buynaksk and Volgodonsk between 4 and 16 September 1999, killing over 300 people and injuring more than 1,000. Russians were understandably terrified; in a bid to calm their nerves, an Interior Ministry soldier was stationed in every building in the capital.

Chechen militants denied responsibility for the blasts, but Putin had no reservations about apportioning guilt. 'If they're in the airport, we'll kill them there,' raged Putin. 'And excuse me, but, if we find them in the toilet, we'll waste them in the outhouse.' It was the first in a series of earthy remarks that would cement his image as a tough-talking, tough-acting leader. Within weeks, some 100,000 Russian troops had flooded back into Chechnya and war had returned to the republic.

Putin's no-nonsense handling of the crisis saw his ratings soar: by the time the March 2000 presidential polls came around, his approval figures were hovering around 60%, despite his refusal to take part in televised debates. Primakov, the one-time favourite for the Kremlin, abruptly abandoned his presidential ambitions amid mounting personal attacks in state-run media and a sudden public passion for the acting president. Putin triumphed in the first round of the presidential elections, taking 53.4% of the vote. International observers praised the 'stable' environment in which the polls were held, but expressed concern over electoral violations and pro-Putin bias in state media.[18]

Less than a decade after crowds had toppled a statue of Felix Dzerzhinsky, the founder of the Soviet Union's secret police, a former KGB officer had risen to the highest post in the land. And Putin did little to alleviate any concerns about his security-services background. He may have spoken of the importance of 'preserving and developing democracy'[19] during his inauguration speech, but among his guests that day at the glittering Kremlin ceremony was ex-KGB chief Vladimir Kryuchkov, the man who had helped spearhead the plot to overthrow Gorbachev. This was not the only cause for concern: on 14 April 2000, a little over two weeks after his election victory, Putin gave his debut address to the State Duma, the lower house of parliament. It was the perfect opportunity, had he so desired, to say that his KGB past was just that – the past. Instead, he chose to threaten his fellow Russians: to warn them of the dangers of associating with Westerners. Putin's comments came even before his maiden televised speech, as he responded to a query from Communist Party leader Gennady Zyuganov on purported 'links' between Western intelligence and Foreign Minister Igor Ivanov.

'If the minister for foreign affairs is observed to be maintaining contacts with representatives of foreign governments outside his official duties, then he, like any other member of the Cabinet, State Duma legislators, party heads *or any other citizen* will be subject to certain procedures in line with the law,' Putin declared tersely.

In fact, there was, as the new president must surely have known, no law forbidding any Russian – be they minister, lawmaker or, even more so, *'any other citizen'* – from speaking to representatives of foreign states.[20]

In the West, where Putin would be depicted for the next few years as 'inching' Russia towards democracy, his Soviet-style warning went largely unreported. In an article the following day, Russia's *Kommersant* newspaper called Putin's words 'ominous',[21] but quickly moved on to other details of his appearance in the State Duma. There would be no outcry. But who could blame the Russians if they chose to turn a blind eye to their new leader's true colours? After the traumas of the Yeltsin era, Putin was their hope for the future.

AN FSB BOMB PLOT?

Putin's victory at the presidential elections was tainted by much more than suspicions of vote fraud and a controversial guest list. On the night of 22 September 1999, six days after what would be the last of the apartment bombings, police in Ryazan, a small city some 120 miles south-east of Moscow, announced they had discovered and defused explosives planted in the basement of an apartment block. Officers had been called to the scene after a local spotted three strangers of 'Slavic appearance' unloading sacks from a car with masked-over number plates. Thousands of residents were hurriedly evacuated, and spent the night and next morning at a nearby cinema. The head of the local FSB, General Alexander Sergeyev, told residents they had escaped with their lives. 'Tonight, you were born a second time,' he said, as his officers searched the area for the would-be bombers.

Some thirty-six hours later, with the authorities in Ryazan on the verge of making arrests in the case, Interior Minister Vladimir Rushailo announced that the sacks had contained hexagon, a powerful explosive found only at FSB bases. Then, something very odd happened. Just thirty minutes later, Putin's successor as head of the FSB, Nikolai Patrushev, informed reporters that the 'explosives' were, in fact, 'sugar' and that the entire operation had been part of a training exercise. The announcement was a surprise to everyone, including the stunned interior minister, Rushailo, who headed an anti-terrorism commission. What was going on? Was this simply a bizarre case of crossed wires? Or an indication of something far more sinister?[22]

Putin's first move as acting president had been to sign an amnesty for Yeltsin and his relatives, guaranteeing them immunity from any criminal charges. In the aftermath of Putin's election triumph, secured largely as a result of his decisiveness on Chechnya, many people soon began to think the unthinkable: had the FSB intended to blow up the apartment block in Ryazan? And, if so, were the bombings in Moscow and elsewhere part of a plot to ensure Yeltsin's freedom from prosecution by providing a pretext for a popular war that would make certain Putin's victory at the polls? As frightening rumours swirled, suspicions were also voiced that the 1999 invasion of Dagestan by Chechen fighters was also part of the plan to secure the ex-FSB chief Putin in the Kremlin.

'Two things brought about Putin's victory: the bombings and the phrase about wiping out terrorists in the outhouse,' noted Russian political analyst Vladimir Pribylovsky. 'They changed the situation by favouring a prime minister nobody knew, with a dubious, dark biography.'[23]

There was no direct proof of FSB involvement, but circumstantial evidence – including interviews with a soldier who claimed to have seen hexagon stored in sacks labelled 'sugar' at a military facility near Ryazan and the bomb expert who was first at the scene – began to mount up. Unconfirmed media reports also said police in Ryazan had detained the would-be bombers, but they had turned out to be FSB agents.

In the aftermath of the blasts, renewed attention was paid to an August 1999 article by the Russian journalist Alexander Zhilin in the *Moskovskaya Pravda* newspaper. Zhilin's report, which cited what he said was a leaked Kremlin document, had warned of imminent attacks in the Russian capital that would be used to manipulate the political situation. 'Tremendous shocks await Moscow,' wrote Zhilin.[24]

Putin, speaking in 2000, expressed outrage at the suggestion that FSB officers had murdered Russian citizens, calling the allegations 'immoral' and part of a 'media war against Russia'.[25] But, despite growing public belief that the authorities were implicated, parliament refused to sanction an official investigation into the incident. Instead, in the summer of 2002, an independent commission was eventually set up to probe one of the murkiest events in modern Russia's history.

Within the next eighteen months, two members of the commission would be dead and a lawyer it employed jailed. The first member of the commission to die, Sergei Yushenkov, a lawmaker, was gunned down in Moscow in April 2003 shortly after registering a political party that had pledged to investigate the apartment bombings. Another member, Yury Shchekochikhin, died in June of the same year in a suspected case of poisoning. The lawyer employed by the commission, Mikhail Trepashkin, another ex-FSB officer, was imprisoned for four years in 2003 on what he alleged were trumped-up charges of arms possession and revealing state secrets. His imprisonment came a week before he was due to present evidence of possible FSB involvement in the bombings to a Moscow court. Another commission member, Otto Latsis, died in 2005 after a jeep crashed into his car. (Other people to die after investigating the blasts were journalist Anna Politkovskaya, shot dead in Moscow in 2006, and former FSB officer Alexander Litvinenko, who was famously poisoned in London in the same year.) There was no proof that any of these people's deaths were linked to their attempts to find out the truth about the disturbing incident in Ryazan, but it was, at the very least, a spectacular series of coincidences.

A number of people from the North Caucasus region were tried and jailed in Russia over the blasts in 2001–4, but their trials – some of which were held in secret – did little to discourage speculation or provide further information on the events of that night.

'The trials were a farce,' said Sergei Kovalyov, the elderly Soviet-era dissident who headed the independent commission into the blasts, when I met him at his south Moscow home. 'They were just held to make it seem like action was being taken. The only way the authorities can disprove suspicions that the FSB blew up the apartment blocks is to carry out a thorough, transparent investigation,' he sighed, the last rays of a winter day shining into the room. 'But this was not done. Putin has created a system in which there is no dialogue between civic society and the authorities, and this makes it impossible to find out the truth about what really happened that autumn.'[26]

STIFLING DISSENT

Aside from his handling of the Chechen crisis, Putin's early popularity was boosted by media comparisons with Max Otto von Stierlitz, the codename of a much-loved fictional Soviet-era secret agent. Ahead of the 2000 presidential elections, the influential *Vlast* magazine put images of both the socialist James Bond and Putin on its front cover under the headline 'Von Stierlitz – Our President'.[27]

'At the end of the 1990s, there was a study carried out into what people thought an ideal president should be like,' recalled Vadim Beriashvili, a historian and one-time Putin supporter. 'The result was – Stierlitz. So that's what the spin doctors offered us: a person from the KGB, a patriot, a believer in a strong state who is tough and never at a loss for words.'[28]

Marat Guelman, a former political consultant employed by both the Yeltsin and Putin administrations, was one of these spin doctors. Along with fellow 'political technologist' Gleb Pavlovsky, he helped 'manage' democracy for Putin during the early years of his rule. The political overseer at state-run Channel One, Guelman was responsible for making sure, through daily and weekly 'analytical sessions', that the influential TV station kept its message in line with Kremlin orders. It was a task that Guelman took to with a genuine zeal; ahead of the 2003 parliamentary elections that saw the decimation of Russia's already embattled liberal parties, a stunning 56% of all coverage on Channel One was dedicated to either Putin or his fledgling United Russia party.[29]

However, by the time of our meeting in the summer of 2013 at a trendy Moscow arts centre, Guelman, a bearded fifty-two-year-old with an earring, had long grown disillusioned with the man whose transformation into 'national leader' he had been instrumental in bringing about. Unhappy with Putin's increasingly autocratic rule, he had walked away from the Kremlin after Putin's 2004 re-election.

'Putin seemed like a good choice to succeed Yeltsin,' Guelman said, shrugging. 'He was eager to learn and he listened. Yeltsin had considered making the previous prime minister, Sergei Stepashin, the new president, but he was worried he would be more independent than Putin. It seems strange now, of course.' He took a long drag of his cigarette. 'Putin was just an instrument,' he went on. 'He was set a task and he went about fulfilling it. He really wanted to fit in, to do well. Of course, no one had any idea back then what he was really like,' Guelman laughed. 'Putin gave no indication of his character whatsoever. We only discovered his true nature after he had won a second term of office. It turned out that even those people who thought they knew him didn't actually know anything about him at all.'

One thing Putin had learned as he rose through the ranks was the power of television. It had helped make him, but it could also destroy him. 'Putin's rise was like a miracle,' said Guelman. 'He went in a matter of months from being this complete unknown to having approval ratings of around sixty to seventy percent. But, because his ascent was so sudden, he and his team were terrified that things could just as easily go the other way again, and just as unexpectedly. That's why television was so important for Putin.'[30]

Yeltsin may have been ruthless when it came to his political opponents, but he had taken no steps to reel in on-air critics, or even the comedians who frequently and cruelly mocked him on national television. Putin wasted no time in taming the media. One of his first targets was NTV, the only national television channel not under the Kremlin's control. Founded by tycoon Vladimir Gusinsky in 1993, NTV was a slick, professional channel renowned for its uncompromising reporting of the First Chechen War, the horrors of which it beamed straight into the nation's living rooms. (Or, more precisely, bedrooms and kitchens: very few Russians are lucky enough to have living rooms.)

Just two days before the March 2000 presidential polls that would confirm Putin as Russia's new leader, NTV aired a talk show on the row over the FSB's 'training exercise' in Ryazan. FSB officials had agreed to appear on the programme in the hope that they could persuade the country there was no substance to the rumours of the security services' involvement in the blasts. But, after an intense grilling by residents of the apartment block where the 'sugar' had been discovered, they came off looking – at best – as if they had something to hide.

If all this wasn't enough to earn the ire of the new man in the Kremlin, NTV's *Kukly* (Puppets) programme, a political satire show inspired by the UK's *Spitting Image*, had quickly come up with a latex caricature of Putin. In perhaps the programme's most infamous scene, Russia's new diminutive leader was portrayed as an evil, infant gnome muttering, 'Waste them in the outhouse!' – the phrase that had helped propel him to power.[31]

The scene was dreamed up by Viktor Shenderovich, a diminutive writer blessed with a caustic wit who would later join forces with the anti-Putin movement. Although Britain's rulers had been forced to grin and bear *Spitting Image*'s puppets, Putin would have no such qualms about lashing out. 'Putin has never been a Western-style politician and our cruel caricature made him hysterical with anger,' Shenderovich told me. 'He took it as a personal insult. He has a serious problem with self-irony.

'We were informed by several sources that he hit the roof. There is no such thing for him as a free press or satire,' Shenderovich added. 'But if only he'd seen what the British did with [John] Major and [Margaret] Thatcher!'[32]

Putin wanted the puppet gone, and Kremlin officials were not shy about making the demand. 'The disappearance of the Putin puppet was put forward as one of the conditions for the survival of NTV by Alexander Voloshin, then the head of Putin's administration,' Shenderovich said. The other conditions, according to former NTV staff, were to cut both critical coverage of Chechnya and investigations into government corruption. But NTV refused to bow to the Kremlin's demands: time was running out for the channel.

Just four days after Putin's inauguration as president on 7 May 2000, the Moscow headquarters of NTV and its parent company, Media MOST, were searched by masked tax police and armed FSB officers. A month later, Gusinsky, the channel's owner, was arrested and charged with embezzlement. He later said he was only released from custody after agreeing to hand his stake in NTV over to the state-run energy giant, Gazprom.

Putin had laid down a marker. The man in the Kremlin would no longer be mocked.

'Authoritarian leaders always start with the media,' Shenderovich said. 'They are all the same. It was only natural then that Putin immediately closed down an independent channel that was the best and most influential in the country.'

In truth, NTV had been no saints. When Yeltsin was facing defeat by the Communist Party leader Gennady Zyuganov at the 1996 presidential elections, the channel had rallied to his side, providing favourable coverage and hushing up a heart attack. The channel later received a generous state loan; critics alleged its refusal to back the authorities was simply revenge for being denied a repeat line of credit. Whatever the truth of the allegations, NTV had at least been independent of the Kremlin. Its takeover meant national television was firmly under Putin's control. Blacklists were introduced and censorship stepped up. Over the next few years, the Kremlin's spin doctors would shape Putin's image into that of not just 'national leader', but national hero.

For Mikhail Shats, a popular comedian from St Petersburg who had made it big in Moscow in the mid-1990s, the first alarm bells began to ring in 2002, when he and his colleagues on the OSP-Studio comedy show were ordered to drop a satirical song about Putin. The song – 'My name is Vova' – was based around a popular hit, but the new version featured brand-new lyrics that took an ever so gentle dig at the president. ('Vova' is one of the possible diminutives of 'Vladimir'). 'My name is Vova / I am the coolest… I fly around the world / chatting about peace / and every day I waste bandits in the outhouse,' went the lyrics.

'After that, censors were posted at every channel,' Shats, a dark-haired, middle-aged man with a fondness for fine cigars, told me. 'They would examine every programme before it was aired and just cut out anything they didn't like about Putin.' He laughed. 'At one point, it became impossible to even make any mention of him at all, however innocuous, on light entertainment programmes.'

The reining in of NTV was just part of Putin's drive to remove any potential threats to his power. Within weeks of his May 2000 inauguration, a presidential decree created seven presidential envoys – most of them drawn from the security forces or the army – to 'supervise' the work of the country's elected governors. This was just the beginning of Putin's move to strengthen his position. In 2003, the country's richest man, oil tycoon Mikhail Khodorkovsky, was arrested on fraud charges widely believed to have been revenge for his funding of opposition political parties, including the Communists. (Putin had gathered the country's top businesspeople together in July 2000 and warned them in no uncertain terms to stay out of politics.) Khodorkovsky had also riled the Kremlin elite with his attempts to open up Russia's oil sector to foreign participation. Along with his business partner, Platon Lebedev, Khodorkovsky was sentenced to nine years behind bars, and his oil company, Yukos, was swallowed up by the state. Like anyone who made vast amounts of money in Russia in the 1990s, as Khodorkovsky did, this bespectacled oligarch's past was hardly likely to have been whiter than white. But Putin was applying the law selectively, as a bludgeon, to pummel his enemies. Despite his pledge to eliminate the oligarchs 'as a class', those who stayed loyal, such as Chelsea FC owner Roman Abramovich, would have little to fear.

By the time the 2004 presidential elections rolled around, Putin's domination of the political scene was almost complete. He had neutered the media, sent a powerful warning to the business community to stay out of politics and was busy rolling back post-Soviet reforms. He had done what he would later admit in a candid moment was the very thing he had set out to do: eliminate the 'feeling of absolute freedom'[33] that had reigned during the chaotic Yeltsin years. For Putin, like his role model, the ruthless, Tsarist-era prime minister Pyotr Stolypin, no price was too high to pay for stability. Putin's main nominal rivals as he stood for re-election – Communist Party chief Gennady Zyuganov and the nationalist Vladimir Zhirinovsky – stepped aside to allow the president a clear playing field. Putin romped home with 72% of the vote.

What had happened to the man who in 1996 warned of the dangers of the 'firm hand that would quickly begin to strangle us all'? Had he simply become disillusioned with the messy nature of democracy? Did he now believe that Russia could not be ruled in any other manner, that an iron fist was the only way to maintain control over his vast and unpredictable homeland? Or perhaps he had not fully understood the nature of a free society to begin with? 'Like anyone who is not a crazy person, he wanted good,' said Yuli Rybakov, a former pro-democracy lawmaker in St Petersburg while Putin was deputy mayor. 'But his idea of good came from somewhere else. What we understand as democracy is, to him, anarchy.'[34]

Putin still had work to do. His control over the regions, many of them vast areas thousands of miles from Moscow, was not complete. Direct elections meant that there was still the chance that voters would plump for the 'wrong' candidate. Something needed to be done to eliminate the last major political force with the potential to challenge the Kremlin: regional governors had to be brought into line. Putin got the excuse he was looking for that autumn.

In September 2004, as over a thousand people gathered to mark the first day of the new academic year in School Number One in the tiny North Caucasus town of Beslan, Chechen militants stormed into the building, herding terrified parents, teachers and many, many children into the gym. For days, the hostages were kept without food and water, as militants wired the school with explosives and demanded the withdrawal of Russian troops from Chechnya. The raid made international headlines, yet state media ran only cursory coverage and lied about the number of hostages. The siege was eventually brought to a catastrophic end when Russian special forces launched a heavy-handed rescue attempt, deploying flame-throwers and tanks before they stormed the building. By the time the smoke had cleared, 334 people were dead, more than half of them children.

'We demonstrated weakness, and the weak get beaten,' Putin thundered in the bloody aftermath of the siege. From now on, he announced, there would no longer be direct elections for governors. They would, instead, be appointed by the president himself. What was more, there would be no more independent members of parliament; in future, candidates would be chosen by the tame parties the Kremlin had allowed into the State Duma. However, beyond a vague promise that this would put an end to the 'epidemic of collapse' that Putin blamed for the slaughter at Beslan, it remained unclear what exactly the loss of the people's right to choose their own governors had to do with the country's worst ever terrorist attack. The answer seemed to be – nothing. 'The plans to scrap direct elections for governors had been drawn up well before Beslan,' Marat Guelman, the former Kremlin spin doctor, told me. 'The tragedy was just exploited to put them into practice.'

Putin's rule had entered a harsher stage. 'Up until 2003, Putin relied on television and other forms of manipulation to maintain and consolidate power,' Guelman went on. 'But after this he began to trust in more established methods, ones that were guaranteed to bring results. Prosecutors, tax inspectors, the courts. You see, television is such a tricky thing, you don't always know what is going to happen. But if you put a person in jail, well, he's not going to win any elections, is he?'

Guelman had long quit politics in favour of his other great love – modern art. He had also passionately defended the protest punk group Pussy Riot before and after their controversial trial and had attended his first anti-Kremlin demonstration just weeks ahead of our conversation. How deep, I wondered, was his regret over his role in Project Putin?

Guelman sighed. 'Look, if Putin had just served one term, from 2000 to 2004, his presidency would have been viewed positively,' he told me, stubbing out a cigarette as he spoke. 'There were more good points than bad – the economy was improving and he was cracking down on regional crime bosses. He managed to fix a lot of the negatives of the Yeltsin era. For me, for a while, the ends justified the means. But, during his second term, well, it became a lot harder to find the positives, let's put it that way.'

THE GREY CARDINAL

The new political reality that took hold in Russia in the 2000s was both shaped and given ideological substance by Vladislav Surkov, a chain-smoking, secretive Kremlin official with a fondness for both chaos theories and the gangsta rap of Tupac Shakur. Widely viewed as the heir to the Soviet Union's shadowy chief ideologue during the Cold War, politburo member Mikhail Suslov, Surkov's genuine role was masked by his official anodyne job title of deputy chief of staff of the presidential administration. But the dark-haired Surkov was Putin's grey cardinal, responsible for the final transformation of state-controlled media into slavishly pro-Kremlin platforms, and the creation of a docile parliamentary opposition that provided the masses with the illusion of a functioning democracy.

It was to Surkov's Kremlin office, overlooking the fifteenth-century, golden-domed Cathedral of the Dormition, that top party officials, leading journalists and other influential figures would come to be issued with 'directives'. It was here that opposition politicians were brought onside and plans drawn up to dirty the names of those who would not submit. Tellingly, the chunky, beige telephones on Surkov's desk had speed-dial options for all the major figures in Russian political life, both pro-Putin and the tame parliamentary opposition.[35]

Born in the provinces in 1964 to a Russian mother and Chechen father, Surkov followed the well-beaten path taken by talented youth to Moscow. He studied theatre for a while and read widely; the American Beat poet Allen Ginsburg was a particular favourite. Like Putin, Surkov also trained in the martial arts. In the late 1980s, he was briefly a bodyguard to the tycoon Mikhail Khodorkovsky, who quickly realized that there was more to his new employee than mere muscle and promoted him to head his bank's advertising and public relations department.[36] Surkov soon gained a reputation as one of the most skilful PR people in the country. But Khodorkovsky would prove unwilling to satisfy Surkov's growing ambitions; the two reportedly fell out after the businessman refused to make his PR manager a full partner. 'I wanted to be like the hero in the movie *Pretty Woman*,' Surkov later recalled. 'I wanted to be a big businessman who's sitting in a big hotel, supervising big events.'[37] In 1999, after highly paid jobs in TV and banking, Surkov was brought into Yeltsin's presidential staff, where he helped launch Putin to the presidency.

Regularly identified by analysts as one of the two or three most powerful men in Russian politics throughout the 2000s, the obsessively secretive Surkov was, however, far from a household name. Most ordinary Russians, it is fair to say, had never even heard of him. And Surkov did everything he could to bolster his mysterious image, rarely making public appearances and declaring that Putin was 'sent to Russia by the Lord'. ('Yeah, as the angel of the apocalypse,' they joked in opposition circles.) Believed to have written a satirical novel, *Almost Zero*, under a pseudonym, Surkov also penned lyrics for the Russian rock group Agata Kristi. The Kremlin's chief ideologue liked to think of himself as an artist. His canvas was Russia.

Possessed of a piercing gaze, Surkov was invested with almost supernatural powers by the anti-Putin movement, whose members loathed and feared him in equal measures. 'He's like the gang member who actually enjoys torturing victims,' a protest figure colourfully described him to me, on condition, naturally, of anonymity.

'He is the lord of darkness,' said an opposition politician, Vladimir Ryzhkov, without irony. 'He has been complicit in all the vileness of the Putin era.'[38]

And so it was Surkov who in 2004 announced that Putinism, this strange new hybrid of Soviet-type authoritarianism and free-market morals, was based on the concept of 'sovereign democracy'. The malleable term drew heavily on the works of one of Putin's favourite philosophers, Ivan Ilyin (1883–1954), an intellectual exiled by Lenin, who believed that Western-style democracy was not only unsuitable for Russia, but also harmful. Instead, Russia, Ilyin believed, required a 'united and strong state power, dictatorial in the scope of its powers'.[39]

Sovereign democracy essentially meant that the state should exert robust controls over a nominally democratic political system, one that was free of any foreign influences whatsoever. The political playing field was open to both the left and the right, and everything in between, but the number-one rule, inflexible for participation, was 'the Kremlin is always right'. Stick to that, and things would go smoothly. Deviate and fall victim to Surkov, the master of black PR. Not everyone was convinced, however, by Surkov's new addition to the political lexicon. 'Sovereign democracy', ran the joke, was to 'genuine democracy' what 'electric chair' was to 'chair'.

All this trickery may have secured Putin in the Kremlin, but there was only so much that Surkov and state media could do to mask the injustices that permeated Russia. Angry protests were sparked in early 2005 by sweeping social-benefit reforms, with well-attended marches taking place in a number of cities. The demonstrations may have fizzled out quickly, and produced no new or viable opposition leaders, but the authorities were rattled. Grassroots movements were also gaining popularity, from campaigns against the often deadly driving habits of government officials to protests against environmental destruction. Even Surkov, with all his dark talents, had been unable to eliminate dissent entirely. Not everyone had signed up to Putin's pact.

3

THE 'ORANGE THREAT' AND THE EARLY DISSENTERS

'*Revolyutsiya Budet!*' (There Will Be a Revolution!) proclaimed a piece of stylized graffiti – the slogan sprayed under a clenched fist – on a wall near my home in central Moscow in mid-2005. In a Russia where the R-word had not been uttered seriously for many years, the sentiment was somehow jarring. Hopelessly dated or a forewarning of turmoil to come? I took a photo. The next day the graffiti was gone.

The clenched fist was the symbol of *Oborona* (Defence), an anti-Putin youth movement openly inspired by the so-called Colour Revolutions that had toppled Moscow-friendly regimes in ex-Soviet republics in 2003–5, as well as an earlier, similar uprising in Serbia. The symbol had been used in one form or another in all of these revolts, and was intended by *Oborona*'s founders to 'elicit shock and rage' in the Kremlin.

The Colour Revolutions had begun with the Rose Revolution in Georgia in late 2003, when protests over rigged parliamentary polls swept a pro-Western politician called Mikheil Saakashvili into power. Events repeated themselves a little over a year later during the Orange Revolution in Ukraine, when around a million people camped out in the country's capital, Kiev, to demand the annulment of the results of disputed presidential elections. The eventual rerun of the vote saw victory for a pro-American candidate, Viktor Yushchenko, who pledged to take Ukraine into NATO. The pattern continued in the spring of 2005 in Kyrgyzstan, when President Askar Akayev (the man whose bald head Yeltsin had once played the spoons on) and his government were toppled following parliamentary polls. All three Colour Revolutions had been viewed with extreme nervousness by Putin and his administration, but it was the loss of Ukraine that was hardest to take. Many Russians, including Putin, consider Ukraine a mere extension of Russia. One in every six people in Ukraine is an ethnic Russian, and millions in the east of the country speak no Ukrainian at all. 'Ukraine is not even a state,' Putin reportedly told George W. Bush in 2008.[1] Putin had been so enraged by the Orange Revolution protests in Kiev that he had urged the outgoing president, Leonid Kuchma, to use force to clear the streets. Kuchma, to his credit, refused.[2]

It was against this background of rising tensions that *Oborona* was formed, when groups of young anti-Putin activists came together in an attempt to up the pressure on the Kremlin. Youth movements had played a leading role in the uprisings in Ukraine, Georgia and Serbia, and *Oborona* was seeking to repeat their success in Russia. Oleg Kozlovsky, a young, well-spoken Muscovite who was one of the movement's leading figures, explained its aims to me as the following: 'Unite the opposition, empower the youth, and help a popular non-violent democratic protest come about.'[3] But turnout at the movement's first rally was modest: a few hundred people attended a demonstration in Moscow in mid-2005 entitled 'That's Enough Putin!'

Times were hard for anti-Kremlin movements, especially those that were so open about their inspirations. State-controlled media had focused heavily on the presence of US pro-democracy groups in both Georgia and Ukraine, airing allegations that the revolts were part of a NATO plot to encircle and eventually invade Russia. Orange suddenly became a very unpopular colour. 'With state propaganda in Russia focused on discrediting both the domestic opposition and the Orange Revolution, it wasn't an easy thing to be linked to both,' admitted Kozlovsky.[4]

Despite *Oborona*'s modest resources and limited appeal, the Kremlin was keen to crack down. The group was frequently targeted by the authorities, with raids on its tiny office and the open harassment of its members. Kozlovsky was even illegally drafted into Russia's brutal army for six months.

Such heavy-handed tactics puzzled many Russia watchers. Why did the authorities feel it necessary to clamp down on marginal groups that had little or no popular support? Surely by doing so, they simply gifted these protest movements both publicity and credibility?

For Kozlovsky, the answer was obvious. 'The authorities understood that, if they allowed small groups to protest freely, these groups could grow very quickly and become uncontrollable. So they wanted to suffocate the revolution while it was still small, by showing society where the red line was,' he said. 'And, for a while, these tactics worked.'

PUTIN YOUTH

The Colour Revolutions taught Putin an important lesson. In the event of the 'Orange threat' spreading to Russia, the Kremlin would require its own protesters. These loyalists would need to be young, physically strong and ready to break up the kind of mass demonstrations that had been seen in Ukraine. Widespread political apathy among young people had played into Putin's hands in the early years of his presidency, but now he needed their active support. There were parliamentary elections approaching in 2007, and presidential polls set for the year after: the Kremlin would need to be vigilant. After all, the Colour Revolutions had all been sparked by disputed vote counts.

With the grey cardinal, Surkov, calling the shots, a massive overhaul of a previously existing pro-Putin youth group, Walking Together, was launched. 'We almost completely lost the youth of the nineties,' Surkov said. 'They had little interest in politics, and perhaps that was even a good thing.'[5] But times had changed. The unguided energies of youth were too potent to be left to chance. To prepare the ground for the impending launch of Surkov's 'super-patriotic' youth organization, pro-Kremlin activists travelled around universities and colleges, outlining the dangers of what they called a US plot to enslave Russia.

In April 2005, a little over a year after the Orange Revolution, Surkov unveiled his latest creation: *Nashi*. The youth movement's name can be translated as 'our', 'ours' or – and most accurately when speaking of Surkov's brainchild – 'one of ours'. Historically used from the nineteenth century onwards to divide the world into friends and enemies, the expression had taken on a powerful political sense in the Soviet period. When interrogating dissidents, a KGB officer frequently began by saying, 'You're not one of ours,' to which a second officer, playing the 'good cop', would reply, 'But you're one of ours, aren't you?'[6] It was a potent choice of moniker and played upon Russians' traditionally strong sense of patriotism and collectivism. You were, the movement's name suggested, with the motherland, or against it.

'The first guys who joined [*Nashi*] were super-patriotic,' said Sergei Markov, a political consultant who worked with Surkov on the project. 'And the first rule was geography. They had to live within ten hours' drive of Moscow so that they could take the night bus and be in Moscow in the morning and occupy Red Square to defend the sovereignty of the state.'[7]

Nashi was not just defensive in nature: its members regularly disrupted anti-Putin protests and beat up opposition activists and journalists. In one notorious incident, *Nashi* members defecated on a parked vehicle belonging to a young protest movement figure. The Kremlin-backed movement treated anti-Putin activists like their enemies, rather than political opponents. With them, it was personal. The youth group also harassed foreign diplomats, notably UK ambassador Anthony Brenton, who was targeted after he attended an opposition conference in the Russian capital. *Nashi* members stalked him for the next six months, even camping outside his house, until the Russian Foreign Ministry belatedly ordered them to back off. To inspire and educate its members, *Nashi* held annual summer camps at a lake north of Moscow, where activists married at mass weddings and attended seminars on Russia and Putin's greatness.

'*Nashi* is worse than a cult,' Oleg Kashin, an opposition journalist who wrote extensively on the movement, told me. 'It's a mixture of cult and criminal gang that combines an almost religious-like belief in Putin with illegal activities.'[8]

The head of *Nashi* from its inception until its disbandment in 2012 was an acerbic, thirty-something named Vasily Yakemenko. Hailing from the tough, working-class Moscow commuter town of Lyubertsy, Yakemenko had rumoured connections to a criminal gang that once routinely decapitated its enemies. The gang also cut off its victims' hands for good measure.[9] While the *Nashi* leader denied any past involvement in organized crime, he made no secret of his ties to violent football hooligans. In 2005, he boasted that, if Russia were to be faced with an Orange Revolution scenario, he would 'summon' thousands of thugs from the Spartak Moscow FC fan movement to disperse 'Western-backed' protesters.[10] 'Ukraine always used to be a Russian colony,' Yakemenko said in the same speech. 'And now it is an American colony. But the real target for the United States is Russia.'[11]

After 60,000 *Nashi* members marched through central Moscow in a show of support for Putin in the spring of 2005, Surkov was rumoured to have promised *Nashi*'s leaders that they would one day inherit Russia. When asked to comment by a persistent BBC reporter, the architect of sovereign democracy sidestepped the question. 'They are young and so naturally they will receive the country. Who else should?' He smiled. 'But I don't think they are up to it right now.'[12] Nevertheless, not long afterwards, Yakemenko was named head of Russia's youth ministry.

THE OTHER RUSSIA

As Putin's rule became increasingly authoritarian in the aftermath of the Beslan massacre and the Colour Revolutions, the previously splintered opposition had little choice but to unite. While world leaders were converging in St Petersburg for a G8 summit in July 2006, Western-style democrats, leftists and nationalists gathered in Moscow to launch the Other Russia opposition coalition. The group's figureheads included some unlikely allies, such as Garry Kasparov, the world-famous chess champ turned liberal politician, and Eduard Limonov, a radical writer and head of the National Bolshevik Party, a direct-action movement that fused the hard left and the ultra-right.

Surkov, watching developments from his Kremlin office, was not impressed. Comparing protest leaders to the violent revolutionaries described by Fyodor Dostoyevsky in his novel *Demons*, the Kremlin's chief ideologue derided the newly united opposition as 'fake liberals and genuine Nazis' – a 'fifth column' in the pay of the West. 'They say they share a hatred of Putin's Russia,' he seethed. 'But it is Russia itself that they hate.'[13]

The Other Russia coalition may have been wracked from the very beginning by internecine conflicts, but its leaders managed to forget about their differences – and egos – for long enough to organize a series of so-called Marches of Dissent. It was at these rallies, which took place in over a dozen cities, that the slogan 'Russia without Putin!' was first aired. Although they never attracted more than a few thousand protesters, the marches punched far above their weight, gaining widespread media coverage both at home and abroad and providing a genuine focus for discontent. For beleaguered opposition activists, they were like a breath of fresh air amid the stifling atmosphere of Putinism. 'I didn't even want to smoke as we marched. Like how you don't want to smoke in the mountains or at the sea. I wanted to breathe,' recalled Valery Panyushkin, a journalist and author who sympathized with the protest movement.[14]

The marches also triggered a predictable response from the security forces. In April 2007, around 2,000 protesters were confronted in central

Moscow by at least four times as many police and Interior Ministry troops. As a police helicopter hovered above and demonstrators chanted, 'We need another Russia', riot police in body armour hauled away protest leaders, while other officers lashed out with truncheons. Police later pursued activists to nearby metro stations, where they made more arrests. State-run TV showed brief footage of the protest, but not the police crackdown. That evening's news bulletin led with Putin attending a martial arts match.

One of the protesters detained that afternoon in central Moscow was Kasparov, the Other Russia co-leader. The world's number-one-ranked chess player for nineteen consecutive years, Kasparov had quit professional chess in the spring of 2005 to concentrate on 'preserving electoral democracy' in Russia. But, despite his considerable financial and personal resources, the chess champ's undisguised fondness for the West severely limited his appeal to ordinary Russians and made him an easy target for the Kremlin. He was also mercilessly hounded by *Nashi* activists; members of the pro-Putin youth group once famously disrupted one of his news conferences with a radio-controlled, flying plastic penis. Kasparov looked on furiously while a bodyguard jumped into the air to swat down the X-rated aerial intruder. Another time, a pro-Putin supporter requested an autograph on a chessboard and then walloped him around the head with it.[15]

Putin was also keen on taking the occasional potshot. 'Why do you think Mr Kasparov was speaking English rather than Russian when he was detained?' Putin asked in late 2007, shortly after the Other Russia leader had been arrested at another protest. 'His deeds were not aimed at his own people but rather at a Western audience. A person who works for an international audience can never be a leader in his own country.'[16]

Kasparov later made the extremely valid points that he was speaking to a US journalist when the police nabbed him, and that – anyway – he was de facto banned from airing his views on Russian national television, but the damage was done.

However, the main problem faced by the anti-Putin opposition throughout the 2000s was neither *Nashi* nor the Kremlin domination of state media. The real drawback was that the majority of the protest movement's 'leaders' led almost no one and inspired even fewer. The Kremlin's opponents were viewed by the vast majority of Russians as, at best, an irrelevance and, at worst, a potentially dangerous throwback to the deprivations of the Yeltsin era. Aside from marginal groups like *Oborona* and the easily sidelined Kasparov, other key protest leaders were Boris Nemtsov and Mikhail Kasyanov, both wealthy former government insiders. Nemtsov was tainted by his time as a deputy prime minister in the loathed Yeltsin government, while Kasyanov had earned himself the nickname 'Misha 2%' for his alleged fondness for kickbacks while first finance minister and then prime minister during Putin's first term.[17] What could they offer Russia that Putin could not? For Surkov, discrediting these men was almost an insult to his talents. 'They are a shadow cast by a lamp on the wall,' mocked best-selling author Sergei Minayev, whose 2006 novel, *Soulless*, was an epitaph for a generation of newly well-off, yet cynical Muscovites. 'Putin is the only competent politician who has appeared here in the last 16 years.'[18]

LIMONOV AND THE NATIONAL BOLSHEVIKS

Not everyone in the early opposition to Putin was as toothless. The Kremlin's most visible and stubborn critic throughout the 1990s and much of the 2000s, Other Russia co-leader Eduard Limonov, at the peak of his popularity, was able to boast a following of thousands of young supporters. Many of them addressed him as '*vozhd*' – the Soviet-era term of respect for Communist Party leaders like Lenin and Stalin. 'Russia is rich in generals without armies,' Kasparov admitted. 'But Limonov has foot soldiers. He commands street power.'[19]

An avant-garde poet who fled the Soviet Union in the mid-1970s, Limonov found his way to New York, where he got to know punk stars like The Ramones and Richard Hell at the legendary CBGB club. 'These punks weren't so different from the artists and musicians I'd been hanging out with in Moscow,' Limonov later told me.

It was during his stay in the States that he penned *It's Me, Eddie*, a fictional memoir of deviant immigrant life. The book earned him international acclaim for its bleak depiction of American society, as well as eternal notoriety in his homeland for its depiction of gay sex with a black vagrant, an unthinkable thing for a Soviet author to have written. A massive success in Europe, Limonov later moved to France, where he was granted citizenship in 1987. But the West's love affair with this uncompromising and complex Russian writer would not last long. When civil war broke out in Yugoslavia, Limonov took a trip to the hills around Sarajevo, where he was filmed shooting a high-powered sniper rifle into the besieged city in the company of Bosnian Serb leader Radovan Karadžić. The incident, captured by Bafta award-winning director Paweł Pawlikowski in his *Serbian Epics* documentary and shown at Karadžić's trial at the Hague, cost Limonov publishing contracts in both Europe and the USA. Limonov maintained he was 'set up' by Pawlikowski, although he also appeared to admit, in print, taking shots at the city.[20]

Limonov returned to Russia shortly after the break-up of the Soviet Union, where he thrived on the uncertainty and anarchy of the post-Communist years. In 1993, he linked up with Yegor Letov, the foul-mouthed father of Russian punk, to form the National Bolshevik Party. The movement's instantly recognizable flag was an explosive mix of Nazi and Communist imagery. 'Stalin, Beria, gulag!' chanted the National Bolsheviks – or *NatsBols*, as they came to be known – on the streets of Russia's cities, their exhortation of the Soviet dictator, his secret-police chief and the labour camps that killed millions designed to provoke Russians suffering from brutal economic reforms. 'Our aim is a national Russian revolution!' Limonov screamed from a stage in Siberia in 1994, as an audience of thousands yelled back in approval. 'We are the largest white race in Europe! Glory to Russia! Law and a new order! A Russian order!'[21]

Punks, skinheads and kids from broken homes flocked to Limonov to seize the opportunity to fight against a system they loathed and that related to them with indifference at best. The *NatsBol* 'prayer', which party members recited en masse at street protests, went like this:

I, a warrior of the National Bolshevik Party, welcome the new day.
In this hour of the united party, I am with my brothers!
I sense the power of all brothers of the party, wherever they may be.
Let my blood mix with the blood of the party.
Let us become one.
Yes, death![22]

The *NatsBols* quickly became veterans of street battles with the OMON, Russia's equally infamous riot police, as well as activists from the pro-Kremlin youth movement, *Nashi*. Seemingly indifferent to long prison sentences and police brutality, the *NatsBols* were streetwise, tough and uncompromising. They got beaten and came back to get beaten once more. Sometimes fatally.

'I was fourteen when I left my home in the provinces to join up with Limonov,' Matvei Krylov, a baby-faced, tattooed activist, told me, as we ate dumplings in a kitschy Soviet-themed café in Moscow. 'I was a skinhead and I'd been reading lots of books about revolution, about Lenin and Trotsky and so on, and Limonov seemed to me to be a living example of all that. He was the father I'd never had. I called him "dad" or "uncle".'[23]

Membership of Limonov's movement came with terrible risks. *Nashi* leader Yakemenko had identified the group as one of the threats to Russia's sovereignty, and pro-Putin thugs targeted *NatsBols* wherever they could find them. 'Lots of my friends were badly beaten, even killed after being set upon in the street,' Krylov said. 'We had to start carrying weapons to defend ourselves.'

In late 2007, just two days before a March of Dissent in Moscow, a young *NatsBol* named Yury Chervochkin was attacked by five men carrying baseball bats. 'Just don't hit my head!' he yelled. Minutes later, he lay unconscious in the snow. He slipped into a coma and died just over two weeks later without ever having regained consciousness. An opposition journalist later said Chervochkin had called him less than an hour before the attack to say he was being trailed by plainclothes police officers, two of whom he recognized. The investigation into Chervochkin's murder was closed in 2009. No one has ever been charged with his death.[24]

Judges, likewise, showed little mercy to the *NatsBols*: seven young men from the movement were sent to penal colonies for three years each in 2004 after storming into the Health Ministry headquarters to protest social-benefit cuts. Limonov also saw the inside of prison cells. In 2001, the former New York punker was locked up for two years on weapons charges after being initially accused of organizing an armed uprising among the Russian-speaking population of eastern Kazakhstan. The evidence against him – the testimony of two youths caught buying guns in central Russia – was widely viewed as flimsy, but there was little international coverage of the trial. Limonov's politics were too extreme to allow his case to become a cause célèbre. The West liked a certain kind of Russian dissident, and Limonov simply didn't fit the bill. Not that Limonov, as he later told me and anyone else who cared to listen, gave a 'fuck about the West'. He wrote eight books while inside.

After his release from jail, Limonov abandoned his nationalist rhetoric, as he joined forces with liberals like the chess grandmaster Kasparov in the Other Russia coalition. There had been a suspicion all long, anyhow, that his far-right posturing had been little more than an extension of his art, a reaching back to the slogans of fascism and Nazism to shine a spotlight on the violent reality of post-Soviet Russia. 'Why would we bother playing with fascism anymore when the Kremlin is already fascist?' he admitted later. 'We are an opposition party. And today the most radical position of all is to fight for democracy and elections – against Putin's fascism. It's far-right fascism that is banal and oppressive now.'[25]

✱

Like any would-be revolutionary leader worth his salt, Limonov had his hideouts. I met the taciturn youth who would take me to one of them at the entrance to a Moscow branch of Mothercare. It was an incongruous start to our meeting, but, for a man who embodied much of the chaos and contradictions of his post-Soviet homeland, it somehow seemed apt.

Limonov opened the door to the sparsely decorated apartment he was using as a base and ushered me through the corridor into a room with walls that were bare save for two large, framed photographs of scenes from his career in alternative politics. With his glasses, greying moustache and goatee, he resembled no one so much as Leon Trotsky, the Bolshevik revolutionary murdered by Stalin. In keeping with the 'dress code for the future' he had outlined in one of his more than forty books, Limonov was clad in black from head to toe.

I got straight to the point. What did Limonov feel, I wanted to know, when his young supporters were killed by the Kremlin's goons or locked up in brutal, disease-ridden penal colonies? Did he regret encouraging them to resist Putin's rule, when the price for this resistance was often so very high? After all, by his own admission, the situation in Russia under Putin was 'bearable'. Russia was not North Korea. Or, come to that, the Soviet Union. Limonov visibly bristled. 'You can't change the world without losing some of the buttons on your jacket,' he replied instantly. 'These young people, they are sane, and they know what they are doing. They are strong, and ruled by passion. Prison is nothing in comparison with the freedom of the country.

'Russia is not yet a fascist state, it's true,' he admitted, staring out at the impressively urban Moscow skyline. 'It's a police state, with no free elections. That's a different thing. But we can see some signs of fascism. I cannot find another state which has created such an enormous lie. Putin wants Russia to seem normal and democratic, but every decision is taken from the position of brutality.'

It was one thing to gather a few thousand people in Moscow and shout anti-Kremlin slogans, but something entirely different to offer serious resistance to a government that controlled the media, the security services and the courts. What, I wondered, was the chink in Putin's armour he hoped to exploit? Did he really believe that he and his allies in Other Russia could bring down Putin?

'We have no chance, if you look at the situation as static,' Limonov shrugged, stroking his beard. 'But, if we apply more and more pressure, we can create a conflict again and again. We are aiming to create a great upheaval in society. If we can do this, everyone will follow us.'

Hidden away in his headquarters, waited on by young men and women who jumped at the sound of his voice, Limonov had lost touch with reality. He may have been able to inspire a hard core of devoted activists, but his appeal could not go wider. Russians are both tired and scared of radical social change, and Limonov is about as radical as it gets. This is, after all, a man who once proposed solving Russia's demographic crisis by forcing 'every woman between 25 and 35 to have four children'. The children would then be taken away from their parents when they began to walk, and educated in a House of Childhood. 'Boys and girls will be taught to shoot from grenade launchers, to jump from helicopters, to besiege villages and cities, to skin sheep and pigs, to cook good hot food and to write poetry,' Limonov wrote, in one of a series of essays for his followers entitled 'Outlines for the Future'. 'Many types of people will have to disappear,' he added ominously.

'Fuck,' Limonov replied, when I quizzed him on the extract. 'I even forgot I wrote that. I feel free to use dreams and thinking in my work. I may be as wrong as hell, but, if so, I'll say, "OK, don't do it." You have too square a view of me,' he sneered.

It was wrong to think of Limonov as a politician. He was, like Surkov, the Kremlin's mysterious ideologue, an artist who had turned his talents to shaping and manipulating events in his volatile homeland. Surkov conjured up the illusion of stability out of chaos, while Limonov worked with the gaudy colours of rebellion, drawing inspiration from friction and contradiction. He could not come to power, because power was not his aim. He was addicted to struggle, to the adrenaline kick of his role as an eternal outsider. 'Life is conflict,' Limonov told me, before I left him.

Putin's hold over Russian politics throughout the 2000s was absolute. Who could rival him? The parliamentary opposition was under Surkov's thumb, while the protest movement's leaders were so convenient for the Kremlin it was tempting to suspect that the grey cardinal had been meddling here, too. Putin seemed to have Russia locked down. But he was about to be faced with a dilemma, the solution to which would both define his long rule and sow the seeds for increasing dissent. Putin had to decide whether to stay or go. In the end, he chose both.

4

MEDVEDEV AND THE SCENT OF CHANGE

As his second term of office hit the midway point, Putin had to make perhaps the most important decision of his presidency. The Russian constitution stated clearly that no president could serve more than 'two consecutive terms'. But Putin had no plans to surrender power. His self-appointed task of reshaping Russia was not yet complete, and there was no one he trusted enough to finish the job. There was also the possibility of eventual criminal charges over allegations of massive corruption, were he to step down without securing a watertight amnesty from prosecution. Even if he had wanted to, quitting was simply too dangerous.

Accordingly, speculation grew in 2006 that Putin would rewrite Russia's laws to enable him to remain in the Kremlin for a third term. It was, after all, a tactic that had been used effectively in neighbouring Belarus by the former Soviet republic's authoritarian leader Alexander Lukashenko. A reworking of the Russian constitution would have posed no problem: by law, there was no need for a national referendum. But

Putin, wary perhaps of international condemnation and possible protests at home, was seeking a more subtle way to hold on to power.

After months of deliberation, Putin resolved, like Yeltsin before him, to appoint an heir. But, unlike Yeltsin, he had no intention of retiring quietly to the countryside. Putin was going nowhere. 'My successor will have to negotiate with me how we divide power,' he said bluntly.[1]

Two main candidates for the presidency emerged: Sergei Ivanov, the hawkish defence minister, and Dmitry Medvedev, a young, liberal-minded lawyer, who was chairman of the state-run energy giant, Gazprom. Medvedev was also a deputy prime minister – a post Ivanov was likewise promoted to in February 2007. The two men seemed to symbolize the two wildly different paths that Russia could take. Ivanov, a former KGB general, promised more of the same as under Putin, while the softly spoken Medvedev offered the tantalizing prospect of reform. In an ideal world, Putin would have let them run against each other. But Putin was not interested in a genuine successor. He needed a malleable heir, one who could be relied on to jump at the sound of his master's voice.

On 10 December 2007, Putin announced he would back Medvedev – at just forty-two, his junior by thirteen years – to succeed him as president. 'I am confident that he will be a good president and an effective manager,' Putin said. 'But besides other things, there is this personal chemistry: I trust him.'[2]

Kremlin insiders suggested Putin and Medvedev enjoyed a father-and-son-type relationship. Indeed, Putin was in the habit of addressing Medvedev as 'Dima' – the diminutive and casual form of 'Dmitry'. Notably, Medvedev did not respond in kind, sticking to 'Vladimir', rather than the much less formal 'Volodya' or 'Vova', when speaking to and of his mentor. 'It's almost a monarchical succession,' noted Olga Kryshtanovskaya, an analyst and member of the ruling United Russia party. 'Putin's nominated his adopted son.'[3]

No one was under any illusions that Putin planned to grant his 'son' too much power. As analysts, pro-Putin politicians and the opposition all hurried to point out, the constitution spoke only of two 'consecutive' terms. It remained silent on a third or even fourth term at a later date.

'If Putin wants to return… there is no doubt Medvedev will give way to him,' said opposition politician Vladimir Ryzhkov.[4]

Even throughout the darkest days of the Soviet Union, Russians joked about their leaders, and Medvedev soon became a target for their barbed humour. 'Medvedev sits in the driver's seat of a new car, examines the inside, the instrument panel and the pedals. He looks around, but there is no steering wheel. He turns to Putin with a quizzical look on his face and asks: "Where is the steering wheel?" Putin pulls a remote control out of his pocket and says: "Oh, Dima, didn't you know? I'll be the one doing the driving."'

PUTIN'S SECRETARY

Putin and Medvedev go back a long way. Both were born in Leningrad (St Petersburg) and both studied law at the city university. But, while Putin grew up in a cold-water, communal apartment in a city still recovering from the horrors of World War II, Medvedev had a relatively comfortable childhood. His father was a lecturer at a scientific institute in the city, while his mother taught part-time at a local teacher-training college. His first-grade teacher, Vera Smirnova, remembers him as a clever and curious student, a '*pochemuchka*' – or, in English, someone who is always asking 'Why?'[5]

While Putin had spent his secondary school years dreaming of a career in the KGB, Medvedev's generation was far more interested in the culture of the West, which was just beginning to infiltrate big cities. Putin had adored Soviet spy films; Medvedev spent months saving to purchase a copy of Pink Floyd's *The Wall* and a pair of blue Levi jeans. In the early 1980s, he also attended concerts by the leaders of Leningrad's nascent underground rock scene. This was real dissident music. Groups such as Akvarium, a Dylanesque folk/rock outfit, and Kino, led by the iconic Viktor Tsoi, were musical outlaws who were banned from recording studios and the airwaves. Venues where these groups were due to perform were often surrounded by the police to stop gigs going ahead.[6]

In the late 1980s, after defending his dissertation, Medvedev got a job teaching Roman and civil law at his old university. He also offered legal services to some of the private businesspeople who had begun operating in the wake of Gorbachev's economic reforms. Unlike Putin in Dresden, Medvedev experienced in full the thrills of perestroika. In 1989, he campaigned for Anatoly Sobchak, his old law professor and Putin's future political mentor, who was running for the new Soviet parliament. It was a bold decision: Sobchak, by now a national celebrity, was urging an end to the Communist Party's monopoly on power. Had Gorbachev's reforms been crushed, Medvedev could have lost his job, at the very least. But the young lawyer threw himself vigorously into the campaign. When a batch of Sobchak's campaign leaflets was confiscated by the KGB, Medvedev sat up all night with other activists, printing out new copies on an old mimeograph machine. Medvedev later said the experience made him feel 'like Lenin' plotting to overthrow the tsar.

It was Sobchak who brought Putin and Medvedev together. In 1990, Sobchak, while head of the Leningrad city government, invited his former campaigner to come and help him out part-time. Medvedev accepted and, a month later, Putin joined the team. The two former law students became friends, and Medvedev would often spend the weekends at the Putin family *dacha* near St Petersburg. When Sobchak became mayor in the summer of 1991, he made Putin head of the city's Committee on Foreign Relations, a post the future president would later hold simultaneously with his position of deputy mayor. Over the next few years, Medvedev would often drop by at the committee's HQ after work to help out his new friend. Visitors to the office recalled that Medvedev sat at a tiny desk in the lobby, and was frequently mistaken for Putin's secretary.

Those evenings in St Petersburg set the pattern for the two men's relationship. When Putin was unexpectedly made acting president by the ailing Yeltsin in 1999, Medvedev received a call asking him to come to Moscow. Putin wanted him as his campaign chief. In just ten years, Medvedev had gone from running off illicit leaflets for a Soviet reformer to organizing the election campaign of the acting president. After Putin's election victory, Medvedev became deputy head of the presidential administration. He made few ripples and ruffled even fewer feathers. Indeed, one of his colleagues at the time, Putin's economic adviser, Andrei Illarionov, said later he was unable to recall a single instance of Medvedev expressing a personal opinion about 'any idea, any project, any movement, any action'.[7] For much of the 2000s, Medvedev combined his duties in the Kremlin with his chairmanship of the Gazprom board, the energy giant that Putin turned into a political weapon in the Kremlin's frequent feuds with post-Orange Revolution Ukraine. Medvedev's job, insiders say, was to sign off on Putin's orders. The curious little boy who could never stop asking 'Why?' had become a loyal Kremlin bureaucrat.

FORWARD, RUSSIA?

Putin's endorsement of Medvedev meant there was never going to be any serious doubt as to the outcome of the March 2008 presidential polls. State TV provided blanket and fawning pre-election coverage of Medvedev, and no genuine opposition candidates were allowed on the ballot. Medvedev won a landslide victory, taking just over 70% of the vote. The Organization for Security and Co-operation (OSCE) boycotted the vote after it was unable to secure visas for its monitors. Those international observers who made it to Russia criticized the polls as unfair.[8] Scattered protests took place in Moscow and St Petersburg, but demonstrators were outnumbered by activists from the pro-Kremlin movement *Nashi*. A crackdown on well-known opposition activists ahead of election day also helped to ensure there would be no Orange Revolution-style uprising.

Two days after Medvedev's election victory, Putin accepted the new president's proposal to become prime minister. In a further sharing out of duties, Putin also became head of the governing United Russia party. The country's most powerful man was now, technically at least, subservient to his protégé. This unheralded power-sharing arrangement soon became known as 'the tandem'. Images of the master and his pupil – the stern but wise Putin and the jovial, almost childlike Medvedev – were soon everywhere.

A Deep Purple-loving rock fan ('I have all their albums: not CD reissues, but the vinyl')[9] with bookish looks and an enthusiasm for technology, Medvedev was initially hailed by both Russia's middle class and Western commentators as an antidote to the tough-talking Putin. His relative youth also made him, as one Western analyst gushed, 'as close as you can get to a post-Soviet generation'.[10] And, of course, unlike many of the Kremlin elite, he had no known links to the security services.

Despite Medvedev's undoubted loyalty to Putin, his political mentor, there were occasional signs that the new president might prove to be his own man. In the weeks before he took office, Medvedev blacked out parts of a keynote speech to civic and cultural leaders written for him in the Kremlin. In place of sycophantic praise for Putin and allegations that the West was seeking to foment revolution in Russia, Medvedev attacked instead what he called the 'legal nihilism' he said was destroying the country. Early on in his one-term presidency, Medvedev came up with his memorable, if slightly clumsy, catchphrase: 'Freedom is better than non-freedom.' He also took a swipe at the concept of 'sovereign democracy', the dominant political philosophy dreamed up by the Kremlin's chief ideologue, Surkov. 'It would be much better to speak of genuine democracy,' Medvedev remarked coldly.[11]

Medvedev also gained plaudits in liberal circles when he gave the first interview of his presidency to the opposition-friendly newspaper *Novaya Gazeta*. Medvedev had promised the interview to the paper's editor, Dmitry Muratov, after one of its journalists, Anastasia Baburova, was gunned down in central Moscow alongside a human-rights lawyer named Stanislav Markelov in January 2009. Baburova was the fourth *Novaya Gazeta* journalist to be murdered since the investigative newspaper was launched in 2000.

Medvedev praised *Novaya Gazeta* in no uncertain terms: 'You never suck up to anyone,' he told its editor, Muratov. He also used the interview to promise his rule would bring Russia not only economic prosperity, but also political freedoms. It was a bold pledge: this was something no

Russian leader in history had ever been able to do. Medvedev wanted to give Russians both sausages *and* freedom.[12] 'All we can do is hope,' a *Novaya Gazeta* reader wrote in the comments section under the interview.

Medvedev laid out his vision for Russia in a September 2009 essay with the oddly Soviet-sounding title of 'Forward, Russia!', in which he called for the sweeping political and economic 'modernization' of his homeland. Labelling the economy 'primitive' and corruption 'endemic', Russia's young president tore into Putin's system. 'Our affairs are far from being in the best state,' he began.[13]

'We need to cultivate a taste for the rule of law, for abiding by the law, respect for the rights of others, including such important rights as that of property ownership. It is the job of the courts with broad public support to cleanse the country of corruption. This is a difficult task but it is doable. Other countries have succeeded in doing this.

'I would invite all those who share my convictions to get involved,' Medvedev concluded, vowing that, however hard 'influential groups of corrupt officials' might try to prevent the rise of this 'new Russia', 'the future belongs to us, not them!'

It was, in parts at least, an electrifying vision and one that inspired, for a brief period, tens of thousands of young Russians disillusioned with the cynicism and corruption at the heart of the country's politics and business.

'When I read Medvedev's "Forward, Russia!", I thought that he really could become an independent politician and carry out the political reforms he had written about,' said the young opposition politician Dmitry Gudkov, when I met him and his wife, Valeriya, in a chic café across from the State Duma. 'We really believed this,' he went on, glancing at Valeriya, who nodded solemnly in response. 'Medvedev captured a genuine feeling of hope.'[14]

Unlike reported technophobe Putin, Medvedev embraced the latest gadgetry, launching a Twitter account (mercilessly mocked) and personally wishing Russians happy birthday via social network sites. Internet users nicknamed him Russia's 'chief blogger'. He also demonstrated a willingness to poke fun at himself, bringing a levity to the Kremlin unimaginable under the austere and terse Putin. When a clip of the country's 'chief blogger' dancing at a university reunion was posted on YouTube, Medvedev responded to an online comment that 'he dances like my dad', with a jokey Twitter post: 'That's about right, probably, age-wise.'[15] Medvedev's spokesperson also later said the president had failed to understand the decision to cut a parody of his dance moves from a primetime television show. 'The president is pretty calm about parodies,' said a Kremlin spokeswoman. 'He's even posted some of the best on his Twitter account.'[16]

It all boiled down to this: the country's 'creative classes' – as urban, educated Russians became known during Medvedev's tenure – might not have been empowered by the country's youngest leader for a century, but there was little doubt they had been emboldened. At times, Medvedev even appeared to be goading liberals into challenging the Kremlin. During a private meeting with leading cultural and public figures in Moscow towards the end of his rule, he reportedly hailed them as 'the best people in our city', and urged them to 'take power!'[17]

However, as Medvedev's presidency reached the end of its second year, it was becoming increasingly clear that the young president was no saviour. His constant talk of reform, without action to back up his statements, reduced his buzzwords of 'modernization' and 'development' to empty, meaningless phrases. Indeed, the only serious reform carried out by Medvedev during his time as nominal head of state was to increase the presidential term of office from four years to six. It was a move that would grant Putin, upon his return to the Kremlin, the opportunity to remain in power until 2024. Medvedev also oversaw the establishment of Anti-Extremism Centres, whose agents would mercilessly persecute anti-Putin activists. True, Medvedev had blocked a number of Putin-backed draft laws on protests and a wider definition of treason that would have made dissent even more dangerous, but he had failed to push through any of his own policies in response.

Medvedev was also unable – or unwilling – to prevent prosecutors bringing new charges against Mikhail Khodorkovsky, the tycoon jailed by Putin after his funding of opposition parties. The decision to arrest the businessman in 2003 had been welcomed by the vast majority of

Russians, and even some foreign businessmen, as a necessary step to reel in the powerful oligarchs. But public sympathy had swayed significantly by 2010, when Khodorkovsky and his business partner, Platon Lebedev, had six years added to their sentences on new charges that were widely seen as politically motivated. The businessmen had first been imprisoned for tax avoidance on oil sold by Khodorkovsky's company Yukos; investigators now claimed they had simply stolen the company's entire output. 'A thief should sit in jail,' Putin declared, even before the trial had ended.

Medvedev was enraged by this blatant interference. 'No official has the right to express their position on a case before the court announces their verdict,' he retorted. His supporters were thrilled by what was, in effect, a public dressing down of Putin.[18]

But Medvedev's bark had no bite. He could not protect Khodorkovsky, and he was also powerless to halt attacks, often deadly, on journalists and human-rights campaigners. In November 2010, Oleg Kashin, the opposition journalist who described the pro-Putin movement *Nashi* as a 'cult', was set upon by two men armed with iron bars as he entered the courtyard of his apartment block in Moscow. The attack, captured by a nearby CCTV camera, was a study in methodical, relentless brutality. *Nashi*'s leader, Vasily Yakemenko, the man who had threatened to send football hooligans after Putin's foes, mocked Kashin as he lay in a coma, calling him a 'zombie'. Although it seemed no one could survive such a sustained battering, Kashin eventually made a full recovery – although one of his fingers was amputated.

Shortly before the attempt on his life, Kashin's photograph had been published – along with other 'JOURNALIST-TRAITORS!' – on the website of another pro-Kremlin youth group, Young Guard, with the words 'WILL BE PUNISHED!' stamped over his face. The group denied any involvement in the attack. Kashin said he suspected *Nashi*'s chief, Yakemenko, who also rubbished the allegation.[19] The savage assault on the journalist made national news, and an emotional Medvedev pledged to 'tear the heads off' Kashin's attackers.[20] (No progress was made in the investigation until the autumn of 2015, when Kashin revealed in a blog post that three men had been charged with the attack. But the authorities refused to even question the man named by the wife of one of the suspects as the organizer of the brutal assault – Andrei Turchak, the governor of central Russia's Pskov region. Turchak had been involved in a dispute with Kashin shortly before the attack, and had reportedly paid the three men some $105,000 to ensure Kashin would 'never write again'.)

However, the biggest symbol of Medvedev's utter failure to combat Russia's 'legal nihilism' was the November 2009 death of Sergei Magnitsky, a thirty-seven-year-old lawyer with the equity fund Hermitage Capital. Magnitsky was arrested in late 2008, shortly after he had alleged a $230 million tax-embezzlement scheme by Interior Ministry officials. In a display of cynicism so blatant it takes the breath away, Magnitsky was detained by the very same officials he had accused of stealing from the state. He would never see his family again. A year later, he breathed his last in a grimy pre-trial detention cell, handcuffed and bruised, and suffering from agonizing and untreated abdominal pains. In a report, the Kremlin's own human-rights council stated that Magnitsky's death was likely to have been the result of a 'beating' and the denial of medical assistance.[21] Both Putin and investigators dismissed the findings of the expert group, and announced the lawyer had died of 'heart failure'. Obscenely, Magnitsky would later be tried posthumously on the tax-fraud charges.[22]

'It was very symbolic for me that I was attacked during Medvedev's rule. And also that Magnitsky was murdered,' a glum Kashin told me. 'Like many other people, I really thought we might see a new Russia after Medvedev came to power. But he cynically exploited our trust.'

Belief in Medvedev's oft-stated desire for reform had been born out of a hope that Russia could really turn itself around, that corruption and nepotism could be rooted out and that an independent media, judicial system and police force could be established. It was a pipe dream. As the reclusive, postmodern novelist Viktor Pelevin pointed out in a novel the year Medvedev came to power, the modernization of Russia would entail, essentially, that 'bureaucrats would not demand kickbacks, judges would ignore telephone commands, natural resources traders would not take their money to London, [and] traffic policemen would live on their salaries'. Most importantly, it would also mean, Pelevin noted astutely, that many of Russia's wealthiest people would have to 'move to *Chistopolskaya Krytaya* [a famous prison]'.[23] Even if Medvedev was genuine about the need for change, there was no way Putin would allow him to deconstruct the system he had spent so many years building up. Modernization and Putinism could not co-exist. Millions watched as their hopes for a fairer, more just Russia were slowly deflated.

✳

Many in Russia's still tiny protest movement had been sceptical to begin with that Medvedev could bring about real, meaningful change. Shortly after the young president came to power, Roman Dobrokhotov, a pipe-smoking, twenty-something veteran of the opposition scene, planned to test how seriously the Kremlin was about reform. 'We came up with the idea of a protest where we would hold up placards with Medvedev's liberal catchphrases on, things like "freedom is better than non-freedom" and "we don't need sovereign democracy",' he laughed, when I met him at a central Moscow club.[24]

'We just wanted to see if the police would disperse us or not,' he went on, raising his voice above the reggae coming from the club's sound system. 'You know, it's easy enough to say all these liberal things, but following through is an entirely different matter.'

The rally never went ahead; instead, Dobrokhotov came up with a much more direct way of drawing attention to the gulf between the new president's 'fine-sounding phrases' and the reality of life in Russia. In late 2008, as Medvedev was halfway through a televised Constitution Day speech at Moscow State University, Dobrokhotov's voice rang out. 'What are you listening to him for? The country is under the censors, there are no elections, and he's talking about the constitution?' Dobrokhotov yelled, continuing to shout even as he was dragged out of his seat by Medvedev's security.[25]

'There's no need to take him anywhere,' Medvedev murmured, almost to himself, as one of his burly bodyguards clamped a hand over

Dobrokhotov's mouth. 'Let him stay here and listen. The constitution was adopted so that everyone has the right to their own opinion.'

The president may as well have been reciting his shopping list for all the attention his security team paid: the activist was ejected from the hall.

For Dobrokhotov, it was a deeply symbolic moment. 'It was a perfect illustration of how the system was set up. If even his own security didn't listen to him, then what else is there to say here?'

THE VIEW FROM THE TOP OF THE PYRAMID

Medvedev's message of reform had not come from nowhere. As the very real Yeltsin-era fear of famine and the total disintegration of the state receded into memory, many Russians, especially in Moscow, began to think about more than mere material gain. Abstract ideas such as freedom and morality, things that hadn't been discussed much since the final heady days of the Soviet Union, suddenly became fashionable again. The growing middle class had travelled to Europe and compared their country unfavourably with what they had seen there. Back in Russia, they started to ask themselves why things should be so much worse in their homeland.

'I and many of my friends, educated and well-travelled people, may have lived in Russia, but we tried to stay aloof from things around us,' Maria, a well-dressed, twenty-something lawyer and a regular at anti-Putin marches, told me when I spoke to her at a fashionable central Moscow restaurant. 'Via internet forums, plus a few clubs and cafés, we tried to create our own little version of a civilized Western country. But, eventually, we realized it was impossible to live like this. We got fed up of pretending, and decided to build in the real world the kind of country we wanted to live in!' She laughed, and took a sip of her green tea. 'I'm not sure why it took us so long to make our minds up to do that, actually.'

Medvedev's constant triumphing of liberal ideas both tapped into and frustrated the growing hunger for change. 'The moment of greatest danger for an autocratic regime is when it begins to reform itself,' wrote the nineteenth-century French political thinker Alexis de Tocqueville. It was a statement that held equally true in twenty-first-century Russia. Meaningful political and social change may have been minimal under Medvedev, but even the hint of reform was enough to inspire Russians dissatisfied with Putinism. A slow but steady drip-drop of dissent began, with small but unmistakable signs appearing almost weekly that Putin's pact was in trouble. Anti-United Russia graffiti began to appear on walls all over town. The readership of opposition-friendly magazines like Moscow's *Afisha* went up. Celebrities started to speak out. From mid-2009 onwards, hundreds of protesters began gathering at a square in central Moscow on the 31st day of every month that had one in defence of article 31 of the Russian constitution, which guarantees the right to free assembly. Demonstrators were frequently dispersed, in keeping with Putin's advice, with a 'whack around the head with a baton' by riot police.[26] 'I don't give a shit about the law,' an officer yelled at a protester at one rally, who promptly posted footage of the outburst online.[27]

Small 'initiative' groups also began to spring up all over the country, but mostly in and around Moscow. Volunteers tackled the issues the authorities could not – or would not – deal with. From the middle-class professionals and students who spent their spare time caring for Moscow's massive vagrant population to Liza Alert, a volunteer group that searched for missing children, these people were suddenly everywhere. This was a new phenomenon for Russia. In the Soviet era, people had been forced into joining social groups and other organizations; with the collapse of the communist state and the onset of bandit capitalism, the vast majority of Russians retreated inwards to focus on providing for their families. The popularity of volunteer groups was a clear sign of a maturing and more independent society.

This frenzy of self-help reached its apex in the baking summer of 2010, when thousands of volunteers risked their lives to battle massive wildfires in the peat bogs around Moscow. The fires occur annually, but rarely on the scale of that year. As thick, choking smoke swept through the streets, I fled with my wife and young daughter from our non-air-conditioned apartment to a nearby hotel. There we kept the windows closed tightly, safe from the tendrils of smog in the corridors outside. Elsewhere in the city, the morgues were filling up fast. Health officials later admitted that the death rate had doubled that summer. But Moscow's mayor, Yury Luzhkov, was unconcerned. His spokesperson said he would not be returning from his vacation, as the smog and the abnormal heat was 'no crisis'.[28] With emergency services incapable of dousing the flames alone, it was left to volunteer groups to co-ordinate their efforts online in an attempt to tackle the disaster. On the surface at least, acts like these may have been apolitical, but they unnerved the Kremlin. Volunteerism not only smacked of the West, but it also had the potential to morph into something more dangerous for the authorities. A new law to regulate the actions of volunteers was quickly drawn up.

Russians were starting to question everything. When veteran rock star Yury Shevchuk unexpectedly launched into a discussion of democracy with Putin at a televised charity dinner in late 2010 ('I have a few questions, the first is about that thing called freedom'), the clip went viral, clocking up some three million hits in a matter of weeks. 'Excuse me, who are you?' interrupted Putin, apparently unaware of the name of one of the country's best-known musicians.[29]

A few weeks later, inspired by the online sensation created by Shevchuk's boldness, Leonid Parfyonov, one of the country's most famous journalists, delivered a blistering condemnation of state media at an awards ceremony. 'The country's leaders are treated as the dearly deceased: you speak well of them or not at all,' a clearly nervous Parfyonov told an audience of media big shots. 'At the same time, the audience clearly thirsts for other opinions.'

Media bosses looked on in astonishment, the emotions on their faces a mixture of shock, embarrassment and admiration for the veteran journalist.[30]

Around the same time, a well-known, ex-Bolshoi prima ballerina called Anastasia Volochkova caused a stir when she quit United Russia in a radio interview. The blonde and statuesque Volochkova had long been one of United Russia's many celebrity faces, adding glamour to otherwise dull election campaigns and a sparkle to party rallies. But now she wanted out. 'That fucking party... [was] shit I was careless enough to step into,' she raged in the radio interview.

Such explicit, public criticism of Putin's party was still rare, and her comments caused a storm. The trigger for Volochkova's anger may have been far removed from politics (a bizarre row over her decision to post topless photos on her blog), but her discontent had obviously been building up for some time.

'Young people today don't care at all about United Russia,' she told me, with a pout, when I went to visit her at her office near Red Square. 'They don't believe in the authorities or in any kind of future. Hosni Mubarak was in power in Egypt for so many years and thought that's how things would go on, but the people overthrew him just like that. Of course such a thing is possible here. If the authorities don't do something to change the situation, the people themselves will.'[31]

It was a truly startling thing to hear from the mouth of a woman who had for so many years been an establishment figure. It was, I reasoned, the kind of prediction the Other Russia leader, Limonov, might have made. But a one-time Bolshoi ballerina and former United Russia loyalist? There could be no doubt – times were changing fast.

Russian anti-Putin activists are keen on using US psychologist Abraham Maslow's theory of human motivation to explain this sudden surge in middle-class dissent in Moscow. Maslow's paper, published in 1943, said that most people have five sets of needs. These start off from the very basic – food and drink – and progress to the need for self-actualization and self-respect. Russia's middle class, they say in opposition circles, are nearing the top of that pyramid. They have solved the problem of how to feed their families and even purchase luxury items; now they want to live in a country where they can experience a sense of their own moral worth. But this is hard to do when you are ruled by a corrupt elite whose sole saving grace is that it has provided a modicum of economic stability, when state TV pumps out crude propaganda all day long, and the law is a weapon used to eliminate political rivals.

'Urban, educated Russians declared that the everyday freedoms so generously bestowed on them by the Putin epoch – the freedom to drink, eat, travel, sleep, read, watch, stick their fingers up their noses – were insufficient to feel a part of Europe,' noted Stanislav Belkovsky, a well-known political analyst. 'They also needed political freedoms.'[32]

Ironically, the people who had benefited the most from Putin's rule were now his biggest critics.

There was also growing unease at the apparent near immunity from prosecution enjoyed by even minor officials. This lawlessness was thrust into the limelight in November 2010, when twelve people – including four children, among them a nine-month-old baby – were stabbed, shot or strangled to death over a suspected business dispute in a house in the small town of Kushchevskaya, in south Russia's Krasnodar region. The crime, even for a country where horrific violence had become the norm, shocked Russia. Eventually, a local town-council member and gang leader, Sergei Tsapok, was arrested and charged with organizing the killings. But it soon emerged that some 200 cases of murder, rape, robbery, assault and grievous bodily harm against Tsapok and his gang had been opened and quickly closed without charge by local police in the decade before the massacre. Another member of the gang, Sergei Tsepovyaz, was fined around $5,000 for covering up the crime. Prosecutors had not even asked for jail time.[33] Opposition figures and media alleged both men were United Russia members, and that Tsapok had even been present at Medvedev's 2008 inauguration. Putin's party belatedly denied this, but the scandal only served to blacken its reputation further.

Volochkova, the ballet star, had described United Russia as a 'criminal gang'. And it was this image of criminality, rather than its weak, almost non-existent ideology that was the party's major attraction for prospective members. In a poll carried out in 2011 by United Russia among people who wanted to join its ranks, just under half said they were looking to earn money on the side.[34] There appeared to be plenty of scope for this. In April 2011, Russia's *Vedomosti* broadsheet reported on the spectacular business successes of the children of leading regional United Russia officials, many of whom had somehow managed to become heads of massive regional companies while still in their early to mid-twenties. The article ran under the mocking headline 'They Were Just Very Lucky'.[35]

In the political vernacular of modern Russia, United Russia is commonly referred to as 'the party of power'. The term, like Surkov's 'sovereign democracy', reflects the essence of Putin's take on the political process. Power, once attained, is eternal. However, by late 2011, despite the best efforts of state media, United Russia's approval ratings had dropped to under 50% nationwide. Putin's ratings were also steadily declining. The number of Russians who felt an 'affinity' for the 'national leader' was now just 24%, a drop of almost half from his finest hour: victory in the 2008 war against Georgia.[36]

ONLINE AND OFFLINE

It was not hard to see the link between this increasing disgruntlement with the authorities and the dramatic increase in internet penetration across Russia. Russian scientists were among the first people in the world to exchange information digitally, and their fellow citizens soon caught on to the possibilities of the medium. When Putin came to power in 1999, just over 1% of Russians were online; by 2011, this had risen to almost 50% of the country, or some fifty-one million people. Putin had taken the decision not to build a Chinese-type wall of censorship early in the 2000s, and the decision was coming back to haunt him.[37]

The Kremlin may have seized control of state television – dubbed the 'Zombie box' by disaffected urban Russians – but an army of bloggers, as well as a handful of opposition websites, were busy documenting the country's many woes. Social networks and online tools such as Twitter and YouTube became the protest movement's most potent weapons. Free of Kremlin control, they not only offered a platform for dissent and a means of publicizing injustice, but also a way of uniting the discontented. 'The internet is the only place where people can find out about what's really going on in Russia,' Oleg Kozyrev, a young media professional and opposition blogger, told me. 'It's also the only place where they can get organized.'

Soviet-era dissidents who had been forced to rely on typescript and handwritten *samizdat* documents to circulate information could only watch in envy.

These online activists would soon learn how to influence the real world. In March 2010, the Mercedes-Benz of Anatoly Barkov, the vice-president of the oil company Lukoil, crashed into a Citroën hatchback in central Moscow, killing the driver, a respected doctor and her daughter-in-law. Police immediately blamed the driver of the smaller vehicle for the accident, but refused to provide footage of the crash from the security cameras lining the highway. Pre-internet, the story would probably have ended there, but the case was seized upon by outraged bloggers and the Federation of Russian Car Owners, an online movement. The row went public, sparking widespread anger at what looked like yet another case of an 'untouchable' going unpunished. Medvedev eventually stepped in and ordered a full investigation into the case. Predictably, the police cleared Barkov later that year, but not before Russia's increasingly politicized online community had sensed its potential strength.

The power of the internet and the growing trend for self-organization would be most effectively harnessed in Khimki, a small town near Moscow, where eco-activists were attempting to prevent the construction of a Kremlin-backed, multimillion-dollar highway through ancient woodland. Led by Yevgenia Chirikova, a local young mother, the activists not only set up camp to defend the forest, but they also blogged relentlessly, raising the profile of their campaign both nationally and beyond Russia's borders.

A petite blonde with a fondness for tank-tops and a penchant for straight-talking, Chirikova had moved from Moscow to Khimki in the early 2000s with her businessman husband, Mikhail, to raise a family in 'the fresh air, away from the traffic fumes'. For a while, everything went to plan. But, one evening in 2007, as the family was walking in the sprawling oak forest next to their apartment block, Chirikova, pregnant with one daughter and busy caring for another, noticed that a number of trees had been daubed with red paint. Curious, she went online. The red slashes, Chirikova discovered, were to mark trees intended for destruction as part of a project to build an $8 billion Moscow–St Petersburg highway through the ancient woodland.

The news acted as a wake-up call for the young mother: 'I knew this highway had to be stopped – the forest is part of Moscow's green belt. Its lungs, if you like. They were getting ready to cut out Moscow's lungs,' she recalled.[38]

'I was such a vegetable back then,' she told me, as we walked through a wintery central Moscow, large flakes of powdery snow falling on her Andean-style hat. 'You know, I'd thought United Russia was some kind of ecological party. Why? Because they had a bear as their symbol! I knew nothing at all about politics. I had never paid any attention. I mean, I only found out about the split-up of the Soviet Union in 1998.'

I laughed at what I assumed to be a slightly weird joke. The collapse of the Soviet Union was one of the most significant events of the twentieth century, the repercussions of which are still being felt today. I found it hard to believe the event had passed her by entirely. But, no, Chirikova was serious. She may have been attentive enough to spot red paint splashed on trees in her local wood, but she had completely failed to notice that her country had changed its name, not to mention its flag and national anthem.

'I only found out when my husband told me one of his colleagues had had problems on the border with Ukraine. "What border?" I asked. "It's the same country." My husband looked at me with these massive eyes,' Chirikova recalled, laughing. '"Not anymore it's not," he said. "Since when!?" I asked him. And he told me all about it. I really hadn't paid any attention at the time. My father always told me politics was a dirty business. And I was busy with my own life…

'It was only because of the forest that I started to find out about things. They'd touched something I cared about a lot, something I loved, and after that I discovered everything very quickly. How the Soviet Union collapsed, about how Yeltsin attacked parliament in 1993, and so on. It was all because of the forest,' she repeated. 'That was my motivation. It was all down to the forest.'

Chirikova's evolution from self-described 'vegetable' to committed political activist reflected a growing awareness in Russia that the passivity and apathy that had dominated for much of the 1990s and 2000s had its dangers. You could shut your eyes to corrupt politicians and their business friends, but eventually they would come and start cutting down your favourite forest. Or worse. As the Russians say: 'If you don't pay attention to politics, politics pays attention to you.'

As soon as her second child was born, Chirikova began to campaign against the highway, whose construction was backed by Mayor Yury Luzhkov and financed by the French multinational Vinci, as well as, reportedly, a businessman close to Putin. Unversed in the realities of political activism, Chirikova began writing letters to City Hall, the Kremlin and anyone else she could think of. She received no replies. Slowly, it dawned on her that the authorities weren't listening. 'The local administration told me, "If you want to live in the forest, then go to Siberia!"' she recalled.

New tactics were needed. Before long, Chirikova and her self-styled 'Defenders of Khimki Forest' were standing in front of bulldozers to stop construction work from going ahead. They slowly gained not only the support and the respect of locals, but also the backing of international environmental-protection organizations.

There was a high price to pay for this uncompromising opposition to the highway. Just six months after Medvedev's pomp-filled Kremlin inauguration, during which he had declared that 'human rights and freedoms' enjoyed the 'highest value' in Russia and that 'we must gain full respect for the law and overcome legal nihilism', Mikhail Beketov, an eco-activist and journalist opposed to the Khimki highway, was ambushed and beaten mercilessly by assailants wielding metal rods. The ferocity of the attack on Beketov was so great that doctors were forced to amputate one of his legs and he lost the ability to speak, because shards of his skull had become lodged in his brain. Beketov died five years after the assault, in April 2013, when he choked on a piece of food. Police had long abandoned the investigation into the attack due to its 'complexity' and 'lack of evidence'.[39] Another highway opponent, Konstantin Fetisov, was also viciously beaten. The modus operandi was exactly the same as in the assault on Beketov; only this time the attackers used baseball bats instead of metal bars. Fetisov survived, but was left with a titanium plate in his skull and a serious speech impediment.

Chirikova escaped physical assault, but the authorities attempted to take her children away from her on the pretext that she was 'mistreating' them, only backing down after a public outcry. 'The whole country rose up,' she told me, exaggerating, it must be said, just a touch.

This brutality was proof that Chirikova's tactics were working. In August 2010, some 3,000 people gathered at central Moscow's Pushkin Square for a rally against the highway, singing along to acoustic sets by opposition-friendly rock musicians. Attendance might not have seemed like much, but, for a country where anti-government demonstrations very rarely attracted more than a few hundred hardcore dissidents, it was a landmark event. Just days after the rally, Medvedev announced the temporary suspension of the highway project. 'For me, Pushkin Square was when the protest movement began in earnest,' Chirikova told me later. This young mother with no previous political experience had proved that ordinary people could affect Kremlin policy. For a country with almost no history of independent civil or political activism, it was a massive step forward.

It is no coincidence that Chirikova's breakthrough came during Medvedev's presidency. This hard-rock-loving lawyer had failed to reform Russia, but his frequent talk of change had uncorked a genie that would prove impossible to put back in the bottle. Change suddenly seemed not only possible, but inevitable. Anti-Putin activists were scheming and dreaming, and for once their ambitions did not seem so outlandish. Watching from afar as events unfolded in Khimki, the man who would soon lead the biggest challenge to Putin's rule had learned some very important lessons.

5

NAVALNY AND THE 'CROOKS AND THIEVES'

The radio presenter's question was far from inspired: after all, it was no secret that Alexei Navalny, the tall, blond lawyer whose anti-corruption campaign had made him the most popular of Russia's online activists loathed Putin and his party with – as he had colourfully phrased it – 'every fibre of my soul'.

But Yury Pronko, the bespectacled and well-spoken talk-show host at Moscow's Radio Finam station, had almost an hour of airtime to fill, and just one guest. And, anyway, it was a professional courtesy to toss an interviewee a few soft questions.

'How do you feel about United Russia?' Pronko asked.

'Very badly,' Navalny replied instantly, fiddling with the black strap of his watch. His piercing blue eyes darted up to the right as he sought for a more vivid expression of his hatred.

'This is the party of crooks and thieves,' he continued, speaking in a slow, steady, almost rhythmic tempo. 'It is the duty of every patriot – and yes, I'm a patriot – to do all they can to destroy this party.'[1]

The mocking nickname was just the slogan that rising discontent had been searching for. Within days, the meme went viral, and then seeped out into the real world. Its popularity would soon vastly outstrip that of its author. By May 2011, some three months after Navalny had come up with the phrase, a poll indicated that one out of every three Russians concurred that 'crooks and thieves' was an accurate description of Putin's party. Around a quarter weren't sure. Just two years later, over half of all respondents would agree.

Navalny's slogan became so popular, so fast, not only because it was so gloriously defiant and truthful, but also because it was extremely funny. The Russian word for 'crook', '*zhulik*', which can also be translated as 'swindler', conjures up images of a small-time villain or a cartoon-style masked robber with a bag marked 'swag'.[2] Navalny had not only insulted the authorities with his slogan, he had also demythologized them in the eyes of millions of Russians. Suddenly, Putin and United Russia didn't look so powerful or frightening, after all.

Like all the best creative work, the slogan had come to its author in a sudden flash of inspiration. '[The nickname] came about entirely spontaneously,' Navalny recalled later. 'If you said to me now, "think up a slogan," I wouldn't be able to do it to save my life.'[3]

POKING THE TOAD

Although it would later seem as if Navalny had emerged from nowhere to challenge Putin with his electrifying speeches and jaw-dropping claims of corruption, he had been involved in opposition politics since the early 2000s. He was a relatively well-known face in both liberal and nationalist circles, but had never been able to make the breakthrough to wider recognition. His online battle against state corruption changed all that.

Navalny had learned much from Chirikova and her battle to save Khimki forest. As the head of a committee on the rights of Moscow residents run by the liberal Yabloko party, activists had asked him to assist with the campaign against the highway, but he had been sceptical. 'I was one of those people who thought that it was senseless to get involved,' Navalny said later. 'I told them to forget about it, not to bother. But they achieved things that no one had thought possible. I was inspired.'[4]

As he observed from a distance the storm that Chirikova and her allies kicked up over the highway project, Navalny realized that party politics and the traditional forms of opposition protest were at a dead-end. Shouting 'Russia without Putin!' in the company of a couple of dozen or so other hardcore activists until the cops dragged you off to a waiting police truck might seem like the noble thing to do, but it wasn't going to win any new recruits. Neither was jumping through the Kremlin's hoops to get permission to form tiny parties that would then inevitably be torn apart by in-fighting. People needed easy-to-understand issues, ones they could rally around, both online and offline. And what was simpler to understand than corruption? It was something everyone in the country had experienced.

With the collapse of the Soviet system and the onset of bandit capitalism, bribery had rapidly become a fact of life in Russia, necessary for everything from getting your child into a good school to opening a business. Everyone in authority, it sometimes seemed, was on the take.

Throughout the 1990s and 2000s, police in Moscow regularly shook down passers-by for real or imagined residency permit violations. Like the Tsarist-era officials expected to seek out bribes to compensate for their almost non-existent official salaries, Russia's police made little secret of the motivation for their frequent demands to see documents, as I discovered one afternoon after being stopped by a gang of cash-hungry cops. 'How else am I supposed to survive?' a large, red-faced police officer replied indignantly, when I complained about his behaviour. 'I have a family, you know? Could you live on 10,000 roubles a month [about $300]?'

Another officer laughed: 'They gave us guns and said, "Do whatever you want."'

At least they were honest about it.

The police who shook me down that afternoon were simply going with the flow. In November 2010, Medvedev admitted that Russia was losing up to $33 billion – a sum equivalent to 3% of its GDP – every single year due to corruption in its state procurement system alone.[5] A report by the Berlin-based anti-corruption watchdog Transparency International put the sum at $300 billion a year, an amount eight times higher than Russia's combined annual spending on health, education and agriculture.[6] Russia is being bled dry by corrupt officials. As the country's deputy prosecutor once admitted in a startlingly frank interview, even a 'mid-ranking corrupt bureaucrat' on a salary of less than $1,500 a month would be able to afford a $600,000 apartment in Moscow 'within a year'.[7]

This culture of corruption means that, while Russia may be swimming in oil dollars, its infrastructure outside the biggest cities continues to crumble dangerously. Travel even a few hours out of Moscow, and the reality on the ground in many of Russia's impoverished and brutal regions has little in common with life in the wealthy capital. Potholed and barely passable roads resemble those found in war zones, state care institutions burn to the ground with an alarming regularity, and failures at poorly maintained substations frequently leave thousands without electricity.

Engrained corruption has also posed dangers for national security. The willingness of police officers and security personnel to accept bribes means it is easy for militants to smuggle bombs on to planes or weapons across Russia at will. In August 2004, eighty-nine people died when two passenger planes were almost simultaneously blown up in mid-air by female suicide bombers who had slipped airport personnel slightly less than $200 to let them on board. A month later, heavily armed Chechen fighters bought their way through dozens of checkpoints on their way to commit Russia's worst ever terror attack in the small North Caucasus town of Beslan.

Navalny was not, of course, the only political activist to target corruption. But he was the first to do so in a way that galvanized mass support. Navalny was not content merely to condemn corruption: he was seeking to prove 'what was stolen, who stole it, where the money went, and who in government is responsible'.[8] He reported the results of all these probes on his increasingly popular blog – 'The Final Battle between Good and Neutrality' – in an attractive and easy-to-read mixture of outrage and weariness. His efforts turned him into a folk hero for thousands of equally discontented twenty- and thirty-somethings. Navalny also had street cred; unlike many figures in the anti-Putin movement, he had never held public office, nor was he a wealthy celebrity like the chess champ Kasparov. He was just an ordinary guy living in a medium-sized apartment with his wife and two kids in an unfashionable Moscow district an hour's drive from Red Square. And now he was taking on Putin and his 'crooks and thieves'.

Navalny's tactics as he dug into the layers of secrecy around Russia's corporate world were very simple: he would purchase a minuscule amount of stock in the organization (for example, 0.00000326% in state oil concern Rosneft),[9] and then set about 'poking' around to see what he could turn up. When he did discover something suspect, he demanded answers. One of the earliest objects of his investigations was Transneft, the state oil-transport monopoly. Kremlin-owned, with the energy minister on its board of directors, the company handled the transportation of over 90% of Russia's oil. No one could ever accuse Navalny of picking soft targets.

'An obvious example [of suspected corruption] was Transneft's charitable donations,' Navalny later explained. 'The company not only has a monopoly on the transport of oil, it is also the biggest giver to charity in Russia, and one of the biggest in the world. In 2007–8, it spent half a billion dollars on charity. But no one ever saw a trace of this unthinkable sum.'[10]

According to its official records, Transneft was spending as much on charity annually as it was on the upkeep of its vast network of oil pipes. Navalny, suspecting the money was being siphoned off, wrote to Transneft to demand to see its records. 'This is charity, not a commercial secret,' he argued.

The company refused, contesting his claim to be a minority shareholder. So Navalny filed a complaint with the Interior Ministry, which opened a criminal case. The investigation, predictably, was stonewalled. But Navalny was inspired by the storm his allegations had kicked up: he would soon allege cases of massive embezzlement at state gas monopoly Gazprom and the government-controlled VTB Bank, among others. In late 2010, while on a six-month fellowship at Yale, Navalny went public with his most startling accusation yet. The target was again Transneft and the scale of the allegations would dwarf the charity scandal. Navalny said he had gained access to official company documents, drawn up at the request of the Accounts Chamber, a parliamentary financial watchdog, detailing what he alleged was the theft of $4 billion of state funds during the construction of the company's East Siberia–Pacific Ocean pipeline.[11] The biggest project of its type in post-Soviet Russia, the pipeline was designed to bring oil to the US and Pacific Rim markets.

'This is not my report,' stressed Navalny, holding up a thin blue folder as he went online with his claims in a short, snappy clip that labelled Transneft 'Pipe-Eaters'. In a typical example of Navalny's offbeat humour, blood dripped down from the clip's captions, horror-movie style. 'This is not the opinion of analysts or experts. This is official Transneft material, prepared and signed by dozens of its employees… Our hair stood up on end when we read this report. It says that billions of dollars were stolen – simply stolen – during the realization of this wonderful national project.' He also noted that the suspected scam was the equivalent of the authorities lifting around 10,000 roubles ($30) from the pocket of every single tax-payer in Russia. 'We have reason to believe that Putin personally provided the political cover for these acts of corruption and thievery,' Navalny said, tapping the table in front of him to emphasize key words. 'Fed up with the thieves? Send this video to your friends!' an on-screen message urged at the end of the clip.[12]

Transneft would not deny the authenticity of the documents, although officials would dispute the size of the losses.[13] As the scandal broke, Putin took the opportunity to praise Transneft for its 'effective' work. Navalny snapped back: 'Sooner or later I'll see they all go to jail. They will all be punished.' He also dubbed Putin a 'toad sitting on an oil pipeline'.[14]

Six months after Navalny went public with the Transneft allegations, in a development reminiscent of the tit-for-tat revenge taken upon the whistleblowing lawyer Sergei Magnitsky, embezzlement charges were filed against the anti-corruption blogger. Navalny's investigations had provoked a reaction. He was now a marked man. 'I'm not ready for my son to become a martyr,' his mother, Lyudmila, wept after the charges were brought in an interview with the *New Yorker*.[15]

In late 2010, shortly after his high-profile accusations against Transneft, Navalny launched *RosPil*, a website devoted to uncovering suspicious-looking tenders for services requested by government entities. The organization takes its name from the Russian word *pilit*, meaning to illegally 'saw off' funds from a business contract. The website's striking symbol is the Russian double-headed eagle gripping two saws in its talons.

RosPil soon made a name for itself by publicizing what appeared to be the spectacular misappropriation of state funds by officials. There was, for example, the $60,000 worth of mink coats that authorities in St Petersburg insisted were intended for patients at a psychiatric institute. The thirty gold-and-diamond wristwatches ordered by a regional governor as 'gifts for local teachers'. The $276,000 Audi saloon ordered by the finance minister of a North Caucasus republic. ('Why should we buy limousines for local bigwigs?' Navalny fumed. 'Most world presidents get around in more modest vehicles.'[16])

All of these tenders, and many, many more, were annulled after readers of Navalny's blog flooded the Federal Anti-Monopoly Agency with complaints.[17]

Navalny's ability to elucidate the ins-and-outs of Russia's deep-rooted culture of high-level corruption in a no-nonsense, easy-to-understand manner won him the trust of tens of thousands of ordinary Russians. It was a remarkable achievement in a country where people had long learned to be cynical about anyone claiming to act in their interests. Within a week of asking for donations from the public to pay lawyers for *RosPil*, Navalny had received over $120,000 in anonymous contributions. Polls indicated that almost 70% of Russians were ready to accept there could be some truth behind Navalny's claims of state corruption.[18] No opposition figure had ever enjoyed this level of public trust.

Navalny also set out to highlight Putin's links to a number of ultra-rich businessmen: Arkady and Boris Rotenberg were once Putin's judo sparring partners in St Petersburg – they are now both billionaires who provide steel pipes and construction services to state-controlled gas giant Gazprom. A company belonging to Arkady, who has known Putin since they were both schoolchildren, was also awarded massive, multibillion-dollar contracts to undertake construction projects ahead of the 2014 Winter Olympic Games in Sochi.[19]

Another man alleged to have benefited from what he says is a casual relationship rather than a friendship with Putin is businessman Gennady Timchenko, the co-owner of the Gunvor Group, one of the world's largest traders in crude oil.[20] Another former member of the St Petersburg judo club where Putin and the Rotenberg brothers sparred, Timchenko has seen his wealth multiply to over $14 billion since Putin came to power.[21] The Gunvor Group is based in Switzerland, meaning Russian tax-payers receive no benefits from its marketing of crude exports from Russian state energy firms.

There is no proof that any of the men mentioned here have committed any crimes, or that the massive fortunes they have amassed are in any way connected to their acquaintanceships with Russia's long-time leader. Timchenko denies profiting from Putin's rise to power and has decried what he calls conspiracy theories.[22] But, for Navalny and other Kremlin critics, it seems suspicious that so many of Putin's friends and acquaintances have grown so rich, so fast.

Other acquaintances to have become extremely wealthy since the early 2000s are the eight men who were part of the shadowy *Ozero dacha* co-operative co-founded by Putin in the St Petersburg countryside in 1998. These men include Vladimir Yakunin, a former KGB officer appointed head of the gigantic Russian Railways state corporation in 2005, and Yury Kovalchuk, who is now a billionaire and major shareholder in Bank Rossiya. Another ex-*Ozero* resident, Nikolai Shamalov, is also a multimillionaire co-owner of Bank Rossiya. In late 2010, Shamalov was reported to be the nominal owner of a lavish palace being built for Putin in south Russia, not far from the Black Sea resort of Sochi. The allegation was made by Shamalov's former business partner, Sergei Kolesnikov, who said state funds had been siphoned off to finance the construction of the $1 billion palace.[23] The Kremlin denied Putin was the owner, yet there was no explanation as to why the building was being guarded by government security. In August 2013, four environmental activists who had helped bring the existence of the palace to public attention were jailed for between eight and thirteen years on extortion charges. The activists alleged the charges were trumped up and said they had been tortured while in police custody.[24] Putin not only wants to rule like a tsar, claim opposition figures, he wants to live like one as well.

Inevitably, claims arose that Navalny, this anti-graft crusader with the potential to hit the Kremlin where it hurt, was a US agent set upon the destruction of Russia. 'American tax-payers spent money on his training at Yale University, which prepares leaders for the so-called "Third World",' said Transneft director Nikolai Tokarev, a former KGB officer reported to have worked in East Germany with Putin. 'We all understand what kind of leaders they prepare there. They rate his type very highly and recommended that the State Department use him in the interests of the United States.'[25]

Navalny hit back, calling Tokarev 'dumb' and suggested it was because of KGB officers like him that 'we lost the Cold War'. 'The main reason I went to Yale was to learn how they investigate Russian crooks abroad,' he explained later. 'It's impossible to try Gazprom and Rosneft in Russian courts.'[26]

Whatever his critics may have alleged, Navalny's time at Yale – where he studied on a course designed to 'sharpen leadership skills and build relationships with other emerging leaders'[27] – was an indication of his support among influential Russians alarmed by entrenched corruption and a lawless business environment. 'I recommended Navalny to Yale,' Sergei Guriev, a prominent economist and government adviser close to Medvedev, told me. 'I wrote that: "This is a guy who does extremely important work for Russia, who goes after corruption in state companies.

These people should be educated and supported and so on." I think it was useful for him. He learned a lot.'[28] Guriev would later be forced to flee Russia over his support for the anti-corruption crusader.

Disillusionment with Putin and United Russia was running so high that, for many, it was irrelevant if Navalny was a US agent or not. 'OK, so Navalny is working for the US State Department,' said Anton Plushenko, a twenty-nine-year-old engineer and former Putin supporter. 'But who is going to give me answers about the crazy government contracts and apartments belonging to members of parliament that he writes about in his blog? Even if he is a triple American spy, who is going to explain all this?'[29]

What motivated Navalny? Why had he dedicated himself so completely to exposing high-level fraud in a country where such activities carried massive risks? 'To be honest,' he said, speaking to a small audience at a Moscow club in early 2011, 'I don't understand why everyone isn't doing this. What's happening to our country is like some old, feeble woman being mugged by a gang of evil teenagers as she walks down the road. But, instead of helping her out, everyone just watches. Or tweets about it.'[30] He is also driven by a loathing for Putin and his allies. 'I understand that hatred as a motive doesn't sound very good,' Navalny confessed. 'But it's eighty percent of my motivation. Otherwise I couldn't have done this for as long as I have.'[31]

MILK, APPLES AND GUNSHOTS

Navalny was born in 1976 into a military family near Moscow. Although his Ukrainian peasant grandmother was a virulent anti-Communist who once hopefully asked a relative if he had 'spat' on Lenin's embalmed corpse after a visit to the Bolshevik revolutionary's Red Square tomb, Navalny's parents were far from Soviet dissidents. His father was a Red Army communications officer and his mother an economist.

'My abiding memory of the Soviet Union was standing in queues for milk,' he would later recall. 'We built space rockets and told each other tall tales of shops with forty kinds of sausage and no queues. As we now know, other countries had both rockets and sausage.'

For the young Navalny, the problems of the slowly decaying Soviet system were all too apparent. 'You had to be a child to sense all the abnormality surrounding us. There was hypocrisy everywhere, but adults already barely noticed it.'[32]

Navalny studied in the mid-1990s at the same south Moscow university as Anna Chapman, the Russian intelligence agent deported from the United States in a high-profile, Cold War-style 'spy swap' in 2010. But the flame-haired former agent, whom I met on a number of occasions after her return to Russia, was dismissive of the opposition figurehead. 'He was nothing worth mentioning,' she told me. She declined to comment further.

After graduation, Navalny worked for a while as a lawyer at a property firm, but his interest in opposition politics had already begun. In 2000, the year Putin won his first term of office, Navalny, then twenty-three, joined Yabloko ('Apple'), Russia's oldest liberal party. The party was led by Grigory Yavlinsky, a Gorbachev-era deputy prime minister and architect of a never-to-be-fulfilled plan to transform the Soviet Union into a market economy. Yavlinsky was hero-worshipped by Russia's liberals over his anti-Chechen War stance and his opposition to the Yeltsin-era 'shock therapy' that had impoverished millions. He had also suffered for his views – in 1994, his young piano-playing son was kidnapped and had three of his fingers amputated. 'The price of taking part in politics in Russia is extremely high: your life, your family, everything,' he later said.[33]

While Yavlinsky may have had all the right liberal credentials, he and Yabloko were commonly dismissed in the Putin era as a rag-tag group of 1990s democrats whose day had come and gone. By the time Navalny came knocking at Yabloko's central Moscow HQ in 2000, the party was little more than an outlet for Kremlin critics to let off steam with a protest vote. Still, for Navalny, the choice wasn't exactly wide: it was either Yabloko or the Communist Party, led by Gennady Zyuganov, an ally of the KGB hardliners who had failed to overthrow Gorbachev in 1991. At least Yavlinsky wasn't on the grey cardinal Surkov's speed dial.

'[For me], there was no alternative to Yabloko. Of course, I didn't believe that Yavlinsky would become president, but I did hope we could create a big democratic coalition,' Navalny explained.

But he would quickly grow disillusioned by the party's lack of ambition.

'No one could understand what I was doing there,' he said. 'This was the start of the Putin era, and almost no one joined political parties because of their convictions. There was hardly any money in it, sometimes none at all, and they were always asking "why don't you go and work somewhere or do something normal?" This really made me mad; it was an admission of their own mediocrity.'[34]

In early 2006, along with Maria Gaidar, the young, dark-haired daughter of Yeltsin's reformist prime minister Yegor Gaidar, Navalny began organizing political debates in clubs and cafés in central Moscow. The idea was simple: two people, one well known, one not so, preferably with opposing views, would get on stage and argue. Navalny moderated the debates, roaming the stage as he variously kept the peace and dropped inflammatory remarks. In a Russia where political discussion had been largely expunged from television and parliament, the project was a hit. Soon, there was standing room only. Magazines and newspapers started to write about the debates. Their success, Navalny says, unnerved the Kremlin.

'The presidential administration thought they were dangerous,' he claimed. 'And soon they started to send in provocateurs to stir things up, so that they could just say, "Look, this isn't politics, these are just a bunch of hooligans."'[35]

If these 'provocateurs' were indeed Kremlin thugs looking to cause trouble, then Navalny took the bait. In the autumn of 2007, as a debate entitled 'Putin's Plan or Putin's Clan?' raged at central Moscow's Gogol club, Navalny confronted a group of hecklers who had begun chucking bottles. The dispute went outside, after which Navalny fired a traumatic handgun – a non-lethal weapon of compliance – at one of them. Photos of the incident show rubber-bullet casings scattered on a blood-stained pavement. It was later reported that the man Navalny fired at was the son of an FSB official.[36] 'People said later I should have fucked him up without a gun, or had a knife with me,' Navalny wrote on his blog. 'But I had no desire to get into a fight with a drunken idiot. As for a knife, I don't believe you can control yourself in situations like that. You get some adrenaline in your blood and you start hacking away like the main character in a Hitchcock film.'[37]

An investigation was opened, but later dropped, under circumstances that remain unclear. In opposition circles, rumours spread that Navalny had earned the powerful protection of one of the handful of liberals in or close to the Kremlin.

The evening Navalny shot at an intruder would be the last of the debates. But they had made a deep impression on the opposition activist. 'It was politics in its purest sense,' he said. 'The debates got written about, and thanks to this people started to discuss important topics. Things like nationalism.'[38]

GLORY TO RUSSIA!

As Navalny's star rose, the Russian online tabloid *Life News*, widely believed to have close links to the security services, posted a short animated clip depicting the anti-corruption blogger as a white-power freak compulsively sieg-heiling his way through the day, the eggs he flipped into his frying pan as he simultaneously saluted the memory of Adolf Hitler metamorphosing instantly into a swastika.[39] As an attack on Navalny, it was hardly subtle. But where had the idea to depict the opposition activist as a Nazi come from? After all, this was a man beloved of Russian and Western liberals alike: 'Russia's best hope', as a writer for *The New Yorker* magazine would soon describe him.[40]

Navalny was, of course, no Nazi. But he was virulently opposed to mass immigration from impoverished Central Asian states like Tajikistan and Uzbekistan, something he believed was 'planting a bomb under our future'.[41]

In July 2006, around a year after deadly clashes had broken out between ethnic Russians and people from the Caucasus region in the

town of Kondopoga, near Russia's border with Finland, Navalny stunned
political allies, friends and family alike by launching NAROD, an openly
nationalist movement. The movement's name signified a people united by
blood, akin to the German word '*volk*', frequently used in Nazi political
slogans. Formed in conjunction with around a dozen other 'nationalist-
democrats', including his great friend Zakhar Prilepin, a shaven-headed
novelist, *NatsBol* and veteran of the Chechen conflict, NAROD declared
its main aim as no less than the rescue of Russia from total destruction.

'If Russia does not acquire a national programme for the future, the
country will split up and disappear from the global political map,' the
NAROD manifesto read. 'Russia needs a new national mindset.'[42]

Positioning itself as the 'first national-democratic' movement in
Russia's 'new history', NAROD called for free elections and an end
to corruption, goals shared by any self-respecting Russian liberal. But
NAROD also demanded the restoration of the 'organic unity' of former
Russian territories, from ancient Kievan Rus to the Soviet Union, and
an amnesty for the handful of Russian soldiers who had been found
guilty of crimes against civilians in Chechnya. Any such amnesty would
have covered men like Yury Budanov, a nationalist hero and former
army officer jailed in 2003 for ten years over the kidnapping, rape and
murder of a young Chechen girl. NAROD's reasoning was that men
like Budanov had been punished for their crimes in Chechnya, while
separatist fighters who had waged war against the Kremlin were free
to take advantage of an amnesty aimed at tempting rebels to surrender
their weapons. All these demands were posted on Navalny's blog below
a smiley face and the slogan 'Imagine no liberals'.

In July 2007, Navalny was expelled from Yabloko after he was
reported to have joined the organizing committee for the Russian March,
an annual rally in Moscow of nationalists and ultra-right groups. At one
march I attended, masked youths threw sieg heils and chanted slogans
in support of ethnic cleansing. Nearby, an old woman held up a portrait
of Stalin emblazoned with the words 'a real Russian nationalist'. How,
I asked her, could Stalin – who hailed from Georgia, the former Soviet
republic on the Black Sea – be a Russian anything? 'Those Jews can

be Russians, yes?' screamed the elderly women, her gold-capped teeth glinting in the winter sun as she prodded me in the chest. 'So why can't Stalin be Russian, eh?'

Navalny, somewhat unconvincingly, argued that the majority of the people on the march were not unhinged neo-fascists and that Yabloko was failing in its duties by refusing to discuss what he believed was the very significant problem of illegal immigration and rising inter-ethnic tensions. 'If we don't want the Russian March to consist exclusively of sieg-heiling youths, then normal people concerned about illegal immigration must go on it,' he said.

Yabloko members were unimpressed.

'Glory to Russia!' Navalny yelled at the meeting called to vote on his expulsion, slamming the door as he left both the room and the party.[43]

Later, and calmer, he expounded on his views. 'I don't see any contradiction in being a liberal and speaking about illegal immigration and crime committed by certain ethnic groups. For me, this is no dilemma at all... A nationalist is a genuine patriot, someone who puts the interests of his nation above his own interests. There is nothing frightening about this.'[44]

*

While there were flare-ups of racial tensions in the Soviet Union, the authorities managed – on the whole – to keep the lid on inter-ethnic hostilities. But, as Russia grew richer under Putin, millions of labour migrants from former Soviet states in Central Asia took advantage of visa-free borders with their gigantic neighbour to flock to Russia. This mass influx of migrant workers is encouraged by corrupt officials who skim as much as 90% off their official salaries, claim Navalny and his nationalist allies.

The sudden arrival of millions of poorly assimilated Muslim migrants in Russia's heartland, twinned with a rise in Russian nationalism, has created an ethnic tinderbox. Scores of people of 'non-Slavic appearance' continue to be murdered or injured every year in Russia in race-hate attacks, with among the most gruesome examples being a nine-year old

Tajik girl stabbed to death by skinheads in St Petersburg and the beheading of a Tajik migrant worker in the Moscow region. In an opinion poll carried out after the murder of the Tajik child, some 20% of people in St Petersburg said they 'understood' the motives of the killers.[45] In another reflection of the popularity of nationalist sentiments, in polls, around 60% of people regularly agree with the far-right slogan 'Russia is for the Russians'.[46]

The situation has also been exacerbated by mutual hostilities in big cities between ethnic Russians and internal migrants from its mainly Muslim, North Caucasus region. Young men from the North Caucasus are far more confident than Central Asian immigrants, and many have been guilty of provocative and confrontational behaviour, often, for example, firing wildly into the air from speeding vehicles during 'traditional' weddings in Moscow. Tensions, predictably, eventually erupted. In late 2010, thousands of masked nationalists rioted under the Kremlin walls, beating anyone who looked 'foreign', after a Muscovite football fan had been killed by a young man from the North Caucasus republic of Dagestan. By the time the violence was over, two people were dead.[47] One of them, a man from the former Soviet republic of Kyrgyzstan, was stabbed to death after being set upon by over a dozen rioters.

These riots were the point at which it became brutally clear that Putin, who had tapped into nationalist passions during his first two terms, had lost the ultra-right. These nationalist groups felt he had betrayed them by both allowing Central Asian migrants to flood into Russia and pumping state funds into Chechnya.

The Kremlin says its generous spending in the North Caucasus republic is an attempt to prevent the outbreak of another war there. But critics say the money is frequently misused by Chechnya's young leader, Ramzan Kadyrov, a former rebel fighter backed by Putin. The popular 'Stop Feeding the Caucasus!' campaign, which Navalny supports, calls for an end to the massive injection of cash into Chechnya and other republics in the region. The campaign's name may be provocative, but it is not hard to see why Navalny and his supporters feel this way, at least with regard to Chechnya.

Flush with Kremlin cash, Kadyrov has spent millions of dollars that could be used to build up Russia's creaking infrastructure on showcase projects and glitzy events, from the construction of a brand-new state-of-the-art football stadium in the capital, Grozny, to a concert featuring Hollywood celebrities like Hilary Swank and Jean-Claude Van Damme to mark his thirty-fifth birthday. 'I love you, Mr Kadyrov,' shouted Van Damme from the stage, while the former militant fighter giggled and clapped.[48] Kadyrov, who denies frequent allegations of torture and other human-rights abuses, has also overseen the construction of one of Europe's largest mosques in the Muslim republic. 'Allah gives it to us,' he laughed when asked where the money for such grandiose projects came from, shortly after he had organized a high-profile match in Grozny between Brazilian international football stars and a team of government officials, which he captained.[49] Along with thousands of other spectators, I watched as Brazil's stars obligingly melted away to allow Kadyrov chance after chance on goal. 'I love him [Putin] very much, as a man loves a man," Kadyrov told *Newsweek* in 2010. "I can do anything while he backs me up.'[50]

✳

Vladimir Tor, one of Navalny's nationalist allies and an organizer of the annual Russian March, is an articulate, well-dressed businessman with a neat goatee. He appears to have little in common with the popular images of nationalist thugs, but his rhetoric is familiar, echoing the ideas of far-right groups across Europe and the United States.

'Putin may be an ethnic Russian, but he does not operate in the interests of his own people,'[51] he told me, sitting in his plush office in front of a large map of Russia. 'He acts in the interests of the oligarchs and his own security elite, people from the former KGB. Ethnic Russians are suffering because of this.

'I am absolutely against immigration,' he added. 'Sociological studies demonstrate that mass immigration from countries with different cultures, ethnic groups and religious beliefs causes problems.

'We can see this most clearly right now in France, where we see a conflict between the traditional population and immigrants from Africa and the Arab world. It's possible that Europe has crossed the point of no return, as far as immigration goes. We do not wish Russia to share the same fate.'

Tor turned his computer screen towards me. 'Look at this wonderful Tajik fellow,' he said, pointing to a photo of a grinning Central Asian labour migrant. 'He raped a fourteen-year-old girl just last week.'

For Tor, it is clear: there is a war going on for the future of Russia.

'As far as all this race-hate murders go, of course, we condemn them,' he said. 'But, really, you know, it would be surprising if they did not occur.' He called for more tea and offered me a bowl of sweets. 'See, I really like this Uzbek porcelain,' he said, as I selected a chocolate from the pale-blue bowl. 'But I would prefer the Uzbeks to stay in Uzbekistan.'

Tor was one of the nationalist figureheads who had held negotiations with police during the right-wing riots that hit central Moscow in 2010, and he predicted that it would not be long before similar scenes once again rocked Russia.

'Anything could trigger the next violence.' He shrugged. 'I would prefer this problem to be resolved by parliamentary means. And I see no reason why it cannot be. But the fewer the legal means to solve the issue, the more violence there is on the streets.'

Ominously, Tor was not shy about boasting of support within Russia's security forces. 'There are… enough people from within the security structures who back us,' he smiled, choosing his words with care.

Navalny usually does his best to ensure his statements stay on the 'moderate' side of the nationalist stance, pointing out that a visa regime for migrants from Central Asia would provide them with rights, as well as obligations to Russian society, but he occasionally lets his guard down. 'These people will NEVER assimilate,' he wrote of a regional scheme to offer migrant workers citizenship. 'And neither will their children or their grandparents. The example of France proves this.'[52] In an even more blatant example of his views, he also publicly referred to Central Asian migrant workers as '*chuchmeky*' – an offensive, ethnically loaded term used mainly for migrant workers from Tajikistan and Uzbekistan.[53] 'And they should stop sitting on their haunches!' he yelled, in reference to the widespread Central Asian habit. 'It really gets to me!' he exclaimed, raising his voice and waving his arms in the air.[54]

He also stirred up controversy with two online clips he starred in for NAROD. In the first, Navalny urged the legalization of guns so that Russians could defend themselves against 'overly large cockroaches' – symbolized in the clip by bearded Chechens and a threatening figure clad in a cloak shouting what sounded like 'Allah Akbar!' Navalny pulled a gun and shot the 'cockroach' dead. 'I recommend a pistol,' he said, smiling nonchalantly.[55]

'This is fascism,' responded Maria Gaidar, the young activist who had helped Navalny organize the debate shows, when she saw the clip.[56]

For the second video, Navalny dressed up as a dentist to urge the forceful repatriation of illegal immigrants. 'We have the right to be ethnic Russians in Russia,' Navalny declared, staring straight into the camera to the accompaniment of jaunty music and footage of Asian-looking migrants being rounded up by police. 'And we will defend that right.'[57]

POWER IN RUSSIA DOESN'T CHANGE THROUGH ELECTIONS

A 'liberal kind of guy'[58] with undisguised nationalist tendencies, Navalny is confusing, contradictory and at times unsavoury, but his talent for tapping into discontent and giving it a voice is unparalleled. His anti-corruption campaign broke through the wall of apathy to achieve what other opposition figures had failed to do: make political activism seem both viable and fashionable. By mid-2010, he was making a name for himself not only as an anti-corruption activist, but also as a politician. In an unofficial online ballot for mayor of Moscow organized by Russia's *Kommersant* newspaper and the *Gazeta.ru* news portal, Navalny came in first, taking some 45% of the vote.

'Navalny is a politician of an entirely different type, of a different generation,' said Leonid Parfyonov, the journalist who had shocked media big shots with his no-holds-barred speech slamming state media coverage of Russia's ruling tandem.[59] The readership of the *Kommersant* broadsheet and the liberal *Gazeta.ru* were hardly representative of the vast majority of the Russian population, but for a young, previously unknown blogger it was a remarkable achievement. An anti-corruption whistle-blower with a foot in both the liberal and nationalist camps, Navalny's appeal was easy to understand. 'He has really great potential,' said Boris Nemtsov, the Yeltsin-era deputy prime minister who was one of the anti-Putin movement's leaders throughout the 2000s. Like Navalny, the alternately brusque and charming Nemtsov – a one-time contender to succeed Yeltsin as president – also sought to expose Kremlin corruption. Unlike Navalny, his rhetoric-heavy, vaguely academic reports failed to achieve the same kind of mass audience. 'Navalny's young, smart and handsome,' Nemtsov told me, in what seemed like a symbolic passing on of the opposition flame. 'He poses a real threat to Putin.'[60]

Russia's liberals had been dreaming of someone like Navalny, a man unencumbered with the political baggage of the 1990s and 2000s; someone with the potential to speak to the masses and the influential intellectuals alike. Inspired, excited and a little afraid of this straight-speaking lawyer, they were more than willing to close their eyes to his nationalist views. 'He is someone who has gone it alone against massive state machinery based on theft, lies and a whole range of inhuman and inhumane activities,' wrote Vera Krichevskaya, the co-founder of TV Dozhd, the hip and slick liberal online channel. 'For me, it's not important if he went on the Russian March or not.'[61]

Navalny had also started to attract allies from the business world. His most notable business recruit was Vladimir Ashurkov, a former top banker and ex-Putin supporter. A well-travelled, middle-aged Muscovite with a penchant for the films of Quentin Tarantino, Ashurkov was a senior executive at Alfa-Group Consortium, one of Russia's largest investment groups, when he stumbled upon Navalny's blog in mid-2010. What he read there 'resonated' with his growing disillusionment with Putin's rule.

'I started reading Navalny's blog and I was very impressed by what he was doing,' the softly spoken Ashurkov told me, in impeccable English, when I met up with him in a Vietnamese restaurant in Moscow. 'He was doing a lot of corporate governance work. This was my area of expertise, so I wrote to him to make some suggestions.'[62]

The decision cost Ashurkov his job, transforming him from a bona-fide member of the business elite – who had once earned a reported annual salary of $700,000 (something I only found out after I'd bought him lunch) – into a modern-day political dissident. 'I really miss being in business now,' he admitted. 'Once you get a taste of it, it's hard to let go. And politics is so frustrating sometimes. Well, most of the time, actually, in Russia.

'Yes, I voted for Putin in the 2004 presidential elections,' he said, shrugging. 'I thought that things were improving, becoming more liberal, at least economically. I believed things were moving in the right direction.'

And now?

'Now power is all solidified in the hands of these crooks and thieves,' he sighed, picking at his food. 'But things can't go on like this forever.'

✳

As 2010 drew to an end, an uprising broke out in Tunisia, and the North African country's long-time authoritarian leader, Zine al-Abidine Ben Ali, was quickly swept from power. The spirit of dissent shifted next to Egypt, and political observers began to wonder if such a scenario might not be about to play out in Russia. After all, no one had predicted the Arab Spring, and sensation seemed to be the order of the season.

Navalny was inspired. Of course, as he freely admitted, there were plenty of differences between Russia and the Arab Spring countries. Demographics alone meant the likelihood of a major revolt breaking out was lower. In Egypt, the average age was a youthful and excitable twenty-four – an age at which anything seems possible – but in Russia it was almost forty – not generally a period in life when people take to the streets. The Russians were a tired nation. And whatever appetite they had for social change had been understandably diminished by two revolutions and a devastating world war.

However, the Russian protest movement also had massive advantages over the men and women who had plotted against dictators in North Africa and the Middle East. Pre-Arab Spring, Navalny had studied at Yale alongside an opponent of the Tunisian regime, Fares Mabrouk, and conversations with the middle-aged Arab intellectual convinced him that the anti-Putin movement had all the tools it needed to bring down its arch-nemesis.

'Fares was always terribly envious of our situation in Russia,' Navalny recalled at a discussion evening at an upmarket Moscow restaurant in early 2011. 'He told me, "Our internet is blocked, we have no YouTube, no Twitter, nothing. You Russians are so lucky! In Tunisia there is absolute totalitarian control."' Navalny laughed. 'They were the last people to believe they could change things. Compared to their situation, everything we have managed to do so far – all our Marches of Dissent, and so on – is just incredible.'[63]

Navalny was by now open about his political ambitions. It was no longer enough to be a 'popular blogger' or an 'anti-corruption activist'. His followers began to call him 'Russia's future president'.[64] They were only half joking.

'If you are serious about fighting against corruption in Russia, then you understand that it is impossible to eradicate without serious political change,' Navalny declared in April 2011. 'But power in Russia doesn't change hands through the ballot box. There will be a confrontation between the corrupt elite and the masses. We don't know yet when this moment will come, but we can work toward it with all our strength.'[65]

In Tunisia, an uprising had been triggered when a young man immolated himself in protest at the corruption that had made his life impossible. Navalny and the anti-Putin opposition were still waiting for the spark that would ignite discontent in Russia.

6

CASTLING AT THE KREMLIN

As revolution raged in the Arab world, Medvedev's supporters continued to hope that the young president would be able to implement his much-needed programme of reform. But it was becoming increasingly clear that, to do so, he would have to win a second term of office. Medvedev's first presidential election victory had been guaranteed by Putin's endorsement, but now he could stand for re-election on his record, or, more precisely, on his pledges to bring about change. A second term, his supporters insisted, would give him the mandate to become a genuine head of state, rather than Putin's puppet.

The decision, however, wasn't Medvedev's to make. He may have been president of the largest country on Earth for the past three years, but he still remained subservient to Putin. People who met the two men together reported that Medvedev was in the habit of carrying Putin's briefcase for him.[1] Not much, it seemed, had changed since the early days of their friendship in St Petersburg.

It was far from certain that Putin would allow the nominal head of state to run for re-election in 2012. Would he risk the possibility of Medvedev becoming an independent and popular president? After all, the dangers of prosecution over allegations of corruption and other suspected crimes were still very real. As Putin's time as prime minister came to an end, mocked-up video footage of Russia's leader standing trial on embezzlement and terrorism charges became a YouTube hit.[2]

Rumours began to grow that Putin was planning a comeback. Throughout the spring and summer of 2011, the issue became unavoidable. It loomed large over Russian politics, the subtext to every political development or debate. In an ominous sign for his supporters, Medvedev was being referred to more and more frequently by Putin as 'Russia's *current* president'. But everyone was guessing. And, besides the occasional tantalizing hint, neither Putin nor Medvedev was telling. The only thing they would confirm was that they would not run against each other. As tensions rose, the Kremlin dismissed Gleb Pavlovsky, an influential spin doctor who had helped engineer Putin's dominance of the political landscape. His crime? Openly calling for a second term for Medvedev.

This lack of any clear information on Putin's intentions was forcing political analysts to scramble for clues wherever they could find them. The results were often bizarre. If Soviet-era political pundits once examined the minutiae of Kremlin protocol to determine the intentions of Russia's rulers, their modern-day counterparts now pondered the when, where and why of Putin taking his top off. Putin had never been one to shy away from showing off his pecs, but now his semi-stripping was of keen interest not only to his many female admirers, but also to political experts. In 2007, as Putin came to the end of his second and final consecutive term as president, a bare-chested photo session in Siberia had been taken by commentators as an indication that he might be content with an elder statesman role. However, as 2011 dragged on, Putin's continued willingness to show off the result of countless hours in the Kremlin gym – 'flexing his muscles' – was suddenly being interpreted as a desire to get his old job back from his hand-picked successor.

Medvedev had not quite rolled over and given up. With just over a year left in office, he made what looked like a belated attempt to stamp his authority on the presidency. On Medvedev's orders, Russia had abstained from a March 2011 United Nations vote on the use of air strikes against forces loyal to Colonel Gaddafi in civil-war-stricken Libya. When the UN Security Council voted to approve strikes to defend the civilian population, Putin hit the roof. Speaking to factory workers in central Russia, he likened the decision to a 'medieval call to crusade'.[3] Medvedev responded with unusual fury. Foreign policy was, after all, the president's responsibility. He summoned journalists to his *dacha*, where, without mentioning Putin by name, he told them any talk of 'crusades' was 'unacceptable'. But he looked nervous as he did so, and it was too little, too late to convince anyone that he could stand up to his political mentor.[4]

Medvedev was growing increasingly despondent. In the summer of 2011, he openly admitted for the first time that he would like to run for re-election, but that he was not able to make that decision alone. 'Any leader who occupies a position such as president simply must want to run,' he told *The Financial Times*. 'But another question is whether he is going to decide whether he's going to run for the presidency or not. So his decision is somewhat different from his willingness to run.'[5] It was an unprecedented humiliation.

THE POINT OF NO RETURN

Despite all the speculation, Russia's political future remained unclear until 24 September 2011, when both Putin and Medvedev addressed a glittering United Russia party congress in south Moscow. Putin was first up, and he used his spot to suggest that Medvedev lead the party at the upcoming parliamentary polls. A camera zoomed in on Medvedev, who did his very best to look pleased at being handed stewardship of an organization that was being more and more frequently referred to as 'the party of crooks and thieves' than it was by its official moniker.

And then it was Medvedev's turn to dish out the gifts.

'I believe it would be only correct for the congress to support the candidacy of Prime Minister Vladimir Putin for president of the Russian Federation,' a tired-looking Medvedev said, after a lengthy preamble. The arena erupted with applause. Medvedev flinched at the enthusiastic approval of his decision not to seek a second term. 'That applause spares me having to explain what experience and authority Vladimir Putin possesses,' he added, as the cheers finally died down.

'This agreement was reached between us several years ago,'[6] Putin told party members, with a smirk that could only be described as mischievous. Medvedev, seated now, grinned weakly at those around him. He looked ashamed at the trick he and his political mentor had pulled. And there was much for Medvedev to feel guilty about. That afternoon in south Moscow, he confirmed that his entire four years in office had been nothing more than a ploy to help Putin sidestep the constitutional ban on two consecutive terms of office. All his talk of modernizing Russia, of taking a joint decision with Putin on whether to run for a second term 'when the time was right' suddenly looked like nothing more than a bad joke.

Reaction was swift. The mood in Moscow and other big cities darkened instantly.

'There is no reason for happiness,' tweeted an anguished Arkady Dvorkovich, an economic adviser to Medvedev.

'We don't need a tsar,' wrote Navalny.

It was a watershed moment for Russia's urban, educated class. It may have been naive to believe that Medvedev could act independently of Putin, but many had nevertheless allowed themselves to hope. What else were they supposed to do? And now those hopes had been dashed. The announcement of Putin and Medvedev's job swap was quickly dubbed 'the castling', the move in chess when the king and rook swap places on the board.

'I got so depressed. I'd hoped that I wouldn't hear the word "Putin" anymore, that Medvedev would become a genuine president,' Maria Baronova, a young activist who would later face criminal charges over an anti-Kremlin rally that turned violent, told me. 'I'd hoped that we might see some real democracy, where real elections take place every four years. But in place of that they promised us that things were just beginning and that they were going to get very bad indeed. September 24 was the point of no return.'[7]

For others, Putin's imminent comeback triggered nightmarish images.

'I had this idea that, you know, Putin might use some really advanced anti-ageing medicine and stay in power for decades more to come,' grimaced Gaya Marina Garbaruk, a young media professional, and one of those young Muscovites with the most to gain from Medvedev's promised reforms. 'I thought: "I don't want to live my whole life only knowing Putin as president!"'[8]

Medvedev's 2008 amendment to the constitution had extended the presidential term from four to six years and Russians quickly did the maths. Putin could remain in power until 2024, far longer than any Russian or Soviet leader since Joseph Stalin. All across Russia, people began to calculate mentally how old they would be when Putin was finally obliged to step down. It did not make for comforting arithmetic.

In place of 'modernization', the new buzzword was one dredged up from the almost two-decade rule of Soviet leader Leonid Brezhnev – 'stagnation'. The *Novaya Gazeta* newspaper ran with the notion of Putin as the new Brezhnev, depicting the presidential shoo-in and his ministers as they might look in 2024: geriatric, feeble and festooned in medals.

A year or so after Medvedev had neutered himself politically in front of the nation, an opposition source, citing a well-known political consultant with Kremlin connections, told me this colourful story.

'The night before Medvedev announced he would not be standing for a second term, he spent the night in Putin's office. Putin's people wouldn't let him home, because they were afraid his wife, Svetlana, would get at him over his decision to step down, and say, "Are you a man, or what?" Putin didn't go home, either. I guess they drank tea until the early hours and discussed Russia's destiny.'

The Moscow-based consultant would neither confirm nor deny the report when I contacted him. But, irrespective of the reality, it is hard to imagine a better illustration/metaphor of Putin and Medvedev's oft-discussed 'father and adopted son' relationship.

Disappointment with Medvedev – soon to be dubbed 'the Pitiful' by politically minded bloggers – would frequently manifest as outright hatred.

'Are you ready to go before a people's court, one that will probably be held in the event of a revolution, to defend your actions?' a young, long-haired university student called Vladimir Kulikov asked Medvedev at a Q&A session in Moscow towards the end of 2011. 'Do you understand that you could even be sentenced to death?'

'Vladimir, that's the bravest question you've asked in your life. And I congratulate you on it,' Medvedev replied, smiling at the young man's impudence. 'And I'll tell you honestly, I'm not afraid of anything.' He smiled again. It must have seemed like the perfect retort. He had softened the student's aggression and answered his query with a no-nonsense reply.

But Vladimir wasn't finished yet.

'Yes, but are you ready to die for your ideas?'

Medvedev, clearly unsettled by this relentless and vitriolic line of questioning, started to speak, changed his mind, pulled an unconvincing Putinesque pose and said he was. Vladimir, satisfied now, nodded.[9]

Putin and his advisers had spectacularly misjudged the public mood, at the very least in Moscow and other big cities. The castling signalled to Russians that their opinions were irrelevant. In his apparent belief that he alone could determine Russia's destiny, Putin was acting like a tsar. 'People saw that the leadership had been fooling them around for four years. That Medvedev was no independent leader, if everything had been decided four years ago. This is when opposition sentiments began to rise,' said Boris Dubin, a sociologist.[10]

Something had changed in the atmosphere. For months, political life in Russia had been on hold as everyone waited to see what Putin would decide. Now, the sense of insult was so strong among Russia's urban, educated classes it was almost overpowering. Reformist Russians had been conned. And now they were angry. The storm warnings were increasing. Putin, however, wasn't listening. But the howls of dissent were about to grow too loud to ignore.

END OF AN ERA OR JUST THE QUEUE FOR THE TOILETS?

Less than two months after announcing his intention to return to the Kremlin, Putin stepped into the ring after a no-holds-barred bout in a north Moscow sports arena. It was the kind of event where he should have been in his element. With two vital elections on the horizon, a fight featuring a Russian champion and an American challenger was the perfect opportunity for the judo black belt to bolster his tough-guy image.

After Russia's heavyweight champion Fedor Emelianenko had played his part and convincingly defeated his US opponent Jeff Monson, Putin greeted the crowd at the Olympiyskiy stadium. 'Dear friends, today is a great holiday for all fans of martial arts,' he began, only to be drowned out by a sudden storm of jeers and catcalls.

Putin was visibly taken aback. He paused for a moment, stumbling slightly over his prepared speech, before raising his voice to continue. But he struggled to make himself heard above the noise. The booing only ceased when Putin praised Emelianenko as 'a real Russian hero', and the crowd broke off from their jeers to show their appreciation of the night's only winner.[11]

It was an incident that was over almost before it had begun. And one that would have gone largely unreported had a clip of the jeering not been uploaded swiftly on to YouTube. Kremlin-controlled state television channels had edited out the booing in reruns of the fight and made no mention of the crowd's apparent anger when faced with the man who had ruled Russia in one form or another for over a decade. The man who was thought to be untouchable.

But the clip went viral and soon became one of the most discussed in Russia.

Putin had, it was true, been subject to public verbal lashings in the past. He had been yelled at by relatives of the scores of sailors who perished when the *Kursk* nuclear submarine sank in 2000. Angry crowds also confronted him in central Russia after devastating wildfires in 2010. But these were both anguished reactions to tragedies. The booing at the sports arena was provoked by the mere sight and sound of Putin. The crowd had judged him; and their verdict was summed up by a single voice that came from the darkness, as Putin stood blinking in the ring: 'Get out of here!'

Not everyone accepted that Putin had been jeered. Kristina Potupchik, the brash spokesperson for the pro-Putin youth movement *Nashi*, was sceptical, declaring bizarrely that the catcalls had come from fight-goers 'anxious' over the long queues for the toilet. Other Putin supporters said the jeers were directed at Monson, the losing fighter.

Navalny was overjoyed by the frantic denials from Putin supporters. They were, he said, doing the opposition's work for them by publicizing the incident. Soon, no one would remember the details, but the image of Russia's long-time leader faced with a hostile stadium would remain and become a valuable symbol of Putin's declining popularity. The jeers and the catcalls, Navalny declared gleefully, marked 'the end of an era'.[12]

Putin's decision to return to the presidency proved to be the biggest mistake of his long reign, providing the opposition with both a focus for their discontent and a pedestal from which their arch foe could be toppled. 'When Putin announced he wanted to become president again, in some respects I was glad. I knew that this would be the start of something,' recalled Roman Dobrokhotov, the activist who had disrupted Medvedev's Constitution Day address. 'We'd been trying since 2005 to get people to go out on demonstrations and stand up for their rights. But we'd never managed to get a critical mass of people together. But, when it became clear they were going to get rid of Medvedev, I knew a wave of protests would begin. People just needed a trigger.'

7

POLLS AND PROTESTS

As 2011 drew to a close, the dissent that had become commonplace during Medvedev's presidency underwent a subtle shift in tone: the feeling now in opposition circles was one of impending confrontation. A potential flashpoint was that December's parliamentary polls. Putin's intention to return to the Kremlin meant the elections were now being seen as a referendum on his decision to flaunt the spirit, if not the letter, of the constitution. His United Russia party enjoyed a clear majority in parliament: the vote was a chance to give Putin a bloody nose.

Something was definitely in the air in the Russian capital that autumn and winter. Glossy magazines started to run lengthy interviews with opposition figures like Navalny. The talk of politics in Moscow's hipster hangouts was increasingly strident. As pre-poll tensions grew, a fellow journalist got blind drunk and daubed the ruling party's now ubiquitous nickname, 'crooks and thieves', all over the walls of his apartment block's common stairwell. His neighbours, he later told me, had been furious, although it was the mess that had angered them, rather than his uncompromising anti-United Russia message.

But many of these newly politicized young Russians faced a major problem: those opposition parties allowed on the ballot at the 4 December 2011 parliamentary polls were opposition merely in name or, like the Communist Party, equally as unattractive to most reform-hungry voters. To overcome this stumbling block to electoral participation, Navalny began promoting a new strategy: 'A vote for any party but United Russia.' It was a simple solution: so simple, in fact, that it seemed strange no one had thought of it before. Navalny's plan caught on fast.

Inspired by the chance to strike a blow against Putin, many young Russians signed up for the first time to act as vote monitors. Casting your ballot against United Russia was all very well, ran the reasoning in online discussions, but you also had to make certain the 'crooks and thieves' did not simply steal your vote.

One of the main attempts to organize independent vote monitoring, Citizen Observer, was set up by Dmitry Oreshkin, a middle-aged political analyst and journalist. 'We want to cover at least five percent of the polling places in Moscow,' he told me ahead of the elections. 'That way, we figure, we will be able to get an indication of how people really vote.'[1] He then outlined to me the myriad ways in which he said the authorities had falsified previous votes, from ballot-stuffing to simply rewriting results once polling stations had closed.

Timofei Markin, the thirty-something owner of a small Moscow business, was one of those who signed up to monitor the December 2011 vote. 'No one but my generation has ever concerned themselves with such things,' he told me when I met him in a fashionable central Moscow café with American jazz on the sound system and German beer on the menu. 'But I feel a sense of responsibility. I have a family and I want to make Russia a better place to live.' When I asked him, for the record, what it was he found so disagreeable about Putin's Russia, he raised his eyebrows in mock astonishment: 'You've been here long enough. Haven't you noticed what kind of a country we live in?'[2]

'Party of Crooks and Thieves' stickers began to appear all over Moscow in the weeks before the elections, going back up again almost as fast as city cleaners could unpeel them. 'One day, your child will ask you, "Papa, what were you doing when the crooks and thieves were robbing our country blind?"' read one of the most persuasive, depicting a small, sad-looking girl.

Seeking to rally support, Putin addressed a massive and glitzy United Russia congress at south Moscow's cavernous Luzhniki Stadium. 'Russia! Russia!' chanted thousands of flag-waving party members and delegates, the sound rippling around the Soviet-era arena. But Putin wasn't happy: 'When you chant "Russia", the sound should fill the entire hall,' he said, clenching his fist and grinning. 'Let's have it again!'

Standing on a dark-blue podium, Putin then turned his attention to what he said were attempts by 'representatives of certain foreign states' to influence Russia's elections. Putin had called foreign-funded vote monitors 'jackals' in 2007, but this time he went biblical, labelling the election watchdogs 'Judas', to wild applause.[3]

Lilia Shibanova, the feisty, middle-aged head of Russia's main independent elections observer group, Golos, countered that Putin's comments had revealed his and United Russia's 'total misunderstanding' of the situation ahead of the polls.

'They have cornered themselves by creating the only governing party, by impeding normal political competition, and turning the political process into a monopoly,' Shibanova said. 'What they'll get are fierce protests.'[4]

2+2=5?

There were lots of puzzled – and angry – faces around on election night. Despite its rapidly declining popularity, official results showed that United Russia had somehow managed to retain its vital parliamentary majority, garnering just under 50% of the vote nationwide.

But the figures just didn't add up – literally, in many cases. In central Russia's Rostov-on-Don region, for example, state television announced that United Russia had taken 59% out of a total of 146% of votes cast, with screenshots of the bizarre electoral mathematics quickly becoming one of the lasting images of the night.[5] There was more scandal when exit polls posted by one pollster indicated that United Russia had taken a mere 27% of the vote in Moscow. It was an estimate that starkly contradicted the preliminary official results, which indicated that Putin's party had, in fact, garnered a far more respectable 47% in the capital. The Public Opinion Fund pollster quickly removed the exit poll from its website, citing a 'technical error'. It must have been a serious breakdown for one of Russia's top pollsters to misestimate the results of national elections by 20%. The Public Opinion Fund denied it had faced pressure to remove the exit poll.

In another indication that something was not quite right with the vote tally, returns often differed dramatically between polling places where independent monitors were present and those without. At five neighbouring polling stations in Moscow, in the two where monitors were in place, United Russia took just 26.3% and 26.6% of the vote. In the polling stations without monitors, Putin's party scooped 92%, 94% and 89.8%.[6]

'I saw a neatly stacked pile of voting papers in the ballot box, a clear case of ballot-box stuffing, but when I yelled, "Hey, stop!" the head of the polling station commission walked up and shuffled them all. Then he shouted: "No one saw anything!"' recalled Markin, the young business-man, who observed voting at a south Moscow polling station.

'Other election officials – all teachers at the school where the polling station was based – were spoiling ballot papers with votes for parties other than United Russia. I was shocked by their behaviour,' he told me, frowning as he recalled the blatant way officials went about ensuring victory for United Russia. '"You teach our children!" I shouted at one of the teachers, in an attempt to appeal to his conscience. "Yeah, mathemat-ics," he answered. "What?" I replied, "2+2=5?"'

In Putin's Russia, teachers are a vital cog in the machinery of vote fraud. Badly paid and with little job security, it is not hard for pro-gov-ernment officials to coerce them into making sure the 'right' party wins.

'Most polling station officials are teachers,' Shibanova of the Golos election monitoring group told me, when I met her at the watchdog's tiny Moscow office. 'Their involvement in vote fraud is a sad indication of the general state of our society, of its degradation,' she sighed. 'Over the years, vote fraud just became a normal thing for them to do. Almost part of the job, in a way. Teachers were either scared into doing it, or paid to do so. Or both.'[7]

In Chechnya, ruled with an iron grip by the pro-Kremlin, former rebel fighter Ramzan Kadyrov, United Russia took 99.5% of the vote. It was in this tiny, mountainous province that Putin had seen one of his worst results at the 2000 presidential elections, taking just under 30%.[8] Just over a decade on, according to Russia's election officials, there was barely a single person left in the still volatile province who did not endorse Putinism. Terrified vote monitors did not even attempt to observe the vote. Kadyrov later said he would have used 'tanks and howitzers'[9] against anyone who dared to protest about the election results. The ludicrous returns in Chechnya were an indication of the darkness of the heart of United Russia's election victory. If this was how Kremlin officials acted when there was no one around to keep them in check, then why believe their denials of mass vote fraud elsewhere?

After Chechnya, the highest returns for United Russia were in a Moscow psychiatric hospital, where 99.5% of inmates had also apparently plumped for Putin's party. The irony, predictably, was lost on no one.[10]

Russia's election committee chief, Vladimir Churov, became an instant figure of hate. A rabid Kremlin loyalist, the man in charge of the vote-counting was best known for his oft-repeated, notorious catchphrase: 'Churov's number-one rule is that Putin is always right.' Post-elections, Churov earned the ironic nickname 'the wizard' for his success in conjuring up yet another United Russia poll triumph.

Despite denial-of-service attacks on independent media websites and popular blogging platforms on the morning of the elections, the internet played a vital role in stirring up public anger. Even as the votes were still being counted across Russia's vast territory, dozens of examples of apparently blatant cases of electoral fraud – ranging from the almost comical use of invisible ink at polling stations to more traditional ballot-box stuffing and multiple voting – were posted online by newly politicized and outraged bloggers. Previous votes may have been no cleaner, but that was before smartphones and the internet had hit Russia big-time. State TV was faithfully parroting the Kremlin's line, but there was nothing Putin could do about the revolt brewing on the web.

'All the people who had monitored the vote for us, some of whom were simply kicked out of polling stations by officials, went home and wrote in their blogs exactly what they had seen,' said Oreshkin, the political analyst who organized independent vote-monitoring in Moscow. 'They helped to raise a storm.'

WE ARE THE POWER HERE!

As the internet buzzed with video after video of vote fraud, Russia seethed. But would this fury stay online, in opposition chat rooms and forums, the twenty-first-century equivalent of the kitchens where Soviet dissidents had gathered to whisper of injustice and their dreams for the future? Or would people take to the streets? No one knew. After all, an entire generation had grown up with no real experience of public protest.

'Up until December 2011, anti-Putin demonstrations usually drew a few hundred people, so I wasn't entirely sure that we would see a big turnout,' said Ilya Yashin, a key figure in the tiny, liberal opposition movement *Solidarnost*, which organized a 5 December 2011 post-election protest in central Moscow. An indication of how low expectations were is illustrated by the text messages that Navalny and Yashin sent each other in the hours before the protest.

'The Communists have got 400 people [at their rally],' wrote Navalny.

'There's a danger we'll get 800,' joked Yashin.[11]

Although still in his twenties, the wiry and talkative Yashin was a veteran of the anti-Putin movement. He knew all about the crushing inevitability of Putin's rule. Inspired by a visit to Ukraine to witness the Orange Revolution, his attempts to spark a similar uprising in Russia had quickly fizzled out. 'I was really worried that people would just stay at home, like always,' he confessed. 'Of course,' he told me, smiling, 'when I arrived and saw how many people had turned up, it was obvious this was the start of something.'[12]

That 'something' was the crystallization of growing discontent into a street protest movement unlike anything modern Russia had ever seen. From early evening onwards, thousands of demonstrators started to gather at a square near the Chistye Prudy (Clean Ponds) metro station, a short walk from the Kremlin. 'Give us back our votes!' chanted the ever-swelling crowd as they stood in a light drizzle under the gaze of a monument to the eighteenth-century playwright and poet Alexander Griboyedov. Each new arrival would do a double-take when he or she saw how many people had turned up, immediately firing off a text message or a Twitter post; the electronic nerve centre of the anti-Putin movement pulsed with an uncommon energy.

It was a scene made for Navalny, whose daring exposés and sharp, ironic humour had earned his blog a massive following. He clambered long-limbed over a fence, and waded through the packed square. 'We exist! We are the power here!' he screamed, wrath incarnate, to the 'nationalists, liberals, leftists, greens, vegetarians, and Martians'[13] who had answered his online call to take to the streets. 'These crooks and swindlers and murderers… they should be afraid of us and they should understand that we hate them!' Navalny raged on, seguing into the nationalist chant, 'We won't forget! We won't forgive!'[14]

For the first time in Putin's long rule, the scent of genuine revolt was in the air. The crowd that night was not made up of fanatical *NatsBols* chanting 'Yes, Death!' or communist pensioners bearing Stalin portraits. These were college students and graduates, office managers and computer programmers: the generation that barely remembers the Soviet Union, and whose frustration at Putin's heavy-handed rule had finally exploded.

The rally had been approved by the authorities, who by all accounts were expecting the usual dozens of hardcore protesters, but, when Navalny and Yashin, the co-organizer of the rally, tried to lead demonstrators on a march towards the nearby election committee headquarters, police moved in.

'This is our city!' chanted protesters as they faced down the cops. 'Putin's whores! Stop obeying the crooks and thieves!' they added, for good measure.

Riot police, taken aback by both the size of the crowd and its naked fury, responded in the way they knew best – by cracking heads and making arrests. Around 300 people would find themselves in police custody by the end of the evening. In the first of many of what can only be described as iconic tweets over the next couple of years, Navalny posted a photo of a police truck full of smiling young faces. Politics, it turned out, could be fun.

Both Navalny and Yashin were sentenced to fifteen days behind bars the next morning, but the decision to imprison – even briefly – the charismatic anti-corruption crusader was a fateful one. Jail time would do nothing to dampen Navalny's fervour, and served only to turn him into an instant figurehead for the burgeoning anti-Putin movement.

Crowd numbers at the 5 December rally might not have been earth-shaking – between 5,000 and 8,000 people were later estimated to have attended but the demonstration went down in opposition folklore. The following summer, a new political party – one of dozens that took advantage of reluctant Kremlin reforms to seek registration – named itself the 5 December movement. 'The day Russia woke up' read glossy party flyers handed out at a mass protest in central Moscow.

✱

The day after the landmark vote protest, social networks buzzed with plans for a new rally the very same evening, this time unapproved, at central Moscow's Triumfalnaya Square. As activists plotted, police rein-forcements and Interior Ministry troops flooded into Moscow. Among them was the notorious Dzerzhinsky Division, a motorized infantry unit named in honour of the founder of Stalin's secret police. 'I've just counted seventeen trucks full of soldiers,' one blogger wrote, posting photos of what she said was a build-up of security forces just outside the centre of the city. 'Take care everyone!'

Aside from the build-up of security forces, thousands of *Nashi* teenagers were bussed in from across Russia, many from as far away as Siberia, to provide a physical presence in central Moscow. They occupied squares across the capital, and shouted slogans like 'Yes to Putin! Yes to the elections!' For reasons that even they were unable to fully explain, some of the *Nashi* activists were dressed up as Storm Troopers, the shock troops fanatically loyal to the Evil Empire in the *Star Wars* films.

Many pro-Putin youth activists covered their faces when approached by film crews. Others openly admitted they were in Moscow for a pocketful of roubles and a trip to the capital. There were, of course, the genuine believers. 'Putin is our only hope,' sneered a lanky teenager, who told me his name was Sergei. 'Are you a foreigner, or what?' he asked. 'A spy?'

As evening approached, anti-Putin demonstrators began gathering near a statue to Soviet-era poet Vladimir Mayakovsky at Triumfalnaya Square, a short distance from the Kremlin. They were met by hundreds of *Nashi* activists and a large contingent of riot police. I elbowed my way through a crowd of protesters to the edge of the square. ABBA's 'The Winner Takes it All' was blasting out from a nearby CD shop. Hardly the soundtrack to a revolution, I thought, but appropriate enough.

'Shame!' shouted protesters, as riot police charged, heads down and batons out, forcing them back further down the central Tverskaya Street thoroughfare, with its glitzy boutiques and expensive restaurants.

'When they attack you, don't just shout "Shame!" Fight back!' yelled one demonstrator.

For now, though, no one was listening. And, besides, what could the protesters be expected to do against the riot police, clad in body armour and well versed in the intricacies of street warfare? Even the strident 'Fight back!' protester had declined to lead by example. Police snatch squads moved in, emerging from the crowd with a portly, well-dressed man. Hundreds more were arrested that evening in Moscow. Worryingly for the Kremlin, the protests were spreading: another 200 people were detained when police dispersed a rally in St Petersburg.

Putin was quick to inform Russians who he believed was to blame for rising political tensions. US Secretary of State Hillary Clinton, he declared in terse televised comments, had 'given a signal' to opposition figures in the wake of the parliamentary polls: 'And with the support of the US state department, they began active work.'[15]

The Kremlin had successfully suppressed any attempts at an Orange Revolution in the wake of the 2004 uprising in Ukraine, but upheavals in the Middle East and North Africa had renewed fears that the United States was set upon regime change in Russia. And, for Putin, things were reportedly getting personal: rumours had circulated that he had become obsessed by the fate of Libyan dictator Muammar Gaddafi, murdered by his own people earlier in 2011 during a NATO-backed rebel offensive.

'People in our country do not want the situation in Russia to develop like it did in Kyrgyzstan or in Ukraine in the recent past,' an uncharacteristically overwrought Putin went on. 'No one in our country wants chaos.'

SWAMPY SQUARE

State-controlled television had, predictably, declined to report on that week's demonstrations, but the news spread rapidly on social networks and via coverage by the independent, online channel TV Dozhd, whose presenters soon took to wearing the white ribbons that became the symbol of the protest movement. As more and more people clicked 'Like' on the Facebook page set up to co-ordinate protests, a wave of enthusiasm swept through a generation of young, educated and middle-class Russians. In Moscow, newly forged political activists attended protest-planning sessions at the capital's hip Masterskaya club or cafés in the former Red October chocolate factory, now transformed into a media and arts complex.

'For the first time, we've realized that the *narod*, the people, don't all worship Putin, as we've been told. That we are not alone,' Yulia Vaynzof, a lawyer friend inspired by the protests, told me breathlessly. 'We kept telling ourselves – and the TV kept telling us and sometimes taxi drivers – that true Russians want this type of ruler and are actually quite happy about all his policies. We are a miserable minority, we are not the people. So we thought we couldn't change the situation. But with the help of the internet we now know that this is not the case and a mass of people are dissatisfied. So I know I am unhappy and my friends are unhappy and friends of my friends and it turns out even the person on the bus that my friends and I had thought was quite happy is also unhappy. The king is naked!'[16]

In the days after the disputed parliamentary polls, some 35,000 people indicated on social networks that they would attend a protest rally, 'For Fair Elections!' in Moscow on 10 December. The development rattled the authorities. In the weeks before the elections, a permit had been given to Sergei Udaltsov, the uncompromising leader of Russia's hard left, for a 300-strong protest on central Moscow's appropriately named Revolution Square. But that was before the sudden shift in the mindset of tens of thousands of Russians. When the FSB 'requested' that Pavel Durov, the young co-founder of VKontakte, Russia's answer to Facebook, close down the pages of groups co-ordinating the protest, he refused. Instead, he posted on his Twitter account an image of a dog in a hoodie with its tongue sticking out. 'The official reply to the special services,' he wrote.

Dominated by a large, granite bust of Karl Marx, Revolution Square is smack-bang between parliament and the Kremlin. And so, faced with the startling prospect of hordes of angry protesters within a stone's throw of the twin seats of state power, the authorities did the only thing they could: they panicked. First, just days before the rally, 'urgent' sewage maintenance work was announced at the site, and metal barriers were quickly put in place around the landmark square. After a public outcry, the work was shelved. Next, reports surfaced of plans to open 'the world's first ice theatre'[17] on the square – with the grand premiere set for the day of the demonstration. Russia's chief doctor also did his bit, warning potential protesters that they faced catching influenza if they attended the vote fraud rally. The authorities were getting increasingly inventive in their desperation. Eventually, sensing that neither the ice theatre nor fear of the flu would deter angry protesters, City Hall called for negotiations; the authorities proposed shifting the site of the rally to the nearby Bolotnaya Square.

Once the favoured location for rallies by the pro-Putin Walking Together youth movement, Bolotnaya Square is also within sight of the Kremlin towers, but it is far less central than Revolution Square. There was also another major drawback: its name (Bolotnaya translates as 'Swampy') lacks the obvious potency of Revolution Square. A compromise would, the more radical of the protesters insisted, be an unacceptable sell-out. But, with Navalny, Yashin and the leftist leader, Udaltsov, in police custody, the moderates triumphed. People would be allowed to gather at Revolution Square, but from there they would be directed by protest leaders to Bolotnaya.

Despite the protest organizers' co-operation with the authorities, the atmosphere ahead of the 10 December demonstration was a potent mixture of expectancy and apprehension. There was simply no telling how the modern-day Kremlin would react to large numbers of angry protesters in central Moscow. Given Russia's history, few were optimistic the day would end without bloodshed: both Soviet and Tsarist-era troops had fired on peaceful demonstrations. Bolotnaya Square's history was also ominous. The one-time location for public executions, the square was where Cossack rebel leader Yemelyan Pugachev, who led a violent uprising against Catherine the Great, was beheaded and then drawn and quartered in 1775. No one was anticipating any decapitations in 2011, but the potential for violence was huge. 'We're all expecting mass arrests,' a US-based editor emailed me ahead of the rally, warning me to file a story immediately if 'security forces gun down protesters in the streets, the Kremlin goes up in flames, or Putin resigns'.

White ribbons – indeed, a multitude of white items, garments and even a woman dressed in white carrying a white cat[18] – were everywhere on the morning of 10 December 2011. The security forces were also out in number. Dozens of police trucks lined the streets around the Kremlin. 'The police are with the people!' chanted a couple of middle-aged protesters, 'For Fair Elections' white ribbons tied to their handbags, as I made my way to the rally. A young officer stared at them blankly from the back of a vehicle. Was he, I wondered, one of the many riot police officers reportedly drafted in from the North Caucasus region, far from Moscow? And what of the rumours that scores of heavily armed Chechen fighters were holed up in an under-repair hotel on the edge of Red Square, just in case things got out of hand? How many hardened gunmen would it take to deal with this crowd of middle-class professionals, veteran dissidents, pensioners and students?

Several thousand people were already milling around the bust of Karl Marx by the time I arrived at Revolution Square. The mood was surprisingly upbeat. 'I didn't vote for these bastards, I voted for the other bastards!' read one placard. Another read: '*Vy nas dazhe ne pred-stavlyaetye*', a taunting and clever piece of wordplay addressed to Russia's rulers that means both 'You can't even imagine us' and 'You don't even represent us'.

Police had set up metal-detection barriers at one of the entrances to the square, but protesters who went through them were immediately informed by megaphone-wielding officers that they should head immediately to Bolotnaya. Protest leaders including Chirikova, the eco-activist from Khimki, were conveniently on hand to lead demonstrators, Pied Piper-style, across town towards the river, to the officially approved protest site.

As the mass of demonstrators melted away, only the Other Russia leader, Limonov, and a few hundred or so of his supporters remained on Revolution Square. Limonov was violently opposed to the compromise on the protest's location. Disgusted by the refusal of protesters to heed his urging to stand their ground, and the sudden tolerance being exhibited by Moscow's police force, he screamed some more, before climbing into a black Volga and speeding off through the winter's first snowfall to his south Moscow HQ. He and his supporters would play no further part in the white ribbon protest movement.

'The protest movement was lost from that moment,' Limonov told me later, still furious. 'The so-called protest leaders betrayed everyone who wanted to see real change in Russia. The only chance was to use the element of surprise and surround the central election committee office, which is not too far from Revolution Square. The police were disheartened and the authorities were panicking – the momentum was with the protesters. Instead, they went to Bolotnaya Square on bended knee. They wanted to become revolutionaries on the cheap, without accepting any of the risks.'[19]

Over at Bolotnaya Square, Putin's comments that the US State Department, soon to become a Kremlin byword for unmitigated evil, was behind the protests were widely mocked by a crowd estimated at around 60,000. 'You tell Hillary Clinton that I'm still waiting for my cash,' a laughing middle-aged man in a floppy hat told me, before joining fellow demonstrators in yet another round of 'Putin is a thief!'

Navalny was still in jail, so Oleg Kashin, the journalist mercilessly beaten in 2010 after being dubbed a 'traitor' by the pro-Kremlin Young Guard movement, read out a letter from the anti-corruption activist. 'Our leader,' Kashin declared. Navalny's message tore to pieces Putin's long-standing pact with his fellow Russians.

'They convinced us that a life lived like toads and rats, a life lived like mute cattle, was the only way to receive the prize of stability and economic growth,' Navalny's letter read. 'But we can see that this cattle-like silence was a gift only for that pack of crooks and thieves that became billionaires. And this gang and its media servants continue to try to convince us that the falsification of the vote in favour of their party of crooks and thieves is a necessary condition for hot water in our taps and cheap mortgages. They fed us this for twelve years. We are sick to the teeth of it. It's time to break the spell of entrancement!'[20]

But among the defiance, no one, least of all the speakers at the rally, had any real sense of what would come next. Was the Kremlin prepared to listen? And what, exactly, did the protesters want? Was this just about a rerun of the elections? Or was it about something deeper, some profound change in the way Russia was run?

'I don't know what's going to happen now,' Igor, a fifty-something engineer who had taken the train from a small town near Moscow to the protest, told me. 'But we have to take this chance to change our country. We'll regret it if we don't.'

The police made no move at all to detain protesters, standing by even when a group of nationalists let off a smoke bomb in the middle of the square. Confounding expectations that the demonstration would end with Moscow's holding cells overflowing with bruised and bloody protesters, not a single person was detained all day. 'Today we acted like the police force of a democratic country. Thank you,'[21] a police representative clambered on stage to tell the crowd, as the event came to a close. It had been a long, strange week in the Russian capital. Later that evening, state-controlled TV channels even led with news of the demonstration in Moscow, albeit without mention of the anti-Putin slogans.

These were exhilarating times for anyone involved in the protests, if even in a minor capacity. There was a sense that history was being made, that Russia's destiny was being decided right there, on the streets of Moscow. The protest movement may have been confusing and chaotic, but its leaders had seized the zeitgeist. For a brief period, it seemed as if they might change Russia forever. 'I haven't seen such things in Moscow for twenty years, since 1991,' marvelled the best-selling author Grigory Chkhartishvili, who writes historical detective novels under the name Boris Akunin. 'There's no way back from events such as these.'[22]

Protests had also taken place in scores of other towns and cities across Russia, from the 10,000 or so who had gathered in Putin's hometown of St Petersburg to the some 500 who demonstrated in Ulyanovsk, Lenin's birthplace. But for most people in the regions, far from the capital, the protests were barely understood, almost inconsequential events. Discontent over corruption and social issues is nationwide, but Moscow was the only city to witness sustained mass protests. It is one thing to vote against United Russia, but it is another thing altogether to keep taking to the streets, time and time again. Especially if, like over 50% of the country, you and your family rely on state jobs or assistance to get by. Few in the country's sprawling provinces truly love Putin, and his

United Russia is widely loathed, but he is the boss, the tsar, and in the regions that still counts for something.

The protest movement was also hindered in the regions by widespread suspicion of the Yeltsin-era democrats in its ranks. Tellingly, when state-controlled television channels deigned to report on the anti-Putin protests, they frequently led with the name of Boris Nemtsov, the deputy prime minister from Yeltsin's government. Navalny was not mentioned once. There was also the fear factor to consider: the security forces are much harsher when dealing with provincial dissent. When up to a thousand people rallied in Russia's Far East port city of Vladivostok in 2008 against the government's plan to raise tariffs on imported automobiles, the Kremlin sent in riot police from Moscow and the North Caucasus to disperse protesters violently.

'The conservative heartland will just sit and watch television to see what's going on in Moscow,' Dmitry Gudkov, the young opposition politician who had believed in Medvedev's pledges of reform, told me when I put it to him that the protest movement was failing to reach out to the regions. 'And if one day, instead of Putin, someone else appears on TV, they'll just continue to watch. They'll say: "Oh, we've got Navalny, now. Or Gudkov. Let's see what they tell us to do." And we will tell them.'[23]

It was an arrogant assumption. But it was hard to argue with the protest leaders' determination to make Moscow the focus of their efforts. Russia's pre-Soviet history is full of examples of the middle class attempting to take a message of revolt to the regions. These forays into the provinces rarely end well; the most vivid example being the intellectuals who flocked into the countryside to stir up rural dissent in the 'mad summer' of 1874, only for many to be handed over to the authorities by the very peasants they had come to liberate for speaking out against 'God and the tsar'. More than a century may have passed since then, but the divide between Moscow's Europhile middle class and the regions is almost as wide as ever.

The revolution, if one was to come, would be made in the capital. From the toppling of Tsar Nicholas II in 1917 to the sudden dismantling of the Soviet Union in 1991, this is how it has always been in Russia.

PRESIDENT PYTHON LOSES HIS GRIP

Five days after the Bolotnaya Square rally, as protest leaders were still rejoicing at the once unthinkable turnout, Putin held his annual, televised Q&A session with the Russian people. Putin began these marathon 'conservations with the nation' in 2001, when he spent two-and-a-half hours fielding questions from people across the country, on a variety of topics. The question-and-answer sessions have grown longer every year, with Putin often issuing orders live on air to regional officials. On one occasion, he invited a little Siberian girl who had complained she had no dress for the New Year to the Kremlin.[24] These televised appearances are politics, showmanship and populism rolled into one.

Questions were, naturally, carefully screened ahead of the 15 December 2011 Q&A show. But there was no way Putin could avoid commenting on the biggest ever demonstration against his rule. The 'national leader' and his advisers had undoubtedly spent the days ahead of the broadcast discussing how best to respond. It appeared they had been unable to agree on their tactics: Putin's answers were confused, at best.

Initially, in a bizarre attempt to take credit for the protesters, Putin hailed the tens of thousands of bright, young (and not so young) Russians who had poured into the streets to voice discontent at his long reign, saying: 'I was happy to see the fresh, healthy, intelligent and energetic faces of people who were actively stating their position. If this is the result of the Putin regime, then I'm truly pleased.'[25]

Had his advisers urged Putin to take a mollifying tone in his 'conversation with the nation' to neuter the protests with praise and pride? If so, Putin was unable to keep to the script for long. With almost visible relief, the ex-KGB man turned to talk of traitors and foreign powers.

'There are, of course, people who possess Russian passports who act in the interests of foreign governments and are paid with foreign money,' he said. 'We will try to work with them, but often this is useless or impossible.

'So what is there to say in this case?' Putin asked. 'I'll tell you what there is to say. "Come to me Bandar-logs."'

It was a memorable moment: faced with unprecedented numbers of 'fresh, healthy, intelligent and energetic' protesters, Putin was attempting to imitate the python Kaa from British author Rudyard Kipling's *The Jungle Book*. Kipling is wildly popular in Russia, arguably even more so than in Britain, and there can have been few educated Russians who would have failed to recall that Kaa's speciality was hypnotizing the wild and anarchic 'outcast' Bandar-log monkeys before swallowing them whole. 'I've always liked Kipling,' Putin grinned.

Putin was not content with comparing the protesters to chattering monkeys. His next target was the white ribbons the protest movement had chosen as its symbol. 'When I saw them on the television – some people had them hanging from their chests – I'll be honest, it's a bit inappropriate, but I decided that it was a campaign against Aids – that they were, pardon me, condoms,' he said.

Such comments had become Putin's trademark, proof of his tough-guy status. But this time his quip fell flat. The joke had failed to register with voters in their thirties, the majority of whom had no idea what the president was talking about. How exactly had Putin managed to confuse a white ribbon with a condom? (Soviet-made condoms were white in the 1980s, it turned out.) Putin suddenly looked not like one of the guys, but hopelessly out of touch. Had Putin lost his feel for Russia, for this new generation who knew little of and cared even less for the Soviet past?

An opinion poll released the following week indicated that Putin's approval ratings had fallen to 36% – his lowest figures since he was first nominated for president by Yeltsin.[26] Was President Python's hypnotic hold over the nation weakening?

Putin may have ridiculed the protesters, but, two days before the second mass protest on 24 December, Medvedev, speaking at the Kremlin's ornate Georgiyevsky Hall, proposed a 'comprehensive reform of our political system'. His suggested reforms included a return to direct elections for governors, scrapped by Putin in 2004, and a loosening of the rules on registering political parties.[27] Protest leaders reacted cautiously. And with good cause. It would later turn out the elections included a Kremlin 'filter' of potential candidates, and that genuine opposition parties such as the Navalny-backed People's Alliance would continue to be denied registration necessary for electoral participation.

Surkov, the grey cardinal of Putin's 'sovereign democracy', continued the conciliatory tone, praising the protesters as the 'best part of our society' in an interview with the *Izvestia* newspaper. 'Of course it is possible to say that those who have gone out on the streets are only a minority. If this is the case, what a minority!' he enthused. 'The fundamental structures of society have shifted, the social fabric has acquired a new character,' he went on, hitting his stride. 'We're already in the future. And this future is restless. But there is no need to be scared. The turbulence, although strong, nonetheless is not catastrophic, but a form of stability. Everything will be fine.'[28]

Surkov's unexpected praise for the anti-Putin protesters caused a storm. Was he attempting to dilute the dissent? Or had he been genuine in his admiration? What exactly was he up to? Whatever his motivations, later that month, Putin's chief ideologue was abruptly reassigned from his post in the presidential administration and shunted to a minor ministerial portfolio. He would, officially at least, play no further part in domestic politics. Was the move a sop to the protesters, or punishment for his outspoken statement? No one was telling. 'Stabilization devours its own children,' Surkov declared. 'I am too odious for this brave new world.'[29]

MELTING POT

Snow had finally come to Moscow by the time Navalny was released from the detention facility where he had been marking time since his arrest at the 5 December post-election protest. Apparently wary of affording the opposition figure too much publicity, the authorities did their best to keep his exact release time a secret. But, despite the late hour and a snowstorm, a throng of supporters were waiting to meet Navalny as he stepped out of a south Moscow prison.

'We went to prison to serve our fifteen-day sentence in one country, but were released in a different one,' Navalny said, after cheers had died down.

He then outlined his strategy for the upcoming presidential elections. 'The party of crooks and thieves is nominating its chief crook and thief for president,' he said. 'All those people that came into the streets in Moscow and across the whole country should become a perfect propaganda machine and explain to all the population that this man is a crook and a thief and he can't be the president of our big and wonderful country.'

Navalny then threw himself into the organization of the next demonstration. The protesters had already forced limited concessions from the Kremlin, now they needed to keep the pressure up. But was public anger strong enough to sustain more protests in the face of uncertainty over what exactly could be accomplished by gathering at state-approved demonstrations and, as a young leftist activist put it scornfully, 'shouting for a while and then heading off home'?

The answer to that question came on 24 December 2011, just two weeks after the Bolotnaya rally, when, despite falling temperatures, a crowd estimated at around 100,000 packed an avenue in central Moscow named after the Soviet-era dissident Andrei Sakharov.

'I've been reading this little book, it's called the Constitution of the Russian Federation,' Navalny said, addressing a mass rally for the first time in his life. 'And it states clearly that the only source of authority is the Russian people. So I don't want to hear any talk that we are appealing to the authorities… Who is the power here? We are the power here!

'With the help of their Zombie boxes, they are trying to prove to us that they are big, frightening beasts. But we know who they are – they are tiny, cowardly jackals,' Navalny yelled, trancing out on his own fury. 'There are enough people here to take the Kremlin,' he raged on, before adopting a softer tone. 'But we are peaceful and won't do that just yet… But next time we will bring one million people out onto the streets!'[30]

Navalny was right to temper his threats with caution. Traumatized by a world war, revolutions and almost total economic collapse at the tail end of the twentieth century, many Russians have first-hand experience of the dangers of rapid political and social change. This is why Putin's message of stability has remained so attractive to so many, for so long. Ordinary people may be angry about corruption, but they are unprepared for the massive sacrifices that overthrowing Putin would entail. As protesters gathered in Moscow, Putin drastically increased wages for security-services personnel. Riot police and investigators drafted in from the provinces to work in the capital already had little love for what they viewed as Moscow's wealthy and pampered protesters; now they had an extra incentive to crack heads, if it came to that.[31]

It is also important to remember that Putin, for all his faults, is one of if not the most democratic leaders in Russia's history. After all, from Ivan the Terrible to Stalin, to Brezhnev and the former KGB chief Andropov, Russia does not exactly have a shining history of free elections and respect for human rights. If Putin is toppled, who or what will emerge to take his place?

And so, despite Navalny's impassioned pledge, one million people would not flood the streets of Moscow at the next anti-Putin rally. But, for now at least, the protesters were going nowhere. On 4 February 2012, after an ill-advised 'break' for the New Year and Orthodox Christmas that sucked some of the momentum out of the movement, tens of thousands of people defied Arctic-like conditions to gather at Bolotnaya once more.

'What shall I sing about?' asked Yury Shevchuk, the bearded, veteran lead singer of the Soviet-era rock group DDT, whose televised debate on democracy with Putin had caused a sensation, as he stepped out on to the stage. 'Freedom!' suggested someone in the crowd, but Shevchuk launched instead into a few unaccompanied lines from the nation's favourite song about the cold: '*Oi moroz, moroz*' (sample lyric: 'Hey, frost, don't freeze me!').

It was an equally apt theme. With temperatures of just below -20°C, that afternoon's protest was by far the coldest of the anti-Putin demonstrations to hit Moscow in 2012. It was also, bizarrely, the best attended, with organizers estimating a crowd of some 120,000. The frost was so intense that day that I abandoned my usual practice of recording interviews on a Dictaphone; my fingers would freeze up painfully whenever I removed my gloves to operate its delicate controls. Russians are, of course, used to the cold, but they usually spend winter days rushing from warm apartments to heated shops and offices, and back again. The willingness of so many people to come out in such conditions sent a powerful message of discontent to Putin.

Gripping on to his acoustic guitar with gloveless hands, Shevchuk picked out the opening chords to his twenty-year-old hit '*Rodina*' – 'Motherland'.[32] All around me, the crowd, even those not too keen on Shevchuk's extensive back catalogue, danced along, jumping up and down and from side to side to keep warm in the freezing conditions.

Who were they, these tens of thousands of Russians who came out on the streets to protest Putin's long rule? For a start, they were well educated: surveys indicated that over 80% of the protesters had studied to university level. Age-wise, the vast majority were between the ages of twenty-five and fifty-five. Politically, their views spanned the entire spectrum, from the hard left to the ultra-right. A mere 30% or so described themselves as 'liberals'.[33] The protests brought them face-to-face with each other, in numbers, for the first time.

'I knew there were lots of people like me who hate Putin and United Russia, and want to see our country become a normal country, without all this corruption and political repression and... and... idiocy,' said Kirill, a young student, gesturing meaningfully upwards at a hovering police helicopter as he searched for the precise words to express his overflowing emotions. 'But, you know, I never thought I'd see so many of them in one place.'[34]

Like Kirill, I was also having difficulty getting my thoughts in order. Standing amid a people shedding their fear and apathy, it was hard not to exalt these suddenly visible demonstrators at the expense of objectivity, to project on to the protest movement my own wishes for Russia. The sins of Putin's regime were so apparent and, at times, blatant that it was tempting to support the nascent street opposition without examining too closely the convictions and ideologies of its figureheads.

But, like some wildly ambitious Russian novel brought to life, the protest movement was populated by a sprawling cast of unforgettable characters, drawing together the moderates and the radicals, the left-wingers and the ultra-right, in a heady and shaky alliance based solely on discontent with Putin's rule. Amid the hipsters tweeting of social reform were sinister nationalists consumed by a rabid hatred for 'traitors to the white race', while old-school liberal democrats stood side-by-side with Stalin apologists. Putin, predictably, homed in on this lack of solidarity. 'There's no one to talk to,' he replied, when asked if he would enter into dialogue with the protesters.

This bewildering diversity was Navalny's dream come true. He had previously called in a controversial report for the NAROD nationalist movement for an alliance between 'representatives of the overwhelming majority of parties and ideologies'[35] as the only way to challenge the Kremlin's grip on power. He must have felt a deep sense of satisfaction as he gazed out at the sea of nationalist, leftist, democratic, monarchist, green and anarchist flags.

Those veteran Soviet-era dissidents observing or even participating in the demonstrations were struck by the lack of a common set of ideals among the protesters. 'We were all different, of course, but today's protesters are even more different from one another than even we were,' said Natalia Gorbanevskaya, one of eight people who took part in a landmark 1968 protest on Red Square against the Soviet invasion of Czechoslovakia. 'We shared certain values on the importance of human rights,' she told me, 'but the values of the people protesting today sometimes contradict each other so much that it's hard to even see a common link between them.'[36]

In a sense, this ideological melting pot was the outcome of yet another of Putin's sins: by so completely eviscerating all other centres of power and influence, Russia's 'national leader' had left very little room for a conventional political culture to develop. As the celebrated Polish journalist Ryszard Kapuściński once noted, when cracks begin to appear in an authoritarian regime, it is not always the best people who emerge from hiding, but those whose 'thick skin and internal resilience have proven their survival'.[37]

All of these groups, for years marginal and largely obscure, were suddenly tussling for leadership of a potentially earth-shaking force.

8

UDALTSOV AND
THE NEW LEFT

Red stars were everywhere in the winter of 2011 and 2012, the flags of left-wing groups fluttering in the wind as disgruntled Russians marched through snowy Moscow to call for new parliamentary elections and, increasingly, Putin's resignation. Every third protester held leftist views of some sort.[1] As the protest movement slowly took shape, a strange alliance was forged between Navalny, the (almost) undisputed leader of the hipsters and the middle class, and Sergei Udaltsov, the fiery hero of the new left. Udaltsov may be the one with the shaven head, but he does not share Navalny's nationalist tendencies, speaking wistfully of the 'brotherly friendship'[2] between the many ethnic groups that made up the Soviet Union.

'I can't say I agree with Navalny on many things,' Udaltsov told me in his trademark rasp, after the initial wave of vote protests. 'But right now we are all working together to create a climate of freedom. After we are successful, the people will be able to decide who they want to lead them.'[3]

Udaltsov has revolution in his blood. His great-grandfather, Ivan Udaltsov, was a Bolshevik ally of Lenin's who has a street in south Moscow named after him, while his uncle and great-uncle were Soviet ambassadors. A lawyer by profession, Udaltsov first became seriously involved in anti-Kremlin protests in 1998, when he helped form the radical Red Youth Avant-garde (AKM) movement, whose emblem was a Kalashnikov rifle and whose members burned images of Putin in public. All of this was met with a general widespread indifference. It would be an exaggeration to say the AKM's members couldn't even get arrested (police were more than happy to oblige), but the movement's impact was confined to a few dozen hard-left activists. Udaltsov later co-founded the Left Front, an umbrella organization for leftist groups, whose slogan is 'The land to the peasants! The factories to the workers! Power to the soviets!'[4] The Left Front's policies include the nationalization of strategic industries and a return to elements of a planned economy, as well as the closure of the Russian stock exchange. Udaltsov's politics are as alternative as his musical tastes: a great enthusiast of US and British punk, such as The Ramones and The Sex Pistols, he is also into 'really heavy, fast underground stuff'.

The authorities had been so concerned that this leftist punk fan would stir up trouble during the parliamentary polls that they detained him on farcical charges of jaywalking on the morning of the vote. After serving five days for 'resisting officers' recommendations to cross the road in the correct place', he was immediately sentenced to another fifteen days in jail on charges dating from a previous protest-related offence. Udaltsov was more than used to jail cells; he once told me he had 'stopped count-ing' after his hundredth arrest.

'Basically, the Kremlin doesn't want Udaltsov out and about on the streets while there are any protests going on,' laughed Ilya Ponomarev, a young, bearded lawmaker who was also one of the co-founders of Udaltsov's Left Front. 'They are really afraid of him leading an angry crowd to the Kremlin.'[5]

With his buzz cut, black clothes and frequent hunger strikes to pro-test his persecution by the authorities, Udaltsov is possessed by a stark asceticism that brings to mind Rakhmetov, the fictional austere nihilist in Nikolai Chernyshevsky's classic nineteenth-century novel *What Is To Be Done?*. The character of Rakhmetov, who ate nothing but black bread and slept on a bed of nails, greatly inspired Lenin, who said the description of the committed revolutionary had 'ploughed him up anew'.[6] Udaltsov is unlikely to sleep on a bed of nails, but there is the sense of another, harsher era about him, as if he has somehow been transported directly to Putin's Russia from the hideout of some hardened gang of Tsarist-era socialist utopians.

'I live very modestly,' Udaltsov told me. 'I spend very little money on myself. Once I even considered forming a party of ascetics.' He took a sip of his black tea. 'I don't really care much about personal comforts.'

Despite this intensity, Udaltsov injected both humour and unpredictability into the protest movement. Responding to state-run media allegations that vote-fraud protesters were all wealthy Muscovites in the pay of the West, Udaltsov leaped on stage at the 4 February 2012 demonstration in central Moscow and snarled, 'I've been wearing this jacket for the past three years! It's you in the Kremlin who are wearing mink coats!' He then took an impromptu straw poll. 'Is there anyone here working in the interests of the United States of America?' he asked, as tens of thousands of protesters shivered in freezing temperatures. 'Is there even one person?'[7] At another protest later that year, he turned up in dark glasses and shouted from the stage, 'Let's all wear sunglasses to the next protest! Black reflects my mood – I'm angry!'[8] He also appeared to seek out confrontation with the police, often leading small breakaway groups of activists on impromptu marches across town after 'official' protests had ended.

This impulsiveness worried some fellow protest figures. 'What's Udaltsov up to now? Anyone know?' I heard one nervous activist mutter, as the Left Front leader made a noisy arrival at yet another anti-Putin rally.

NOSTALGIC FOR COMMUNISM

Along with a widespread nostalgia for the Soviet era, socialist ideas have remained extremely popular in Russia, with polls regularly indicating that, more than two decades on from the collapse of the Soviet Union, around a third of Russians still consider communism the best political system for the country. A Western-style democracy is favoured by around a quarter of the population, while around 20% are content with Putin's 'sovereign democracy'.[9] After Putin's United Russia, the Communist Party has the second biggest share of seats in parliament. Some analysts even claimed that the Communists would have won the disputed 2011 parliamentary polls, had it not been for the theft of millions of votes by Kremlin-friendly election officials.[10]

It is important to understand the motivations of those millions of Russians who vote for the Communist Party. It is not the gulags or one-party elections that these people are hankering after, but rather the social safety nets and the sense of a national ideology that the Soviet authorities supplied. After all, very few people alive today went through Stalin's Great Terror; the Soviet Union they miss is the one of state-subsidized holidays to the Black Sea, the 1980 Moscow Olympics, and the comparative calm and lack of rampant crime. It is true that dissidents and critics of the Soviet regime were sent to gulags in the 1970s and 1980s, but, unlike during Stalin's era, there was no random, all-encompassing terror. Under Brezhnev, if you did not speak out, the KGB would not, as a rule, come for you.

'Things were better in the Soviet Union than they are now,' Ponomarev, the opposition lawmaker and Left Front co-founder, insisted. 'It was a strong state with many social guarantees. Of course, there were problems. There was no freedom of speech or guarantee of human rights. But today's Russia is no better, in that respect.'

Leftist sentiments in Putin's Russia are also encouraged by the country's appalling record on wealth inequality, which has been labelled the highest in the world by the financial-services company Credit Suisse. 'Worldwide, billionaires collectively account for 1%–2% of total household wealth; in Russia today 110 billionaires own 35% of all wealth,' the Swiss company reported in 2013.[11] Compare this with the desperate situation in some of Russia's poorest regions, where up to 30% of the population survives on less than $200 a month.[12] People in big cities like Moscow and St Petersburg may be better off than ever before under Putin, but large swathes of the country are still wallowing in Third World-style poverty.

Healthcare, which under the constitution is supposed to be free for all, is also criminally undeveloped. Outside of central Moscow, state hospitals remain inhumane institutions, where medical care is primitive or almost non-existent. Fundraising campaigns for what should be routine yet life-saving operations are common. As I was rounding up my research for this book, visitors to Moscow's biggest chain of bookshops were being asked to donate towards the cost of an $80,000 heart operation for a fourteen-year-old girl. The state, quite clearly, had other priorities. The Russian authorities are also failing to take care of the country's old people. UN global studies on quality of life for the elderly place Russia seventy-eighth out of ninety-one countries, below Nepal, Ghana and Romania. Even in Moscow, where pensions are significantly higher than in the rest of the country, it is common to see old men and women begging on the streets.

And all this in a country that possesses the world's largest natural gas reserves, the second-largest coal reserves and the ninth-largest crude-oil reserves.[13] To add insult to injury, Russia also overtook Saudi Arabia in 2011 as the planet's top oil exporter.

'We should all be living like kings and queens, you know?' a friend in central Russia noted, with understandable anger.

THE KREMLIN'S NIGHTMARE

In early 2012, with Moscow still in the grip of vote protests, Udaltsov's Left Front forged a partnership with the Communist Party and its veteran leader, Gennady Zyuganov. The two made for odd allies as they signed off on the co-operation agreement at a Moscow news conference, with Zyuganov's suit, tie and Communist Party pin in sharp contrast to Udaltsov's black top, jeans and shaven head.[14]

'This is a historic and significant moment,' Udaltsov declared, as he put pen to paper. And, indeed, it was the first time that one of Russia's established political parties had entered into an alliance with representatives of the emerging street protest movement. Under the agreement, the Left Front would support Zyuganov at the 2012 presidential polls, while the Communist leader pledged to back the demands of the 'For Fair Elections' protesters, if elected.

The deal sparked speculation that the Communists were moving closer to outright, genuine opposition, shaking off years of tepid, token resistance to Putin's rule. Rumours quickly spread that Zyuganov, pushing seventy, had offered Udaltsov leadership of the party.

'If they are willing to put this trust in me, then I'd accept it,' Udaltsov commented later. 'What we are after is rev-o-lu-tion,' he growled, his eyes aflame as he enunciated the word.

Zyuganov later denied he had made the offer,[15] but just the prospect of the streetwise and uncompromising Udaltsov leading the party that had ruled the largest country on Earth for seven decades was surely the stuff of nightmares for the modern-day Kremlin.

The continuing popularity of socialist ideas in Russia means the potential for a powerful left-wing political party is huge. Under Zyuganov, the Communist Party does not fit the bill. Opposition merely in name, the party has little appetite for confrontation. When the vote-fraud protests began in late 2011, Zyuganov initially accused demonstrators of being in the pay of the West and of seeking to foment Orange Revolution-style regime change. The party's refusal to move on from its Soviet past (its flag, for example, still features a hammer and sickle) has stunted not only its own development, but also that of the left throughout Russia. Operating in the shadow of the Communists is not an easy thing to do. It was a task made even harder in 2006, when the Kremlin's chief ideologue Vladislav Surkov conjured up A Just Russia, a centre-left party designed to cater to leftist-minded voters turned off by the Communists. The apex of Russia's Potemkin parliamentary opposition, the party's leader Sergei Mironov had never been shy about where his loyalties lay. Ahead of the 2004 presidential elections, Mironov had declared with no apparent embarrassment that he would vote for Putin, despite being – on paper at least – a rival candidate. Mironov was so loyal to Putin that he would even 'oppose' him, if ordered to.

While clearly no believer in economic equality for all, Putin has also shown a willingness to flirt with Communist imagery and ideology. Putin's campaign ahead of the 2012 presidential elections was based in part on leftist ideas, such as a much-trumpeted umbrella alliance with trade unions and other groups under the distinctly Soviet-sounding title of the All-Russia People's Front. He also brought back the Soviet anthem, albeit with new words, shortly after coming to power in 2000. 'If we accept that we cannot use the symbols of previous epochs, including the Soviet epoch… then we must agree that our fathers and mothers lived useless, senseless lives. That they lived in vain,' Putin said, commenting on his decision. 'I cannot accept this with either head or heart.'[16] But Putin's respect for the Soviet past is based on emotions, rather than economics.

The emergence of Udaltsov and a new wave of socialist activists threatened to damage both Putin's carefully honed image and the monopolization of the leftist vote by the Communist Party and A Just Russia. 'There is a real hunger for genuine leftist groups,' Alexei Sakhnin, a leading Left Front member, told me. 'That's what makes us so dangerous. The Communists are fakes and no one buys Putin's mock leftism. But we are the real thing.'[17]

Tellingly, a public-opinion survey by state pollster VTsIOM indicated that Udaltsov was one of the few high-profile protest figures to have seen his popularity ratings increase after the initial series of election fraud rallies.[18] Udaltsov might not be a new Lenin, but any future economic downturn clearly had the potential to play straight into the hands of this new breed of leftists.

A LONG POLITICAL WINTER

Udaltsov breathed politics, fielding dozens of calls a day from journalists and allies, and always willing to discuss developments with the crowds that seemed to follow his every public move after the start of the vote-fraud protests. That was not to say, however, that he was easy to pin down for an in-depth interview. I'd grown used to meetings falling through at the last minute, as Udaltsov was summoned to court, detained or called in for questioning. 'Marc, we'll have to put the interview off,' he would tell me, on around a dozen occasions, often calling as I was already on my way to our rendezvous point.

I finally cornered the Left Front leader ahead of a meeting with supporters in a side-room at a central Moscow news agency. I'd grown used to seeing a furious Udaltsov lead anti-Putin rallies, or being dragged off by swarms of riot police, and it was revealing to witness him chair a meeting of some dozen or so supporters, a mixture of enthusiastic twenty-somethings and earnest middle-aged activists.

'Come on, guys, we're trying to have a meeting here,' Udaltsov scolded.

'I didn't say anything,' countered a slim young woman, defensively.

'Whatever,' said Udaltsov. 'But let's keep it down a bit, yeah? They won't invite us back here otherwise.' The Left Front leader frowned, and took his place at the head of the table. Suddenly, plotting an anti-Kremlin uprising didn't seem half as exciting as I'd imagined.

Although still in his mid-teens when the Soviet Union disintegrated in 1991, Udaltsov was devastated by the collapse of the socialist system. 'My parents were real believers in communism. They still are,' he told me, when we spoke during a break in the protest planning. 'When the Soviet Union split up, I picked up on their distress. I took it very badly. The Soviet Union was a great country,' he said, looking straight at me, as if daring me to assert otherwise. 'To break it up was a terrible idea. It wasn't just some social or political experiment. We lost our homeland.'[19]

The collapse of the Soviet Union may have been welcomed in the West, but it caused misery for millions of people across its fifteen republics, as ethnic violence rocketed, poverty soared, and family members and relatives scattered across the Communist state's vast territory suddenly found themselves living in newly independent countries.

I reminded Udaltsov of Putin's famous statement that the Soviet Union's break-up was the 'greatest geopolitical tragedy of the twentieth century'. Was he, I wondered, in agreement on at least one thing with his arch-nemesis?

Udaltsov looked uncomfortable. He obviously wasn't used to concurring with Putin on anything. He pursed his lips. 'For those people who lived in the Soviet Union, yes it was,' he said finally. 'But it's really not important who said this, Putin or whoever.'

If Navalny is grilled incessantly over his nationalist sympathies, then Udaltsov faces equally intense questioning on his attitudes to Stalin. And not without justification: this is, after all, a man who wore a Stalin T-shirt to his wedding in 2001. More seriously, Udaltsov had also consistently refused to condemn the Soviet dictator's reign of terror unequivocally.

'You have to understand that the late 1990s, the early 2000s were very different times,' Udaltsov told me. 'When I used to walk around in a Stalin T-shirt, it was like a red flag to the liberal democrats who had ruined the country. Before Putin established himself in power, everyone was dreaming of a strong hand to rule the nation. And that was symbolized by Stalin, of course.

'Now, my attitudes have changed somewhat. Stalin is a black-and-white figure for me. He achieved huge breakthroughs and massive progress in industry and infrastructure – this is indisputable. But at what cost? His rule was built on terror. This is a separate issue. Stalin was a genius, yes. An evil genius, perhaps, but a genius all the same.'

But surely, by the same logic, I countered, Hitler was also a black-and-white figure? After all, the Nazis built superb roads… 'Don't dumb things down,' Udaltsov snapped, clearly irritated by the argument. 'Stalin didn't just kill people for his own pleasure. All the people around him wanted to serve and please the father of the nation. Sometimes they went overboard,' he said, in an uncanny echo of the 'good tsar, bad boyars' reasoning that had kept Putin in power for so long.

For the average Westerner, any discussion of the rights and wrongs of Stalin's three-decade rule might seem like a purely academic exercise, and one with an obvious conclusion. In Russia, where the dictator's popularity had been steadily rising since Putin's ascension to power, the debate is far more relevant. Stalin is not coming back. But the Russians' respect for an 'iron fist' has never gone away. For many in the opposition movement, the prospect of Udaltsov coming to power is a terrifying one. ('Udaltsov has the mentality of a ruthless dictator,' one activist told me, off the record. 'I really hope he doesn't come out on top.') It was an understandable fear. What was the sense in toppling Putin only to replace him with a man whose politics were potentially far more authoritarian?

As attention turned to the May 2012 presidential polls, Udaltsov spoke often and loudly of the need for a nationwide trade-union strike to force the Kremlin to make genuine concessions. It would have been an incredibly effective tactic, and one that would have terrified the authorities. But the likelihood of the country's workers coming out en masse against Putin is almost non-existent. There is no tradition of trade-union militancy in Russia. During the Soviet era, the trade unions were state-run organizations that did little more than organize holidays for workers and summer camps for their children. Unlike in the West, they played no part in seeking to improve workers' rights. Since the Soviet collapse, attempts to build genuinely independent trade unions have been largely thwarted by the almost complete lack of a functioning legal system that workers can turn to. Workers who try to organize themselves in Putin's Russia also often face pressure and threats. Moreover, many of the country's leading unions have been integrated into the United Russia network. The Left Front had begun reaching out to the unions, but even Udaltsov didn't seem too convinced by the plan for a national strike. Fortunately for the revolutionary firebrand of the Russian new left, he had plenty of others in reserve.

'If the elections are fixed again, we will also call on people to put up tents and not to leave the streets until the results are annulled or until the authorities quit the political scene altogether,' Udaltsov told me.

While, for many in the protest movement, the battle to bring down Putin consisted of a long, methodical slog to bring about change slowly, Udaltsov viewed events through a prism of pure revolution. But would enough people listen to this radical left-winger seeped in the tradition of socialist insurrection? Would hundreds of thousands of bankers, office workers and computer technicians really be willing to follow Udaltsov as he led them into a confrontation with baton-wielding riot police? Somehow, it seemed unlikely.

'We need to get a million people out on the streets of Moscow,' Udaltsov went on. 'Otherwise, the Kremlin will simply crush the protest movement. And we will face a long political winter.'

Udaltsov was right to be anxious. The protests against Putin's rule would soon provoke a terrible backlash. For now, though, this would-be socialist hero was free to continue his scheming and dreaming. 'My comrades are waiting for me,' Udaltsov told me, as our talk came to an end, gesturing in the direction of the meeting room, where the protest-planning had resumed.

Deepening discontent with Putin's rule had highlighted dangerous fault lines, from shameful wealth inequality to rising ethnic tensions. And divisions were about to grow even deeper. The liberal world of opposition Moscow was moving towards a head-on clash with the powerful Orthodox Church, its Kremlin allies and Russia's conservative masses. Five young women were getting ready to put on their brightly coloured balaclavas.

9

PUSSY RIOT VS THE KREMLIN

The special-forces officer sat down on a bench next to the metal cage the three defendants would be kept in throughout the pre-trial hearing and began to polish the barrel of his Kalashnikov absent-mindedly. Glancing up at the two dozen or so journalists crammed into the tiny Moscow courtroom, he took off his black ski mask to wipe the sweat from his brow, and warned off a press photographer who had pointed a camera in his direction. Outside, in the courthouse's narrow, oak-panelled hallways and sprawling yard, more brawny officers from Russia's elite *spetsnaz* unit kept a vigilant watch.

Despite the high-level security, the defendants were not terrorists or crime bosses, or even businesspeople charged with multi-million-dollar fraud. The suspects, who had already spent more than four months in custody, were three young women from an all-female punk group called Pussy Riot, detained that spring after a brief anti-Putin protest in Moscow's biggest cathedral. Putin's spokesperson had said the 'national leader' found the group's actions 'disgusting' and the women, two of whom had young children, were now facing up to seven years in a brutal, TB-ridden penal colony far from the capital.

The defendants were already over an hour late and it was becoming unbearably hot in the courtroom, where the air-conditioning system had briefly spluttered into life at around eleven, before packing up for the humid summer afternoon. Deciding the risk of losing my place in the courtroom was infinitely less dreadful than succumbing to heat exhaustion and thirst, I pushed through the tightly packed journalists and stepped outside. 'Free Pussy Riot!' came the chant from the street, where dozens of the group's supporters and a smaller number of religious activists had gathered. I made my way towards the noise and out through the metal crowd-control barriers, securing as I did so a promise from a court security guard that I would be allowed to re-enter.

After the dullness of the courtroom, the central Moscow side street was a kaleidoscope of colour and impressions, as Pussy Riot supporters, many wearing the group's trademark bright balaclavas, argued furiously with Orthodox Church activists, who were holding wooden religious icons. Other believers, some clad in black 'Orthodoxy or Death!' T-shirts, prayed long and hard.

'God does not suffer evil-doers!' a small, enraged young man with a wisp of a beard repeated over and over to a twenty-something woman in an oversized Pussy Riot T-shirt. 'God is not evil! God condemns evil!'

'God forgives everyone!' responded the slim, black-haired woman, whom I would later find out was an anti-Putin activist called Tatyana Romanova. 'Yes, he forgives everyone!'

The young man reached out a thin arm and slapped Romanova hard on the cheek. 'That's sacrilege!' he screamed. 'Sacrilege! And I'll strike again any blasphemers who say that God forgives evil. He does not!'

Romanova, I thought, to make a timely biblical point, really should have offered the other cheek. But, instead, she strode off down the street in search of a police officer, the still furious Orthodox activist in pursuit.

Footage of the slap later went viral among Russia's opposition bloggers.

'That's the first blow in the holy war,' commented one. 'What's next? The inquisition?'

CHURCH AND STATE

After decades of the suppression of religious freedoms by the Soviet authorities, Orthodox Christianity made what church leaders hailed as a 'miraculous' comeback in the newly independent Russia. By the time the vote-fraud protests broke out, roughly 70% of Russians identified themselves as Orthodox Christians,[1] around double the level when the Soviet system collapsed. Religious icons, once destroyed en masse by the atheist Bolsheviks, were suddenly everywhere again. Getting your child baptized was now the norm. This religious zeal was typified by a campaign in the summer of 2008 to build dozens of tiny, wooden Orthodox churches across the country in the space of just twenty-four hours. On a visit to the west Siberian city of Omsk, I watched as weary builders raced against the setting sun to hammer in the final nails on a new place of worship.

Despite his years of service in the Soviet-era KGB, the feared security agency in the world's first officially atheist state, Putin has done his utmost to project a pious image since taking over the presidency from Yeltsin at the turn of the millennium. He has made a great show of celebrating religious holidays and receiving blessings from the influential heads of the Russian Orthodox Church, first Patriarch Alexei II, and then his successor, Patriarch Kirill.

And so, with protests against vote fraud having transformed into a broader demonstration of discontent with Putin's rule in the run-up to the presidential vote, the support of the country's spiritual leaders was vital. On 8 February 2012, Putin took part in a televised meeting at Moscow's ancient St Daniel's monastery with representatives of the country's major religious faiths.

Russia's chief mufti, rabbis, Catholics and even a Buddhist lama were all present at the monastery, seated around Putin at a large shiny table as cameras recorded the meeting for the evening news. In recognition of his status as head of the country's largest confession, the seat at Putin's right-hand side was reserved for sixty-five-year-old Patriarch Kirill.

Relations between the Orthodox Church and the authorities had been growing steadily warmer; just three months before the monastery meeting, Kirill had been awarded residency in the Kremlin. The government had also handed over large swathes of real estate to the Church and made promises on the introduction of Orthodox religion lessons in schools. The constitutional separation of Church and state was on shaky ground, critics cried.

But Kirill had so far failed to provide a public show of support to counter mounting discontent. Instead, he had called the vote-fraud protests a 'lawful negative reaction' to corruption. True, he had issued a vague warning about the danger of 'internet manipulation', but there was nothing resembling the kind of backing that Putin and his campaign staff were undoubtedly counting on. And, in a worrying sign for the Kremlin, other figures within the Orthodox Church had also begun to speak out.

'As a result of the particular way in which power is set up in our society today, this arrogant attitude toward the people has become the abnormal norm,' well-known Moscow priest Revd Father Zuyevsky said at a sermon in early 2012, which he then posted online. 'Those in power are not only conceited, they refuse to allow anyone else but themselves the right to decide what is good and what is bad.'[2]

And Zuyevsky was not the only priest to criticize the Kremlin.

'People of the most varied convictions are now gathering on the square, but they are united by one thing – their unwillingness to live like this any longer,' said Archpriest Alexei Uminsky, a popular Moscow priest and host of a state television programme about Orthodoxy. 'The same thing is happening right now in the Church.'[3]

But, on 8 February 2012, after Putin had outlined his vision for the country's many faiths to those gathered at the centuries-old Moscow monastery, Kirill delivered what was expected of him. His speech left no doubt in the minds of the country's millions of Orthodox believers as to whose name God wanted them to tick on the ballot paper.

'The 1990s saw the destruction of the political system, the economy, society and the country,' Kirill began, recalling the 'heady' Yeltsin era. 'This period was comparable to the Time of Troubles, the Napoleonic invasion, Hitler's aggression and the civil war. On each of those occasions arose the question – would the country survive?

'But what were the 2000s?' he went on. 'Through a miracle of God, with the active participation of the country's leadership, we managed to exit this terrible, systemic crisis. The country escaped the danger zone and began to turn itself around.'

The head of the Orthodox Church then turned his head to look at the former KGB officer to his right. 'As the patriarch, sworn to speak the truth, I have to say this openly – you personally played a massive role in correcting this crooked path in our history. I wish to thank you.'[4]

Putin nodded in recognition of the patriarch's praise, but said nothing. It was clear, however, that the Kremlin had secured what it had been after. The modern Russian state had lacked legitimacy in the years since the break-up of the Soviet Union, with no obvious ideology or vision other than an all-embracing patriotism. An alliance with the Orthodox Church and its thousand years of unbroken history invested it with an invaluable sense of solidity.

Close co-operation with the Kremlin was nothing new for the Orthodox Church. Outlawed after the Bolshevik Revolution, when priests were murdered and churches destroyed, Stalin allowed a controlled revival of Orthodoxy during World War II, in a bid to improve public morale. But its patriarchs were handpicked by the Kremlin. Unsurprisingly, the Church was riddled with KGB agents and informers. Anatoly Oleynikov, the last deputy chairman of the KGB, revealed in 1991 that a mere 15%–20% of priests had refused to collaborate with the security services.[5]

In an all-too-brief period of openness following the failed 1991 coup attempt by KGB hardliners, researchers gained once unthinkable access to the spy agency's archives. One of these researchers was Gleb Yakunin, a dissident Orthodox priest who had spent five years in a Soviet jail. Elected to parliament in the year before the Soviet collapse, Yakunin had always suspected large-scale KGB infiltration of the Orthodox Church. But what he discovered when he studied the archives shocked him. The Soviet-era Orthodox Church, he declared, was 'practically a subsidiary, a sister company of the KGB'. Yakunin urged church leaders to admit to their KGB past. Instead, less than two years after making his discoveries, he was defrocked by the Orthodox Church. When he continued his calls for a full investigation into the Church's collaboration with the Soviet spy agency, he was excommunicated.[6]

From the archives studied by Yakunin, who cross-checked the known travel itineraries of leading clergy with journeys made by agents, it seems likely that both Kirill and his predecessor, Patriarch Alexei II, were KGB operatives. Active cogs in the system of repressive state control. Kirill's codename as he worked his way up the Church hierarchy is believed to have been 'agent Mikhailov'. He is also alleged to have made a fortune as part of a tobacco and alcohol imports scheme run by the Orthodox Church in the 1990s. The Church denies both sets of accusations. It was no proof of anything, of course, but both Kirill and Alexei II were photographed downing a shot of vodka with Soviet leader Leonid Brezhnev in the 1980s.

When Russia experienced a religious revival in the 1990s, the Orthodox Church was protected by its history of Soviet-era persecution, making it almost invulnerable to attack. But Kirill's 'miracle of God' statement was like a red flag to the protest movement. From now on, the Church was fair game.

In early 2012, in an interview with a well-known television presenter, Kirill fended off suggestions that he led a luxurious lifestyle, one that critics said was inappropriate for a man of the cloth. Ukrainian media reports claimed the patriarch had worn a $30,000 Breguet watch on a visit to Kiev, but Kirill denied ever sporting the timepiece. Any photographs of him doing so had likely been doctored, he suggested. But eagle-eyed bloggers quickly discovered a photograph of Kirill wearing the watch on the Orthodox Church's official website. The wristwatch was quickly airbrushed out of the photo. Unfortunately for the Church, the inattentive editor left intact the telltale refection of the luxury watch on a varnished table, triggering a storm of online mockery. An embarrassed spokesperson for Kirill said the watch had been deleted by a 'secular' employee who had made an 'absurd mistake'. The original, undoctored photograph was quickly returned to the website. The patriarch had been caught out in a lie. Another scandal involved a mysterious woman said to be living at a luxury apartment registered in the patriarch's name. The Orthodox Church denied Kirill had done anything untoward, and said it was under attack by 'anti-Russian' forces seeking to erode its authority.[7]

VIRGIN MARY, DRIVE PUTIN OUT!

The most potent symbol of Russia's 'return to the faith' is the colossal Christ the Saviour Cathedral that stands on the bank of the River Moscow. The original cathedral was destroyed in 1931 on Stalin's orders to make way for a never-to-be-erected Palace of Soviets. At 415 metres, the proposed building would have been the tallest in the world at the time. According to design blueprints, it was to be topped by a gigantic statue of Lenin, from whose eyes beams of red light would shine out across Moscow at night. But the ground under the demolished cathedral proved too waterlogged to support such a vast edifice, and in 1958 a huge open-air swimming pool was opened on the site instead.

With the demise of the Soviet Union, the Christ the Saviour Cathedral began to rise again, with work funded by a host of oligarchs and the state arms-trading company Rosvooruzheniye. I visited the building site in 1997, and watched as workers scuttled around the heights of the vast under-construction edifice. By 2000, its golden domes would again dominate the skyline of the upmarket Kropotkinskaya district, where the local metro station had been constructed using marble from the original cathedral.

The modern-day cathedral is mired in controversy, with many Orthodox believers uncomfortable with the numerous commercial activities that take place on its sprawling territory. Directly underneath the Christ the Saviour Cathedral is a huge underground parking lot with space for hundreds of vehicles, charging prices that reflect its prime downtown Moscow location. Cathedral grounds also contain tyre-changing services, a chemist, halls available for rent for private functions, and shops hawking pricy religious souvenirs to the millions of worshippers who visit it each year. All profits are tax-free.

The cathedral is also where Russia's leaders come to celebrate religious holidays in front of the TV cameras, dutifully crossing themselves as bearded priests light sweet-smelling incense and choirs sing songs of praise in Church Slavonic. Within sight of the Kremlin towers, it is hard to think of a better target for any activists wishing to attack the growing ties between the Russian Orthodox Church and the state.

Less than three weeks on from Kirill's televised endorsement of Putin, five young female activists and a handful of opposition journalists mingled with the worshippers and tourists making their way into the cathedral.

Once inside, the young women slipped on the multi-coloured balaclavas that would soon become the headgear of choice for young female would-be revolutionaries the world over and made their way to the area around the altar.

'Virgin Mary, drive Putin out! Virgin Mary, become a feminist!' the Pussy Riot members yelled, alternately high-kicking and crossing themselves, the words echoing off the cathedral's arched marble ceilings. 'Patriarch Gundyayev believes in Putin – that bastard, he should believe in God instead!' they screamed, using the head of the Russian Orthodox Church's 'secular' surname.[8]

'Shit, shit, holy shit!' the group just had time to shout before church security dragged them away, and escorted them out of the building. In a show of respect for religious traditions, a security guard waited until one of the Pussy Riot members had finished crossing herself before pulling her to her feet.

'What a nightmare,' said one onlooker, as the women were led away. 'They should have their heads torn off for that,' muttered another.[9]

Later that evening, a punk soundtrack and additional earlier filmed footage was added to the recording of the group's forty-second a cappella performance. The clip was then put online with the title 'A Punk Prayer: Virgin Mary, Drive Putin Out!'

Despite its shock value, the protest appeared to be little more than a colourful skirmish in the anti-Putin opposition's wider war. After all, the group was notorious for its provocative musical performances, none of which had resulted in serious consequences for anyone involved. Just a month prior to the cathedral protest, for example, eight women from the group had raced through a track called 'Putin's Pissed Himself' on a snowy Red Square. Police briefly detained the musicians, and released them later that day without pressing criminal charges. Pussy Riot had also performed on the roof of a detention facility where protesters arrested after vote-fraud demonstrations were being held. No criminal charges were brought that time, either.

There was certainly no reason at all to suspect the group's 'punk prayer' would make international headlines and turn Pussy Riot into a household name in the West, drawing in a cast of international celebrities and politicians from Paul McCartney to Hillary Clinton and Nobel Peace Prize winner Aung San Suu Kyi.

✱

On the eve of Putin's March 2012 election victory, some thirty police officers and anti-extremist agents detained Pussy Riot members Nadezhda Tolokonnikova, twenty-two, and Maria Alyokhina, twenty-four, near a west Moscow metro station. After seven hours of questioning, during which officers made it clear to the suspects that the case was being handled 'at the very highest level',[10] charges of 'hooliganism as part of an organized group' were brought. The quaint-sounding nature of the offence belied its seriousness – the maximum punishment was three years behind bars. And, when charges were altered to include the phrase 'with the aim of inciting religious hatred', the two young mothers were suddenly looking at seven years in a penal colony. Two weeks after the initial arrests, police detained a third suspect, Yekaterina Samutsevich, twenty-nine, and the scene was set for the most controversial trial in modern Russia's history. All three suspects were denied bail. Even the intervention of Russia's justice minister, Alexander Konovalov, who stated publicly that there was no reason to lock up the women, was insufficient to secure their release. Red Square and detention centres, it appeared, were all fair game for Pussy Riot's musical protests, but not the symbol of the modern Russian state's increasingly symbiotic relationship with the Orthodox Church. Someone very high up had been angered by Pussy Riot's actions.

The women were stunned to find themselves facing such serious charges. 'Nadya [Tolokonnikova] thought there was a 0.1% chance they would be jailed for the cathedral protest,' her father, Andrei, a trained doctor turned part-time poet who had known of the group's plans, told me. 'After all, the Red Square protest had been just as high profile. But I told her that I thought they would find some way to jail her for it. But Nadya was under the illusion that she knew the rules of the game. I told her there are no rules. It's impossible to talk Nadya out of anything though.'[11]

The case was quickly picked up on by human-rights groups. Amnesty International recognized the women as prisoners of conscience less than a month after their arrest, and the Kremlin's own human-rights council would also call for their release. As the story began to make international news, the US rock band Faith No More became the first of dozens of Western musicians and actors to support the group when they invited the still-at-large Pussy Riot members on stage at a concert in Moscow.

It would be wrong, however, to think of Pussy Riot as a normal rock or punk group. With no constant line-up, the group does not play conventional, pre-announced gigs, nor does it release recordings on CD or vinyl. In fact, it has nothing whatsoever to do with the music industry.

Pussy Riot draw their influences from a wide range of sources, from the 1990s feminist US punk rock Riot Grrrl movement to the avant-garde art of the early Soviet-era OBERIU (The Union of Real Art) collective. Founded in 1928 in Leningrad by the absurdist writers Daniil Kharms and Alexander Vvedensky, OBERIU specialized in jarring, hallucinatory poetry and prose. The experimental collective also carried out unconventional public performances, with Kharms once surprising residents of Leningrad with a rooftop appearance. Criticized by the Soviet authorities for 'deflecting the people from the building of socialism',[12] Kharms and Vvedensky both later perished in Stalin's prisons.

'Pussy Riot are Vvedensky's students and heirs,' Tolokonnikova would later say. 'His principle of the bad rhyme is dear to us. He wrote, "Occasionally, I think of two different rhymes, a good one and a bad one, and I always choose the bad one because it is always the right one.""[13]

Tolokonnikova, a slim and dark-haired Siberian with a pout soon to grace the covers of magazines the world over, had earlier made the news in Russia when she took part in a bizarre bout of public sex in a Moscow biology museum to 'commemorate' Medvedev's 2008 presidential inauguration. The performance/protest was organized by the notorious *Voina* (War) art group, whose previous stunts had involved drawing a gigantic, erect penis on a St Petersburg drawbridge opposite FSB headquarters, and throwing live cats at staff in a McDonald's in central Moscow. Four days after having sex on the floor of the museum with her husband, Pyotr Verzilov, a co-founder of *Voina*, Tolokonnikova gave birth. 'I couldn't have just stayed at home and done nothing,' she replied later, when asked if she regretted taking part in the unorthodox protest against Medvedev's inauguration. 'I would have felt even worse.'[14]

Alyokhina, a curly-haired vegan and aspiring poet, went through the court hearings in a haze of apparent bewilderment at the Soviet-style legal proceedings unfolding around her. As the trial began, she told the judge that she was unable to plead because she could not understand the nature of the charges. 'You have a higher education!' snapped the judge. Like all three defendants, Alyokhina had no doubt that Putin was behind their prosecution. 'If I cannot hear my child's voice because of my criticism of the authorities, then welcome to 1937,'[15] she said as the suspects were remanded in custody by a Moscow court, in a reference to the year that was the peak of Stalin's Great Terror.

Samutsevich, the smallest, oldest and only childless suspect, was perhaps the most complex of the trio. A former computer programmer with tomboy looks, she would largely forego outright anti-Putin soundbites at court hearings in favour of an analysis of the system of control that the former Soviet security services officer had constructed. She also put forward the most in-depth explanation as to why the group had chosen to protest in Moscow's largest cathedral.

'That the Christ the Saviour Cathedral had become a significant symbol in the political strategy of the authorities was clear to many thinking people when Vladimir Putin's former KGB colleague Kirill Gundyayev took over as leader of the Russian Orthodox Church,' Samutsevich told the court, glancing down occasionally at a scrap of paper. 'After this happened, the cathedral began to be openly used as a flashy backdrop for the politics of the security forces.[16]

'Our sudden musical appearance in the cathedral violated the integrity of the media image that the authorities had spent such a long time generating and maintaining, and revealed its falsity,' she explained, hands stuffed in pockets, her features fixed in a mixture of disgust and punker boredom.

In the aftermath of the three women's arrest, both influential Orthodox Church figures and ordinary believers called for leniency as a demonstration of Christian forgiveness. Pussy Riot had, some argued, simply been acting in the centuries-old Russian tradition of 'holy fools', those half-witted prophets given licence in medieval times to say out loud what others could not. The most famous was Saint Basil, the outspoken critic of Tsar Ivan the Terrible, who has an onion-domed cathedral named after him on Red Square.

But, for many older Orthodox Christians, Pussy Riot's performance had brought back painful memories of the Soviet persecution of believers, when the faith was routinely ridiculed in public as part of the country's official atheist ideology, and Christians imprisoned in the vast gulag system were subject to grotesque parodies of church services.

'There was a great deal of public mockery of religious services, priests, vestments, etc., both in marches, performances, films and cartoons in the 1920s and early 1930s in Soviet Russia,' Andrei Zolotov, an Orthodox journalist and expert on the Church's relations with society, told me. 'That's why any contemporary art that also ridicules the faith is so disturbing to church people.'

Patriarch Kirill was in no mood for clemency. Speaking in a televised March 2012 sermon, he portrayed the performance as a demonic assault on the Church and all it stood for. 'The devil laughed at us,' he said. 'But there are those who seek to downplay this sacrilege. My heart breaks from bitterness that amongst these people there are those who call themselves Orthodox.' The group and their supporters, the patriarch went on, 'believe only in the strength of propaganda, in the strength of lies and slander, in the strength of the internet, in the strength of the media'.[17]

Those members of Pussy Riot still at large hit back in a blog post.

'We were deeply saddened that you allowed the Church to become a weapon in a dirty election campaign and urged the faithful to vote for a man who is as far as can be from God's truth,' the group said. 'You cannot believe in an earthly tsar if his deeds contradict those values for which the Heavenly Tsar was crucified.'[18]

MEDIA MACHINE

Tolokonnikova was first into court for the 4 July 2012 hearing that would determine when the group's trial was to begin for real. Handcuffed to a burly police officer, she smiled and laughed her way to the metal cage, dark shadows under her eyes. 'In Russia, anyone can end up in handcuffs,' she said, shrugging. 'There is nothing unique about this.'

Her husband, Pyotr Verzilov, wiry and bearded, held up a news-paper report of Faith No More's show of support. He gave his wife the thumbs-up, but was prevented from handing the newspaper over by a special-forces officer.

Wearing a T-shirt bearing a clenched fist and the Spanish Civil War slogan '¡No pasarán!' ('They shall not pass'), Tolokonnikova alternately strode around her cage and slouched on its wooden bench as she waited for the hearing to begin.

'What are conditions like inside?' asked a journalist.

'OK,' she said. 'I mean, OK for a prison.'

To the left of the metal cage, the group's three lawyers were trying to wade their way through thick sheaves of legal documents. 'They handed this to me when I got here and said you have an hour,' complained lawyer Nikolai Polozov, a bespectacled Orthodox believer who had taken on the case over what he called the 'legal nihilism' of the allegations. He would later reveal that he had been given an informal warning that his defence of Pussy Riot could see him disbarred.

'The investigation is fulfilling a political order and the court is going along with this,' Polozov said when the court hearing began. 'It was common to deny suspects the right to acquaint themselves with case materials in Stalin's Soviet Union and Nazi Germany.'

The judge stared straight ahead, fixing her gaze on some point on the far wall. Was she even listening? Courts in Russia are widely believed to operate to a system of 'telephone justice' – highly placed officials call judges and tell them what decision to make in important cases. So who could really blame her if she chose not to pay attention? There was nothing Polozov could say that would have any effect on the court's ruling.

Violetta Volkova, a larger-than-life, short-tempered lawyer who had represented almost all of Russia's long-suffering opposition figures at one point or another, was even blunter than Polozov. 'This is a farce,' she said, staring at the state prosecutor. 'You have falsified documents and I really don't understand how you can do such things without feeling ashamed.'

To no one's surprise, the court ruled against the defence team's request for more time to study the case materials. Tolokonnikova was led out of the courtroom, the police officer she was handcuffed to squeezing her past journalists. 'There is only one person to blame for all this, and his name is Vladimir Putin,' she said.

After the hearing, I struck up a conversation with a red-faced police officer outside the court. Why, I wanted to know, did the suspects have to be handcuffed and kept in a cage? The cop stared at me. 'What about the way those guys who rioted in London were treated?' he said, referring to the mass disturbances in the UK the previous summer. 'I bet they were kept in cages at their trials, no?' He didn't seem convinced by my insistence that cages were not a part of the British judicial system.

'Those women spat in my soul,' he went on, choosing not to push the cage debate further. 'This lot only care about bringing Russia down,' he added, waving in the direction of the group's supporters. 'They'd sell us all out to the West.'

The policeman's fury symbolized the growing divide between Russia's liberals, with their Western attitudes and fashions, and the socially and religiously conservative majority, who found Pussy Riot's cathedral protest both incomprehensible and indefensible.

There was genuine anger among some believers, as I found out when I quizzed worshippers at the scene of the high-profile protest. 'Those bitches should be put away for life,' a young woman snapped, as she stood in brilliant sunshine on the steps of the Christ the Saviour Cathedral. It didn't seem a very Christian attitude and I asked her how she could reconcile her fury with Christ's teachings. I was genuinely curious. 'Yeah, of course, Christ taught people to forgive their enemies, but, all the same, they should go down for life,' she replied. 'I'd have dealt with them right on the spot.'

This growing split in society was later neatly summed up by Putin himself, when he told state television in October 2012 that he was interested in not only the ideas of 'intellectuals', but also the thoughts of 'real Russian people'. It was a revealing moment, and one that would come to symbolize growing attempts to portray opposition to his long rule as somehow un-Russian.

Putin also challenged a foreign journalist to translate the 'obscene' name into Russian in a rare TV interview. When the journalist at the Kremlin-backed Russia Today channel declined, Putin lashed out. 'I know you understand it perfectly well, you don't need to pretend you don't get it,' he said. 'It's just because these people made everyone say their band's name too many times. It's obscene – but forget it.'[19]

But this was something Putin, strangely, seemed unable to do. Aside from the Russia Today interview, the president would address the subject – unprompted – on a number of other public occasions, most notably at the annual Valdai club gathering of foreign political analysts and journalists. Putin, it appeared, just couldn't stop saying 'pussy'.

The persecution of Pussy Riot was shocking, and said much about the selective use of the legal system in Putin's Russia. But the group's impending trial also posed a genuine dilemma for the nascent protest movement's figureheads: support the suspects and be tarred with the same brush as Tolokonnikova and her 'orgy in the museum' friends. Condemn Pussy Riot and lose the backing of the 'creative class', for whom the group had become a cause célèbre.

'Pussy Riot is an incredibly convenient theme for the authorities,' sighed Yevgenia Chirikova, the eco-activist and protest leader. 'The entire opposition movement has become Pussy Riot for ordinary people. As if we were all dancing in that cathedral. I mean, it really was disgusting what they did. I go to church to communicate with God,' she told me. 'Why is this "holy shit"? But it was also disgusting to detain young mothers over this. That's also unchristian.'[20]

Navalny, an Orthodox believer, expressed outrage over the harshness of the treatment of the women, but condemned their 'repulsive' actions. 'I'd be angry if my daughter did something like this,' he fumed. 'But I don't see why they can't be put under house arrest. Why lock them up? They are no danger to society. When deciding the issue of the freedom of even the most disgusting people we have to stick to legal norms. The case has a clear political element.'[21]

The authorities had wasted no time in exploiting Pussy Riot to damage the protest movement. A documentary on the state-controlled NTV channel portrayed the group as pawns of foreign powers intent on destroying 'holy Russia'. The programme featured an interview with an investigator involved in the case who announced that the group was made up of 'revolutionaries and demons'. Suitably spooky music was played whenever the women's faces appeared on the screen. Another interviewee also compared the group to Nazi ideologist Alfred Rosenberg, who had urged the wartime destruction of the Russian Orthodox Church as a necessary step towards conquering the Soviet Union. And the man behind Pussy Riot? Why, NTV alleged, it was Boris Berezovsky, the former Kremlin insider who had fled Russia after falling out with Putin in 2000. By now a massive Putin critic,

Berezovsky had boasted in 2007 that he was funding 'revolution' in Russia. He denied, however, any links to Pussy Riot, but said he would have been 'proud' to have been involved with the group.[22] The Kremlin's propaganda may have been crude, but it was effective: the Pussy Riot saga effectively killed off the opposition's hopes of making allies of millions of conservative Russians.

Tolokonnikova's husband, Pyotr Verzilov, laughed sharply when I asked him if Pussy Riot was in the pay of demonic Westerners. A fluent English speaker with dual Russian and Canadian citizenship, Verzilov grew up in Toronto, where he 'got a feel for Western culture'.[23] Tolokonnikova later visited Toronto with him, attending lectures by the American feminist philosopher Judith Butler. Still in his mid-twenties, Verzilov had quickly become the group's de facto spokesperson and he was clearly relishing his moment in the media spotlight. 'Pussy Riot is a machine placed inside the media,' he declared, when I journeyed with him to the pre-trial detention centre where Tolokonnikova was being held. 'It's designed to draw attention in the West to what's going on in Putin's Russia. And the group has succeeded.'[24]

He shrugged, however, when I suggested the group's performance had also supplied the Kremlin with a powerful propaganda weapon in its fight against the protest movement. 'We know that lots of people believe all that rubbish they see on TV,' he said, smiling and stuffing his face with breadsticks as we drove through a beat-up residential zone. 'We need a revolution of the mind before we can change Russia. But this could take a very long time. It could take some fifteen years or so to see real change. That's what we are most afraid of.'

After Tolokonnikova's arrest, Verzilov had been left to care for the couple's four-year-old daughter, Gera, and Putin had become a bogeyman figure for the pre-schooler. 'Gera's been making plans to bust mummy out of jail,' Verzilov laughed. 'She's been telling people that Putin has locked her up in a cage. Her nursery-school teacher even called me recently to ask if she could please not tell everyone quite so often that "Putin is evil, but my mummy and daddy are fighting him".'

THEY HAVE NOT REPENTED

As the Pussy Riot story began to attract international attention, influential Moscow archpriest Vsevolod Chaplin became the Church's de
facto point man on the rapidly escalating row. An outspoken figure,
Chaplin (his surname, not his title) quickly became the man to turn to
for a memorable quote or two.

'God is waiting for their repentance. He has revealed this to me, like
he revealed the gospels to the Church,' he said, as initial hearings into the
case got under way in Moscow. In another interview, he alleged Pussy
Riot's protest was symbolic of the 'Satanic rage' the country's opposition
forces had unleashed against the Orthodox Church.

Eager to meet a man the Supreme Being deemed worthy of a one-to-
one chat, I went to visit Chaplin – a forty-four-year-old bearded asthmatic
with a fondness for visiting underground rock clubs[25] – at the central
Moscow cathedral where he was rector.

In over fifteen years in Russia, I have yet to shake the feeling of
unease that I experience whenever I enter an Orthodox church. Under
the onion domes of Russia's Orthodox churches, the relation between
God and humanity is one of pure surrender and unquestioning devotion. There are no pews in Orthodox churches. Worshippers stand at
services, often for hours on end, among clouds of thick incense smoke
and prayers intoned in Church Slavonic, a language all but incomprehensible to modern-day Russian speakers. Entering an Orthodox
church from the busy, chaotic streets of Moscow is like stepping into a
time machine. Unlike, say, Church of England places of worship with
their trendy priests and Facebook posts for family fêtes, there is almost
no concession to modernity.

Chaplin was busy when I arrived at the poetically named Cathedral
of St Nicholas under the Three Hills. As I waited outside his office, I
watched an elderly female worshipper praying. Her head covered in
accordance with Orthodox rules, she crossed herself and kissed an icon,
then stood silently in front of it. There was an almost tangible sadness
about her. I suddenly felt uncomfortable, as if it was somehow wrong to

be observing her prayers. It was a timely reminder that, for many Russians worn down by their country's numerous problems, the Orthodox Church offers a comfort they are unable to find elsewhere.

'A Christian country should act decisively when one of its holy places is attacked,' Chaplin intoned, as we sat in his spacious, yet oddly ramshackle office.[26] He was wearing his billowy, black priest's cassock, from whose depths he would occasionally pull out his cell phone. The Kremlin and Patriarch Kirill had frequently suggested that an act of 'sacrilege' such as Pussy Riot's cathedral protest would be clamped down on just as severely in any Western country. But it was a fact that in the United Kingdom, for example, gay rights campaigner Peter Tatchell had in 1998 been fined the grand sum of £18.60 for interrupting the Archbishop of Canterbury's Easter sermon with a protest at the pulpit. And even in Russia, in 1995, a performance artist named Alexander Brenner had disrupted a service in central Moscow's Yelokhovo Cathedral by rushing into the church and chanting, 'Chechnya! Chechnya!' He was punished with a night in the cells and a small fine. Why were Pussy Riot different? I asked. Why was the Church unwilling to do the Christian thing and forgive the group?

'If someone insults me personally, then of course I will forgive them,' Chaplin responded. 'But, if someone insults my faith or my God, I wait until they change their position and admit that they acted wrongly.'

I had not so long ago returned from a reporting trip to the Iranian capital of Tehran, where I had seen at first hand the power of the Islamic Republic's many mullahs. And, while, clearly, the differences between Iran and Russia were vast, recent events had made me wonder if Russia might not also be heading in the same direction.

So what I wanted to find out from Chaplin was this: was the Orthodox Church seeking the same kind of power that Iran's Shiite clerics enjoyed? The question sounded insane as soon as I had asked it, and I was about to cover my tracks by qualifying my words, but Chaplin was already answering. My query, it turned out, was not so crazy, after all.

'For a Russian Orthodox believer, it is normal for the state and the Church to co-operate in harmony with each other,' he told me. 'They should have the same values and co-operate in the majority of spheres.

'The separation of the secular and the religious is a fatal mistake by the West,' Chaplin went on, before pausing for breath. 'It is a monstrous phenomenon that has occurred only in Western civilization and will kill the West, both politically and morally. I don't believe the political system in the West today is any better for a Christian than the Soviet system.'

It was an astonishing statement. Although I was sure he knew them, I reminded the archpriest of the facts. Some 200,000 clergy and believers were executed by the Soviet authorities between 1917 and 1937, according to a 1995 presidential committee report.[27] 'The more representatives of the reactionary clergy we shoot, the better,' Lenin had said. Thousands of churches were destroyed, and those that survived were turned into warehouses, garages or museums of atheism.

But Chaplin just nodded when I asked him to reconfirm that he believed contemporary Western society was as bad for a Christian as the Soviet Union. 'Yes. Of course, of course,' he replied instantly. He looked bored with the discussion.

Chaplin had recently met Navalny for informal talks and smiled when I reminded him of the encounter with the opposition figurehead. 'He's obviously a clever person, but it's difficult for me to agree completely with everything he says,' he said. 'But it's clear that such people should be drawn into national politics. I hope that Russia's future political life will develop through dialogue, and not through revolution and chaos.'

Russia had seen more of the 'revolution and chaos' that Chaplin so feared in the past hundred years than many countries had suffered in their entire modern history. A clear sign, the archpriest was adamant, of God's fondness for Russia and its people.

'If God loves someone or something, he creates difficulties,' he concluded, as he stood up to signal the end of our meeting. 'If a person is living a sated, peaceful life, this means God has forgotten about him. This life is but a preparation for the next, real life, and it is through suffering that God prepares us.'

So did God love Pussy Riot? After all, Moscow's pre-trial detention centres were well-known places of suffering. And even the prosecution had, in a widely reported slip-of-the-tongue, referred to the defendants as 'the injured party'.

'Without repentance there can be no forgiveness,' Chaplin reiterated, apparently citing God once more, as he sidestepped the question. 'And I do not see that they have repented.'

As the date of Pussy Riot's trial drew nearer, pleas for leniency flooded into Russia from across the world, including from celebrities such as Madonna and Elton John. Noble Peace Prize winner Aung San Suu Kyi added her voice to the appeals. 'I would like all the members of the group to be released,' she said, joking that only people who sing 'really terribly' should be prevented from doing so.[28]

Dozens of Russian celebrities and cultural figures also signed an open letter calling for the Kremlin to show mercy. In an echo of the famous *The Times* editorial, 'Who breaks a butterfly upon a wheel?' on the 1967 jailing of Rolling Stones members Keith Richards and Mick Jagger on drug charges, Soviet-era pop icon and Kremlin favourite Alla Pugacheva declared a custodial sentence for the group would be like 'shooting sparrows with a cannon'.[29] Even Boris Grebenshchikov, the veteran Russian rock legend turned Buddhist, broke his self-imposed silence on worldly issues to condemn the prosecution of Pussy Riot. 'The justice system that this is being performed under is not worthy of the name of justice,' he told me, peering out from behind dark glasses as we sat near the banks of the River Volga.[30] But the Kremlin does not enjoy being dictated to: Tolokonnikova and co stayed behind bars.

Like the pleas for their freedom, Pussy Riot's 'punk prayer' would also go unanswered. The Virgin Mary, if she had heard, appeared in no mood to drive Putin out. The 'national leader' was heading back to the Kremlin.

10

PUTIN'S RETURN

It was around -12°C in central Moscow's Pushkin Square when Udaltsov pledged he would not be going home until Putin had quit politics. Bareheaded and clad in his beloved black jacket, the leader of the Left Front movement certainly wasn't dressed for a long wait. And given it was less than twenty-four hours since Putin had returned to the presidency, triumphing at the 4 March 2012 elections with almost 64% of the vote (but tearfully claiming victory with less than a third of the ballots counted), it seemed a most unrealistic demand.

'Television is informing us that these were the most honest elections ever,' Udaltsov told a crowd of over 20,000. 'So why the hell are troops occupying Moscow? I'm not leaving this square today until Putin goes!' Some people laughed. Others responded with a sustained chant of – what else? – 'Russia without Putin!' Udaltsov waited until the noise had died down. 'I'm not joking. I'll be standing over there,' he said, pointing vaguely in the direction of a statue of Russia's nineteenth-century national poet Alexander Pushkin.

True to his word, when the speeches were over, Udaltsov – joined by Navalny, Yashin and opposition lawmaker Ilya Ponomarev – stayed put in the centre of the square, clambering up on to an iced-over fountain. The allotted time for the rally had ended, meaning the protest leaders and the some 2,000 people who had stayed on with them were liable to arrest, but the presence of Ponomarev, the slight, bearded socialist who was also a member of Udaltsov's Left Front movement, technically transformed the gathering into a legal open-air meeting between a member of parliament and his constituents. But Moscow's tooled-up and psyched riot police had little time for the finer nuances of Russian law.

'Remember that this is a peaceful protest,' said Navalny through a megaphone, as police circled. 'Don't get into any fights. There'll be many more camps later. And one day we'll make a camp so big that no one will be able to break it up.' Russia's opposition was still dreaming of an Orange Revolution; it was also painfully aware that it had taken one million protesters, many camped out in tents in central Kiev, to force change in Ukraine.

Udaltsov, hailed by Navalny as the 'hero' of the night, shoved his hands in his pockets and glanced around warily from his vantage point on the fountain. Minutes later, a police officer was shouting through his own megaphone: 'Your protest is unsanctioned! Disperse immediately!'

A group of grassroots activists had announced their intention to encircle the Kremlin after the end of the Pushkin Square rally, but the plan was thwarted by the presence of hundreds of police officers lining the road to the seat of Russian state power. Instead, as news that Udaltsov and Navalny were serious about a showdown spread among departing protesters, many returned via the warren of subways that extends from the square, swarming past police and back into the thick of things.

'You are acting in violation of the rules of the Russian Federation!' shouted Ponomarev, the legislator, as police moved in to 'retake' the fountain, which was now covered in a light sprinkle of freshly fallen snow. Bodies tumbled as officers broke through an impromptu human ring to pull people down, all this lit up intermittently by camera flashes from around a dozen press photographers. The fountain cleared, police linked arms and moved forward in a sweeping motion, trampling indiscriminately anyone too slow to get out of their way.

I leaped on to a low wall to avoid being crushed by cops, only to be screamed at to 'get down from there!' by another officer. I weighed up the odds, and ignored him until riot police had rushed past me.

Beneath the statue of Pushkin, a young man stood waving an opposition flag. The police appeared not to notice him, drifting past as if he were somehow invisible. 'I'm not leaving until our demands are met,' said the young, fresh-faced activist, who told me his name was Gleb. But wasn't he afraid? After all, Russia's riot police are not the gentlest of souls. 'No,' he told me, genuinely baffled by my question. 'Why should I be afraid?'

Helpless in the face of well-trained and equipped riot police, the protesters were finally pushed out of the square, spilling out on to the central thoroughfare, Tverskaya Street. From there, hundreds of them ran in the direction of the Kremlin, holding up traffic and chanting anti-Putin slogans until police chased them away, detaining many more in the process. A police helicopter buzzed over the capital's famous skyline for hours afterwards, until the last cries of 'This is our city!' had long faded away.

Of course, the protest leaders hadn't really believed they could bring Putin down by occupying a snowy fountain in central Moscow. Navalny called the stand-off with police an 'experiment' to gauge the mood of protesters.[1] 'It's good to be irrational sometimes,' Udaltsov laughed, when I quizzed him later. 'It keeps your enemy on their toes.'

IF NOT PUTIN, THEN WHO?

There had been little doubt that Putin would return to the presidency. How could there have been? He had faced off at the polls against four Kremlin-approved candidates, none of whom had been expected – or, indeed, themselves expected – to present anything resembling a genuine challenge. Not only had Putin and Medvedev decided behind closed doors who would become president in 2012, but the Kremlin had also controlled the exact nature of the electoral campaign, selecting and moulding malleable 'rivals' into shapes that suited its ever-shifting agenda.

Putin's main rival, on paper at least, had been the veteran Communist Party leader, Gennady Zyuganov. He had failed to triumph in three presidential elections ahead of the 2012 polls, and came in a distant second this time, with just over 17% of the vote.

The other three candidates allowed on the ballot were:

1. Mikhail Prokhorov, a lanky tycoon and owner of American basketball team the Brooklyn Nets. Clearly intended to appeal to the disaffected middle class, he had, however, admitted discussing his candidacy with the Kremlin and was widely seen as part of Putin's game plan to divide and confuse opponents to his rule. He took almost 8% at the polls.

2. Vladimir Zhirinovsky, the eccentric nationalist who in the past had threatened to seize Alaska from the United States and launch nuclear weapons at Japan. His 2012 election campaign included a pledge to clone famous Russians, such as nineteenth-century composer Pyotr Tchaikovsky. He won just over 6% of the vote.

3. Sergei Mironov, the A Just Russia party head who had voted for Putin in 2004, despite running against him. Eight years on, he had pledged to make a real go of things. Less than 4% of voters believed him.

Putin's move to retake the Kremlin was also aided immensely by the fear factor: he had been in power in one form or another for so long that, for many voters, it was truly impossible to imagine the country without him. 'If the Russian people choose another president, I don't know how this will affect my life. It could get better, or it could get worse,' said a young Putin supporter in February 2012, her nose red with cold, as she argued with a protester in central Moscow. 'But "better" is the enemy of "good enough",' she continued, citing a well-known Russian saying. 'My life is OK as it is now. And I'm not ready to risk it getting worse.'[2]

Playing on these fears, a well-timed, slickly produced video clip was released online ahead of the March 2012 presidential polls. The clip had the snappy title of *Russia with No Putin – Apocalypse Tomorrow*, and racked up almost a million hits in a few weeks.

'In Moscow, the opposition has been chanting "Russia without Putin",' intoned a stern voice over images of protesters and spooky, horror-movie-style music. 'But just imagine that there is no Vladimir Putin. What would await Russia without Putin?'

The answer, according to the clip, was this: deadly street fighting between nationalist gangs and Islamists from the North Caucasus, catastrophic inflation, mass unemployment, near famine, civil war and – eventually – the incursion of NATO troops on the grounds of protecting the 'peaceful, civilian population'. As if all this wasn't enough, Russia also risked being stripped of the right to hold the 2014 Winter Olympics. 'Russia without Putin? Choose for yourself,' concluded the narrator, as the music reached a crescendo and the screen filled with images of corpses and ultra-violence.[3]

State-run television channels were more restrained than the authors of the *Apocalypse Tomorrow* clip during the brief election campaign, but their coverage was heavily focused on Putin. Channels justified this blanket coverage of Putin's comings and goings as 'newsworthy' items about the prime minister. Documentaries glorifying the ex-KGB man as the nation's saviour and protector from the Kremlin's new bogeywoman, Hillary Clinton, were also aired by state TV. Such was his confidence, Putin did not even feel the need to take part in televised debates with his nominal rivals, sending underlings to convey his message of 'stability' and 'economic growth' to voters.

Patriarch Kirill's endorsement of Putin's first term as a 'miracle of God' had also added a spiritual dimension to the elections: vote 'right' or your soul was in danger of eternal damnation. 'I was at Mount Athos monastery recently and the first thing they asked me there was "Are you for Putin or against?"' smiled a slightly tipsy, middle-aged man with a gold tooth at a massive pro-Putin election rally in Moscow. 'I replied, "It's a political matter." "No," they said. "It's a spiritual thing. Are you for him or not?" I said, "As a matter of fact, I am." And they absolved me of all my sins.'[4]

Critics alleged the tens of thousands of people who attended rallies like this in support of Putin were state employees or students who had been forced to attend. Others, they said, had been bussed in from the provinces and handed mass-produced placards. Unlike the talkative protesters at anti-Kremlin rallies, people at these shows of support for Putin were generally tight-lipped. One person notably broke his silence, however. 'Are they letting people go yet?' a miserable-looking middle-aged man asked me ahead of Putin's appearance at the Soviet-era Luzhniki sports arena in the spring of 2012. 'I want to go home,' he sighed sadly. He refused to give his name. 'I don't need any trouble, you know?' Nearby, a placard that read 'Putin is our president!' lay abandoned in a puddle of slush.

While allegations of vote fraud had sparked massive protests after the 2011 parliamentary polls, Putin's victory at the presidential elections served only to dampen the spirits of the protesters. There was a grim acceptance that, despite the inevitable election-night trickery, Putin really was the most popular politician in Russia. Even the independent Golos election watchdog recognized that Putin had won the polls, albeit with some 50% of the vote rather than the reported 64%.[5]

Putin's critics lacked a figure they could rally around – there was no one they could point at and say, 'This is your true leader! We demand a recount!' In Ukraine, in 2004, furious protesters had swarmed into the streets of Kiev to chant that vote fraud had cost the pro-Western candidate, Viktor Yushchenko, the presidency. But it is hard to get people as excited about state media bias or the slow but steady construction of a police state. In the vernacular of the newsroom, such topics simply aren't 'sexy' enough to ensure mass protests.

But Putin's hold on power was founded on a strange contradiction. In 2012, a poll revealed that, while 63% of Russians approved of Putin's policies, only 41% thought the country was heading in the right direction, and 'confidence' in Putin was at a mere 37%. In other words, while Russians were unhappy with what was going on in their country and had little hope that Putin could rectify matters, they still approved of his actions. Bemused, I called the head of the Moscow-based Levada pollster to ask for an explanation.

'There is a mechanism at work here that protects and relieves Putin of responsibility and puts the onus on lower levels of authority – the government, regional authorities, and so on,' said Levada Centre head Lev Gudkov. 'It's a classic case of "good tsar, bad boyars".'[6]

It was a point aptly demonstrated by an online clip popular among opposition supporters just before the presidential elections.[7] The first half of the video showed a dozen or so Russians complaining about miserly salaries, corruption, low living standards and other social ills. They were all then asked, 'Will you vote for Putin?' Every single one said yes. 'He's someone you can trust,' explained a smiling young woman, apparently blissfully aware of the contradiction.

In one remarkable vote at Moscow's infamous Butyrka remand prison during the presidential polls, 96% of inmates had ticked Putin's name on the ballot box. But this was no blatant case of poll fraud, as Olga Romanova, an opposition figure who had monitored the vote, told me. 'It was an honest result,' she said, still amazed over a year after the elections. 'I talked to all of the inmates as they voted and saw their ballot papers. Instead of just ticking the box next to Putin's name, they had all written their names, cell numbers and the charges against them on the voting slip. They all hoped that it would help them somehow; that someone would come and see they had voted in the "right" way. Russians have a great respect for the boss, for the man at the top.

'It was a real problem,' she laughed. 'The prison boss was distraught because he feared a scandal and it was bad for me because I was worried people would ask me, "How did you monitor the vote?" But he really did get ninety-six percent.'[8]

Russia's opposition was also hampered by a widespread perception, encouraged by state media, that there was no viable alternative to Putin. 'If not Putin, then who?' went the common rhetorical question. Of course, for many within the protest movement, the answer was very simple: 'Navalny'. Some of the opposition figurehead's supporters had urged him at least to make an attempt to register for the polls, but he had been languishing in a pre-trial detention centre when the deadline for lodging applications passed. Not that Navalny, even in the unlikely event of the Kremlin approving his candidacy, would have stood a chance of defeating Putin; he may have been the rising star of opposition politics, but his nationwide recognition rating as of March 2012 was a mere 25%.

I put the 'If not Putin, then who?' query to Gennady Gudkov, a former KGB colonel who was also one of the few genuine opposition members of parliament. I'd barely got the question out, before Gudkov began to fume. 'If in a country of 145 million people there are no other worthy figures for the post of president, then all I can say is woe to a people who cannot formulate a normal political system,' the portly, moustachioed Gudkov growled, as we crawled through a central Moscow rush-hour a few months after Putin's return to the Kremlin. 'They also said, "If not Stalin, then who?" "If not Brezhnev, then who?" Under the current system, anyone can become a great leader, so to speak, without having any outstanding qualities.'[9]

A few days after our conversation, Gudkov became only the second ever legislator to be expelled from Russia's parliament without a court decision, a move he called 'pure payback' for his outspoken views. His ejection – and loss of his parliamentary immunity from prosecution – had been requested by investigators, who wanted to charge him with allegedly fraudulent business activities. Unsurprisingly, United Russia lawmakers had been happy to oblige, shouting 'Judas' as Gudkov made his final, furious speech to parliament.

BLOOD AT THE SWAMP

Udaltsov's 'irrational' bid to seize a central Moscow fountain for the opposition had injected a burst of energy into the protest movement, but numbers at a rally in the capital the weekend after Putin's election win were noticeably down on the jaw-dropping attendances of that winter's

'Snow Revolution'. As some 20,000 people milled around one end of the New Arbat thoroughfare and listened to speakers go through the motions – Navalny had declined to give a speech – it suddenly felt like the end of a brief period of resistance to Putin's rule. 'Putin's election win was a blow,' said Dmitry Oreshkin, the independent vote monitor and analyst. 'Lots of people began to think, "Why should I just go out and protest if the machine just keeps grinding on?"'[10] The speeches over, demonstrators drifted off home.

The game, it seemed, was up. Moving in for the kill, state television broadcast images of the tail end of the New Arbat rally, when just hundreds remained in front of the stage, while a senior United Russia official taunted and insulted protesters who had worn the white ribbons of the anti-Putin movement, comparing them to the White Brotherhood religious cult blamed for a number of suicides across the former Soviet Union in the 1990s.

'Like the White Brotherhood, the White Ribbons movement sees itself in an exclusive light,' wrote United Russia's Andrei Isayev. 'The presence of a political sect made up of far from stupid, charismatic, energetic people is a danger – an infection. And this sect, like any infection, is attempting to exploit an unfortunate situation to cause an illness that can kill the organism – in other words, our country. We need to think about what to do with it.'[11]

Isayev may have been guilty of a gross exaggeration, but there was an element of truth to his 'sect' claims. 'This is our sacred land! Our holy place!' an enthusiastic activist shouted at a rally in Moscow's Chistye Prudy district to mark the first anniversary of the initial elections protest. I half expected him to kiss the ground. The protests had given many people a reason to live, a purpose to their otherwise routine or desperate lives, inspiring a religious-like fervour that frequently found an outlet in a growing idolization of Navalny.

Almost by inertia, protest leaders called for a demonstration in central Moscow on the eve of Putin's 7 May inauguration. Expectations were low. The protest was due at the start of *dacha* season, when Muscovites traditionally flee the hectic capital for the countryside. Few, or so the reasoning went, would have any inclination to head down to Bolotnaya Square once more. Even the choice of 'Swampy' square for the rally apparently symbolized that the protest was going nowhere.

'We didn't think anything was going to happen at all. We thought it would be a dull kind of protest,' recalled Yelena, a friend and protester who got caught up in the violence. 'Friends of mine came with their kids. And then, suddenly, it all kicked off.'

The weather was good that afternoon, the first warmth of the coming summer after a long winter and a brief, wet spring. The first indication that, as is so often the case in Russia, events weren't about to play out to the generally accepted scenario came when people looked around themselves and realized that crowd numbers were much higher than anyone had expected, although still down from the peak of that winter's protests. The next sign that something other than the usual 'protest/ chant/home' was at hand came when scores of aggressive, masked young men – not at all typical Swampy Square protesters – materialized, as if from nowhere, amid the marchers.

But no one had very long to reflect on these things. In a flash, the mood shifted from good-humoured to tense, protesters suddenly forced up against each other, sweaty in the unseasonably warm weather, as riot police inexplicably blocked off the entrance to the square, sparking shouts, anger and, all at once, a sit-in.

Udaltsov, inevitably, was in the midst of the throng, megaphone in hand, urging the diverse protesters, including Navalny, to 'sit down!' on the short stretch of road that leads to the landmark Bolshoi Kamenny Bridge, and from there to the Kremlin. 'We are the power!' protesters chanted, as riot police linked arms and pushed up again. Left Front flags waved in the breeze as protesters shoved back against riot police, Udaltsov carried along by the wave of demonstrators. A cheer went up as police lines cracked for a second, leaving the road to the bridge open, and then split, allowing dozens of protesters to break clear in a brief bid to take their discontentment to the Kremlin's walls. Police rounded up the runaway protesters, someone let off a smoke bomb, a white balloon floated into the sky, and then the day descended into the violence that pro-Putin officials had been warning for months was part of the 'US State Department-backed' protest movement's plan.

Riot police lashed out with truncheons at protesters, some of whom hit back with long poles, shorn now of their flags, while a dazed and helmetless officer swirled around, eyes blazing with anger. Protesters toppled portable toilets to block police charges as OMON riot squad helmets bobbled almost comically in the Moskva River. Someone tried to pitch a tent – the Kremlin's nightmare! – and even managed to crawl inside for a few brief minutes before police ripped it up. The authorities had reportedly been so paranoid about the prospect of protesters establishing an Orange Revolution-style tent city in the centre of Moscow that police had even searched state television vehicles for camping gear ahead of the rally.

Putin's allies in the media had a field day, with Peter Lavelle, the US-born, pro-Kremlin hawk, comparing protesters to Nazis on the state-funded, English-language TV channel Russia Today. 'These are not people looking for peaceful change here,' sneered Lavelle, as he watched footage of clashes. 'There are radical forces out here, there are nationalists out there, there are radical socialists out there. Put them together, gentlemen – nationalists-socialists. These people want violence.'[12]

As street fighting raged, Maria Baronova, a brash, blonde aide to the opposition lawmaker Ilya Ponomarev, lectured a phalanx of young Interior Ministry troops guarding the road to the Kremlin. 'You have been issued with a criminal order,' she shouted over the buzz of a low-flying helicopter. 'They hanged generals for criminal orders at the Nuremberg trials. And our soldiers hanged German soldiers. That's how they deal with those who commit crimes.

'My friends, you know the tsar in the Kremlin is violating the constitution,' she went on, gesturing at the storm raging behind her. 'Be heroes, like these people. We didn't think anyone was going to turn up to our protest today, but look – just look – there are 100,000 people here.'

'What tsar?' interrupted the soldiers' equally young-looking commanding officer, rolling his eyes. 'Look, girl, there has been no tsar in

Russia since 1917. He's the president of the Russian Federation. Formerly the prime minister.' He ordered his troops to take a step forward, to press up against and push back this mouthy activist.

Baronova was going nowhere: instead, she leaped on his words. 'It's a coronation that's going to take place tomorrow,' she half wailed, half mocked. 'He's anointing himself.'[13]

Back at Bolotnaya Square, Udaltsov had extracted himself from the crowd and jumped on to the stage, armed with not one but two megaphones, resulting in a sudden, startling vicious squeal of feedback. He just about had time to shout 'Russia will be free!' before police dragged him away.

'What are the grounds for arrest?' someone asked from behind the stage.

'That's just how it is,' said Violetta Volkova, the lawyer representing Pussy Riot.

'Next!' joked activists as a tense-looking Navalny accepted another megaphone, prodding at its buttons as he did so to check it would actually work.

'We're taking you in,' a police officer said, suddenly shoving his way past an activist.

'Taking me in?' Navalny did a double-take. 'I haven't done anything yet,' he muttered, as officers grabbed hold of him, prising him away from the stage. 'Everyone stay here!' Navalny screamed suddenly. 'Don't disperse!'

Still wired for sound for a documentary on the protests, Navalny engaged in a breathless discussion with the arresting officer, who had twisted his arm painfully behind his back. 'Don't move or I'll break your arm, got me?' the officer said as he pushed him in the direction of a holding cell.

'I'll jail you later,' Navalny replied, through gritted teeth.[14] He later revealed that 'later' meant post-Putin, when he or another opposition leader was secure in the Kremlin and the retribution would begin. 'I'll do everything I can to make sure Putin, Rotenberg, Timoshenko and everyone else on the list goes to jail,' Navalny explained, spitting out the names of Putin's business associates with a disgust he didn't even bother to try to disguise. 'They and that police officer are all linked to the loathsome, thieving authorities.'[15]

By late evening on 6 May, as the sun dipped beneath the Kremlin's still-intact towers, the last protesters had been dragged from Bolotnaya Square, and teams of street cleaners had moved in to hose down patches of blood and gather up discarded flagpoles and flyers. In the smoky, opposition-friendly cafés around Red Square, activists were nursing their wounds with alcohol, coffee and cigarettes, and plotting how to spoil Putin's inauguration day.

'If we don't get out on the streets tomorrow, then all of this will have been for nothing,' urged Roman Dobrokhotov, the pipe-smoking protester who had disrupted Medvedev's Constitution Day speech. He needn't have worried. Thousands of protesters had no intention of simply staying at home to watch Putin be crowned king of the Kremlin again. All the talk of the demise of the protest movement had been premature. There was a new energy – even a belief – about activists. Putin's return was a body blow, but it was also a challenge.

STAY AWAY FROM PROTESTS

Investigators quickly classified the clashes at Bolotnaya Square as 'mass riots'. A senior United Russia official described the unrest as an 'attempt to launch a coup'. In truth, the violence at the rally had been entirely unspectacular. A few heads had been cracked, a few flagpoles had been thrown and a lot of people had gone home with impressive bruises. I'd been in Trafalgar Square in London in 1990, at the poll-tax riots that led to Margaret Thatcher's resignation, when police and tens of thousands of protesters fought frenzied battles all day long, as windows were smashed, cars blown up and buildings set ablaze. In comparison, Bolotnaya had been nothing more than a minor scuffle. It was, in fact, not much more violent than the regular brawls between fans of rival Moscow football teams.

However, over the following months, police would charge almost thirty people – from leftist activists to students, from an unemployed artist to a pensioner – with either inciting or taking part in the violence. Raids in connection with the unrest took place nationwide, from the west European enclave of Kaliningrad to Siberia's Novosibirsk.

Maria Baronova, the activist who had confronted the soldiers guarding the path to the Kremlin, was one of the first to be charged. Kalashnikov-toting officers broke down the door to her Moscow apartment when they came looking for her. But she was not at home, having fled to the suburbs as storm clouds gathered over the opposition. After first forcing her son's nanny to lie face down on the floor, investigators confiscated anti-Putin booklets, laptops and strips of white ribbon from her apartment. When investigators finally located her, Baronova was barred from leaving Moscow ahead of her trial, and charged with inciting mass disorder. She was luckier than many other suspects, the majority of whom were tossed into grimy pre-trial detention facilities and held there for over a year. However, like other anti-Putin activists with children, Baronova would face unwanted visits from the social services. 'They came and asked me why we had children's books in English in my house,' she told me later, rolling her eyes at the absurdity of it all.

Other detainees included twenty-one-year-old former marine Denis Lutskevich, who was arrested after trying to pull a female friend away from a riot police officer. Lutskevich was so severely beaten while in custody that his body was still covered in bulbous welts when he appeared in court. Another protester, Yaroslav Belousov, a political science student, was alleged to have 'thrown rocks and pieces of asphalt, broken through the cordon and attacked police officers'. But video footage from the square showed him lobbing what looked like a lemon at riot police in full body armour.[16] Like the vast majority of other suspects, he was refused bail – even though he had no previous convictions. One suspect, Artyom Savyolov, was charged with running and shouting opposition slogans: this constituted 'participating in mass disorder'.[17]

One of the most high-profile detainees was Alexei Gaskarov, a leading anti-fascist activist, who was charged and taken into custody more than a year after the unrest. Video footage shows Gaskarov attempting to pull an enraged riot police officer off a fallen demonstrator: he received a vicious kick to the side of the head for his troubles. The only suspect to plead guilty, Maxim Luzyanin, a thirty-six-year-old gym owner, was sentenced to four and a half years in jail – an ominous sign for those who had not been so eager to co-operate with investigators.[18] The investigation also led to the death of thirty-six-year-old activist Alexander Dolmatov, who killed himself in a deportation centre in the Netherlands in January 2013 after being denied political asylum by the Dutch authorities.

Not a single law-enforcement officer would face charges, despite widespread footage of riot police – or 'cosmonauts' as they are known due to their bulbous, visor-equipped helmets – beating defenceless protesters. In fact, a number of officers said to have been injured at the protest were later awarded much sought-after apartments in Moscow in recognition of their 'bravery'. Moscow mayor Sergei Sobyanin made a great show of visiting these officers in hospital, and promised them their attackers would face criminal charges. (When opposition lawmakers went looking for the officers, however, they were unable to find any. Hospital staff told them the entire scene with Mayor Sobyanin and the 'wounded' riot police had been set up for the cameras.[19])

The Kremlin was sending a message to society with the seemingly haphazard selection of protesters detained in the wake of the Bolotnaya unrest. The charges against them were a none-too-subtle signal to ordinary Russians to stay away from demonstrations, even legal ones. 'The Bolotnaya case is directed against run-of-the mill participants in the protest,' said Baronova, the activist whose apartment was raided by police. 'It's targeted at those anonymous people who came out on to the streets because they were fed up of the lies and the injustice. In response, they were shown that it was precisely small and anonymous people like them who would be jailed. And that no one would defend them, because they were no one.'

And the masked youths who had appeared from seemingly nowhere? Members of an unofficial public investigation alleged that they had been hired by the authorities to provide a much-needed pretext for a clampdown. Indeed, the Kremlin's own human-rights council would state in a report that police had provoked the clashes, a finding dismissed out of hand by the authorities.[20] Putin's spokesperson, Dmitry Peskov, regretted just one thing: that police had not been tougher. 'Protesters who hurt riot police should have their livers smeared on the asphalt,' he said.[21]

OCCUPY GHOST CITY

Putin's motorcade sped through the empty streets of the Russian capital, sunlight glinting off the sleek black jeeps and motorcycles accompanying his armoured Mercedes to the Kremlin. With hundreds of protesters still roaming Moscow in the wake of the ill-fated Bolotnaya Square rally, security forces had blocked off access to much of the city centre. Burly, monosyllabic riot police stood guard at the entrances to side-streets along the president-in-waiting's route. Images broadcast live on state television showed an apparent ghost city devoid of life.

Putin's inauguration in May 2012 for a third presidential term was not so much a national celebration of sovereignty as a highly disciplined military operation. And the number-one threat to the head of state? The Russian people.

The comparison with US President Barack Obama's inauguration in Washington some six months earlier was striking. Over a million Americans had lined the streets of the US capital to congratulate Obama on his re-election. But the risk of protesters embarrassing Putin on his big day was too great, the Kremlin had decided. Better the unfavourable comparison with Obama than the possibility of, say, a lone demonstrator stepping out in front of the motorcade – and the world's TV cameras – holding an English-language banner that said simply: 'Putin is a thief'.

Just a short walk from the New Arbat, the central thoroughfare that Putin's motorcade would race down before heading towards the banks of the Moskva River, riot police had earlier raided the Jean-Jacques café, a well-known opposition hang-out, arresting anyone wearing white ribbons. 'Is white a criminal colour now?' yelled an activist, as police trucks began to fill up. But the police were not exclusively picking off members of the white-ribbon 'sect' – they were also eager to detain anyone who simply looked as if they might not be entirely thrilled with Putin's return to the pinnacle of state power.

By the time I arrived at the scene, after having been forced to take a long detour around police barriers, scores of people had already been arrested and shattered glasses lay on the pavement outside the café. Riot police lined the streets in brilliant sunshine, lashing out occasionally with batons.

'Get out on the streets, and return the city to the people!' chanted a group of young protesters, earning the applause of a couple of young mothers at a nearby playground. Police moved in quickly to make arrests (but left the mums and their toddlers in peace).

'What are you doing?' yelled a balding, middle-aged man, as officers hauled him off to a police truck for the apparent crime of speaking to a news crew.

For some protesters, it was all too much. 'Is this how the president wants to start his rule?' asked a distressed young woman, tears mixing with mascara. 'He's afraid of his own people.'

✱

When Occupy activists began setting up protest camps across world capitals in the autumn of 2011, there had seemed little prospect of the movement spreading to Russia, where a no-nonsense police force and a weak and divided opposition appeared to present insurmountable obstacles to any form of prolonged public display of dissent.

However, from the morning of Putin's inauguration onwards, hundreds of protesters spent the next three days and nights roaming through central Moscow's squares and boulevards, dodging police snatch squads, before – amid unconfirmed rumours of rank-and-file police discontent over mounting arrests – setting up camp in the fashionable Chistye Prudy area around a statue of nineteenth-century Kazakh poet-philosopher

Abai Kunanbayev. 'We're at the monument of some obscure Kazakh,' Navalny tweeted shortly before he was detained once more. Udaltsov, in a development greeted with mock astonishment by online activists, was also nabbed. Both men were sentenced to fifteen days behind bars for 'disobeying police orders'.

Wary of provoking riot police who had strict orders to break up any Orange Revolution-type activity, activists refrained from pitching tents. Police surrounded the impromptu camp, close to where the first vote-fraud rally had taken place in the aftermath of the December 2011 parliamentary elections, but made no move to disperse protesters.

'When Occupy started in America, we started discussing how it had all been organized,' said Isabelle Magkoeva, a young, dark-haired activist, who played a key role in the running of the camp. The rising star of Russia's new left, Magkoeva had become a familiar face as anti-Putin protests rocked Moscow. 'After the protests against Putin's inauguration, when everyone was still wandering the streets, we put our ideas into practice," she told me.[22]

However, unlike the global Occupy movement, which was intended to draw attention to corporate greed and wealth inequality, the target of the Moscow Occupy activists was Putin's political system. In a startling show of unity, anti-Putin activists from the far right and the hard left, and all those in between, worked together at the camp to provide security, a field kitchen and clean-up teams. Hatred of Putin, it again became clear, was stronger than any ideological differences.

Like the protesters at that winter's mass rallies against vote fraud, the people at the camp were some of Moscow's best-educated and richest residents. More than 90% had a higher education of some sort, while 60% described themselves as specialists (computer programmers, lawyers, translators and lecturers were among the more popular professions).[23] From conversations, it appeared that most of them had been to the United States or Europe. It was tempting to draw comparisons between these well-travelled, middle-class protesters and the Decembrists, the nineteenth-century army officers who challenged Tsar Nicholas I after returning from the West full of liberal ideas. The Decembrists were crushed, with the majority executed or exiled to Siberia. But, for the authorities, their rebellion was a clear sign of dangerous discontent at the heart of the empire. The defiance of the young anti-Putin activists at Occupy sent a similar warning to Russia's modern-day rulers. Many of these young professionals had no clear memories of life in the Communist era; they also had no intention of being dictated to by Putin and his allies in the security services.

By the third day of the camp, some 3,000 people had gathered around the monument to the Kazakh poet, holding impromptu debates, strumming guitars and swapping stories from the protests. 'We're not going to force Putin out, of course, but we have a right to express ourselves,' Nikita Belov, a pale-looking student, told me as he perched on a low wall of a pond. Behind him, two young girls with acoustic guitars entertained the crowd with a song from the Soviet-era cartoon *The Bremen Town Musicians*,[24] injecting new relevance into the animated film's rock-influenced soundtrack, which reportedly infuriated high-ranking officials when it was performed at the Kremlin in the late 1960s. 'Freedom,' sang the crowd, joining in with the song's refrain.

In a typical example of Moscow hipster ironic humour, anti-Putin activists adopted the previously obscure (in Russia, at least) Kazakh poet Abai Kunanbayev as the symbol of their camp, reading his works and vying with each other to extract from them the quote most appropriate to their situation. The camp became known as Occupy Abai. 'Are you going down to Abai tonight?' became a common question that week among opposition activists.

'What are you all doing here next to our poet's statue?' asked a bemused, middle-aged Kazakh woman when I visited one afternoon, shaking her head in disbelief as she took in the sight of hundreds of activists sitting and strolling around the monument to Kunanbayev.

'He's become, well, the unofficial symbol of our anti-Putin movement,' said a young blonde woman wearing a homemade 'I rock the boat' T-shirt, a white ribbon tied around her wrist.

'Do you even know anything about him?' asked the Kazakh woman. 'And, besides, what are you all protesting for? Putin won the elections, didn't he? The people voted for him. If not Putin, then who? Who do you lot want to see in charge?'

'Any of these people here could run Russia, no problem,' said another activist, a long-haired young man, gesturing at those around him.

Unfortunately, at that very moment, one of the numerous vagrants rejoicing in the chance for a free meal at the camp lurched past. The woman, unconvinced, walked off.

The Occupy Abai camp had been set up and organized by grass-roots activists, but it quickly became a showpiece for Ksenia Sobchak, a blonde celebrity turned protest figure. Sobchak, the daughter of Anatoly Sobchak, the late mayor of St Petersburg and Putin's political mentor, is a socialite best known for hosting a dumber-than-dumb reality show. She is widely rumoured to be Putin's goddaughter, something she has always denied. Her mother was also at the time a senator in Russia's upper house of parliament. I'd been following Sobchak's unabashedly banal career with morbid curiosity for years, and had jokingly predicted to friends that 'Russia's Paris Hilton' would one day turn against Putin and team up with the radicals, *à la* Patty Hearst, the American newspaper heiress and socialite who had joined a group of US urban guerrillas in the 1960s. It was, then, a real shock to see the former *Playboy* cover girl running around Moscow with hardened anti-Kremlin activists. She first came out as an open dissenter at the Sakharov Avenue protest, addressing bemused demonstrators, who greeted her speech with jeers. But her embracing of the protest movement – and one of its leaders, Yashin – was a powerful indication of the protest movement's pulling power. These anti-Putin activists had once been ridiculed as deluded fanatics; now they were hobnobbing with the stars.

Not everyone was thrilled by Sobchak's daily high-profile visits to Occupy Abai. 'She really got on my nerves,' Magkoeva, the Occupy activist, grumbled. 'She didn't spend a single night at the camp, but would just come around every now and then and say, "How's it going, cats?"'

On the sixth day of the opposition camp, around a dozen well-known Russian writers led a march from Pushkin Square to the Occupy strong-hold. 'The aim of our experiment is to determine – can Muscovites walk

freely around their own city or do they need a special pass?'[25] declared
Boris Akunin, the best-selling writer turned protest figure. It turned out
they could: police stood by, but made no move to break up the unsanctioned rally as some 10,000 people streamed through the leafy boulevards
of central Moscow.

'The authorities have to understand that they need to be respectful
when they talk to the people,' the bald and bespectacled Akunin told
supporters as they strolled towards the camp on an unseasonably warm
May afternoon. 'If they chase after them with truncheons, nothing good
will come of this. The more aggressive they are, the quicker everything
will end for them.'

But, while the country's best-loved writers had been able to score
a minor victory over the authorities, they were under no illusions: the
days when the printed word could rattle the Kremlin were long gone.
The Soviet authorities may have been terrified of the power of dissident
poets and novelists, but today, with the vast majority of the population
numbed by state-controlled television, they are a minor irritant, at best.

Putin's spokesperson, Dmitry Peskov, had pledged the camp would
be broken up, the fate, he said, of such protests 'all over the world'.[26]
And, on the morning of 16 May, using the pretext of complaints from
locals over the 'noise', riot police moved in, dispersing sleepy activists.
Attempts to establish other camps elsewhere in the city were swiftly
curbed before they could take root. A year on, with Putin's assault on
the protest movement in full swing, memories of Occupy felt somehow
unreal, as if the entire camp had been one mass illusion held together
by sheer will-power.

'Occupy Abai was the best time for a lot of people,' recalled Magkoeva,
the young activist. 'We felt like we were really doing something, like
we were influencing things. But I don't think it will happen again. The
authorities have become a lot harsher since then. They won't even let
small groups congregate without permission. It's a miracle, really, that
we managed to keep the camp going for a week.'

Magkoeva was right. The following year, in the summer of 2013, riot
police swooped instantly on a group of some fifty activists who arrived

at the Abai Kunanbayev monument trailing white ribbons and balloons behind them. 'This is an illegal march, you are all wearing white,' a police officer told a small, dark-haired female activist.

'So what?' she responded instantly. 'So what if I'm wearing white?'

In no mood for debate, police began dragging activists into waiting police trucks, pulling a blonde, middle-aged woman away from her small son. 'Mum! Mum!' the boy cried.

'Have you all gone out of your minds?' the dark-haired activist yelled at police, pushing back at an officer almost twice her size. 'I mean, completely crazy?'[27]

Putin's fightback was under way. But things were about to get much worse for the protesters who had dared challenge his long rule.

11

TIGHTENING
THE SCREWS

Exactly two months before his controversial May 2012 inauguration, Putin was asked if he intended to 'tighten the screws' on the protest movement's figureheads upon his return to the Kremlin. The question was posed in jokey tones, and Putin's answer came with a corresponding grin. 'Certainly,' he said. 'Where would we be without that? Don't relax!'[1]

No one was entirely sure how serious he was. Analysts had suggested Russia might see a new Putin in his third term; a softer, less authoritarian leader who would not be so quick to clamp down on dissent. For all his lack of a cutting edge, Medvedev had changed the language of political discourse, introducing liberal catchwords and expressions into the abrupt lexicon inherited from Putin's first two terms. Would Putin simply ignore his predecessor's legacy and revert to type?

The first real suggestion that Putin's smile had been merely a partial mask for his true intentions had come as protesters were still roaming around the Occupy Moscow camp. Citing Kremlin sources, the well-connected socialite Ksenia Sobchak reported that the authorities were planning to jail both Navalny and Udaltsov for at least two years each. This, the former reality-TV-show host warned, would be an 'explosive' move.[2]

In a none-too-subtle hint of what to expect from his third term, Putin snubbed a G8 summit in the United States to make his first foreign visit as president to Belarus, the former Soviet republic ruled over by President Alexander Lukashenko, an eccentric and authoritarian former collective-farm boss frequently referred to in the West as 'the last dictator in Europe'.

But Putin was far wiser than the North African and Middle East dictators who had enraged their people with bloody crackdowns during the Arab Spring; he knew when to hold off and when to retreat. He also knew to strike only when the moment was absolutely right, when his enemies were at their most vulnerable, crushing his foes like Kaa, Kipling's python, to whom he had once gleefully compared himself: Putin's revenge was unhurried, methodical and precise.

THE ANTI-PUTIN MOVEMENT'S BUGBEAR

To begin with, a swathe of laws intended to make dissent harder and more dangerous were fast-tracked through a compliant parliament. First up that summer was a new law that dramatically raised the potential maximum fines for violations of laws governing protests. Hot on the heels of this came a proposal to force 'political' non-governmental organizations (NGOs) funded even in part from abroad – such as the independent elections watchdog Golos – to label themselves 'foreign agents'. NGOs protested that the term, with its clear association with espionage, would discredit them entirely in the eyes of the public. Most, including the country's oldest human-rights organization, the Moscow Helsinki Group, said they would rather shut down their offices than co-operate. The law also attracted biting international criticism. 'It's a simple way to get people out of the debate and to get the views you don't like out of the debate,' an exasperated Thorbjørn Jagland, head of the Council of

Europe, said when I spoke to him in July 2012. 'Some of those executed during the Stalin era were also called foreign agents.'[3]

Other laws rushed onto the books included a reversal of Medvedev's decision to decriminalize libel, and a frighteningly vague new definition of high treason, which meant that anyone dealing with foreigners in a professional capacity also now faced the threat of imprisonment. 'I might even be guilty of treason by talking to you about election fraud,' Lilia Shibanova, the head of Golos, told me when I spoke to her shortly after the law had come into force. She laughed, but nervously. Unsettlingly, neither of us really knew if the law extended to vote monitors speaking to foreign journalists.[4]

Not all these laws were immediately put into practice, but their mere existence meant the authorities had acquired powerful new weapons in the fight against the protest movement. 'What is all this legislation?' exclaimed Sergei Kovalyov, the former Soviet dissident who had investigated the 1999 apartment bombings. 'It makes your hair stand on end!' And this from a man who had served time in a Brezhnev-era gulag.[5]

Although no one really had any doubts that this swathe of controversial new laws had been dreamed up in the Kremlin, the NGOs and protest-fine bills had been proposed in parliament by a young United Russia legislator named Alexander Sidyakin, who denied he was acting on orders from above. A virtual political unknown before the onset of the protests, Sidyakin quickly became the anti-Putin movement's bugbear. It was a role he clearly relished, stamping on a white ribbon in parliament and accusing the handful of opposition lawmakers who wore them of betraying the motherland. 'This rag is a symbol of disgrace!' Sidyakin sneered, rocking violently back and forth at the podium. 'The people who wear it want to see our country on its knees.'[6]

Sidyakin was quickly making a name for himself with no-holds-barred attacks on the opposition. There were even those who suggested his rising star might eventually take him all the way to the Kremlin. After all, Putin would not rule forever.

The first thing I noticed when I entered Sidyakin's office was a large black and white framed photograph of the late Indian civil-rights activist

Mahatma Gandhi. It was, I thought, a bizarre choice for one so scornful of protests and protesters. But not entirely original: I recalled that Putin had recently – just a month before, in fact – expressed his unreserved admiration for the man who led India to independence. (Putin went so far as to compare himself to Gandhi, suggesting that both he and the Indian civil-rights leader were both 'pure democrats'.)

'I like his tactics of non-resistance,' Sidyakin said with a shrug, when I quizzed him over the Gandhi photograph. He offered no further explanation, and I decided not to push him.[7]

His features set in an apparent permanent frown that even the occasional attempt at a smile did little to offset, Sidyakin was nevertheless a far more complex figure than the one-dimensional ogre he had been portrayed as by the opposition. He would later refuse to vote on a politically motivated law banning the adoption of Russian children by American families ('Children should not be bargaining chips,' he tweeted), and, during our talk, he suggested the Pussy Riot members should be released on bail. 'But this is just my personal opinion, you understand?' he stressed.

Critics of Sidyakin's law on 'political' NGOs alleged the legislation was part of a drive by the authorities to eliminate all independent voices in Russia. 'Political' or not. And they seemed to have a case; the law was also later used to clamp down on a vast range of non-political groups outside the Kremlin's control, from pollsters and wildlife sanctuary trusts to public-health support organizations. The Kremlin's own human-rights council – whose members would soon resign en masse in protest at state interference in their work – had also criticized the law. But Sidyakin was unconvinced. 'The United States is trying to influence Russian politics,' he said. 'There's no debating this – I mean, they openly fund NGOs. Why else would they do that? This is dirty money for dirty ends.' He dismissed suggestions that Russian businesses were afraid to finance NGOs such as Golos, the election watchdog. 'I don't believe that's true,' he said simply. 'Why would they be afraid?'

Sidyakin only really grew animated when discussing the opposition movement. 'I assure you,' he went on, in a statement that mixed real

venom with a show of startling honesty, 'all this democratic rhetoric…
if the opposition takes power, they will immediately become exactly the
same as us. Or even worse.

'They will also become subjects of criticism,' he went on, skipping
ahead as if suddenly aware of the implications of what he had just said.
'The authorities are not a hundred-dollar bill,' he laughed. 'Not everyone
is always going to like them. But when people see today's opposition,
when they realize that these people could come to power, they make a
choice in favour of the current authorities.

'Navalny,' Sidyakin went on, spitting out the name of the protest
leader, 'is a crook himself. How can he label two million members of
United Russia all crooks and thieves? All these doctors, teachers, cultural
figures in the party – are they all crooks? This comment will backfire on
him.' The way he said this last sentence, it sounded like a threat.

The interview over, Sidyakin unexpectedly offered to see me out of
the State Duma. As I searched in my pocket for my temporary parliamentary pass, I pulled out my passport.

'That your British passport?' asked Sidyakin. I nodded warily. 'Cool,'
said the author of the 'foreign agents' law, smiling and giving me the
thumbs-up.

It was a bizarre moment. How much of Sidyakin's anti-West rhetoric
was genuine, and how much mere posturing? Later that year, Sidyakin
headed to San Francisco for his winter vacation.[8]

NO FORGIVENESS! NO MERCY!

In June 2012, on the eve of another anti-Putin protest in Moscow,
security forces launched early-morning raids on the homes of opposition figures, including Navalny, Udaltsov and Ksenia Sobchak. The
searches, ostensibly carried out in connection with the unrest ahead of
Putin's inauguration, were clearly timed both to disrupt preparations
for the following day's demonstration and to send a message to protesters. After all, Navalny wasn't even a suspect, but a mere witness to

the violence that officials had labelled a 'coup attempt'. That, however, didn't stop masked investigators threatening to carve through the door to his family's apartment with an electric saw when his wife, Yulia, was slow to open up. After they'd gained entrance, seven masked officers turned the Navalnys' apartment upside down, while two of their colleagues, armed with Kalashnikovs, startled the neighbours by standing guard outside the building. After a thirteen-hour search, investigators hauled away almost all the family's digital devices, including their children's camera.[9]

Across town, police had also turned up at the modest flat where long-time anti-Putin activist Ilya Yashin was officially registered. (Under Russia's residency laws, every person must be registered at an address.) But Yashin was not at home; he was sleeping at the much more luxurious apartment of his new love interest, Ksenia Sobchak, in one of Moscow's most elite neighbourhoods. When the doorbell rang, a bleary Sobchak, expecting her cleaning lady, opened the door in a negligee to eight officers, some of them toting weapons. 'You should have got married to a dependable KGB guy, rather than hanging out with this bad company,' one of the officers said, as a colleague read aloud love letters from her ex-boyfriend in front of Yashin, who was by now wide awake.[10]

During their search, officers confiscated a million dollars and half a million euros, which they discovered in crisp, white envelopes in a safe. The authorities suspected the cash was to be used to fund the protests, but Sobchak said she didn't trust banks and preferred to keep her money at home. 'It's my business how I store my cash,' she later complained. 'I can keep it in envelopes, in jars, under the carpet. However I want. Some people like to tie rubber bands around their cash. I don't – it tears the ends up. Do I have to explain all this to investigators?'[11]

The funds were only returned to Russia's It Girl months later, after a lengthy court battle handled by one of the country's top lawyers.

'It was demeaning,' said a weary Sobchak, after the raid, as she spoke to reporters outside her apartment building. 'They wouldn't even let me get dressed. I was made to stand half naked in front of a mass of police officers. It was like it always is in Russia – they were more interested in humiliation than finding anything out.'

No charges were brought, but the raid was an ominous sign for opposition figures. If even Sobchak, with her close family connections to Putin, was now a target, then no one was safe.

With numbers at protests falling, the security services had begun to circle. Navalny was the first to feel the extent of Putin's wrath. The Kremlin's number-one foe had been living with the threat of serious criminal charges since 2010, when investigators opened a probe into allegations that he had embezzled funds from a state timber company. The accusations – which came shortly after Navalny's claims of massive corruption at the state oil-transportation company Transneft – stemmed from his work in 2009 as a voluntary adviser to the liberal governor of central Russia's Kirov region. The case had been looked into by investigators on two occasions, and charges were initially brought in 2011. However, they were withdrawn in the spring of 2012 due to a lack of evidence.

Navalny's joy was short-lived. Less than two months later, Alexander Bastrykin, Russia's chief investigator, met with regional subordinates in Moscow to discuss their work. 'There's this person called Navalny,' the broad-shouldered Bastrykin thundered, teeth bared in fury, at a Kirov investigation official. 'You had a criminal case against that man. Why did you close it on the sly, eh? There will be no forgiveness! There will be no mercy!'[12]

Days later, the probe was reopened, yet again.

Unfazed, Navalny then publicly accused Bastrykin of owning undisclosed real estate in the Czech Republic, posting documents on his blog that appeared to back up the claim. 'The man responsible for all investigations and the entire struggle against corruption is a swindler, a fraud and a foreign agent,' Navalny wrote.

Bastrykin denied the allegations.[13]

Revenge was swift: less than a week later, the opposition figurehead was charged once more. But, while Navalny had initially been accused of stealing some $15,000, investigators were now claiming he had embezzled

$500,000. They provided no explanation for the dramatic increase. With acquittal rates in criminal cases in Russia standing at less than 1%[14] – lower even than during Stalin's Great Terror – the protest leader was under no illusions that he could beat the charges.

The Kirov charges were just the first in an increasingly Kafkaesque cascade of allegations against Navalny. In the following months, he would also be accused of defrauding a now-defunct liberal party in an alleged advertising scam, despite the insistence of its former leaders that no money had gone missing. Navalny's brother, Oleg, a Post Office employee, was also sucked into his elder sibling's woes: in April 2012, investigators launched probes against both men, accusing them of embezzling funds from French cosmetics company Yves Rocher and a Russian firm called MPK.

'The good news is I don't have a sister,' Navalny declared dryly. 'I'm not going to lie,' he went on. 'This is unpleasant. It's one thing when the Kremlin's crooks come at me. I'm ready for this. My wife's ready. But when they start on my relatives, that's a different thing altogether.'[15]

Just for good measure, investigators also alleged the anti-corruption crusader had fraudulently obtained his licence to practise law.

Charges against Navalny were, as a Russian journalist put it in a memorable turn of phrase, 'flying from the pens of investigators like woodchips from a sawmill'.[16] But journalists were not the only ones having trouble keeping track of the protest leader's legal problems. 'A year ago, I had zero criminal charges against me,' Navalny told protesters at a subdued rally on the first anniversary of Putin's return to the Kremlin. 'Now, there are four... or six? I've already lost count and got confused myself.'

Moscow's hipsters responded to the litany of allegations against Navalny with typical irony. 'According to preliminary information, Alexei Navalny stole the end of the world,' read one tweet, just days after the predicted 21 December 2012 Mayan apocalypse had failed to materialize.

'Navalny stole the peaceful dreams of those crooks and thieves,' another quipped.

The protest leader gave the simplest explanation: 'I stole everything there is to steal,' he joked. But his humour was becoming increasingly dark.

*

The wild enthusiasm that had infected the opposition had dissipated. The failure of Navalny's pet project, the Coordination Council, was neatly symbolic of its inability to capitalize on the energy of the mass protests. Mainly online voting for the much-hyped council, a belated attempt to give protest leaders at least a semblance of electoral legitimacy, took place in the autumn of 2012. In an indication of the anti-Putin movement's diversity, places on the forty-five-member-strong council were reserved in equal measure for liberal, leftist and nationalist candidates, although the majority of activists were elected as non-affiliated figures.

'This is the biggest project ever carried out in the new Russia without the participation of the government,' raved Navalny, who took the largest share of the vote.[17]

But the numbers of voters fell far below the half a million that opposition figures had hoped for. Just over 100,000 had registered to vote, while some 88,000 had managed to cast ballots. The figure, as critics hurried to point out, was less than 0.1% of Russia's total number of registered voters.

Disappointment over voting numbers was soon overshadowed by the let-down that was the Coordination Council itself: within months of the first session, it had become clear that the ideological differences among the group's members were unbridgeable. Moreover, personality clashes and bureaucratic haggles meant the council quickly became bogged down in petty and time-wasting rows. Many members stopped attending meetings. Others simply quit. 'I can no longer allow myself to waste my precious time on convincing clever, grown-up people of the obvious,' said writer Andrei Piontkovsky, as he withdrew from the council.

Despite – or maybe because of – the opposition council's lack of success, the authorities wasted no time in targeting its members. More than half would report harassment of some form or another. It soon began to look as if the Coordination Council's sole achievement had been to provide the security forces with a handy 'Who's Who of the Kremlin's Foes' as they set about dismantling the protest movement.

Putin's tightening of the screws after Medvedev's unsuccessful attempts at reform followed a pattern with deep roots in Russian history. Throughout the nineteenth and twentieth centuries, endeavours to introduce more liberal forms of rule invariably provoked a clampdown by subsequent leaders. After the 1881 assassination of the reformist tsar Alexander II by radical revolutionaries, his successor Alexander III rooted out liberals from the government and cracked down ruthlessly on dissent. In the Soviet era, the 'thaw' introduced by Nikita Khrushchev was followed by years of stagnation and political repression under Leonid Brezhnev. Not for nothing is there a school of thought that holds that authoritarian rule is Russia's natural state.

'We are not the West. We have our own civilization. You are all subjects of his majesty in the Kremlin,' Vladimir Zhirinovsky, the flamboyant, ultra-nationalist leader of the inaccurately named Liberal Democrat Party, once told the country's liberals. 'There will be no democracy in Russia. No independent courts. No press freedom. Either accept it or leave.'[18]

Zhirinovsky is a political eccentric, but his words captured a very real sense among millions of ordinary Russians that only a strong leader – an autocrat – could rule their vast and unpredictable country effectively.

In a sign of the darker mood that gripped both the authorities and their foes in the wake of Medvedev's departure, Putin laid flowers that autumn at a newly erected monument in Moscow to Pyotr Stolypin, Russia's authoritarian prime minister between 1906 and 1911. Putin's role model of choice, Stolypin had hanged thousands to ensure stability.

Even Medvedev was going with the flow. 'They often tell me I am a liberal,' he told a meeting of United Russia activists. 'But I can tell you frankly: I have never had liberal convictions.'[19]

PUTIN'S ENFORCER

If the Communist-era authorities were able to jail dissidents simply on the basis of 'anti-Soviet agitation and propaganda' – in other words, even the mildest criticism of the state – the modern-day Kremlin was forced to come up with at least a pretence to lock up its opponents. That was where Alexander Bastrykin and his Investigative Committee came in.

Like so many of Putin's top allies, the hot-tempered Bastrykin and the 'national leader' go back a long way. Once university classmates in St Petersburg, Bastrykin was working as an obscure legal academic when Putin was elected to his first presidential term in 2000. Keen to surround himself with known and trusted faces, Putin engineered his former classmate's gradual rise. In return, he would receive his unquestioning loyalty.

In 2007, Bastrykin was appointed head of the newly formed Investigative Committee. Initially subordinate to the prosecutor general's office, the organization was transformed by Putin in 2011 into his own personal law-enforcement agency. When election protests broke out later that year, it was the Investigative Committee, rather than the FSB, that led the subsequent clampdown. Bastrykin's enthusiasm for his task drew comparisons to J. Edgar Hoover, the long-time FBI chief with a similar distaste for dissent. 'Bastrykin takes his orders directly from Putin,' Navalny said after a protest rally. 'And he'll do anything he's told.'

Bastrykin's usefulness for Putin had also earned him an apparent immunity before the law. In the summer of 2012, in the wake of the horrific murders of twelve people in south Russia's Krasnodar region, *Novaya Gazeta* journalist Sergei Sokolov wrote an article railing against the small fine ($5,000) handed down to a reported United Russia member who had destroyed vital case evidence. Sokolov called United Russia 'gangsters' and accused Putin and Bastrykin of being the 'servants' of criminal gangs. Enraged, Bastrykin had the journalist driven into a forest near Moscow and threatened to have him killed. 'They'll cut your head off, and your legs will be somewhere else. No one will find you, and, if they do, I'll investigate it myself,' Bastrykin was reported to have told Sokolov.[20]

After an outcry and protests outside the Investigative Committee offices, Bastrykin offered an apology: 'I had no right to get mad, but I did. I am sorry.' But no charges were brought against Bastrykin. In fact, no probe into the threats was even opened; investigators ruled there was no case to examine. An apology from their boss, they declared, would suffice.

Putin's authoritarian tendencies had been all too apparent throughout his first two terms of office, but he had largely avoided wild excesses. His unleashing of Bastrykin on the opposition in the wake of the protests revealed fully the darker side that everyone had always suspected was there. Political repression was the order of the day, and it didn't matter how absurd the charges against opposition leaders were.

Bastrykin's emergence as Putin's personal enforcer was underlined when Vladislav Surkov, the architect of 'sovereign democracy' whose black PR and constant behind-the-scenes trickery had divided and discredited the Kremlin's foes for near on a decade, made an abrupt departure from the government in the spring of 2013. True, Surkov had already been demoted once, in the wake of the 2011 election protests, but the resignation – or was he pushed? – of Putin's puppet-master just as Bastrykin came into his own was deeply symbolic of the growing trend for outright repression.

'Surkov leaving is more confirmation that in [a] choice between murderers and thieves, Putin is going with the murderers,' said chess champ turned Kremlin critic Garry Kasparov. 'No subtlety needed now.'[21]

The irony that Surkov's departure from the political scene had been one of the demands of the protesters who had filled the squares and boulevards of central Moscow was lost on no one. In Putin's Russia, it really is better to be careful what you wish for.

THEY ARE TAUGHT NOT TO THINK OF US AS PEOPLE

One of the clearest indications of these new ultra-aggressive tactics came in August 2012, when a court ruled on an appeal by Taisiya Osipova, a young opposition activist who had been sentenced to ten years behind bars on hotly disputed drug possession charges.

The original sentence was widely condemned as unnecessarily tough: Osipova, the diabetic mother of a five-year-old girl, was arrested in 2010 after police claimed to have found some four grams of heroin at her apartment in the west Russian city of Smolensk. Osipova alleged the police had planted the drugs on her after she had refused to incriminate her husband, a senior activist in Eduard Limonov's Other Russia party. The sentence was overturned on appeal in February 2012 after then President Medvedev had criticized it as 'too harsh' and called for a new probe.[22] The authorities refused, however, to free Osipova on bail.

At the retrial, Osipova's claim that police had planted the drugs was corroborated by a witness, who passed a lie-detector test. Based on this new evidence, the judge threw out the charges stemming from the search of her apartment. Two other drug-related charges, however, were upheld. The prosecutor asked for a four-year sentence. For Osipova, who had already been in custody for almost two years, freedom was suddenly looking a lot closer.

Her optimism was misplaced.

The judge sentenced her to eight years, twice the amount the prosecution had asked for, cutting just two years from the original jail term. Osipova was clearly shell-shocked. Limonov called the ruling 'a terrifying revenge'.[23] At court that day to lend his support, Udaltsov said it was a 'spit in Medvedev's face'.

Some six months after the controversial court ruling, with Osipova in a penal colony in central Russia's Tver region, I met up with her husband, Sergei Fomchenko, and the couple's now seven-year-old daughter Katrina. Like many of Russia's radical underground activists, Fomchenko sported a buzz cut and was dressed all in black. He refused my offer to buy him and his daughter lunch. 'It wouldn't feel right,' he mumbled. His daughter was a typical, bubbly seven-year-old, named after the devastating hurricane that had hit New Orleans as she tossed and turned in her mother's stomach in the summer of 2005.

'As far as we are aware, it was an unprecedented ruling,' Fomchenko told me as we sat in a crowded Moscow café a short walk from the Kremlin. 'Our lawyer has been unable to find another example in Russian legal history of a judge jailing someone for twice the number of years the prosecutor requested.

'It was an order from above,' he went on. 'The Other Russia party might not have been involved in the white-ribbon protest movement, but Taisiya was on all the lists of political prisoners they drew up.'

We turned back to the details of Osipova's arrest, Fomchenko leaning forward to make himself heard above the chatter. 'They wanted to set me up, to prove that I was running drugs between Moscow and Smolensk to raise funds for Other Russia,' he said. 'But Taisiya wouldn't play along. So they framed her. The witnesses the police cited were members of pro-Kremlin youth movements that had been specifically sought out by the police.

'This is a conveyer belt of injustice,' he told me. 'These people have no conscience; they set up and put away women with kids younger than Katrina for eight, nine, ten years. They are all in cahoots with the real drug dealers, but because they have to make it look like they are fighting the trade in heroin they bust small-time users or plant drugs on people. In my wife's case, they simply adapted these methods for political ends. They don't care that she is innocent. Anti-extremism agents and FSB officers are taught not to think of us as people.'

Fomchenko, the right side of his face heavily scarred with what looked like a knife wound, was unconvinced by Udaltsov's suggestion that the ruling had been in some way a signal to society that Medvedev's liberal stance was a thing of the past.

'The white-ribbon protesters like to make out there was some battle among the political elite, and that if Medvedev was still in power he would help them,' he said, slowly shaking his head. 'But we don't buy this – they are all part of the same team. Medvedev's weakness sparked the protests. If he'd been tougher, Putin might not have felt the need to return.'

Osipova had made headlines in her hometown of Smolensk in April 2003, when she strode on stage at a public meeting chaired by the city's governor, Viktor Maslov, a former FSB chief, and slapped him in the face with a bouquet of red carnations. 'You are getting fat at the expense of ordinary people!' she yelled, before she was ushered out by security.

Maslov had been accused by activists in Smolensk of enriching himself as governor at the expense of local infrastructure, as well as darker crimes, including involvement in a series of brutal murders. He denied the charges.

After the attack on Maslov, which saw Osipova handed an unexpectedly light one-year suspended sentence, the couple continued to organize and take part in protests in both Moscow and Smolensk. They soon became targets for the authorities, including 'Centre E' – the anti-extremism department.

'When Taisiya was seven months pregnant, she came home after a walk to find all four gas rings on the oven had been turned on, but not lit,' Fomchenko said, still clearly shocked by the attempt on the lives of his wife and unborn daughter. 'It was clear someone had done it. I mean, you might forget to turn off one ring, but all four?'

I was unsure of exactly how much we could discuss in front of Katrina – while she seemed to be paying no attention to our conversation, we were, after all, discussing her mother, who was likely to remain behind bars for the remainder of her childhood years. 'It's OK,' said Fomchenko. 'She knows everything. Some of her relatives tried to make up some story at first, but there's no point. I try not to politicize her though,' he went on. 'Although she said recently, "Dad, I hate the police." If she asks what Other Russia are about, I tell her we are fighting against injustice, and she says, "Ah, like in that cartoon I saw the other day."' He smiled. Katrina cadged some cash off him and went to buy a cake.

Under Russian law, mothers of children under the age of fourteen convicted of non-violent crimes can apply for a stay of sentence. Osipova's application was turned down without explanation shortly after her initial conviction. The ruling compared starkly with the 2010 decision by a court in east Siberia's Irkutsk to grant a stay of imprisonment to a young woman named Anna Shavenkova, who killed one pedestrian and crippled another for life when her vehicle went off the road. Video footage of the crash showed Shavenkova get out of her car and check it for damage, without so much as a glance in the direction of the two women who lay crumpled like rag dolls just metres from her. She did not even call an ambulance. Shavenkova was sentenced to three years behind bars, but because she became pregnant shortly after the crash she was not due to start serving her sentence until 2024. She was later pardoned without serving even a day of jail time.[24]

It is as depressing as it is predictable that Shavenkova is the daughter of a local influential United Russia member.

'It's almost too obvious even to say out loud, you know?' Fomchenko grimaced. 'But there's one rule for people like us, and one rule for the elite. They will never allow my wife a stay of imprisonment.'

Like the Pussy Riot case, Osipova's imprisonment was an indication of the Kremlin's thirst for revenge. Both cases were proof of the pettiness and cruelty at the heart of Putin's system. For those who took on the authorities, the stakes were high.

'The Russian authorities have the mentality of wolves,' Fomchenko told me, before I left him and his daughter. 'If you attack, you have to be sure to take your target down. If not, expect to be eaten alive.'

12

PUSSY RIOT – THE VERDICT

In a darkly comic twist of fate, charges against Pussy Riot were filed on the day that Russian Orthodox believers traditionally ask each other for forgiveness for any insult they may have caused over the past twelve months.[1] The coincidence set the tone for the group's nine-day trial in August 2012, a surreal cocktail of religious dogma and political theatre that had even Putin loyalists cringing with embarrassment.

The prosecution's case rested on trying to prove that Pussy Riot's performance was a deliberate insult to believers and contained no political elements whatsoever. Pussy Riot, the indictment read, had attempted to 'shake the spiritual foundations' of the modern Russian state. It was almost an admission of weakness. How strong were these foundations if they could be threatened with collapse by five young women in tight stockings and colourful balaclavas?

For a country where the very mention of God was once at best taboo and at worst a sure-fire ticket to the gulag, the group's trial was a startling revelation. Dissident and poet Joseph Brodsky had irritated a Soviet court in 1964 with his insistence that his talents came 'from God'. In Putin's Russia, a witness's belief in the Almighty was a boost to his or her credibility. It also signified loyalty. 'Are you an Orthodox believer?' the mumbling and baby-faced prosecutor asked state witnesses as they took the stand. 'Do you celebrate Church holidays and observe all the fasts?'

The suspects, enclosed in a glass bulletproof box known as the 'aquarium', offered an apology to any believers offended by their performance, but stressed again the protest was not anti-religion. 'I thought the Church loved all its children,' Alyokhina said. 'But it turns out it only loves those children who love Putin.'[2]

Amid the worldwide media glare, former Beatle Paul McCartney added his voice to the long list of celebrities calling on the Kremlin to release the group.[3] Putin, in London for the Olympic Games, remarked that there was 'nothing good' in the group's protest, but he hoped the court would not treat the suspects 'too harshly'.[4] His comments sparked much speculation. What exactly was Putin's definition of 'harsh'?

Back in Moscow, the court dialogue was becoming stranger and stranger, blending Salem-witch-trials-type testimony with Stalin-era court practices. One witness, Lyubov Sokologorskaya, the elderly caretaker of the cathedral's candles, spoke in a near whisper of the group's 'devilish twitching' at the altar.

'How does she know how devils twitch?' defence lawyer Violetta Volkova asked. 'Maybe she's seen some?'[5]

The question was struck by the judge.

'They were wearing dresses that bared their shoulders and were very bright in colour,' Sokologorskaya told the court. 'And they had hats of different colours too. And their tights were different colours! This was blasphemy, sacrilege and an insult to my feelings, and my faith, and my ideals, and a defilement of my personage and my life choice! The pain has not subsided.'

'Is "holy shit" an offensive phrase?' Volkova asked.

'We already established that these words offend God!' the prosecutor yelled.[6]

Another witness for the prosecution, Sergei Beloglazov, a security guard at the cathedral, said he had been so traumatized by the group's brief performance that he had been unable to work for the previous two months.

'Do you find the word "feminist" insulting?' Tolokonnikova asked, when she was permitted to stick her head out of the 'aquarium' to pose a question.

'I do,' responded Beloglazov. 'For an Orthodox believer, it is an insult, an obscenity.'[7]

The defence team had requested permission to call thirteen expert witnesses at the start of the trial, but the judge would allow them to call just three.

'Even in Soviet times, in Stalin's times, the courts were more honest than this one,' Nikolai Polozov, one of the group's three lawyers, shouted, sparking a barking fit from a huge guard Rottweiler that was guarding the women, lest they attempt a daring escape.

Another prosecution witness rambled about 'hell being as real as the Moscow metro', and said Pussy Riot had declared 'war on God'. One of the witnesses, who had only seen the performance online, said watching the clip was 'painful'. Especially when he watched it over and over again.[8]

The days dragged on, surreally, with court sessions lasting ten or even eleven hours. Dazed by the hallucinatory weirdness unfolding in the courtroom and pummelled by the punishing schedule, the suspects started to drift in and out of proceedings. 'We didn't even understand why we were there, most of the time,' Samutsevich told me later. 'It was like they didn't need us to be in court at all. And we were all so tired. We wouldn't get back to our cells until late, and then they woke us up while it was still dark to get us ready for the start of the next morning's session.'[9]

For the group's lawyers, the trial was an excruciating experience. 'I've been working on this trial day and night. I sleep in my car,' Volkova wailed during a break.

On top of their physical torment, they also faced professional humili-ation: no amount of reasoned argument was going to get their clients off. Faced with the starkness of their situation, it was little wonder that they often lapsed into political rhetoric.

'There's a sense right now that we're not in twenty-first-century Russia but in some alternate universe in a fairytale like *Alice in Wonderland*, like *Alice Through the Looking-Glass*, and right now this whole ludicrous reality will disappear and crumble like a house of cards, and three imprisoned girls will rise and return home to their families, to their children,' a weary Volkova told the court as the trial came to an end.

'These women are not here now because they danced in church in the wrong clothes, in the wrong place, and prayed incorrectly, and made the sign of the cross the wrong way. They are here for their political beliefs. The words of the song, the words of the prayer that they performed – it is a political song, a political prayer addressed to the Blessed Virgin.'[10]

Tolokonnikova used her last words before sentencing to draw comparison between the group and the dissidents frequently locked up in psychiatric asylums by the Soviet authorities.

'[We] are in jail but I don't consider that we've been defeated. Just as the dissidents weren't defeated,' she told the court. 'When they disappeared into psychiatric hospitals and prisons, they passed judgement on the country.'[11]

Pussy Riot had no need to pass judgement on Putin's Russia; the rest of the world was doing that for them. 'They realize in the Kremlin that the Pussy Riot trial has caused more damage to Russia's international image than the 2008 war with Georgia,' said Marat Guelman, the ex-Kremlin spin doctor. 'I tried explaining to them that everything they are doing is counterproductive, that this nightmare is not the women's fault, but their fault. But we are all hostages to Putin's emotions now.'[12]

PUTIN LIGHTS THE FIRES OF REVOLUTION

On the morning of the verdict, Pussy Riot supporters took to the streets of Moscow, dressing statues across the city in the group's trademark balaclavas. Alexander Pushkin, the country's nineteenth-century national poet, got a bright-yellow one. 'What kind of people would do that?' asked a bemused elderly onlooker as two young men scrambled down from the statues of Pushkin and his wife. Across town, at an east Moscow metro station, a group of World War II partisans immortalized in stone were decked out in red and blue balaclavas.

Hundreds of the group's supporters later gathered in front of the Khamovnichesky courthouse on the bank of the Moskva River in anticipation of the verdict. Among them was Udaltsov. A committed atheist, the Left Front leader nevertheless had no doubt as to what awaited the judge and prosecutors if Pussy Riot were jailed.

'They will roast in the fires of hell!' he told the crowd of protesters. 'We stay here until the ruling is announced! And, if they go down, we go nowhere!' he shouted.

Riot police quickly moved in to hustle him away to a waiting police truck. Chess grandmaster turned opposition politician Garry Kasparov fared no better when he turned up – he was grabbed halfway through a speech and carried away, each arm and leg gripped by a burly riot cop.

The world's media had also turned out for the verdict, and it was only the judicious use of my elbows and my press card that got me into the courthouse.

Judge Marina Syrova wasted no time once the suspects had been enclosed in their 'aquarium'. Under Russian law, the verdict is announced at the very beginning of the court session, but the sentence is not made public until the entire ruling has been read – a tortuous process that can sometimes take days. Inhaling deeply before she pronounced sentence, Syrova declared swiftly that all three women were guilty. Tolokonnikova rolled her eyes in mock astonishment. Her husband, Verzilov, tweeted furiously, as he had done throughout every court hearing.

Syrova then began to read the ruling and would hardly draw breath for almost the next three hours. The group members, she said, were sane and aware of both the 'rules of society and the Church' when they carried out their 'so-called punk prayer'. She noted, however, citing mental-health evaluations that revived unsettling memories of Soviet-era punitive psychiatry, that all three suffered from 'mild personality disorders' reflected in Tolokonnikova's case in 'a desire for self-realization' and a tendency to 'voice her opinions'.

Halfway through the reading of the ruling, Pussy Riot supporters blasted out the group's new recording outside the courtroom. Tolokonnikova clasped her hands in apparent prayer as the track's jagged guitars and words 'Putin is lighting the fires of revolution!' drifted into the stuffy courtroom.

Judge Syrova paused, waited until police had moved in to silence the sounds of dissent, then continued to read. The chanting of 'Shit, shit, Holy Shit!' in the cathedral, she said, was an indication that the performance had been anti-religion, not a political act. The words 'Virgin Mary, drive Putin out' had been added to the online version of the song later, she ruled, her mention of the track's infamous chorus bringing a smile to the faces of the women in the glass-and-steel cage. The group had, she went on, 'plotted to appear in the cathedral in inappropriate clothing' and 'undermine civil order'.

The court ruled that neither a fine nor a suspended sentence would be sufficient to 'correct' Alyokhina, Samutsevich or Tolokonnikova. Judge Syrova sentenced each of the accused to 'two years in a penal colony'. The sentence was the same as that handed down to a police officer who had recently killed a fifty-two-year-old suspect in Russia's Volga city of Kazan by inserting the neck of a champagne bottle deep into his anus, causing fatal internal injuries.[13]

Tolokonnikova's father, Andrei, was relieved the group's sentence was not harsher. 'I thought they'd get more,' he admitted to me later.[14]

'Only the street can give an answer to this verdict,' tweeted Pussy Riot lawyer Mark Feigin from the courtroom. And, as riot police stood guard, the street gave its response. A chant of 'We will not forget, we will not forgive' broke out as the news filtered through. 'Down with the police state!' chanted the crowd, which had by now swelled to around a thousand, as officers moved in to make arrests.

'Putin wrote this verdict,' said Navalny, who had turned up at the courtroom in time to hear it being read. 'He's shown everyone here, the whole of Russia, that he doesn't give a damn about anyone else's opinions.'

As police snatch-squads picked off protesters, two young men held up a quickly improvised banner that read: 'You are fucking insane!' Police quickly wrestled the banner out of their hands and dragged them away. Minutes later, a young activist clad in a Pussy Riot-style balaclava almost sparked a diplomatic scandal when she clambered up a fence and into the grounds of the nearby Turkish embassy to escape arrest. Riot police, apparently unaware of the finer points of international law, scaled over the fence in pursuit. 'Fuck, come back, you aren't allowed in there!' screamed a senior officer, his words drowned out by the noise of the protesters, who were now chanting 'Virgin Mary, free Pussy Riot!'

An elderly woman, who gave her name only as Olga, shook her head. 'If they'd sung "Virgin Mary, help Putin", they'd be in parliament by now,' she told me. 'Even if they'd danced naked in the cathedral.'

Right next to us, a young man in a Pussy Riot T-shirt set off a smoke bomb. 'Help protect your homeland,' he appealed to a passing riot officer.

'I know where my homeland is,' the ruddy-faced officer shouted back.

As chaos raged, Verzilov told a crowd of journalists what it would take to free his wife, Tolokonnikova. 'The only thing that can save our daughter, my wife and all of us is a revolution,' he said calmly. 'And so that's what we are going to have.'

PUTIN JOINED THE KGB AFTER THEY'D STOPPED SHOOTING PRIESTS

A much-discussed article by Russian journalist Roman Volobuyev in the immediate wake of the verdict raised the spectre of the violent radicalization of young protesters. It was, Volobuyev suggested, just a matter of time before largely peaceful anti-Putin activists offered a more violent form of resistance. The time was ripe, he wrote, for Russia to get its own Red Army Faction, a reference to the violent radical activists who terrorized West Germany in the 1970s and 1980s.[15]

In the weeks that followed the jailing of Pussy Riot, a number of wooden crosses were chopped down across Russia's regions, continuing a

form of protest that had seen a topless Ukrainian feminist take a chainsaw
to a cross high above Kiev on the morning of the verdict. A previously
unknown movement called The People's Will (which took its name from
the nineteenth-century revolutionary group responsible for the assassination of Tsar Alexander II) claimed responsibility for the destruction of
the crosses, which it said was revenge for Pussy Riot's jailing. A senior
Moscow priest, Dmitry Smirnov, said the acts of vandalism amounted
to a 'declaration of war' against the Church.[16]

The row over Pussy Riot had also sparked a rise in Orthodox militancy, with fringe groups announcing plans to patrol near churches to
protect them from 'desecration'. In other incidents in Moscow, Orthodox
activists tore a Pussy Riot T-shirt off a member of the public, harassed
staff at a downtown museum of erotica and picketed a 'blasphemous'
art exhibition. These were all minor events, but they worried liberal
Russians, who feared that the authorities were becoming more strident
in their attempts to impose their ideas of morality on society.

As tensions simmered, I took a train to St Petersburg to meet Vitaly
Milonov, a strident Orthodox activist and head of the city's lawmaking
committee. Milonov's recent legislative proposals included granting full
citizenship to embryos, and drafting women who had not given birth by
the age of twenty-three into the army. He had also authored a controversial law banning the promotion of a positive image of homosexuality
to minors in St Petersburg, earning his hometown the reputation of 'the
least gay-friendly city in Europe'. The law would soon be adopted at a
national level. He was, in short, Archpriest Chaplin's vision of the Church
and state working in 'harmony' made flesh.

'I cannot be Christian at church, without being one at work, as
well,'[17] Milonov told me, as we spoke in the city's Legislative Assembly,
a grand nineteenth-century former palace. There was no Putin portrait
in his spacious office. Instead, Milonov, a chubby, bespectacled thirty-
eight-year-old, sat under a framed photograph of Patriarch Kirill. 'The
Church is the most important government institution, one that shapes
the state,' he said, his desk cluttered with religious icons. 'The Church
must not be in opposition to the state. It must nourish the authorities

with its wisdom.' He smiled. 'This is an acceptable, even desirable, state of affairs for Orthodox believers.'

But the foundations of Christian belief in Russia are not as strong as they appear. While some 70% of Russians describe themselves as Orthodox Christians, an eye-opening opinion poll revealed in 2012 that a staggering 30% of these 'believers' do not, in fact, believe in God.[18] They are self-confessed atheists who wear baptismal crosses because in Putin's Russia this has become the accepted thing to do. For many, the poll's authors suggested, Orthodoxy is simply an extension of statehood. To say you are an Orthodox Christian is, in many respects, to say you are an ethnic Russian. And no more.

Milonov listened with a pained expression on his face as I related all this to him. 'Oh, I don't believe that,' he said, and called for tea.

We moved, inevitably, on to Pussy Riot. Milonov denied outright that Patriarch Kirill had been guilty of meddling in politics with his pre-election endorsement of Putin. 'The Orthodox Church is not political and it will never make an official political statement,' he told me. I must have looked particularly unconvinced, because Milonov backtracked seconds later. 'Of course, Patriarch Kirill's "miracle of God" comment was a political statement of sorts,' he admitted. 'But that was because he realized that the country would suffer greatly if Putin did not remain in charge. But look,' he said, stretching out his palms, 'all authority is from God. Any act of God is a miracle for Orthodox believers.'

A former assistant to opposition lawmaker Galina Starovoitova, who was assassinated in St Petersburg in 1998, Milonov joined the ruling United Russia party after becoming disillusioned with liberal politics. 'Today's liberals are exactly the same as the Bolsheviks were a century ago,' he sneered. 'They are extremely aggressive towards those who don't agree with them. They are ready to hang us all. The Bolsheviks killed priests, you know? Thousands of them.'

Surely, I suggested, the former Soviet spy agency officer, Putin, had more connection to the Bolshevik murderers of priests than the likes of Pussy Riot and their supporters did?

Milonov was sceptical. 'Putin's belief in God is very deep,' he said. 'A person who rules Russian cannot be a non-believer, because the Lord would give him faith.

'And, besides,' he went on triumphantly, as if he had just recalled the fact, 'Putin joined the KGB after they'd stopped shooting priests.'

A FREED PUSSY RIOTER

As the group's October 2012 appeal approached, Medvedev boosted his liberal credentials by urging the court to 'Free Pussy Riot!' Of course, he didn't exactly put it quite so vociferously, saying instead that, while he was 'sickened by what they did, by their looks, by the hysteria that followed what had happened', he believed that the group's continued incarceration was 'unproductive'.[19]

On the morning of the appeal, six weeks after the original ruling, Samutsevich threw proceedings into disarray when she told the court she wished to change her lawyer. She gave no explanation for the decision, but her reasons soon became clear. At a rearranged court session one week later, her new attorney, Irina Khrunova, a slick blonde who struck a stark contrast to the lumbering Volkova, avoided any mention of politics in the courtroom and asked the judge to take into consideration that Samutsevich had been unpacking a guitar when she was apprehended. She had not had time to participate in the group's protest. Therefore, Khrunova reasoned calmly, her client should be freed.

After a short recess for deliberation, the judge agreed. 'I am releasing you on a suspended sentence,' she said, as cheers rang out in the hallway outside, where dozens of journalists and supporters were watching the trial on a large screen. 'But any violation of your probation terms will mean an immediate return to custody. Do you understand?'

'Yes, yes, I do.' Samutsevich beamed, understandably overjoyed.

Alyokhina and Tolokonnikova were not so fortunate. Their defence team had argued that Putin's and Medvedev's public comments on the case meant a retrial was necessary, but the judge somewhat unconvincingly denied reading or hearing the president's or prime minister's opinions.

Samutsevich hugged her two fellow group members and walked out of the court into a rainstorm and a media scrum.

'I'm overjoyed. This is real happiness,' her elderly father told me, as the world's news crews pursued his daughter down a Moscow side street. 'I didn't expect this at all.'

Samutsevich's unexpected release triggered wild speculation. Had she done a deal with the authorities? Was her release an attempt to split Pussy Riot? Or perhaps the Kremlin just wanted to rescue some of its battered international image? Tellingly, no one at all was naive enough to suggest that Samutsevich's release was purely down to the strength of her lawyer's argument.

✳

Mr Samutsevich's bewilderment at his daughter's release was almost matched by my astonishment when, around a week after walking out of jail, the freed Pussy Rioter suggested meeting in a suburban McDonald's. Anti-establishment political activists in the West, I noted, tended to attack McDonald's, not give interviews in them. 'I didn't think of that,' Samutsevich said, blushing ever so slightly. 'Let's go somewhere else.' So we did.[20]

After almost seven months in a Moscow pre-trial detention centre, Samutsevich had a lot to catch up with, not least the full extent of the international row that had raged over the group's arrest and trial. 'People don't seem to be able to grasp that there is no internet in a pre-trial detention centre,' she said with a smile, as she sipped coffee in a much nicer café just down the road from McDonald's. 'It was really tough to find out what was going on – although I saw on TV that Madonna had supported us.

'I've noticed people looking at me since I was released,' she added, dressed in a grey shirt with pointed white collars that gave her an oddly priestly air. 'We were in a bar the other day and someone sent over a glass of cognac.'

Her time in jail had made her acutely aware of what she called the all-invasive system of control that Putin and his former colleagues in the security services had constructed. 'Of course, I'm happy to be out,' she said. 'But, you know, there's not so much difference between prison and the outside world. Russia is like one big prison. In or out, you are always under someone else's control.' She also seemed to have become slightly paranoid, dropping references to 'people in white cars who drive around listening to mobile-phone conversations'.

Despite Pussy Riot's call for the Virgin Mary to 'drive Putin out', Samutsevich insisted Russia's problems went far deeper than the president. Simply removing Putin from office, she said, was unlikely to guarantee a bright and shining future for the largest country on earth.

'People just made out that we were just against Putin and that's as far as it goes,' she said. 'We get emails from young girls saying they also want to fight against him, and what can they do to help. But it's all a bit more complicated than saying simply, "Putin is the symbol of evil."' She laughed. 'The problem is the way the authorities manipulate society, and our entire system of education, which doesn't teach people to think for themselves. Of course, this state of affairs is beneficial for the authorities, but it's also the reason why we have such a system of government. If we had a more open society, we wouldn't have such authoritarian leaders.' She sighed, as if in acknowledgement of the utter hopelessness of the classic Catch 22 she had just described.

Pussy Riot were lauded in the West, but in Russia there was widespread hostility. In an opinion poll, only 6% of Russians said they sympathized with the group. Almost half considered a two-year sentence too light. Even Navalny, I informed Samutsevich, had said he found the group's protest 'disgusting'.

'Did he say that?' she asked. 'I guess he had to keep his conservative followers happy.' But she looked confused, upset even. 'As for attitudes here, well, of course, many people were brainwashed by all the vile stuff they said about us on television. I've had time to watch some of it. But we were championed in the West because people there are used to fighting for their rights. Our protest was in a form that was instantly recognizable.

Also, in the West there is the idea that Putin is one of the most macho world leaders, and so it was a very attractive image there for people to see his regime being taken on by a group of feminists.'

After the confidence and aggression of Navalny and the political dogma of Udaltsov, there was a refreshing simplicity to Samutsevich. She was no politician and had no apparent ambitions to be one. She was just a young woman who had protested against something she believed to be very wrong. 'We were so irritated by Patriarch Kirill's statements that Putin had "rectified the course of history",' she told me, genuinely baffled. 'He's just one man. How could he do that?'

Samutsevich looked vague when I asked her if the group had taken into account the impact their protest would have on believers. Had they considered the unpleasant comparisons their performance would trigger with the Soviet-era mockery of the faith? Had they felt any concern that the group might have caused genuine distress to believers, to people like the woman I had observed praying in Archpriest Chaplin's cathedral?

'Yes,' she admitted, 'the protest had the potential to offend people who are ignorant of what is happening in society. But we deliberately chose to go into the cathedral at a time when there was no service going on and very few people were there. We left as soon as security asked us to. If anyone there had come up to me and said, "Why did you do that?" I would have apologized.

'I don't want to get into a discussion of my own beliefs,' she continued, after a pause in which she weighed up her words, 'but, you know, hypothetically at least, I think God would have approved of our protest.'

The Pussy Riot trial demonstrated to the world the Kremlin's pettiness and cruelty, but, in terms of the protest movement's battle to remove Putin from power, it was little more than a gaudy and damaging sideshow. Instead of consolidating the opposition, the group's provocative appearance in the Christ the Saviour Cathedral served only to encourage anti-Western sentiments among Kremlin officials and their supporters in the Orthodox Church. Stung by middle-class dissent in Moscow, Putin turned now to Russia's conservative heartland for support.

13

DARK DAYS

Putin's assertion that US Secretary of State Hillary Clinton was behind the unprecedented protests against his rule triggered frenzied anti-Western rhetoric from both state media and pro-Kremlin figures. Almost overnight, the aggressive xenophobia that had always been on the fringe of Russian politics seized centre stage.

Shortly after Putin's March 2012 election victory, the state-controlled NTV channel broadcast claims that white-ribbon protesters were being paid 'cookies and cash' by the US State Department to attend demonstrations. The thirty-six-minute film,[1] set to a background of nervy, ominous music, sparked a thousand-strong illegal protest outside the station's Moscow headquarters. Another NTV documentary, on the same theme, revealed what it claimed was an intricate web of 'internet bloggers' being manipulated by Navalny and his alleged US allies as they attempted to foment regime change in Russia. 'I really regret what I did,' mumbled one such repentant 'blogger', a wild-eyed, greasy-haired youth. 'I mean, these people really wanted to organize a coup.'[2]

Putin wasn't being completely paranoid. The Kremlin believed it had good reason to be wary of the United States, which Russian officials insisted had backtracked on a verbal pledge that NATO would not expand up to their country's borders following the fall of the Berlin Wall (the United States says no guarantees were given), and had arrogantly dismissed Moscow's concerns over Washington's plans for a missile shield in Europe.

It was hardly unexpected, either, that the timing of the January 2012 appointment of Stanford professor Michael McFaul as US ambassador to Russia was met with undisguised suspicion. A former senior adviser to the National Democratic Institute, which was tied to the uprisings in Serbia, Ukraine and Georgia, McFaul is an expert on regime change in post-Soviet states. He is also the author of a book with the provocative (to the Kremlin, at least) title *Russia's Unfinished Revolution*. McFaul denied he had been sent to Russia to help topple Putin. He also pointed out that he was the author of the 'reset', the much-vaunted yet ultimately ineffective bid to boost US–Russia ties during the Medvedev presidency. However, when he met with opposition figures and civil activists on just his second day on the job, state-controlled media erupted. Channel One ran footage of McFaul's guests arriving at the US embassy under the title: 'Receiving instructions from the new ambassador'. McFaul's protestations that he had met with Kremlin officials during his first day on the job were ignored.

'McFaul is no expert on Russia,' rasped Mikhail Leontiev, a rabidly pro-Kremlin political commentator given five minutes to pontificate on whatever he sees fit after the main evening news bulletin on Channel One. 'He's an expert solely on the promotion of democracy,' he added, his face wrinkling in distaste. 'Has Mr McFaul come to Russia to work at his speciality – that is, to finish the revolution?' he asked viewers. He also accused the new ambassador of training Navalny – 'the Internet Führer' – to seize control of the country.[3]

Kremlin-controlled media and pro-Putin figures sought to portray the US State Department ('*Gosudarstvenny departament*' in Russian, but commonly truncated to '*Gosdep*') as an all-powerful, nefarious organization set upon Russia's ruin. Given this demonization of the United States, it was somehow apt that McFaul's official residence in Moscow was Spaso House, a Neoclassical Revival mansion that had served as the setting for a ball thrown by Satan himself in Mikhail Bulgakov's classic Stalin-era novel *The Master and Margarita*.

'We were surprised, as a government, to have "*Gosdep*" become this evil word,' a still clearly dismayed McFaul told me when I spoke to him at the US embassy. 'And, personally, as the author of the reset, it was rather surprising to land here and be in this…' he searched for the right words '…different configuration.'[4]

This outbreak of anti-Americanism was less about Kremlin worries over Washington's intentions than a desire to create a necessary external enemy. 'The Russian authorities are always inspired by the Soviet past, and, when the protests started, they simply looked back to see what worked then,' Andrei Soldatov, a respected investigative journalist and expert on Russia's security services, told me. 'And even in the early 1980s, before perestroika, that was anti-Americanism and a belief in Western plots – ideas which were quite common among even ordinary people.'[5]

The Kremlin's tactics worked. Opinion polls in early 2012 suggested that around two-thirds of Russians believed the West could be behind the protests. As vote-fraud demonstrations rocked Moscow, the Kremlin organized massive anti-West and pro-Putin rallies across the capital. The official slogan of one rally in central Moscow was: 'We have something to lose!', its symbol an orange snake being strangled by a fist.

'If you want a fight, we are ready for a fight,' yelled rally organizer and TV anchor Sergei Kurginyan. 'We are the majority!'

Other speakers warned that the opposition wanted to 'hand over' control of Russia's nuclear weapons to the United States.

State media later claimed some 140,000 had attended the public show of support for Putin, who did not put in an appearance. But independent media and observers mocked the official figures as wildly inflated, and insisted that many of those who had shown up to wave United Russia flags and chant 'Yes to Putin! No to Orange Revolution!' were state employees who had been herded to the rally from factories, schools and offices across Russia.

THE ADOPTION BAN

These anti-Western attitudes boiled over when the United States adopted a law introducing visa bans and asset freezes against Russian officials suspected of human-rights abuses. The bill was known as the Magnitsky Act, in honour of the lawyer Sergei Magnitsky, whom human-rights officials claimed had been beaten to death in a Moscow detention facility after alleging massive fraud by Interior Ministry officials. Despite being opposed by both President Barack Obama and the US State Department, who feared it would harm already tense bilateral relations, the Magnitsky Act became law in late 2012. The law was lobbied for in Congress by Russian opposition figures, in particular Yevgenia Chirikova, the eco-activist who had so inspired Navalny, and Boris Nemtsov, the Yeltsin-era minister and co-founder of the RPR-Parnas opposition party.

'We had the whole team against us – Putin, Obama and the State Department,' laughed Nemtsov, when I met him after the act had been signed into law. 'Of course, we realize that there are a lot questions to the US over its own record on human rights,' he went on, turning serious. 'But I don't care. Let them solve their own problems. This law is against corrupt, murdering officials in Russia and that's all I am worried about.'[6]

The adoption of the Magnitsky Act gave rise to a great rage among Russian officials, many of whom not only were keen on taking vacations in the United States, but also owned property and other assets there. In early 2013, the State Duma's ethics-committee chief, United Russia lawmaker Vladimir Pekhtin, was forced to step down after Navalny posted documents on the internet showing he owned undisclosed luxury property in Miami.[7]

Putin said the Magnitsky Act would 'poison' ties with Washington,[8] and Russian officials warned of both tit-for-tat and 'asymmetrical' responses.[9] Within months, Moscow had slapped its own visa and asset bans on US officials suspected of human-rights abuses against Russian citizens. The move triggered much mirth, both in Russia and beyond: the independent online TV channel Dozhd ran a mock news report of

US politicians lamenting the law. 'This is a nightmare, when we drew up the Magnitsky Act, we didn't believe such a thing was possible,' a distraught 'congressman' complained. 'We have all our money in Russian banks! And what about our vacations? Every summer, we fly to Russian cities like Voronezh, Samara or Saratov – but no more. Now we'll have to spend our holidays in Paris or London. What kind of a life is that?'[10]

But Russia's 'disproportionate' response to the Magnitsky Act was no laughing matter: on 1 January 2013 Putin signed off on a law that banned American nationals from adopting Russian children. Exceptions would not be made even for seriously ill orphans or those in the final stages of a move to the United States, children who had already grown close to their new parents. Opponents of the ban argued it effectively condemned Russian children in state care to lives of misery in underfunded and often brutal institutions. Shortly after the ban was introduced, footage emerged of small children being beaten methodically and mercilessly in an orphanage in eastern Russia by the very people who were supposed to be caring for them.

'Just imagine, there are some sick children, without mums or dads, living in terrible children's homes,' seethed Russian actress Tatyana Dogileva, in a raw, emotional online appeal for a rethink of the ban. 'Their parents have already come to see them, from America, and said, "We are your mum and dad." They've already shown them the house where they will live,' she went on, shaking with rage. 'And then the politicians play their dirty, awful games.'[11]

Russian families, due to a variety of reasons, from cramped apartments to a lack of state support, showed little inclination to adopt: they had taken in just 7,400 children in 2011 from some 70,000 available for adoption,[12] while US families had adopted at least 60,000 since the collapse of the Soviet Union. One justification for the bill, which Putin called an 'adequate' but 'emotional' response to the Magnitsky Act, was the deaths of some nineteen Russian children at the hands of their US adoptive parents since 1991. Lawmakers made no mention of the some 2,000 children killed by adults, frequently by their own parents, every single year in Russia.[13]

The Orthodox Church backed the ban. Its spokesperson, Vsevolod Chaplin, said that children adopted by American families 'do not go to heaven'. Svetlana Goryacheva, a politician from the Kremlin-created A Just Russia party, managed to outdo even Chaplin in the controversy stakes, stating that one in every six children sent to adoptive families in the United States would be used for organs or sexually abused, while the other five would be trained for 'war against Russia'.[14]

Russia's urban, educated class, including, remarkably, a handful of government figures – Dmitry Livanov, the education minister, and Olga Golodets, the deputy prime minister responsible for social issues – rose up against the law. 'What's Putin going to do next to spite the United States? Burn down an old people's home in the Moscow region?' went the popular joke. Critics also pointed out that the Kremlin had chosen not to close down a controversial but lucrative NATO transit hub in central Russia in retaliation. The hub, which both Russia and the United States deny is a 'military base', is designed to ease NATO's withdrawal of non-lethal equipment from Afghanistan.

In mid-January 2013, around 30,000 people marched through the centre of Moscow, some carrying signs portraying Putin as a child-killer. Yekaterina Lakhova, one of the United Russia legislators who had proposed the ban, paid a visit to the rally for research purposes, but left early due to the cold. 'These people are always disgruntled about something,' she sniffed before hurrying back to her chauffeur-driven State Duma vehicle.[15]

In the days after the adoption-ban protest rally, state media went into overdrive, running reports on the 'abuse' of Russian children in the United States, frequently to the backdrop of a crying young girl standing in front of the American flag. 'First the liberals wanted everyone to support that dirty hooliganism in the cathedral,' said Dmitry Kiselyov, the presenter of a programme on the Rossiya 1 TV channel. 'And now they are urging everyone to protest against a ban on the export of children.'[16]

When a three-year-old Russian child died in Texas in what was eventually ruled an accident by US officials, the Kremlin's ombudsman for children's rights, Pavel Astakhov, immediately accused – on Twitter, no less – his American adoptive mother of murdering the boy.[17] 'The death of a Russian child was no tragedy for US congressmen or US senators,' the head of the Russian parliament's committee on family issues, Olga Batalina, lamented in a televised address to fellow lawmakers. 'In fact, his death was no tragedy for anyone in the United States.'[18] (The Russian government later offered a belated apology for such 'emotional' comments.[19]) This propaganda campaign was crude, but effective. A poll later that week indicated that just over two-thirds of all Russians supported the adoption ban.[20]

RUSSIA IS A US COLONY

As the adoption row raged, one of the authors of the ban, United Russia lawmaker Yevgeny Fyodorov, gave an interview to supporters in which he called for a campaign of 'national liberation' from the United States. In barely coherent comments, Fyodorov, a heavy-set, bespectacled former deputy minister of atomic energy and a Cabinet adviser, praised Putin's rule, but said Russia had been an 'American colony' since the collapse of the Soviet Union. It was now time, Fyodorov declared, to root out the 'US agents' who had infiltrated the government.

'Putin cannot change the system,' he told three young and captivated supporters from his embryonic Free Russia movement in an interview that was later posted online. 'We have to wait for the system to collapse itself. Ahead of this, ten million people must take to the streets in support of Putin. If they do not come out, direct American control will be imposed.

'It's time to create a website containing photographs of fighters from the occupying army,' he went on. 'It's time to draw up a list of enemies.'

Described by a blogger on *LiveJournal*, Russia's most popular blogging platform, as 'two hours of hell', the interview transformed Fyodorov into Russia's media curiosity of the month.[21] Even by the standards of Russia's parliament, home over the past two decades to a Kremlin-backed psychic, a Ponzi scheme conman and an allegedly Mafia-connected crooner, Fyodorov stood out. Intrigued, I arranged to meet him. Such was Fyodorov's newfound fame, however, that our interview was pushed back by over an hour while he rounded off his media engagements for the day. I killed time in the State Duma's cheap and not entirely cheerful café, surrounded by parliamentary assistants and even a lawmaker or two.

As I waited, I reviewed again Fyodorov's statements from the now infamous interview. I started to underline the most extreme, but gave up halfway through. I was, I realized, underlining almost everything he'd said. As I finished off my State Duma tea and sandwiches, Fyodorov's assistant, a ginger-haired, twenty-something called Denis, sat down next to me. 'You're reading about the interview that was posted in *LiveJournal*,' he noted, frowning. 'The one that caused all the fuss.'

I had planned on asking Denis what it was like to work for someone who held such unorthodox opinions, but I quickly realized his employment in Fyodorov's office was no coincidence. Denis handed me a business card that identified him as a member of Free Russia. The group's slogan: 'The Motherland! Freedom! Putin!'

'We plan for ninety percent of the country to join the movement, but we'll keep the party core small. Quality over quantity,' Denis told me, smiling now, as he thought about the good times to come. 'But that's all in the future. The people aren't ready yet.'

'When will they be?'

'We're working on that.'

✳

Fyodorov wasted no time on pleasantries. Sitting opposite a framed photo of an unsmiling Putin, model Russian spacecraft to his right and a Stalin mug on his desk, he told me that 'Russia's constitution was written by US advisers after the Cold War. Putin is leading a drive for national liberation from the United States, but as president he can't come out and say this outright. But, if you look carefully at everything he says, it's very clear. The adoption ban is just part of Putin's fightback.'

So where were the occupying forces? I asked. I hadn't noticed many US soldiers on the streets as I made my way to parliament that morning.

Fyodorov blinked rapidly. 'There are NATO troops in the Soviet republics of Estonia, Latvia and Lithuania,' he told me. 'There are also,' he went on, hardly pausing for breath, 'US agents of influence within the government.'

'Who?' And how, I wondered, did he know?

'It is obvious by their actions. I'm talking about those members of the government who opposed the adoption ban.' Fyodorov stopped short, however, of accusing Foreign Minister Sergei Lavrov – who had also expressed doubts over the wisdom of the ban – of being an American agent. 'I do not tap telephones,' he told me, calmer now. 'I can only judge people by their political actions and these two have made it very clear.'

It was a startling statement, even by his standards, from a man who had been one of the founders of United Russia in 1999. I asked how many of his fellow party members shared his opinions. Fyodorov pursed his lips. I had, it seemed, offended him. 'Just wait a minute,' he said, holding up a hand to cut me off. 'These are not *views* – these are facts. No?'

We had been talking at this point for less than half an hour, but my brain had already started to go numb. I hadn't even had a chance to pull Fyodorov up on his apparent belief that EU members Estonia, Latvia and Lithuania remained a part of the long-defunct Soviet Union. I shrugged, wary of unleashing another verbal onslaught, and Denis, who had joined us for the interview, laughed.

'Navalny is a US agent who operates on the streets,' Fyodorov continued. 'Government ministers operate in the interests of the United States from within a position of authority. But they are all controlled by the same forces. We need to draw up a list of agents of occupation. We need to determine exactly who these people are and then inform the country.'

There was, I argued, no doubt that the United States had strategic interests it was working hard to implement. Its military forces had also been guilty of some horrific crimes against humanity. But surely this overriding obsession with America was unhealthy and obsessive? And talk of 'enemies of the people' – the Soviet-era term used to justify mass executions and the gulags – was also not only irresponsible, but dangerous. I was annoyed with myself: I had vowed not to get into a row with Fyodorov, but here I was, scrapping it out with him.

Fyodorov heard me out, and then shook his head. 'No one would argue that there exists conflict and competition between countries, right?' he responded, evading a straight answer. 'This is all just a part of this.'

Fyodorov is the logical result of the Kremlin-backed xenophobia poisoning Russian politics. I'd assumed before our meeting that his outlandish statements were a bizarre form of self-promotion to back up his ambitions to lead United Russia's parliamentary faction. But I was wrong. Fyodorov is sincere. He really does believe in a vast web of conspiracy that involves government officials, the anti-Putin movement and the United States. Looking into his eyes, I saw the fanaticism and warped suspicions that led the Soviet Union to murder millions of its own citizens. The temperature had not fallen below freezing in Moscow, but I felt a sudden deep chill as I walked quickly away from the State Duma.

THE 'GODLESS' WEST

Putin had begun to build a new Russian national identity founded on conservative and traditional values, while warning that the West was in a deep moral crisis. The Kremlin insisted that political correctness and official acceptance of homosexuality in the West were indications that the United States and European countries were now godless nations. Ironically, this was the very same insult hurled at the officially atheist Soviet Union for many years by conservative Americans and Europeans. History had come full circle.

'Many Euro-Atlantic countries have moved away from their roots, including Christian values,' Putin seethed in a keynote speech in the autumn of 2013. 'Policies are being pursued that place on the same level a multi-child family and a same-sex partnership, a faith in God and a belief in Satan… This is the path to degradation,' Putin declared. He added that Russia considered it only 'natural and right' to stand up for Christian values.[22]

The Kremlin's encouragement of traditional values sparked a rise in Orthodox vigilantism. Fringe groups such as the Union of Orthodox Banner Bearers, an ultra-conservative movement whose slogan is 'Orthodoxy or Death!', gained prominence; their leader, Leonid Simonovich, an openly anti-Semitic monarchist, had even been honoured by Patriarch Kirill for his services to the Orthodox Church. The Banner Bearers, dressed in their uniforms of black paramilitary gear festooned with death-head skulls, regularly picketed Pussy Riot court hearings. They also attacked LGBT activists who protested in the summer of 2013 against a new law that effectively banned any public references to a homosexual lifestyle. I met up with Banner Bearers on a number of occasions that year, first visiting the studio where its members turn out Orthodox art – including 'Orthodoxy or Death!' T-shirts – and then with its leader, Simonovich.

'Have you read *The Protocols of the Elders of Zion*?' Simonovich asked, as he sat munching on a blueberry muffin in a Moscow coffeehouse. 'You should, then you'll understand everything that's going on.' He waved away my argument that the book, which was first published in Russia in the early twentieth century and outlines a 'Jewish plot' for global domination, had long been proved to be an anti-Semitic hoax. 'Open your eyes,' he said, smiling knowingly.[23]

The anti-Putin opposition was not immune to such controversial sentiments. 'To be gay is to go against God. I mean, the Bible says to "go forth and multiply", yes? Gays can't do that,' the eco-activist Chirikova told me, when I met her in central Moscow in early 2013. 'I feel sorry for gays with all their diseases, but I am against what they do.' She smiled. 'I have very traditional values.'

✱

Life in Russia was beginning to resemble the dystopian future imagined by author Vladimir Sorokin, who in a 2006 novel had depicted an insular, uber-religious and patriotic Russia where order is maintained by a modern-day version of the *oprichniki*, the notorious, black-clad security agents who enforced Ivan the Terrible's draconian laws. 'As a writer, I am, of course, satisfied,' said Sorokin, seven years after his *Day of the Oprichnik* was released. 'As a citizen, not so. But it's all coming true. I wouldn't be surprised if tomorrow they ordered a return to monarchism and Putin is anointed tsar. The grotesque has long become part of the air we breathe.'[24]

Tsar Vladimir? It was an unlikely turn of events. But, although Putin may not have had his eye on any thrones, he was searching for other ways to consolidate his power. The protest movement had failed, for now, to bring him down, but he had been weakened. The reputation of the party he headed in all but name, United Russia, had been ravaged by Navalny and his allies. The president needed a new vehicle, but one that would remain distant from the potentially damaging complexities of everyday politics.

In the summer of 2013, Putin was elected by a show of hands and mass chanting of his name as leader of the People's Front movement, a Soviet-style amorphous alliance of thousands of individuals and organizations, from factories to trade unions to reindeer herders. The organization had been founded ahead of the 2012 presidential elections, but had lain largely dormant since.

Many organizations simply signed up their members for the People's Front en masse, without consulting them. But, beyond its stated intention to operate as a platform for grassroots activists with a 'constructive agenda', the movement had no clear ideological base and no plans, for now at least, to participate in elections. So what was its purpose? The Kremlin's spokesperson, Dmitry Peskov, said simply that the movement would be 'based around Putin'.

'Now the stupidest question ever: "Who are we going to nominate as leader of our movement?"' asked film director Stanislav Govorukhin at the movement's founding congress, as delirious delegates broke into a chant of 'Putin! Putin!' 'Shall we vote?' Govorukhin asked.

'No!' came the reply, the camera panning over hundreds of faces filled with a childlike awe.

'This is pure and simple fascism,' fumed Lev Ponomaryov, the veteran head of the For Human Rights organization, when I visited him at the group's bustling and chaotic central Moscow headquarters. Someone, I had noticed as I entered the building, had daubed 'Foreign Agent' in white paint on the organization's door. No one had apparently yet found the time to scrub the graffiti off.[25]

'These people are simply grouped around Putin to support blindly whatever he does or says,' Ponomaryov, a bearded seventy-three-year-old and former ally of the late Soviet dissident Andrei Sakharov, told me. 'This is the kind of thing that went on in Italy under Mussolini.'

Two days after my visit, Ponomaryov and his rights workers would be kicked out of their offices by private security guards backed up by riot police. Across town, the independent voting watchdog Golos had fared much worse: it had been temporarily forced to shut down its operations after falling foul of the 'foreign agents' law. 'Putin is sick with spy mania,' said Shibanova, the head of the watchdog. 'It sits in him, like a vaccination, from his KGB past.'[26]

From the criminalization of residency-permit violations (met by a memorable, but quickly stamped-out protest on Red Square by some dozen activists holding a banner that read 'Fuck off with your registration!') to the NGO, protest fines, treason and the so-called gay-propaganda laws, it was as if Putin had decided to make a genuine effort to live up to his reputation as a freedom-hating KGB agent, albeit one possessed of an Orthodox Christian zeal. Another law, approved by parliament on the same day as the 'gay propaganda' legislation, made it a criminal offence to 'insult' the feelings of religious believers. 'Putin's trying to create an atmosphere of totalitarian fear,' Marat Guelman, the former Kremlin spin doctor, told me. 'All Medvedev's talk of modernization has entirely disappeared.'

As the protest movement faltered, Putin was picking off his enemies, one by one. Pussy Riot were behind bars, Navalny was facing ten years in a prison camp, NGOs were coming under unprecedented pressure, and the white-ribbon movement had been smeared with allegations of Western funding. Next, Putin would unleash his allies in the security services on the new left.

14

NEXT TARGET – THE NEW LEFT

It was a scene that had become overly familiar: Udaltsov being led away by police. Detained scores of times on protest-related charges in less than a decade, the Left Front leader had long given up trying to keep track of his numerous arrests. It was a running joke among the Moscow opposition that the protest movement's most uncompromising figure only had to show his face on the streets for the cops to pounce. 'You'll never guess what…' Navalny had tweeted earlier that year, 'Udaltsov's only gone and got himself arrested again.'

This time, though, rather than dragging him out of a crowd of protesters, or nabbing him on a trumped-up charge as he made his way to a demonstration, masked officers simply raided the shaven-headed socialist's south Moscow apartment early one sunny autumn morning.

If Udaltsov's previous arrests had been on relatively minor protest-related charges, the officers who arrived at his modest home in mid-October 2012 were on far more serious business. The leftist figurehead was being charged with plotting violent revolution; the allegations based on grainy footage broadcast to the nation by the enthusiastically pro-Putin television channel NTV.

'This is arbitrary repression,' Udaltsov said, giving the V for Victory sign as officers hustled him past waiting reporters. 'The only thing I am guilty of is telling the truth. I hope society will not stay silent.'

Two elderly women, sitting on a multi-coloured bench near the entranceway to Udaltsov's nine-floor apartment block, glanced up briefly as their neighbour was shoved into a waiting police vehicle. They said nothing, and looked entirely unsurprised. But was their indifference really so unexpected? After all, Udaltsov had been accused, tried and judged on national television – the infamous 'Zombie box'. For the majority of Russia's population, those who got their news exclusively from state media, Udaltsov was a violent extremist, and a traitor to boot.

THE GEORGIA CONSPIRACY?

On 5 October 2012, NTV aired a video it said showed Udaltsov, two other leftist activists and an influential Georgian politician, Givi Targamadze, discussing a plot to topple Putin. The poor quality of the footage meant it was impossible to identify with any certainty any of the people in the film.[1]

'I've got this outrageous idea, but I like it,' laughed the rotund figure identified as Targamadze, as he outlined a seemingly far-fetched plan involving Chechen fighters, the criminal underworld, explosions on the Trans-Siberian Express and prison riots. The documentary also alleged the men had organized the unrest in central Moscow on the eve of Putin's May 2012 inauguration. The aim of the plot described by the figures in the video was to seize power simultaneously in Russia's eastern and western extremes: the Baltic exclave of Kaliningrad (squeezed between Poland and Lithuania) and the Pacific port of Vladivostok, creating what was described as a 'logistical' nightmare for Putin. 'He'll have to get permission to send Russian troops through NATO states, yeah?' an off-screen voice cackled. 'And, by the time he's got that, it'll be too late.'[2]

The footage was aired some four years after Russia and Georgia had briefly gone to war over the breakaway republic of South Ossetia, which Georgia's fiercely pro-American president, Mikheil Saakashvili, had long vowed to recapture. Tensions between Russia and Georgia, a tiny, former Soviet republic on the Black Sea, had also been raised by Saakashvili's drive to achieve NATO membership for his country, adding to the Kremlin's fears of encirclement by Western forces. Despite a crushing and humiliating defeat for Saakashvili's party to the pro-Russia opposition at vital parliamentary elections earlier in 2012, Georgia was still seen as a hotbed of US influence, a land of anti-Kremlin plots where rabid Russophobia flowed as freely as the country's famous wines.

It could not have been worse for Udaltsov if he had been accused of conspiring with the devil himself. And the devil was unlikely to pay so well: the NTV documentary alleged Udaltsov was being paid $35,000 a month for his part in plotting Putin's downfall.

Independent media and activists quickly pointed out apparent holes in NTV's version of events: identical footage of 'Udaltsov' and his comrades, which the channel said had been filmed in June 2012 in Minsk, Belarus, had been used to accompany two completely different sections of dialogue. Targamadze, the former chairman of the Defence and Security Committee in the Georgian parliament, repeatedly denied ever meeting Udaltsov. 'First the Russian law-enforcement authorities identified a goal – to arrest Udaltsov,' he said. 'Then, with this goal in mind, they began gathering together a collection of absurdities.'[3]

Udaltsov dismissed the film as 'lunacy', suggesting it was a frame-up put together by the security forces. Intriguingly, however, he would not rule out that he may have actually discussed such things with close friends, but not – he insisted – with representatives of foreign states.

'The film shown on NTV is a montage,' Udaltsov said when I met him in central Moscow after the film was aired. 'And the quality was so low, even I couldn't say if that was me or not. They are trying to accuse us of organizing mass disorder. Which implies action. Action,' he repeated, for emphasis.

'We could sit here, drink some tea or something stronger, and say anything,' he went on. 'Like, it would be good to organize an uprising, or whatever. And, if they are filming us, they can use this for whatever purpose. There was no meeting with Givi Targamadze. I don't know how they put that recording together, if they took fragments of real conversations from wherever or however. But I can say one thing: neither I nor my friends planned any mass disorder with Georgian or Western special services.

'Our aim has always been to inspire people to peaceful protest, to fight for their rights,' he went on, angry now. 'They needed to weaken us, to pressure us, and they thought this up. Putin got afraid after the first big protests, and, when the movement started to lose momentum, he took his revenge. It's very simple.'[4]

The day after the film was shown across Russia's vast territory, the Investigative Committee launched a probe into the footage. Within days, its stern spokesperson, Vladimir Markin, would declare the video was 'genuine' and showed no signs of doctoring. But where had the channel come across the video? Wasn't it the job of the security services to seek out and identify plots to sow discord on Russia's streets and topple its elected leaders?

NTV journalist Alexei Malkin would later clear up the puzzle for everyone: an 'unknown Georgian', he told a Moscow court that month, had handed him a disc containing the footage as he was walking down the street.[5] Court reports did not indicate if Malkin was smirking when he made the claim. (Attempts to speak to him for this book were unsuccessful.)

For the protest movement, however, things were suddenly a lot clearer. 'We can now say that NTV has become a part of the security structure,' said Sergei Parkhomenko, a well-known journalist and opposition activist.[6]

For a TV channel once lauded as the future of independent media in Russia, it was an ignoble fate.

As police hustled him into the headquarters of the Investigative Committee that October morning, Udaltsov relentlessly tweeted the details of his arrest: 'Stay strong and kick things off to the max! They are putting me away!' Then, later: 'Don't stay quiet!'

But, to everyone's surprise, including his own, Udaltsov was released later that evening pending further investigation. 'Investigators are playing some kind of strange game,' he said, as he left the towering steel-and-glass offices of the Investigative Committee.

But what game? Was Udaltsov's unexpected release a hint for him to get out of the country while he still could? A fugitive from the law is, after all, much easier to discredit than a political prisoner.

'After investigators released Udaltsov from custody, he was under close observation. But at one point the people trailing him vanished,' Left Front activist Alexei Sakhnin told me later. 'He was given a clear signal. They expected him to escape to some civilized country, and to quit the political arena.'[7] As the authorities circled, Sakhnin would later seek political asylum in Sweden.

However, Udaltsov had no intention of fleeing Russia. 'It wouldn't be right,' he told me, when I asked him if the idea of getting out of the country had crossed his mind. 'I'd be letting down all those people who put their trust in me.'

THEY TORTURED ME FOR TWO DAYS!

Konstantin Lebedev, one of the other two leftist activists alleged to have featured in the NTV clip, was taken in for questioning the same day that Udaltsov was charged. Unlike Udaltsov, however, Lebedev was kept in police custody. The whereabouts of the third suspect, a thirty-something east Siberian named Leonid Razvozzhayev, were unknown. He was immediately placed on the federal wanted list.

'Neither my loved ones, nor my comrades know where I am right now,' wrote Razvozzhayev in a 19 October 2012 blog entry. 'I'm a Siberian, from the taiga, so I can live for a long time in extreme conditions. I do not intend to play by their rules.'[8]

It was a defiant statement from the fugitive Left Front man, a long-time activist and aide to the opposition lawmaker Ilya Ponomarev. But Russia's security forces were already on his trail, something Razvozzhayev appeared to understand far too well.

'If, in the nearest future, I should be arrested or anything bad happens to me, do not believe anything they say about me,' he warned. 'I am of sound mind, and sober memory.'[9]

Immediately after posting on his blog, Razvozzhayev paid a visit to the office of a partner organization of the United Nations High Commissioner for Refugees (UNHCR) in Kiev, the capital of Ukraine, with the aim of seeking political asylum. During a break in a lengthy discussion with an official, he stepped out into the street to buy some food. He would not return. UNHCR officials were perplexed. 'We are concerned that a person has disappeared in the middle of the day, and nobody knows what happened and how,' said a spokesperson for Ukraine's UNHCR office.[10] Razvozzhayev had even left some of his belongings behind at the office.

Some forty-eight hours later, he turned up in Moscow, in police custody. But how had he got there?

Two strikingly different versions of what had happened to the Left Front activist after he vanished in Kiev soon emerged. According to Russian investigators, Razvozzhayev had been stung by pangs of guilt over his 'betrayal' of his homeland, jumped into a taxi and rode all the way to Moscow, where he turned himself in and wrote a ten-page confession implicating himself and other key protest figures in the alleged foreign-funded plot.[11]

Razvozzhayev had a somewhat different explanation.

'Tell everyone they tortured me! For two days!' he shouted to a waiting journalist and film crew as he was led out the back door of a Moscow courthouse by police. 'They abducted me in Ukraine!' he said, leaning back to speak, before he was bundled into a police van.[12]

The footage went viral, and sent a chill through the protest movement. 'Are they going to return to the traditions of the 1930s, when the Stalinist secret police invented vast, phony conspiracies and went on a killing spree of political dissidents?' asked Ponomarev, as the discussion raged over his assistant's claims.[13] Was Putin becoming drawn into a vicious cycle of political terror?

Razvozzhayev's full version of events would only become known after a visit by Zoya Svetova, a journalist and member of Russia's independent prison watchdog, the Public Oversight Commission, to his cell on 23 October. Razvozzhayev spoke 'very fast, jumping from topic to topic', Svetova would later recall. 'He was nervy and confused, but it was clear, he needed to speak.'[14]

This was what he had to say about what happened that afternoon in Kiev.

'There were four men, one was without a mask – I could recognize him again if I saw him. They pushed me into a minibus and stuck a thick, black hat over my eyes so that I couldn't see anything and tied my hands and legs up with sticking tape.'

Continuing to speak rapidly, Razvozzhayev said he had been driven to the Ukrainian border, transferred into another minibus and then taken to the basement of an abandoned house, where he was handcuffed and kept without food and water.

'They kept me there for two days,' he told Svetova and other prisoners' rights workers. 'They told me: "If you don't answer our questions, your children will be killed." Their main aim was to get me to testify.

'For the first twenty-four hours, they kept stressing that I was in Ukraine, and no one knew anything about my whereabouts. They said anything at all could happen to me. They said: "Either you tell us something interesting, or you will no longer exist. We know you have an eight-year-old daughter, and that your sixteen-year-old son goes to protests. We know where your wife works. So think."

'When I refused to say what they wanted to hear from me, they said they would give me a truth injection that would make me tell them everything, but that could also leave me an idiot for the rest of my life. They brought me a bowl, in case I vomited. Maybe they were calling my bluff, but I decided not to risk it... and told them what they wanted to hear.'

Razvozzhayev's claims united the splintered opposition council, if only briefly. 'They abducted Razvozzhayev and stuck him in a basement,'

Navalny said. 'And now we're going to discuss who is a nationalist, who a liberal and who a leftist?'[15]

However, Razvozzhayev's allegations made barely a ripple among ordinary Russians, most of whom were desensitized after decades of state terror.

Two days later, when his lawyer was finally allowed to visit him, Razvozzhayev retracted his confession. Investigators were unfazed. 'If Razvozzhayev or his supporters believe his testimony is key to this case, then I have bad news for them – we have plenty of other evidence,' said Markin, the Investigative Committee's increasingly busy spokesperson.[16]

Over the next few months, in a litany of allegations that grew more and more outlandish, investigators would accuse Razvozzhayev of illegally crossing the border with Ukraine, slander (by now a criminal offence) over his torture claims and, bizarrely, robbing a businessman of 500 fur hats in his east Siberian hometown of Angarsk in 1997. The last of these charges saw Razvozzhayev shipped off to Siberia in late December 2012, even though the statute of limitations on the case had expired. His lawyers expressed fears the activist could be tortured or even murdered in the far-off prisons of eastern Russia.

'They are trying to get him to confess again, to implicate Udaltsov and other protest leaders,' said a near-hysterical Vyacheslav Ivanets, Razvozzhayev's lawyer, when I called him in Siberia. 'They have special rooms here where hardened inmates torture or even kill fellow prisoners on the orders of prison staff.' Frequently denied access to his client, Ivanets was clearly distressed by the situation. 'Sorry if I seem over-emotional,' he said. 'But it's terrible what's going on here. They are doing all they can to break Leonid.'[17]

After almost four months in Siberia, Razvozzhayev was finally returned to Moscow in March 2013. His appearance in court shocked his supporters. Gaunt and drawn, his hair having begun to grey, the leftist activist compared his experience in the prisons and holding cells of east Siberia to the infamous US detention facilities Abu Ghraib and Guantanamo Bay 'put together'.

'Beatings and humiliations, as well as complete disregard for the law, are far from a complete list of the ways they tried to get me to confess,' he told a court hearing. 'Even though I'm an atheist, I began to pray. And, to be honest, I think it was only this that got me through.'[18]

A KREMLIN AGENT?

In March 2013, in a development that shocked opposition activists, the third suspect in the case, Konstantin Lebedev, filed a guilty plea. He would also, his lawyer said, be testifying against his former 'comrades' – Udaltsov and Razvozzhayev. A trial was quickly arranged, and Lebedev was sentenced to two and a half years in a penal colony.

'I wasn't tortured,' said Lebedev, who had grown a bushy, Tolkienesque beard while in custody. 'I admitted organizing the mass riots on May 6, 2012 with Udaltsov, Razvozzhayev and Targamadze. I also confessed to organizing future unrest with them. I don't feel like a traitor. The people involved in this knew the scale of things – they also knew the possible scale of the consequences.'

One of the potential acts of sabotage discussed by the figures in the NTV video was the bombing of the Trans-Siberian railway, the train journey so beloved of Western travellers looking for adventure in Mother Russia. 'Of course, there was no possibility at all of blowing up the Trans-Siberian,' Lebedev said in a courtroom interview. 'But you have to understand that Razvozzhayev is a very impatient guy. He was unhappy that he was living off his wife. He always wanted to become a professional revolutionary, so that he wouldn't have to think about business and his relatives would get off his back. He grew convinced that he needed to play the Georgians for their money. He wanted to seem crazier than he really was.'[19]

Lebedev's testimony gave rise to speculation that he was a Kremlin agent who had infiltrated the new left.

There was no proof that Lebedev was working for the authorities. But his background was extremely suspicious. A former member of the pro-Putin youth movement Walking Together, Lebedev had been press secretary for the group – which specialized in destroying books by 'immoral' authors – from 2001 to 2004. He then apparently experienced a complete transformation in his political views, going over to the opposition just in time to take part in Ukraine's Orange Revolution.

Intrigued, I dug into Lebedev's past. But, with the security services reportedly trailing protest figures, no one would say much. 'Look, this is a very dangerous subject right now,' a leftist activist told me. 'No one is going to speak about it.'

Another activist, from the liberal wing of the opposition, confided that she had seen evidence that Lebedev had regularly reported to the pro-Kremlin youth movement's leader Vasily Yakemenko. Again, there was no solid proof of this.

Udaltsov continued to maintain that he had never met Targamadze. But his allies in the protest movement were increasingly of the opinion that Lebedev had introduced the Left Front leader to the Georgian politician with the aim of getting him to incriminate himself on tape.

'I am certain that Lebedev was an agent from the beginning,' said Navalny. 'He carried out the role he was sent to do. He brought Udaltsov and Razvozzhayev to the meeting with Targamadze and recorded it all himself.

'It was a political trap – some crazy and incomprehensible Georgian muttering some nonsense about blowing up the Trans-Sib. What was Udaltsov supposed to do? Run out of the room in a panic?'[20]

The story later took another unexpected twist when Georgia's outgoing president, Mikheil Saakashvili, admitted that he had ordered Targamadze to meet up with the activists in both Belarus and Lithuania. The purpose of the meeting, Saakashvili told the US-based BuzzFeed website, was to encourage a 'colour revolution' in Russia. But he strongly denied funding any coup attempt. Top Saakashvili allies confirmed the conversation in Minsk had taken place, but said there had been no talk whatsoever of violent insurrection. All Targamadze had done, they said, was to ask the activists to smear a kind of catnip on the walls of the FSB headquarters in Moscow, so that stray cats would swarm over the building. Lebedev had also spoken of this bizarre plan in his courtroom interview. Targamadze, however, continued to deny ever meeting the leftist activists, and expressed surprise at Saakashvili's comments. It was a development that created almost as many questions as answers.[21]

The protest movement was consumed by conspiracy theories, suspicions and in-fighting. As the autumn of 2012 turned into winter, the atmosphere grew darker: activists who had once been happy to talk began to watch their every word, and fears of phone-tapping and police surveillance were widespread. Nerves were frayed and tempers short. Later that winter, Udaltsov came to blows with supporters of Eduard Limonov, trading punches on a patch of snowy ground. If the initial anti-Putin protests had triggered wild euphoria, the Kremlin's crackdown was like a nervy, slow comedown off a brief but joyous trip. It was payback time.

In February 2013, Udaltsov was placed under strict house arrest, without access to a telephone or the internet, after the authorities said he had breached the terms of his release from custody by continuing to organize illegal demonstrations. It was the first time the Russian authorities had imposed such a punishment on a protest leader, suggesting that the Kremlin had been paying attention to events in China, where the tactic was commonly employed by Beijing to stifle dissenters. Udaltsov was able to keep his online presence alive via messages passed on to and posted online by his supporters, some of whom were arrested after gathering outside his apartment on his thirty-sixth birthday. But his physical absence from the protests was noticeable: things were far less, to use one of Udaltsov's favourite terms, 'hardcore'.

'I'm getting some bad ideas behind these four walls,' Udaltsov told a judge at a rare public appearance that summer, as his lawyers unsuccessfully appealed for an end to his house arrest. 'I was going to write a letter to Putin, but what's the point?' The hearing over, Udaltsov was marched out of the courtroom and hurried past waiting supporters. Turning back briefly, he rasped, 'Stay strong! Don't give up!' And then he was gone.

THE COLLAPSE

The charges against Udaltsov were just part of the protest movement's agonies. As the Kremlin's clampdown gained pace, disillusionment and despair reigned. In late 2012, on the first anniversary of the landmark mass rally that kick-started the anti-Putin movement, some 5,000 demonstrators gathered for an illegal protest near the FSB headquarters in central Moscow. 'Winter go away!' they chanted, but there was little sign of a thaw in sight. I watched as protest leaders were picked off one by one as their followers gathered around the Solovetsky Stone, a monument to the millions of victims of Soviet-era repression. A hard core of activists stayed until the very end, scrapping it out with police in the snow and ice before they too were dragged away. There would, of course, be more protests after this one, but, for now at least, the authorities had won. No one was dreaming of revolution in Russia anymore. The talk was almost exclusively about getting out.

In Khimki, protest leader Yevgenia Chirikova had unsuccessfully run for mayor of the city, her bid in part spoiled by a rival campaign by a bizarre Kremlin-backed trash rocker named Spider, who loudly accused her of being a US agent. But, despite the smears and inevitable vote-rigging, it was clear, from conversations with locals and early opinion polls that Chirikova would have lost anyway.

Perhaps, though, she was lucky she had failed. In mid-2013, Yevgeny Urlashov, the opposition-friendly mayor of Yaroslavl, a city north-east of Moscow, was pulled from his car 'by the scruff of his neck' by masked police when his car stopped at a roadblock late at night.[22] He was charged the next morning with soliciting around a million dollars in bribes. Urlashov, who had abandoned United Russia to join the protest movement in the wake of the election protests, was elected by a landslide in 2012 after independent vote monitors had swarmed into the city to ensure a fair vote. He now faces up to fifteen years in jail on charges that he and his supporters say are politically motivated and a warning – yet another – to the Kremlin's opponents. For those members of the protest movement who had argued against the growing radicalism, it was a slap in the face and a wake-up call. 'The arrest of Urlashov showed once again that it is impossible to reform the system from within,' said Ilya Yashin, the opposition activist. 'Real reform requires the removal of Putin from power.'

The Kremlin's tactics were hardly new, though; Urlashov may have been the most high-profile mayor to go down, but more than fifty non-United Russia mayors from small towns had been forced from office and jailed after being charged with crimes between 2008 and 2012, the golden era of Medvedev's 'liberalism'.[23]

Pro-Putin officials had urged Russians unhappy with the way the country was being run to participate in the electoral process instead of taking to the streets, but it is becoming increasingly unclear how they are supposed to do that. Four days after Urlashov was detained, the Navalny-backed People's Alliance party, headed by former top banker Vladimir Ashurkov, was denied the registration that would have allowed it to take part in elections.

'It's already stupid to hope,' wrote journalist Catherina Gordeeva, in a much-discussed article. 'We, with all our hopes, have lost.'[24]

Just days after the publication of Gordeeva's article, an organization in south Russia called Social Justice began collecting signatures for a petition calling for Navalny, Udaltsov and other opposition figures to be stripped of their citizenship and exiled from Russia. 'We do not need traitors!' an angry middle-aged woman declared. Another, not content with deportation, called for them all to be shot.[25]

One of the most popular songs at the 2011–12 protests was 'Change' by the Soviet rock group Kino. 'Our hearts demand change, our eyes demand change, and in our laughter and in our tears, in the pulsing of our veins, we are waiting for change!' went the song's lyrics, penned by the group's iconic vocalist, Viktor Tsoi.

'Yes, changes took place,' Oleg Kashin, the journalist beaten during Medvedev's one-term presidency, noted bitterly. 'Just not the ones that people were dreaming about.'[26]

It was another Tsoi lyric that perhaps better summed up the dark aftermath of the protests: 'I knew things would turn out bad, but I didn't know so soon.'

15

THE PEOPLE'S WRATH

The protest movement may have been cracking up under relentless Kremlin pressure, but the discontent that inspired its challenge to Putin's rule was going nowhere. Regional issues – economic, environmental and social – continued to stir up dissent in the country's provinces. Massive increases in payments for housing utilities triggered demonstrations in central and north Russia in the spring of 2013, signalling new dangers for the authorities.

Around the same time, I began to hear reports of rising tensions in central Russia's fertile Black Earth region, known for centuries as the country's 'breadbasket', where locals were unhappy about a Kremlin-backed nickel-mining project. The dispute was a classic example of the arrogance and intransigence of Russian officials when faced with popular discontent. Opinion polls had indicated that 98% of locals were against the extraction project,[1] which they feared would prove catastrophic for both their health and local agriculture. A series of well-attended protests had even made national news. But regional officials – let alone the Kremlin – were not listening. Appeals for a referendum on the proposed mining had been stonewalled and the activists had – predictably – been subject to a smear campaign that painted them as Western agents seeking to spark unrest. Their homes had also been raided by police and FSB agents.

The fears that nickel would bring disaster to the area were well founded. Nickel extraction has blighted towns and cities across Russia, most notably north Siberia's Norilsk, which has been transformed by nickel-ore smelting into one of the most polluted places on Earth,[2] with life expectancies some ten years lower than Russia's already unenviable average of sixty-nine (and just sixty-four for men).[3]

I had ties with the area: it was in the region's biggest city, Voronezh, that I had first met my wife, Tanya. As the year went on, we started to hear more and more from friends and acquaintances about the resistance to the project. One of the leaders of the Black Earth protest movement was Konstantin Rubakhin, a thirty-seven-year-old poet and former Channel One analyst, who had spent part of his childhood in a tiny, picturesque village in the region; his family still owned a home there.

'News about the project was a massive shock,' Rubakhin, tall, fair-haired and dressed all in black, told me when I met him at Masterskaya, a club-cum-café tucked just out of sight of the Kremlin's walls. It was here that activists had organized election protests in the delirious winter and spring of 2011 and 2012. 'I'd been living away from the area for over ten years,' he went on, 'but I immediately returned to help fight against the project.' Rubakhin was all too aware of the risks of environmental activism in Russia. 'I've taken steps to defend myself,' he told me, flashing a traumatic pistol, a handgun that shoots rubber bullets at high velocities. Like Razvozzhayev, the Left Front member abducted by the security forces in Kiev, Rubakhin was also an aide to the leftist lawmaker Ilya Ponomarev. But he was reluctant to link the discontent simmering over the nickel-extraction project with the anti-Kremlin demonstrations that had rocked Moscow.

'What's going on in the Black Earth region is something else, completely different,' he told me, raising his voice over the music at the club as he repocketed his weapon.[4]

WE USED TO SEE ALL THOSE PEOPLE MARCHING IN MOSCOW...

A week after meeting Rubakhin in Moscow, I took an overnight train to the Black Earth region, where he met me on an icy platform before driving me to see the woman who had helped spearhead the anti-nickel campaign. 'Nickel brings death,' said Nelly Rudchenko, a jolly fifty-something housewife who sold headscarves for a living. We sat in her chaotic yet cosy home in the village of Novokhopyorsk (population 6,849). 'This is the heart of Russia, and these people are going to kill it,' she told me, pronouncing her words with the soft 'g' of the region. As we spoke, her husband brought us a hearty breakfast and Rubakhin, who had been up all night planning the eco-activists' next move, snored away loudly on a couch. 'This land is our richest resource and they have no right to destroy it for some nickel,' she said, spitting out the name of the metal with a sudden anger. 'But this is all the influence of the West, which teaches people to live for today, and not to care about the future.'[5]

Rubakhin was right when he said that the dissent triggered by the nickel project was far removed from the Moscow-based white-ribbon movement, but there was a growing understanding among the Black Earth activists of the motives of the anti-Putin protesters. For Rudchenko, and many other locals, the nickel project had radicalized their political views, breaking the spell cast by state-controlled television. 'We all used to watch the Zombie box and hear all these wonderful things that our leaders say,' she smiled, appropriating the anti-Putin movement's disparaging nickname for Kremlin-backed television. Her husband nodded in agreement. 'When we first saw all these people marching in Moscow against Putin, we were amazed. "Why would they do that?" But, when we started to face our own problems here, we quickly began to understand. We know now that the authorities have no respect for the people.'

The Black Earth protests might have been directed specifically against the nickel project, rather than the Kremlin, but these were encouraging signs for the anti-Putin movement's leaders. Not that they showed much interest in getting involved besides the occasional retweet of Rubakhin's updates. One exception was eco-activist Chirikova, who paid a visit to the region to support the nickel protesters. 'It's very easy to get people to take action when their health, the health of their children is threatened,' she told me, back in Moscow. 'It's harder to get them involved when it concerns more abstract concepts, even like vote fraud. And that's entirely understandable.'

The experiences of the Black Earth region protesters were similar to those Chirikova had gone through while battling the Kremlin-backed highway. She had also spent months writing letters of complaint, before realizing that only direct action would make a difference. It also took Chirikova time to understand the link between her local problem and the wider implications of Putin's rule. It was a connection the Black Earth activists had yet to make.

FSB officers had recently turned up at Rudchenko's modest home, rifling through her boxes of headscarf material in search of evidence, after an official was slightly injured in a scuffle with activists. 'Of course, I never in my life thought I'd have my house searched by the FSB,' she said, smiling. 'My family has roots here that stretch back centuries. We have always lived peacefully and quietly. The 1917 Bolshevik Revolution, World War II, the split-up of the Soviet Union, these events had hardly any impact on our way of life, And now this nickel is going to destroy us all.'

Rubakhin's house deep in the countryside had also been searched. 'My father told me this was actually the fourth time our house here has been raided since it was built,' the Moscow-based activist said with a wry smile. 'The other three times were by the KGB.'

The spread of the internet had, inevitably, played a major role in fomenting this unexpected dissent in Russia's conservative heartland. 'Before, we would all have been isolated from one another, with no way of finding out if what they said on television was true,' Rudchenko said. She gestured towards a computer underneath a religious icon. 'Now almost every home in the village is linked to the internet. This makes it easy to organize ourselves.'

THE CURSE OF NICKEL

We drove deep into the countryside, towards the site of the planned mining project, already cordoned off and guarded round the clock by security guards employed by UMMC, the mining company that had won the Kremlin's tender for extraction rights. I had slept badly on the train and the motion of the vehicle and the pale sunlight streaming through the car window lulled me to sleep. Rubakhin woke me from my doze to point out a nature reserve threatened by the nickel project. Huge bison had once roamed the sprawling Khoper Reserve, but it was an extremely rare breed of water mammal called the Russian desman that activists were now trying to protect. 'The mentality of the local administration is just amazing,' Rubakhin laughed. 'I told an official any nickel mining in the region would kill the Russian desman off, and he said, "What do you want to worry about those animals for, anyway? There are hardly any of them left."'

The Black Earth region's Cossacks, descendants of the fierce horse-men who once guarded Tsarist-era Russia's borders, were among the most vocal opponents of the nickel project. A group of them had been camped out in the area since the start of the year, keeping watch over the land. It was these Cossacks who erected a massive cross to 'protect' the countryside from what one of them described to me as the 'curse' of nickel, after an order by the Orthodox Church barred local priests from becoming involved with the protests. 'Churches round here really started to empty after that,' Rudchenko told me, as we walked slowly towards the metal cross, with snow falling in large, powdery flakes. A white-bearded Orthodox priest would later bless the nickel-extraction site on behalf of the UMMC mining company, sprinkling holy water over excavators.

Around a hundred anti-nickel protesters – including elderly women, Cossacks in uniform and activists from across the political spectrum – had gathered at the remote site, many of them carrying religious icons and singing hymns. 'The Cossacks are in the vanguard of the struggle, as it has always been in Russia,' bellowed the Cossack leader, or *ataman*, a tall, fair-haired man with a weather-beaten face. 'They thought they could fool us, but you can't fool the people.'

The crowd began to mutter, suddenly displeased. Had the *ataman* said something out of place? But no. The object of their sudden discontent was far across the frozen fields. From the road opposite, a figure dressed all in black had been filming participants for a good ten minutes before driving off. 'FSB,' whispered someone behind me, as the protesters made their way across the field to confront UMMC's security guards. 'What will you do when the mining starts and we come here to stop it?' a plump, middle-aged woman asked a security guard, as she threw dog hair and salt on to the cordoned-off land. ('It's a spell! Witchcraft!' she told me, with a wink.) 'Will you shoot us?'

The head of security, stocky with a drooping moustache, shook his head. 'No,' he said, 'of course not.'

The woman was overjoyed. 'Well, thank God for that!' she said, and clapped.

The brief confrontation over, the activists tramped back across the snowy fields. I caught up with the *ataman*, whose name I had found out was Igor Zhitenyev. In the immediate aftermath of the anti-Putin protests in Moscow, as part of its bid to reach out to the conservative heartland, the Kremlin encouraged a Cossack revival across Russia. Cossacks began patrolling a number of Russian cities on the lookout for illegal immigrants and other wrong-doers. They also took part in raids on art galleries and theatres deemed to have displayed 'blasphemous' material. But historically the Cossacks' relationship with the authorities is a complicated one: these free spirits may have helped the tsar's troops to suppress peasant revolts brutally, but they also boast a proud tradition of rebellion and non-compliance. Indeed, as the anti-nickel Cossacks proudly informed me, the eighteenth-century Cossack rebel leader Kondraty Bulavin once hid out with his followers in the nearby Khoper woods. 'We shall die as one rather than remain silent before the wicked deeds of evil men,' Bulavin had declared.

His modern-day counterparts were equally defiant. 'The authorities have sold out the people,' Zhitenyev told me as he and his Cossacks walked away from the drilling site. 'I was speaking to local administration officials recently and I told them: "The people are against the extraction of nickel." "What people?" they laughed. "You lot aren't the people."

'But if we aren't the people, then who is?' the Cossack leader asked, clearly baffled 'We are a simple people, we don't need much. Those officials steal and build themselves mansions, and we always just thought, "Ah, to hell with them," and got on with our lives. But now they are even threatening our way of life. And our lives.

'I really don't know what's going to happen if they start mining here,' he went on. 'Lots of people say, "I'd give my life to stop the nickel. At least then I won't have to feel ashamed in front of my kids after they destroy the land."'[6]

A PRECEDENT FOR THE WHOLE COUNTRY?

Back in the village of Novokhopyorsk, activists gathered at a makeshift HQ in a local house to discuss further tactics. The fussy housewives, potbellied market traders and middle-aged Cossacks sitting around a table laden with sausage, vodka and fruit were a far cry from the Moscow hipsters at the heart of anti-Putin protests in the Russian capital. Significantly, though, one thing the Black Earth activists had in common with the Putin movement was the presence of nationalist and far-right elements among its ranks. 'There are people in our eco-movement who believe all that Kremlin propaganda, that the anti-Putin demonstrations are funded by the US State Department, and so on,' Rubakhin admitted, with a grimace.

Anti-Semitic slogans were also common at anti-nickel rallies. 'They were shouting "Kill the Jews *and* the Yids!" at a recent protest,' one of the handful of liberal activists in the movement told me later. 'It's a real dilemma for me to attend such events,' he said. 'On one hand, I'm against any nickel mining, but, on the other hand, do I really want anything to do with such people?'

Concerns that the authorities would launch a violent crackdown were ever present among the activists. As more than one person had pointed out to me, it was only 300 miles or so from the region that in 1962 Red Army troops had shot dead more than twenty striking factory workers in the city of Novocherkassk. Details of the massacre only became public after the collapse of the Soviet Union. (It would not have done for a 'workers state' to be seen to be gunning down workers.) 'We've got nothing to be worried about,' declared Rudchenko, perhaps a little too insistently. 'They are not going to shoot us. We've got the internet and everything today. They wouldn't dare.' She turned to me and smiled: 'Eat up!'

While the activists admitted that UMMC was unlikely to back down over the project, unless nickel prices fell, many of them were pinning their hopes on Putin seizing the chance to make himself look good in the region. And there was precedent for a presidential about-turn. In 2006, after local protests, Putin ordered changes to the planned route of an oil pipeline set to pass close to Siberia's Lake Baikal, the world's deepest body of fresh water. But not everyone was optimistic that history was about to repeat itself.

'What do you think?' asked Oksana, a middle-aged housewife turned activist, as I set off the next morning to catch my bus. 'Do we have a chance of stopping the project?'

I told her that, if they could bring the issue to wider public attention, and get public opinion on their side, then they had every chance of forcing a U-turn. After all, I assured her, Russia's fragile democracy may be 'managed', but the authorities are still relatively sensitive to public opinion. Oksana wasn't convinced. 'I'm not sure,' she sighed, as she tidied up the dishes and bottles left over from another night of heated eco-debate. 'Maybe, if Putin was different. But he's so stubborn. We all know he really hates to be seen to back down.'

The violence that the Black Earth activists had so consistently predicted finally erupted in June 2013. After a demonstration in the village of Novokhopyorsk, some thousand protesters, headed by Cossacks bearing religious icons, made the long trek to UMMC's on-site drilling equipment. Once there, they simply tore down fences that had been erected to protect the expensive machinery and set it alight. Police and security guards scattered. Huge plumes of smoke bellowed into the pale-blue sky as protesters trailed away from the site. Months of peaceful protest had brought little or no result whatsoever, but what Rubakhin called the 'people's wrath' led swiftly to a pledge from the authorities to investigate the legality of the nickel project. 'Russians are a very patient people,' the Cossack leader Zhitenyev had told me, before the assault on the mining site. 'But, when they lose hope, there's no telling what they will do.'

It was a scenario that had been played out many times in Russia's long history, from the ultra-violence of nineteenth-century peasant uprisings to the vigilante youths – the 'Primorsky Partisans' – who launched a spectacular war of terror against what they called corrupt and criminal police officers in Russia's Far East in 2010.[7] 'What has happened today in the Black Earth region could act as a precedent for the whole country,' predicted an opposition journalist in an online report as UMMC's machinery burned. He could barely disguise his excitement.[8]

Tensions had exploded in the Black Earth. In Moscow, they were building once more. All eyes in the protest movement were on a small town in central Russia where Navalny was fighting for both his freedom and his political future. Putin's crackdown was continuing. Another show trial was under way.[9]

16

END OF THE LINE FOR NAVALNY?

Navalny, flanked by his wife, Yulia, and the towering man-mountain of a bodyguard who had accompanied him almost everywhere since the onset of the protests, jumped off the train onto the platform in Kirov, the small town in central Russia where he was alleged to have embezzled half a million dollars. It was 17 April 2013, the first day in a trial that would determine exactly how far the Kremlin was willing to go in its crackdown against the protest movement. Few failed to note that the trial was to take place in a city named after Sergei Kirov, the Bolshevik whose 1934 assassination was used by Stalin as a pretext for the start of his Great Terror.

'I feel great!' an assured Navalny told the scrum of waiting journalists, many of whom, like myself, had travelled from Moscow on the same overnight train. He then strode off, journalists and film crews in tow, for the nearby courthouse, newly painted that week for the high-profile trial. Navalny might have exuded confidence, but his wife looked tense, lost in her thoughts. 'He's doing all this for us, for me and my children,' she had declared before the journey to Kirov, smiling weakly. 'I've never once asked him to stop.'[1]

Navalny had worked in Kirov for a number of months in 2009, having been invited to the city by the governor Nikita Belykh, a young liberal politician installed by Medvedev. According to investigators, Navalny had abused his position as Belykh's unpaid aide to pressure officials at a state-run timber company, Kirovles, to sell timber at knockdown prices to a company owned by a business associate named Pyotr Ofitserov, who was also set to stand trial. It was a complex case, made even more so by its apparent lack of logic. As both Navalny and a host of independent legal experts pointed out, Ofitserov's company had bought 14.5 million roubles worth of timber and sold it for 16 million. How then could anyone have embezzled 16 million roubles? Investigators had offered no explanation in the indictment as to how they had come up with the figure. 'They just plucked it from thin air,' Navalny said to journalists in Kirov after the opening court session. He also joked that he would give some free timber to anyone who could make head or tail of the prosecution's case.

One of his lawyers, Vadim Kobzev, was even more bemused, when I spoke to him before the trial. 'What does it mean he pressured Kirovles to sell the timber for an unfavourable price? Aren't negotiations over prices what capitalism is all about?' Just like at the Pussy Riot trial, it was *Alice in Wonderland* logic again.[2]

Navalny had been offered one last chance to co-operate with the Kremlin, when an offer was made via intermediaries in late 2012 to drop the charges in return for a pledge to stay away from street protests. But he refused to enter into negotiations and made a point of attending the unsanctioned rally outside the FSB headquarters in December 2012.[3] 'Am I going tomorrow?' he had asked ahead of the rally in a defiant blog post. 'Why, of course I am.'[4]

Putin denied that the charges were politically motivated. 'Those who fight corruption must be crystal clean themselves,' he declared.[5] He did not, however, mention Navalny by name. In fact, the president had not yet once uttered the protest leader's surname. Was he being superstitious? Or was he simply worried about lending him an air of legitimacy?

WAKING UP KIROV

Navalny's supporters had travelled to Kirov in the days before the trial, and set up a makeshift headquarters on a street opposite – appropriately enough – a Stalin-era anti-corruption HQ. By the time the protest leader arrived in town, they were already gathered for a noisy rally outside the courtroom, shocking bleary-eyed locals with their cries of 'Putin is a thief' and 'Russia without Putin!'

Nikolai Lyaskin, a long-time activist involved with the Khimki forest campaign, urged the people of Kirov to 'show some courage'. 'This is your city!' he yelled into a megaphone. But Kirov was largely indifferent to Navalny's plight; despite the posters and stickers that activists had plastered across town, on bus stops, lamp posts and benches, few people knew – or cared – much about what was going on. Nowhere was the gulf between the protest movement and the majority of provincial Russians greater or more obvious than on that sunny April morning. 'I kind of hoped more people would turn up,' Lyaskin said, shrugging despondently, after police had ordered him to turn off his megaphone.

The crowd outside the court was not only made up of journalists and Navalny supporters. There were also some two dozen members of a pro-Kremlin youth group, many chanting 'a thief belongs in jail!' the phrase Putin had used to justify the imprisonment of the oil tycoon Khodorkovsky, who by 2013 had spent a decade in prison.

It was, as the Russians say, 'only the lazy' who had failed to note the similarities between the two men's cases. Both had threatened to loosen the Kremlin's stranglehold on power, and both had been hit with trumped-up fraud charges. But even Khodorkovsky, who had reportedly incensed Putin with his funding of political parties, had not offered such a direct challenge to the authorities as Navalny. And, while the oligarch had transformed himself into an anti-regime martyr while behind bars, his 2003 arrest was generally popular, even among future members of the protest movement. Navalny's prosecution had far more potential to damage the authorities, with deep splits reported among the political elite as to the wisdom of any custodial sentence.

A handful of elderly women had also been drawn to the commotion outside the court. 'They can't say things like that about the president,' one of them, a grey haired pensioner called Vera, told me, shaking her head. 'They should be ashamed of themselves.'

I wandered over to the increasingly noisy pro-Putin activists, many of whom were, despite their frenzied chanting, covering their faces with placards and refusing to speak to the media. 'They've all been paid to come out here and shout their vileness,' a Navalny supporter laughed. 'Of course they are embarrassed.'

One of those who agreed to chat, a young, dark-haired student who gave his name as Yevgeny, told me he wanted to see Navalny go to prison because the money he was suspected of stealing could have been used to 'do up' the city's notoriously bad roads. 'I'm not interested in Navalny's claims that Putin and his associates are corrupt,' he sneered, apparently sincere. 'I realize Russia sells a lot of oil and gas, but I don't care what happens to that money. It's not my business.'

I later repeated Yevgeny's complaint to a middle-aged taxi driver. 'Of course,' he laughed, as we juddered into and out of a pothole. 'Navalny is totally to blame for these fucking roads. You know, I don't think there have been any repairs to the roads here since before World War II. When was that Navalny born?'

✳

Navalny may have tried to project confidence as he stepped off the train in Kirov, but, in truth, he sensed the dragnet closing around him. Many of his financial backers had withdrawn their support in the face of Kremlin pressure, while others, like Alexander Lebedev, the London-based tycoon and joint owner of the *Novaya Gazeta* newspaper, were facing politically motivated criminal charges of their own.

'Man is weak. People are afraid. I can't expect each of them to be some kind of heroic person,' Navalny told the *New York Times* of his trial, sitting in the Moscow office where his staff had recently discovered a snooping device.[6]

Other supporters had been forced to flee Russia by a campaign of intimidation. The most high profile, Sergei Guriev, a highly regarded, US-educated economist who had advised Medvedev's administration, abruptly left Russia for France in May 2013 after investigators had questioned him over a report he had written for the Kremlin's human-rights council on the Khodorkovsky case. Guriev, whose report concluded that the second set of charges against the tycoon should be dropped, denied allegations he had received money from Khodorkovsky or anyone connected to him. But his real crime, he and many others believed, was making a symbolic donation of some $300 to Navalny's anti-corruption fund. Fearing imminent arrest, the middle-aged, bespectacled economist jumped on the next available flight to Paris, where his wife and children had been living for the past three years.

Guriev was no rabble-rousing protest leader, no radical activist calling for Putin's overthrow. He was a well-respected professor who had earned international recognition for his work as rector of Moscow's New Economic School. He was, in short, the kind of person Russia badly needed. His sudden departure, one blogger wrote, triggered 'a sense of imminent catastrophe'.[7]

'An informed person told me there is a list of friends of Navalny and there is a special operation against those people — and I am on the list,' Guriev told me by telephone once he was safe in France. 'Some of my high-ranking friends told me that as long as there is a special operation — a very important term in modern Russia — they will not be able to find out anything about this and they will not be able to help me. I have done nothing wrong and I do not want to live in fear.'

Guriev laughed dryly when I asked him if he saw his persecution as symbolic of the darkening political mood in Russia. 'Medvedev asked me to speak publicly on the Khodorkovsky case,' he said. 'When Putin came back to power, I am being interrogated about this. It's pretty clear.'[8]

Following Guriev's departure, both Garry Kasparov, the chess champ turned protest leader, and Masha Gessen, a high-profile opposition journalist, declared that they, too, would be staying out of the country until the political climate improved.

Not everyone was convinced it would. 'Nothing will ever change,' Oleg Kashin, the protest figure and journalist, had written miserably. 'Everything will be exactly the same as it is now and was a year ago and a hundred years ago. And, if there is a difference between "then" and "now" and "tomorrow", then it is purely cosmetic.'

I WANT TO BECOME PRESIDENT

Ahead of the trial, Navalny issued his biggest challenge yet to Putin. 'I want to become president,' he said in an interview with TV Dozhd. 'I want to change life in the country. I want to change the way it is ruled. I want to do things so that the 140 million people who live in this country, who have oil and gas coming out of the ground, do not live in poverty or dark squalor and live normally like in a European country.'[9]

The announcement immediately upped the stakes. It was one thing to jail an anti-corruption blogger who belonged to no political party; locking up a potential presidential candidate was another matter altogether. A few weeks later, Navalny also declared he would stand in mayoral elections in Moscow in September 2013; that is, of course, if he could get on the ballot.

There was little doubt that Navalny would be found guilty of the charges against him: the man set to preside over the trial, Sergei Blinov, a softly spoken, baby-faced regional judge, had handled 130 cases in his career, with exactly zero acquittals. The head of the Kirov court, Konstantin Zaytsev, was upfront about the likelihood of a guilty verdict, explaining that Russia's judicial system was so 'effective' that only watertight cases came to court. Why, he recalled, he himself, in a career that stretched back decades, had only once acquitted a suspect. And even that ruling was later overturned.[10] It made one wonder, really, why they were bothering with the trial in the first place.

The only uncertainty was this: would the authorities imprison Navalny or hand him a suspended sentence? 'It's either the Belarus model, where they simply lock everyone up,' said Yashin, the activist and long-time Navalny ally, when I met him ahead of the trial. 'Or the Chinese model, where they put people under house arrest or slap them with suspended sentences.'[11]

Under Russian law, a criminal conviction of any kind would bar Navalny from ever running for public office. The 'Chinese model' would also be likely to soften international criticism of his prosecution, and prevent him becoming a martyr for the protest movement. 'If they jail Navalny, he will become a Russian Nelson Mandela,' opposition figure Boris Nemtsov told me. 'It's that simple.'[12]

The authorities had not even attempted to hide the political nature of the charges. 'If a person tries with all his might to draw attention to himself, even, you might say, tries to taunt the authorities – says, "Look at me, you're all covered in dirt and I'm so clean" – well, then the interest in his past increases, and the process of exposing him naturally accelerates,' said the Investigative Committee's increasingly influential spokesperson, Markin, who was widely believed to be voicing Putin's opinions. He also suggested Navalny would be able to continue his fight against corruption from 'a penal colony' and mocked the Western forces he said had 'prepared' the activist to take over in Russia. 'They mixed Russia up with Georgia or some other Third World country,' Markin seethed. 'But Russia is a world power.'[13]

The verdict was just part of the story: by charging Navalny with corruption, the authorities had thrown the dirt he had dug up back in his face, associating him in the minds of the public with the corrupt officials he had sought to expose. A much-vaunted Kremlin campaign against corruption had also co-opted Navalny's raison d'être; state-controlled TV had taken to airing hysterical exposés of officials accused of demanding bribes and kickbacks. Opposition activists dismissed the campaign as a sham: indeed, its most high-profile victim, Defence Minister Anatoly Serdyukov, may have been fired over allegations of massive corruption at the ministry, but he was charged merely with 'negligence', an offence punishable by a maximum of three months behind bars.[14] Few believed the ex-minister would do time. Shortly after his dismissal, Serdyukov took up a new, highly paid post at Rostekhnologii, the state hi-tech corporation.

'It's very important for them that they can mention me and corruption in the same sentence every night on the news,' Navalny said to journalists in Kirov, clearly affronted by the Kremlin's tactics.

And Putin's plan was working. 'Navalny? Isn't he some official who stole a load of money from the budget? Like they all do?' said a giggly twenty-something woman called Svetlana when I carried out a random survey of passers-by on the first day of the trial in Kirov.

'He was in the governor's team, right?' opined Kirill, a middle-aged man with a bald patch just like Lenin's. 'That means he's corrupt.'

Others had no opinion whatsoever. 'I've got enough worries getting money for my medicine and what have you every month,' said an elderly woman in a purple hat. 'And you want me to worry about some Navalny?'

THE TRIAL

The trial dragged on through the summer, the incessant message 'Navalny – corruption' drummed into the heads of state TV's massive audience by one-sided news reports. The authorities had refused to have court proceedings moved to Moscow, Navalny's stronghold, and – predictably – both his supporters and journalists began to turn up at court less and less often. Even by day five, where once it had been necessary to queue overnight to stand a chance of claiming a place at the 'trial of the year', now it was possible to drift in a few minutes before the start of proceedings. Much of the trial was taken up with the tedious study of case-related documents and the cross-examination of the prosecution's witnesses, not all of whom were able to get their stories entirely straight. A key witness for the prosecution, former Kirovles official Vyacheslav Opalev, who had previously been handed a four-year suspended sentence after he had pleaded guilty to conspiring with Navalny, mixed things up entirely, telling the court that the anti-Putin activist had forced him to sell the timber, rather than colluding with him. When his error was pointed out to him, he covered his face with his hands. 'You are driving me crazy!' he yelled, under cross-examination, triggering laughter from the courtroom.

The prosecution would call almost three dozen witnesses, the majority of whose testimonies appeared to prove that Navalny had done nothing illegal. The cross-examination of the prosecution's witnesses over, Navalny's defence team prepared to call its own. But Judge Blinov was having none of it, and ruled that the court would not be hearing any witnesses for the defence, as it was not clear 'what they could say in the courtroom'.

'I'm in shock,' Navalny responded. 'It was clear they wouldn't allow some. But all of them? How is the defence supposed to operate, if not a single witness is allowed into court?'[15]

A few days later, after the judge had grudgingly allowed a handful of defence witnesses to speak, Navalny 'congratulated' the court on the occasion of what would have been the 130th birthday of Franz Kafka, author of *The Trial*. 'He predicted almost precisely what's going on in this court,' an unsmiling Navalny said.

The very next day, as an activist sat in court reading a newly purchased copy of Kafka's classic novel of unthinking, totalitarian terror, prosecutors requested a six-year jail sentence for Navalny and five years for his co-defendant Pyotr Ofitserov.

Navalny, for once, seemed at a loss for words. 'Everything will be OK,' he said as he stepped outside the courtroom during a break in proceedings, smiling nervously and hugging his wife. But he looked shocked. He had always insisted he was fully aware of the dangers of his uncompromising battle against Putin, but now the abstract threat that had shadowed him through his years of opposition, the heated debates in smoky Moscow clubs, the sensational exposés of multimillion-dollar corruption schemes and the heady street protests was close enough to reach out and seize him. And with many more criminal cases in the pipeline, once he found himself in the brutal, disease-ridden world of the Russian penal system, six years was unlikely to be the limit of his incarceration.

By the time Judge Blinov returned, Navalny had still not regained his usual composure. Standing to address the court, he apologized first to his co-defendant, Ofitserov, and his family. 'Stop torturing this man and his family,' he urged the judge and prosecutors, pausing to collect himself. 'Everybody realizes that Ofitserov is here entirely accidentally… To put a person in prison for an economic crime, a businessman was needed, and Pyotr Ofitserov turned out to be this businessman.'[16]

These were Navalny's 'last words' before sentencing; he had a long tradition of final statements to live up to, from the dissident poet Joseph Brodsky's insistence that God had gifted him his literary abilities and there was nothing the atheist Soviet state could do about it to the defiance of Pussy Riot as they were shipped off to penal colonies.

'If anyone thinks that I or my colleagues will cease our activity because of this trial or the Bolotnaya trials or the many other trials going on all around the country, they are gravely mistaken,' Navalny continued, calmer now, as if soothed by his own rage.

'Some may think that this is not the best place for me to put forward conditions, to make threats or plans for the future – I don't agree. I think this is the best place. And I declare now that I and my colleagues will do everything possible to destroy this feudal regime – to destroy the system of power under which 83% of national wealth belongs to 0.5% of the population.'[17]

It was an uncompromising message, but it was nothing he had not said before. But what, really, was there new to say? Lines had been drawn long ago and both sides were entrenched. There were no converts to be made, no enemies to be turned.

After Navalny had spoken, Ofitserov, who had sat quietly through most of the trial, a pained look on his face, stood to address the court. A chubby father of five facing mounting financial problems, he recalled how he had been offered a deal by investigators. How the authorities had proposed he testify against Navalny in exchange for a suspended sentence, to 'make things easier on himself'. Although, like all normal people, he said, he had no desire to go to jail, he had turned down their offer and the chance of freedom that went with it.

'I don't regret my decision,' Ofitserov went on. 'I believe men should take responsibility for their actions. I mean, one day my children will grow up and ask me about all this. How would I have explained myself to them?'[18] He shrugged sadly and sat down. He had nothing else to say. Judge Blinov, I was not the only one to note, was unable to meet his gaze.

✱

Navalny had jokingly compared the trial in Kirov to a television drama; like all the best examples of the genre, the next episode threw up an unexpected twist. Initially, however, as the court convened again on 18 July 2013, everything seemed to be following the usual scenario. Judge Blinov declared both defendants guilty as charged and jailed Navalny for five years and Ofitserov for four.

'Whatever. Don't get bored without me. And most importantly – don't stay idle,' Navalny tweeted. 'The toad won't chuck himself off the oil pipeline,' he added, using his usual nickname for Putin.

Within minutes of the sentence being handed down, both men were being led away in handcuffs. Navalny looked back at his wife and parents and offered a weak smile. Ofitserov's despairing wife had to be pried away from him by court security.

Reaction in Moscow was swift. Activists had previously made plans for a 'public discussion' of the verdict in Manezhnaya Square, adjacent to the Kremlin. As the news flashed that Navalny and Ofitserov had been sent down, thousands of protesters poured into central Moscow. Police were ready for them, and had blocked off the area. Not to be deterred, demonstrators swarmed over the road and stood in lines many deep outside the State Duma, Russia's parliament. 'Freedom!' they chanted, as passing vehicles hooted their support, and scores of young protesters clambered up on to the windowsills of the State Duma to scrawl anti-Putin graffiti on its walls. The crowd soon swelled to at least 10,000, easily the biggest ever unapproved, spontaneous political demonstration in modern Russian history. 'We want to live in a country that lives by the rule of law, not by the rule of dictatorship,' a young woman said, her dark hair tied back, a 'Navalny' sticker on her T-shirt. Riot police initially seemed unsure of how to react, but, when protesters chanting

'Revolution!' attempted to block a nearby central road to traffic, they moved in to make arrests.

The protest in Moscow that afternoon was a stunning indication of Navalny's popularity among the capital's middle class and younger generations. Many of the protesters were still in their teens, others in their early twenties. No other political figure in Russia had the ability to inspire such a turnout without resorting to the 'rent-a-crowd' tactics employed by Putin in his presidential campaign.

However, not everyone outside the State Duma that afternoon was a Navalny supporter. Many protesters freely admitted that they found his right-wing views off-putting, but had gone to rally against a blatant case of political repression. A five-year jail sentence for a protest leader was a dangerous precedent. 'I went because I'm against locking people up for their political beliefs,' said Isabelle Magkoeva, the leftist activist and bitter Navalny critic who helped set up Moscow's short-lived Occupy camp.

'Like many other people I went to protest against Navalny's jailing because it was a clear example of injustice,' Maria Kuchma, a young graduate student, told me. 'But as a political leader I find Navalny very worrying.'

Elsewhere, things were moving fast. Just hours after Navalny and Ofitserov had been jailed, as demonstrators began to make their way into central Moscow, the prosecutor requested the two men be released on bail pending their appeal. It was an unprecedented move. Things like this simply didn't happen in Russia. Why had the prosecutor originally asked the judge to jail Navalny and Ofitserov without waiting for the result of their appeal if this was, as he now claimed, an infringement of their rights? And anyway, since when had anyone in Russia, least of all the state prosecutor, cared about the law? Well-known lawyer Vadim Klyuvgant even suggested the prosecutor had no legal right to challenge the decision, as he himself had requested it.[19] The prosecutor's about-face was a blatant example of the judiciary's lack of independence. Analysts and legal experts were almost unanimous – someone higher up had called the prosecutor and told him to get Navalny out of jail. 'Putin doesn't like surprises,' Gleb Pavlovsky, the former long-time Kremlin adviser, told me. 'The authorities simply weren't prepared for the size of the crowd outside the State Duma.'

Less than twenty-four hours after they had begun serving their sentences, Navalny and Ofitserov were released on bail. The protest leader couldn't resist a joke, and asked the judge to check if the prosecutor had not perhaps fallen victim to body snatchers. There was, he reasoned, simply no other way to explain the prosecutor's dramatic U-turn.

As the train that brought Navalny back to the capital pulled into north Moscow's Yaroslavl station early on 20 July, the hundreds of supporters who had gathered to meet the opposition leader began to cheer. It might not have been as earthshaking an event as Lenin's arrival by steam train in St Petersburg in 1917, after years in exile, but as Navalny addressed the swelling crowd, it was hard to shake off the sense that a tiny piece of history was being made. 'If it wasn't for you, we wouldn't be standing here,' Navalny said through a megaphone, as wary police looked on. 'We are a massive, powerful force and I'm so glad that we are starting to realize this!'[20] Standing next to him, Ofitserov raised his clenched fist.

Navalny was portraying his release as a triumph for people power. But had Putin really buckled under pressure? Or was there another explanation for the protest leader's unexpected freedom?

'NAVALNY'S WITNESSES'

The day before he was sentenced to five years behind bars, Navalny had managed to get on the ballot for the September 2013 mayoral elections. His release on bail meant he would now be free to participate in his first ever election campaign. Speculation quickly arose that the unprecedented decision to set Navalny free had been taken solely to allow him to run in the polls – and lose. The incumbent mayor, Sergei Sobyanin, a Kremlin-appointed Putin ally from the oil-rich Siberian region of Tyumen, was seeking to legitimize his rule at the ballot box after the return of direct elections for the post (one of the concessions forced by the protest movement). Navalny, he was sure, would make the perfect opponent. After all, with state media and the Moscow city budget at his command, Sobyanin's victory was all but assured. The white-haired mayor was even genuinely popular with large sections of the city's voters for his efforts at transforming Moscow into a comfortable urban environment, including the revamping of city parks. So why not boost his own status with a resounding election win over the biggest thorn in the Kremlin's side? A humiliating defeat for the protest movement's brightest star would also deal a damaging blow to its claims to represent the Russian people. Indeed, Sobyanin was so keen to have Navalny run that he instructed district councillors to approve the protest leader's participation – thereby ensuring he overcame the so-called Kremlin filter designed to keep inconvenient candidates away from elections.

Navalny flatly rejected, however, suggestions that his freedom was part of a wider political intrigue. The spontaneous demonstration at the State Duma, he insisted, had left Putin with no choice but to retreat, at least temporarily.

'Putin changed his decision because he knew that thousands of people were getting ready to take to the streets,' he told Ksenia Sobchak, the socialite TV-show host turned protest figure, in a widely watched online interview after his arrival back in Moscow.

Sobchak, echoing the opinion of most analysts, was sceptical. After all, 10,000 or so protesters was nothing compared to the tens of thousands that had flooded the streets of Moscow in the winter of 2011–12, albeit at approved demonstrations.

'Look,' Navalny went on, 'those 12,000 people were angry, they were mainly young men under the age of thirty-five – yeah, they might have simply gone home later, but then again they might have burned down the State Duma. This is Putin's traditional aikido style. Take a step back, and then, when they turn around, whack them on the back of the head with a hammer.'[21]

There were more outlandish explanations for Navalny's freedom.

'Obama called and ordered that Navalny be set free,' declared Yevgeny Fyodorov, the United Russia lawmaker who had called for a campaign to 'root out' the 'traitors' in the Russian government. 'As a US agent,' he said, eyes flashing wildly, 'Navalny is untouchable. He could walk around the streets of Moscow hitting people if he wanted, and nothing would happen to him.'

Others, like Eduard Limonov, the writer and ex-*NatsBol* leader, who was by now penning a column for the pro-government *Izvestia* newspaper, wondered aloud if Navalny had made a deal with the authorities to get out of jail. 'This whole Navalny story is beginning to smell really bad,' he wrote.[22]

If Navalny was being set up as a fall guy by Sobyanin, then the plan backfired. The opposition figurehead and his team quickly put together a slick, Western-style election campaign, the likes of which had never been witnessed in Russia. His years of online campaigning meant Navalny had already got his message across to the middle and creative classes. Now he would have to reach out to those Muscovites who got their information almost solely from state media, and who, if they used the internet at all, it was for online chat, sports or pornography, but not political debate.

Sobyanin, taking his cue from Putin's election campaign style, declined to take part in debates with opponents. Or even to meet voters. Instead, he relied on loyal state media to reach out to Moscow's millions of residents for him. As a result, Navalny claimed the city's streets, squares and parks, frequently giving up to three stump speeches a day. Blacklisted from national TV, Navalny and his supporters set up so-called 'cubes', colourful candidate information stands manned by enthusiastic campaign volunteers that popped up like mushrooms across the rainy city. 'Change Russia, starting with Moscow!' was the Navalny campaign slogan, and stickers bearing the phrase were soon plastered everywhere. Navalny had once been a little-known blogger preaching to the converted. Now his face – and message – was on almost every corner.

Navalny's campaigning style, he revealed, had been picked up from watching election scenes in US TV dramas like *The Wire*.[23] The hardest-working candidate the city had ever seen, he even descended into the metro to hand out copies of his campaign newspaper. City authorities were unsure how to react to this flurry of activity, sending workers to cut down, often aggressively, pro-Navalny banners from the balconies of private apartments, and even briefly detaining the protest figurehead at a well-attended election rally in an east Moscow park. Police also raided an apartment where a group of activists known as the 'Brothers of Navalny' were turning out 'illegal' election campaign material. Two young supporters, one of them Oleg Kozlovsky from the now defunct Orange Revolution-inspired *Oborona* movement, were detained for ten days, but no one explained what was illegal about the material. On top of all this, state-run television compared Navalny to Hitler.[24]

Navalny was fighting not only for the mayor's office, but also for his freedom. A good showing at the polls would make it that much more difficult for the authorities to send him back to prison. And his relentless campaigning was slowly winning over voters. His ratings, at just 3% before the start of the campaign, began to rise steadily. Equally importantly, Navalny's nationwide recognition ratings passed the 50% mark for the first time.[25] The election campaign was transforming him from a protest leader into a national politician. 'I wasn't too sure about him before, but he makes a lot of sense,' a young office worker on his lunch break told me, when I watched Navalny speak in north Moscow. 'He's not afraid to speak the truth.'

Navalny's liberal supporters had urged the opposition leader to tone down his nationalist rhetoric during the mass anti-Putin protests, and the anti-corruption crusader had listened. But now he returned to the theme, blaming migrants for rising crime and publicly backing rioters who that summer had called for the expulsion of Chechens from a southern Russian town.[26] He also pledged to hire a private security firm to deal with urban problems, including that of illegal immigration. 'Much of his nationalism is based on pure ignorance,' an exasperated high-profile liberal backer told me, insisting on anonymity. But, for the large part, liberals were happy to close their eyes to Navalny's nationalism.

There was a pattern emerging here: Russia's liberals had supported

Yeltsin's deadly attack on the rebellious leftist and nationalist forces that had holed up in parliament in the autumn of 1993 because they were terrified of a return to Communist rule. Their modern-day counterparts backed Navalny because they were scared Putin would reign forever. It was a choice fraught with risk. The shelling of parliament-concentrated power in the hands of the president: Putin merely had to apply the final touches to make his powers dictatorial in scope. What would liberal support for Navalny lead to? The dangers were obvious enough. In the weeks after the mayoral election, a south Moscow region erupted into nationalist violence following the murder of a young ethnic Russian, allegedly by an Azerbaijani national. 'White power!' rioters shouted, as they attacked a market where scores of migrants were employed. The authorities responded by rounding up over a thousand migrants. Writing on his blog, Navalny said the rioters had been forced into 'primitive and desperate measures'.

There were other causes for concern. Navalny's volunteer campaigners, who numbered around 10,000, many of them in their early to mid-twenties, were gaining a reputation for fanaticism that rivalled that of the pro-Putin youth group *Nashi*. Fellow protest leaders, TV presenters, bloggers and anyone else who dared to question Navalny's actions quickly found themselves facing a barrage of abuse and personal attacks. One person who became a target was eco-activist Yevgenia Chirikova, who announced she would not vote for Navalny at the mayoral polls unless he included a green element to his programme.

'I was accused of being a traitor... programmed by the KGB, a drunkard,' Chirikova recalled. 'They told me that God sees everything and would punish me. If this is how they act when Navalny is fighting for power, what are they going to be like when he takes power? What makes them any different from *Nashi* members?'[27]

And Navalny saw nothing wrong with all this. 'I would like to call on my supporters to be themselves: that is, tough and uncompromising,' he said, defiantly, when handed the opportunity to make an on-air plea for his followers to be tolerant of opposing views. 'I want them to tell it like it is. I need people who are like me.'[28]

Navalny's supporters were so willing to attack his detractors because they had ceased to see their idol as a mere politician or protest leader. For the young men and women who laboured that summer at his campaign HQ, or walked the streets to convert the unbelievers, Navalny was the saviour, the Moscow messiah come to lead Russia to the promised land of transparent government and free wi-fi on every corner. Stanislav Belkovsky, a veteran political analyst who had known Navalny for years, mockingly dubbed the protest leader's saucer-eyed followers 'Navalny's Witnesses'.[29]

This willingness to seek a saviour figure that will rescue Russia from itself has roots in the country's turbulent history. The leaders of the four great rebellions that shook Russia in the seventeenth and eighteenth centuries were all hailed by the lower classes as the saviour come to punish the evil-doers and eradicate sin and suffering. The Bolsheviks who swept the tsar from power in 1917 famously pledged to establish a workers' paradise on earth, and the cult of personality that emerged around Stalin has few parallels in modern history. Later, both Yeltsin and Putin were greeted as saviours who would magically put right all wrongs and drag Russia into a bright and shining future. And now it was Navalny's turn to be hailed as the hero of the hour who would wipe away the mistakes of the previous 'false' messiahs. This pattern of a Russian Leader/Saviour who is then discredited and disgraced seems set to repeat forever. 'To change Russia, we need to start not so much with Moscow, but ourselves,' noted Belkovsky, the analyst.

'VOVA, I'M BACK'

No one, with the exception of 'Navalny's Witnesses', had seriously believed that Navalny could defeat Sobyanin at the elections, or even force him into a run-off. Opinion polls in the days before the vote gave the protest leader just under 20%. Sobyanin was on almost 60%, far more than the half of the votes he would need to avoid an embarrassing second round.

The authorities, wary of triggering streets protests and confident of a Sobyanin victory, were reported to have ordered 'clean' elections. But, as voting day progressed, exit polls indicated that a major shock could be on the cards. An unexpectedly strong showing by Navalny meant the authorities had a decision to make. Stay honest, or resort to vote fraud to ensure the 'right' result? As midnight approached, reports came in that an urgent meeting was being held at Moscow City Hall, with the involvement of presidential administration staff.[30] 'It looks like there is going to be a second round,' Navalny told cheering supporters in the courtyard of his election campaign's HQ.

And then the official results were announced. Sobyanin had just scraped victory in the first round, election officials declared, taking 51%, while Navalny had garnered 27%. Navalny called foul and pledged a campaign of civil disobedience, if a second round of voting was not held. But his anger could not disguise his satisfaction. Even the disputed 'official' results were a massive victory for the protest leader, and a boost to his chances of staying out of jail. Turnout had been low, with just a third of Moscow's registered voters casting a ballot, but the results still meant that over 600,000 people in the capital had put their trust in Navalny. For a candidate barred from mainstream TV networks, it was a stunning result and no less than a reshaping of the political landscape. Navalny had received more votes than the candidates from the four traditional opposition parties combined. Enthused by their hero's breakthrough, Russian opposition journalists began writing articles with headlines such as: 'When Navalny Becomes President'.[31]

The next evening, some 25,000 Navalny supporters gathered on Bolotnaya Square, the scene of the violence on the eve of Putin's inauguration. There was a heavy security presence, and tensions were high as a police helicopter hovered overhead. 'Recount! Recount!' chanted the crowd, the majority holding up blue 'Navalny' placards. The mood was defiant.

'The authorities stole the second round from us!' a balding, middle-aged man named Stanislav Kuzmin told me. 'We're going to force a recount. Whatever it takes!' His wife, a pale blonde, nodded enthusiastically.

Navalny, however, had other ideas. There would be no promised campaign of civil disobedience. Better this show of force before his trial, he had reasoned, than an unnecessary confrontation.

'When the time comes, and it may well come, when I will ask you to take part in unsanctioned demonstrations, to overturn vehicles and light flares, I will tell you straight out,' Navalny said, after high-fiving members of his campaign staff as he clambered on to the stage.

Like Putin, Navalny was learning how to bide his time. Besides, the Kremlin had got the message. Navalny was no longer an upstart protester, or 'some blogger', but a national politician with a growing following. A few weeks after the elections, in tacit admission that his foe had reached a new level, Putin would utter Navalny's name for the first time.[32]

✱

Navalny was being increasingly compared with Yeltsin. Not, of course, with the President Yeltsin whose drunken antics had so embarrassed Russians in the 1990s, but with the younger, healthier Yeltsin, who had inspired millions in the final years of the Soviet Union. Both men were tall, fiery speakers with the common touch: like Navalny, Yeltsin had also battled against high-level corruption. 'Vova, I'm back', read the caption under a composite digital image of the two men's faces that made the rounds online that autumn.[33] Yeltsin had famously outmanoeuvred Soviet leader Mikhail Gorbachev's attempts to sideline him politically: would Navalny do the same to Putin?

The first test of Navalny's newfound political weight came on 16 October 2013, as a court in Kirov heard the appeal against his five-year jail sentence. Unable or unwilling to hold off with his relentless attacks on Putin and his allies, just a week ahead of the appeal, Navalny published a report on the foreign-based children and grandchildren of Vladimir Yakunin, the ultra-patriotic, ultra-Orthodox head of the Russian Railways company. 'He's set his family up comfortably in Switzerland and England, but has the cheek to teach us about patriotism,' Navalny fumed. 'And to tell us that anyone who is against him and Putin is an enemy of our country.'[34] Navalny was still raging about Yakunin as he set off on the train to Kirov.

Back in Moscow, Navalny's supporters prepared to take to the streets again in the event of his jail sentence being upheld. But there was no need. The appeals court ruled to soften Navalny's sentence to five years suspended. Ofitserov also got four years suspended. Both men were barred from leaving Moscow without police permission for the duration of their punishment. 'And we'd got the tents and the snacks ready,' an activist tweeted, as preparations for another invasion of central Moscow were called off.

'They'll come in handy, another time,' Navalny replied.

Navalny's supporters celebrated. But it was a hollow kind of victory. Of course, as Navalny admitted, freedom was far better than the prospect of 'battling mosquitoes in a prison cell'. Politically, however, Navalny had been isolated. Under Russian law, he would be banned from running for public office until at least mid-2018, after both the next parliamentary and presidential polls. The probationary nature of his sentence also meant he could be sent back to jail at any time, should he be detained for even a minor offence. He was also facing a number of other criminal charges, any one of which could see him jailed for up to ten years.

'We are simply so used to the lack of justice that, when the authorities give an innocent person five years suspended, we are happy and congratulate one another,' Navalny commented. 'If anyone thinks I am going to get scared and stay away from demonstrations in case they jail me again, then they are wrong,' he added. 'I did what I believed to be right, and I will keep on doing what I believe to be right and necessary.'[35]

Navalny's freedom sparked speculation that the Kremlin had decided to back off, at least temporarily, from its hard line against dissent. With Russia set to host the 2014 Winter Olympics in its Black Sea resort of Sochi, Putin could do without the headache of another high-profile political prisoner. And, of course, by not jailing Navalny, the authorities had prevented him turning into an anti-regime martyr that the beleaguered protest movement could rally around.

On the ground, little had changed. Putin remained in the Kremlin. United Russia, though damaged, was still the largest party in the State Duma. Judges and the courts continued to operate to a system of telephone justice. Udaltsov and his fellow Left Front activist Razvozzhayev were still behind bars, facing ten years on coup charges based on footage aired by state TV. And, ominously, in the autumn of 2013, the authorities made a return to the Soviet-era abuse of psychiatry for political ends when Mikhail Kosenko, a suspect detained after the unrest ahead of Putin's return to the presidency, was ordered to undergo psychiatric treatment for an undefined period.

In October 2013, protesters marched through central Moscow to call for the release of political prisoners. The turnout that afternoon was around 5,000, far fewer than the tens of thousands who had filled the squares of the Russian capital at the height of the anti-Putin protests. Marching past the watchful eye of riot police, the crowd broke into the familiar chant of 'Russia without Putin!' But there was a weariness about the rallying cry. The belief that had sustained the protest movement, I realized, had gone. People had come out on to the streets time after time, been jailed and beaten for their beliefs, and nothing had changed. If anything, things had got worse. It was a brutal truth. Navalny, walking with his wife, Yulia, in the centre of the crowd, sighed. 'The opposition's fight is endless,' he said. 'And rather exhausting.'

Three days later, investigators charged Navalny and his younger brother, Oleg, with another case of embezzlement. The Kremlin might not have been planning to lock up its number-one foe just yet, but it was keeping Navalny on the shortest leash it could find.

17

'NATIONAL TRAITORS'

Putin may have balked at jailing Navalny, but there were plenty of Kremlin critics still languishing behind bars. In normal circumstances, the notoriously stubborn former KGB man would have paid little attention to international appeals for their release. But as Russia geared up to host the 2014 Winter Olympic Games, Putin was faced with the unsettling prospect of his pet project being marred by uncomfortable questions over these troublesome opposition activists. More significantly, a number of world leaders were considering staying away from the Games in protest at Russia's human-rights record. For Putin, this was unacceptable. The Winter Olympics were a chance to showcase what he regarded as Russia's resurgence – economic, political and religious – under his long rule. And so, with less than two months to go until the start of the Games, Russia's long-time leader initiated a wide-ranging amnesty bill that would see the early release of some 20,000 prisoners, including some of his bitterest foes.

Among the high-profile prisoners who benefited from the amnesty were Pussy Riot's Alyokhina and Tolokonnikova, who walked out of their snowy prison camps in December 2013 with just two months left to serve of their two-year sentences. 'Russia without Putin!' shouted Tolokonnikova, as she emerged from captivity into the glare of the media spotlight. Neither of the activists were under any illusions as to the reason for their release. 'This is not an amnesty. This is a hoax and a PR move,' said an unrepentant Alyokhina. 'If I'd had the chance to turn it down, I would have done.' Tolokonnikova was of a similar opinion, calling the amnesty 'cynical and disgusting'.[1] It was a win-win situation for Putin. With public opinion in Russia firmly against the Pussy Riot activists, there was little danger in their early release. They were, after all, hardly going to lead an enraged mob in the storming of the Kremlin walls. And by freeing them, Putin ruled out the danger of the Sochi Games being marred by a sea of 'Free Pussy Riot' T-shirts and banners. Others released under the amnesty included a number of the protesters arrested after the clashes on the eve of Putin's May 2012 inauguration, as well as international Greenpeace activists, who had been seized while protesting Russia's gas drilling in the Arctic.

But the biggest surprise of this bout of unexpected clemency came when Putin announced at his annual end-of-year news conference that he would pardon Mikhail Khodorkovsky, the former oil tycoon and staunch government critic. 'Not long ago he appealed to me for a pardon. He mentions humanitarian considerations, as his mother is ill,' Putin told reporters.[2] This was a genuine sensation for two reasons: first, Khodorkovsky had not fallen under the terms of the amnesty, and, second, investigators had been making noises about bringing a fresh set of criminal charges against Russia's once richest man. Speculation immediately arose among opposition activists that Khodorkovsky, who had just nine months of his sentence to serve, had been threatened with a new jail term if he refused to file an appeal for a presidential pardon. Upon his release in December 2013, Khodorkovsky flew straight to Western Europe, where – despite an initial statement that he had no plans to become involved in politics[3] – he would quickly become a figurehead of sorts for the swelling numbers of the opposition-in-exile. Domestically, though, Khodorkovsky's political appeal was limited to a small group of isolated liberals.

The amnesty did not mean freedom for Taisiya Osipova, the young mother who had been sentenced to eight years on hotly disputed drug-possession charges, which her supporters said were revenge for her refusal to incriminate her husband, a radical opposition activist. 'Putin just wants to make sure that the most well-known prisoners are out of jail before the Olympics, so as to avoid any unpleasant questions at the Games. But Taisiya's case hasn't gained anything like the attention of the Pussy Riot trial, for example,' Osipova's lawyer, Svetlana Sidorkina, told me. 'There are plenty of people left behind in jail who shouldn't be there.'

Left Front leader Udaltsov and his long-suffering sidekick, Razvozzhayev, were also among those whose alleged crimes were considered too serious for the amnesty.

Yet it would take more than the early release of a few internationally known opponents of Putin's rule to polish Russia's tarnished image. Prior to the Games, Russia's parliament passed a law banning the promotion of 'non-traditional sexual relations' to minors. Immediately labelled an 'anti-gay' law by critics, this was legislation designed solely to shore up support for Putin among more conservative Russians, and it triggered an inevitable spike in violence against members of the country's beleaguered lesbian, gay, bisexual and transgender community. For gay activists, it was as if Putin had decided to legalize already widespread discrimination and prejudice. Protests against the law were met with violence by Orthodox Christian activists chanting, 'Moscow is not Sodom!' as police stood by and watched.

In the West, the controversial law was widely condemned by everyone from the US State Department to British actor Stephen Fry, and led to loud and frequent calls for a boycott of the 2014 Winter Games. But Putin was furious at what he called 'clearly orchestrated attempts'[4] to discredit the Sochi Olympics. After all, as the Kremlin and its allies argued, Russia's new law did not make homosexuality illegal, nor were jail sentences stipulated for those who broke it. Indeed, Putin lost no time in pointing out that a dozen US states, including Texas and Florida, still had – albeit unconstitutional – anti-sodomy laws on the books. The Russian law also paled in comparison to harsh anti-gay legislation in both Saudi Arabia and Qatar, both staunch US allies. For Putin, the American and European criticism was a clear case of double values. His sense of injustice and anger at the West would simmer throughout and beyond the Games.

Startling claims of corruption also dogged the run-up to the Olympics, which were estimated to cost an eye-watering $51 billion. This was three times the price of the much bigger 2012 Summer Olympics in London, and more expensive than all previous twenty-one Winter Olympics put together.[5] In one particularly notorious case, a road built especially for the Games cost an estimated $9 billion, making its construction almost four times as expensive as NASA's project to send the Curiosity Rover to Mars. The Russian version of *Esquire* magazine estimated that the thirty-mile road could have been paved with a six-centimetre layer of truffles for the same price, or a one-centimetre layer of black caviar.[6] When the newly freed Pussy Riot turned up in Sochi to protest Putin's vanity project, they were horse-whipped for their trouble by a group of irate Cossacks. Pro-Kremlin bloggers suggested the punk activists had organized the attack on themselves as a publicity stunt.

'The Games are nothing but a monstrous scam,' boomed Boris Nemtsov, the former deputy prime minister turned opposition leader, when I spoke to him ahead of the opening ceremony in Sochi. In a damning report, Nemtsov and fellow political activist Leonid Martynyuk alleged that some $30 billion of the total cost of the Winter Olympics had been skimmed off in 'embezzlement and kickbacks' by Putin's businessmen friends.[7] The report, entitled 'Winter Olympics in the Subtropics', was posted online,[8] and handed out on the streets of Moscow and other Russian cities in the form of a glossy brochure. 'Putin needs these Games to prove how great he is,' Nemtsov seethed. 'But his friends and the businessmen around him need the Olympics to improve their ratings in *Forbes* magazine's richest people in the world listings.'[9]

The accusations were rebuffed by angry Russian officials. One man who undoubtedly benefited from the Games, however, was Putin's childhood friend and ex-judo-sparring partner, Arkady Rotenberg, whose companies received orders for Olympic construction projects worth around $7 billion – more than the total cost of the 2010 Vancouver Winter Olympics.[10] Predictably, state media declined to report on the corruption allegations, and the majority of Russians remained blissfully unaware of the row. 'Are you making all this up?' asked an astonished Sochi taxi driver when I reeled off the facts and figures behind the Games.

MAIDAN

By the time the lavish Olympic closing ceremony rolled around on 23 February 2014, gay rights and corruption scandals were the least of Putin's problems. Instead, the Kremlin's attention was focused firmly on neighbouring Ukraine, where, after months of rallies and vicious street fighting, protesters had toppled the country's president, Viktor Yanukovych. The demonstrations had been sparked by Yanukovych's last-minute decision to back out of a trade deal that would have put Ukraine on the path to European Union membership in favour of closer ties with Russia, but they had quickly morphed into a wider show of anger over widespread corruption and nepotism.

Ukraine's unexpected change of heart on the European Union agreement came after threats by Russia of devastating trade sanctions, as well as thinly veiled warnings that a shift westwards would 'lead to political and social unrest'[11] in the former Soviet state. The Kremlin also had a juicy carrot to go with its stick, in the form of billions of dollars in subsidies, debt forgiveness and duty-free imports.[12] Putin had already seen Ukraine slip out of Russia's sphere of influence once, after the 2004 Orange Revolution, and he clearly did not want a repeat. He had also envisaged Ukraine as a vital part of the Moscow-led Eurasian Economic Union, a fledgling trade alliance, which already included Belarus and Kazakhstan, and which was seen in some hardline Kremlin circles as a first step towards the partial resurrection of the Soviet Union.

However, neither the Kremlin nor Yanukovych had counted on the depth of pro-European sentiments in Kiev and the west of Ukraine. On the same day that Yanukovych announced that Ukraine was backing out of the European deal, Mustafa Nayem, an Afghan-born journalist who had spent most of his life in Kiev, penned a Facebook post calling for a demonstration on Independence Square, popularly known as Maidan, in the very centre of the Ukrainian capital. Although fewer than a thousand people turned up that evening, within weeks, provoked in part by an ill-advised and heavy-handed attempt by riot police to clear the square, the protests had swelled dramatically. What had begun as a low-key, poorly attended demonstration rapidly transformed into a series of rolling protests bringing together pro-Europe activists, leftists, nationalists, football hooligans, miners and hundreds of thousands of ordinary people in the biggest show of dissent in the former Soviet Union for over two decades. There was also an undisguised anti-Putin element to the demonstrations, although – despite claims to the contrary by Kremlin-run media – this did not translate into widespread anti-Russian sentiments. 'We love Russians, but despise Putin,' read a prominent banner at the Maidan protest camp.

As heavy snow fell, and temperatures plunged, protesters and police fought running battles for control of Kiev, and thick, acrid smoke from the burning tyres set alight by Maidan activists drifted through the streets of the Ukrainian capital. By the time Yanukovych had been forced from office, escaping to Russia with the Kremlin's assistance, over a hundred protesters were dead, many gunned down by security forces, while yet others were murdered by still unidentified snipers.

The shockwaves of the Maidan revolution were felt instantly in Russia. 'When the oil revenues run out in Russia, when it becomes clear that Putin cannot rule, the same thing will happen here,'[13] Russian journalist Vladimir Gromov predicted in an article published by the opposition-friendly website Snob. Less than forty-eight hours after Yanukovych had been deposed, Russia's protest movement took to the glitzy streets of central Moscow. 'If there is no freedom in Russia, there will be a Maidan!' shouted a middle-aged man, as some 1,500 people gathered opposite the Kremlin in protest at jail sentences handed down to the demonstrators detained on the eve of Putin's inauguration for a third term. Jittery riot police pounced instantly, wrestling the protester to the ground, before dragging him away to a police truck. Before the evening was out, hundreds of people would likewise find themselves in police custody.

The chanting of 'Maidan!' that evening was not the only indication that Russia's opposition had been fired up by events in Ukraine. Inspired by Kiev's barricades of burning rubber, a few hardcore activists had hauled tyres to the demonstration, where they were promptly nabbed by police. Other copycat tactics were also in evidence, such as the singing of the national anthem and the unfurling of the Russian flag, both clear nods to the rousing displays of patriotism by Kiev's tenacious protesters.

However, it would take more than simply adopting the symbols of the Maidan protests to topple Putin. Russia's mainly middle-class protesters had so far failed to display anything like the determination of their counterparts in Kiev. With Udaltsov still under house arrest, and his Left Front activists leaderless, there was also a distinct absence of anyone in the movement willing to rough it up with riot police. The uncomfortable truth was that any sustained attempt to dislodge Putin would most likely require – as in Kiev – nationalist forces to provide much of the muscle.

'For Russia to get its own Maidan, we'd need the participation of at least 7,000 nationalist activists alongside 150,000 other protesters,' Dmitry Dyomushkin, the ex-head of Russia's outlawed, ultra-right Slavic Union movement, told me. 'In this case, we'd see an escalation, victims and open confrontation, and so on. But so far the protests have all been hijacked by liberals.'[14] It was unclear, however, if Dyomushkin alone would be able to recruit such numbers to his cause. Aggressively anti-Putin, he had triggered a split in Russia's nationalist movement with his support for the Kiev protests, and made enemies of many of his former allies on the far right. 'They want to rip me a new asshole,' he laughed.

There were also formidable logistical obstacles to sustained street protest in Moscow. Unlike in Ukraine, where western regions seethed with anti-government sentiment, organized dissent has never taken hold in Russia's provinces, where there is a deep distrust of the figures driving the Moscow-based opposition to Putin. In Ukraine, the Maidan tent camp was supplied by activists making daily runs from opposition-held cities such as Lviv and Ivano-Frankivsk. In Russia, any protest camp in Moscow would be likely to be targeted by Putin loyalists shipped in from the mainly conservative heartland.

Equally as significant in Ukraine was the existence of genuine opposition parties with the organizational skills to support the months-long protests in Kiev. In Russia, where Putin has tamed parliament, filling it with fake opposition parties that provide the masses with the illusion of democracy, genuine opposition is impoverished and low on resources. Unlike Yanukovych, Putin also controlled national television, something he would use to devastating effect against the protest movement in the aftermath of Maidan.

Russia, then, was not Ukraine. And Putin was no Yanukovych.

'In Ukraine, the protesters defeated the monster at the end of level one,' went a joke, which did the rounds online in the spring of 2014, comparing the two revolutionary struggles to a computer game. 'But in Russia, they are up against the Big Boss.'

✳

He might have appeared to hold all the cards, but the 'Big Boss' was taking no chances. Less than a week after Maidan activists had celebrated their unlikely victory at Yanukovych's deserted presidential residence near Kiev, Navalny was placed under house arrest in connection with fresh allegations that he and his younger brother, Oleg, had embezzled hundreds of thousands of dollars from a Russian subsidiary of the French cosmetics company Yves Rocher. He was also barred from using the internet, eliminating at a stroke the opposition leader's most devastating weapon in the ongoing 'Battle between Good and Neutrality'. This time, public reaction was minimal: there were more riot police than opposition activists in central Moscow on the evening of the court ruling that would see Navalny confined to his apartment for the next year. With Udaltsov likewise under house arrest, the Kremlin had successfully neutralized the anti-Putin protest movement's leading lights, without making a martyr out of either man.

Still, there were other dangers on the horizon for Putin. The Maidan revolution had thrown up the – albeit distant – possibility that Ukraine could eventually transform into a genuine European democracy, a development that would pose a significant threat to Putin's autocratic rule. 'The Kremlin has spent a long time convincing Russians that our troubled history – the Soviet era, the massive wartime destruction, all the revolutions we've seen, and so on – is the reason why living standards here are so much lower than in, say, England or France,' Marat Guelman, the former Kremlin spin doctor turned Putin critic, told me in the wake of the Ukrainian uprising. 'But if Ukrainians, who share a common past with Russia, can now build a prosperous, democratic country, then this will prove a real problem for Putin. Russians will start to ask, "Why can't we do the same thing here?"'[15]

Accordingly, as Kiev crackled with revolutionary euphoria, Kremlin-controlled media launched a wildly successful campaign to discredit the Ukrainian uprising in the eyes of the Russian public. In a series of broadcasts that grew more hysterical with each passing week, Ukraine's revolution was portrayed as the work of a 'fascist junta' backed by Western powers set on the destruction of Mother Russia.[16]

Almost every family in Russia lost someone during World War II, better known across the former Soviet Union as the Great Patriotic War, and the invocation of the spectre of fascism played on powerful historical memories. This was an old Kremlin trick. In the 1950s, Marshall Tito, the maverick socialist leader of Yugoslavia, had been routinely referred to by Kremlin officials as part of a 'fascist clique', despite all the evidence to the contrary. Flash forward some sixty years, and Putin was employing the Soviet Union's tactics against the new government in Ukraine. And by virtue of their open support for the Maidan protests, Putin's critics at home were tarred with the same brush. In February 2014, I witnessed the bizarre scene of Kremlin supporters chanting, 'Fascism will not pass!' at an opposition-led, anti-fascist rally in central Moscow to commemorate the 2009 murders of human-rights lawyer Stanislav Markelov and journalist Anastasia Baburova by a neo-Nazi gunman. 'So-called anti-fascists hide under the cover of anti-fascism to promote their fascist ideas,' a ruddy-faced Putin activist told me, trying hard not to get entangled in his own twisted logic.

There were, of course, far-right groups involved in the Maidan demonstrations, and the new Ukrainian government would also later be guilty of a shameful appeasement of nationalist sentiments. Other far-right activists were also involved in clashes that resulted in the deaths of dozens of pro-Moscow supporters in Odessa, a city on Ukraine's Black Sea coast. But the Kremlin deliberately and massively exaggerated their numbers and influence. The previously obscure Ukrainian nationalist movement Right Sector was transformed by Kremlin-run television channels into a modern-day bogeyman. In the immediate aftermath of the Maidan protests, Right Sector was mentioned more times by Russian state media than even Putin's ruling United Russia party, and three times as frequently as the Communist Party.[17] 'Moscow metro ticket prices are going up again – those Right Sector bastards!' Russian opposition activists joked darkly.

In an indication of Right Sector's true popularity among Ukrainians, its leader, Dmitry Yarosh, took just over 1% of the popular vote at Ukraine's 2014 presidential elections. Indeed, between them, Yarosh and Oleh Tyagnibok, of the ultra-nationalist Svoboda party, garnered fewer total votes than a Jewish candidate for the presidency, Vadim Rabinovich, who captured just over 2% of the ballot.[18] Nevertheless, eager to keep the myth of 'Nazi Ukraine' alive as long as possible, Russian state TV erroneously reported on election night that Yarosh was in the lead in the race for the Ukrainian presidency, with 37% of the vote.[19] The source for the figures was the website of Ukraine's election committee, which had reported an online attack by suspected pro-Russia hackers ahead of the polls.

'CRIMEA IS OURS!'

As Ukraine's interim government struggled with the hazards and complications of a post-revolutionary situation, Russian troops without insignia seized military bases and other key buildings in Crimea, a sun-kissed peninsula in the south of Ukraine with a large ethnic Russian majority. Next, heavily armed gunmen, including Igor Girkin (nom de guerre Strelkov), a shadowy self-proclaimed Russian military intelligence officer, forced Crimean lawmakers to vote for a 16 March 2014 referendum on the territory's future.[20] Two days after more than 95% of Crimeans had voted to join Russia in a hastily arranged and internationally criticized referendum, the Kremlin annexed the peninsula, citing its right to self-determination (a 'right' that Russia had twice sent troops to Chechnya to prevent it exercising). Putin later admitted, however, that the plan to seize Crimea had been hatched in advance of the vote.[21]

The Ukraine crisis invested Putin's presidency with a new potency and significance. In the months before the Maidan protests broke out, his ratings had slumped to an all-time low of 61%. It was, of course, a figure that would have made most Western leaders envious. But for a politician with total control over state media, the courts and the security forces, it was a poor return. His message of stability was less and less relevant to a generation that had little memory of the chaotic 1990s. From an ill-advised publicity stunt that saw the president pose as the head of a flock of cranes, to a stilted televised admission that he and his wife, Lyudmila, were no longer a couple, Putin had gradually become a figure of fun. The capture of Crimea, gifted to Ukraine from Russia by Soviet leader Nikita Khrushchev in 1954, changed all that. For many Russians, the return of the peninsula was the righting of a deep historical wrong. The phrase 'Krym – Nash!' – 'Crimea is ours!' quickly became the slogan of choice for Kremlin supporters, while Putin's approval rating soared to over 80%.

'Congratulations on your return to your native harbour!' roared the president at a Red Square rally to celebrate the slickly implanted Kremlin operation to annex the peninsula, as an ecstatic crowd waved Russian and Soviet flags. The opposition was not immune to such jingoism. Udaltsov and some of his leftist allies, ruled by an undisguised nostalgia for the Soviet era, were among those who applauded Crimea's annexation the longest and hardest.

Eduard Limonov, the Kremlin's former public enemy number one, was another cheerleader for the seizure of Crimea. His enthusiasm for Russia's new foreign policy even saw him publicly appeal to the Kremlin to ban 'hostile' media outlets, such as the opposition newspaper *Novaya Gazeta*, and strip their journalists of Russian citizenship. The appeal was published in the pages of *Izvestia*, a pro-Kremlin newspaper where Limonov had begun writing a weekly column.[22] For a man who had once spoken openly of the need for a new Russian revolution to drive Putin from office, it was a remarkable turnaround. Yet Limonov saw nothing out of the ordinary in his transformation from Kremlin foe to Kremlin-friendly newspaper columnist. 'Putin has finally come around to my way of thinking,' he told me.

Navalny also welcomed the return of the peninsula to Russia, if not the role played by Russian troops in its seizure. 'I think that, despite the fact that Crimea was captured with egregious violations of all international regulations, the reality is that Crimea is now part of Russia,' he said in a rare radio interview from house arrest. 'Let's not deceive ourselves. And I would also strongly advise Ukrainians not to deceive themselves.' He also stated bluntly that he would not return Crimea to Ukraine if he were to become president of Russia. 'Is Crimea some sort of sausage sandwich to be passed back and forth?' he asked, bizarrely.[23] Was Navalny pandering to populism? Or was this, as his detractors claimed, yet more evidence that he was not the man to lead Russia towards a genuinely democratic future?

Navalny's views were shared by many, but by no means all of his fellow opposition figures. But even those in the anti-Putin movement who cautiously welcomed Crimea's return to its 'native harbour' were aghast at the possibility of open conflict with neighbouring Ukraine. On a brilliantly sunny afternoon in late March 2014, some 30,000 'free souls', as one opposition blogger called them, rallied in central Moscow to protest Putin's aggression. Predictably, state TV portrayed the protest as a poorly attended event with only a random collection of half-baked radicals present. In the minutes before the rally began, a journalist from the Kremlin-controlled NTV channel stood in front of a still empty street – one that would soon be packed with protesters – and reported on the 'minimal' turnout. When I quizzed the NTV journalist over her undisguised duplicity, she snapped, 'You do your job, and I'll do mine,' and turned swiftly away from me on her high heels.

If the state media's 'job' was to foster a hatred of Ukraine's new authorities, as well as the domestic opposition, then it was carrying out its mission with enviable success. It was a task that became even more important in the aftermath of the Maidan protests, when the Kremlin fomented separatist rebellion in eastern Ukraine's Donbass region. Led initially by passport-carrying Russian citizens, the conflict would claim almost 7,000 lives by the summer of 2015, and plunge relations between Russia and the West to a post-Cold War low. Although Putin would consistently deny that Russian troops were in action in the Donbass, a swathe of evidence, from the capture of Russians soldiers on Ukrainian territory to the sighting of Russian military hardware in the self-declared Donetsk and Lugansk people's republics, left little doubt about Kremlin involvement. Despite Putin's denials, Russia was, for all intents and purposes, at war. All of which made the opposition more vulnerable than ever.

Daily quick-fire television images of Ukraine's burning cities and corpse-strewn landscapes, all accompanied by a nervy, incessant soundtrack, served to put millions of Russian TV viewers into what Professor Valeriy Solovey, a Moscow-based media expert, described as a 'trance-like state'.[24] As fighting intensified, Russia's Channel One aired a purported eyewitness report from a 'refugee' who said she had witnessed a young boy being crucified by 'fascist' forces loyal to Kiev. The young boy, the distraught women informed millions of Russians on the evening news, had been seized from his mother, a rebel supporter, and nailed to a noticeboard on Lenin Square in Slavyansk, a town in eastern Ukraine. The only problem was there is no Lenin Square in Slavyansk, and locals told independent Russian journalists that they had heard nothing of this gruesome story, which appeared to have been inspired by an episode of the popular US television series *Game of Thrones*. The woman was also not a resident of Slavyansk. Months later, a Channel One spokesperson admitted the report was false.[25] But the damage was done. Anyone now expressing even the mildest opposition to Russia's policy on Ukraine was fair game.

Even the July 2014 shooting down of Malaysian Airlines flight MH17 by what an overwhelming body of evidence suggested was a group of separatists armed with a Russian surface-to-air missile system failed to turn the tide of public opinion against the Kremlin. In the immediate aftermath of the downing of the passenger jet, with the loss of all 298 people on board, Russian state-controlled media flooded the airwaves and internet with a bewildering array of conspiracy theories. These ranged from speculation that Ukrainian forces had fired at the plane believing it to be Putin's personal jet (which was nowhere near eastern Ukraine at the time) to the outlandish suggestion that US President Barack Obama was blaming Russia for the attack because he was angry that Putin had dared to be late for a meeting on the sidelines of the G20 summit in Mexico in 2012.[26] The fact that separatists and Russian news programmes had triumphantly reported the downing of what they initially believed was a Ukrainian military plane, on the afternoon that flight MH17 was blown out of the sky, was conveniently forgotten.[27]

The West's decision to punish Russia for its annexation of Crimea and actions in Ukraine with increasingly tough economic sanctions served to consolidate support for Putin, who spoke often and loudly about what he called a US and European conspiracy to bring Mother Russia to her knees. 'We are living on a war footing now,' said Dmitry Oreshkin, the political analyst whose vote monitors had helped spark the 2011–12 protests. 'The social contract that kept Putin in power for so long is now irrelevant. There is no longer any talk of stability and economic prosperity.'[28] Instead, loyalty and a willingness to make sacrifices for the good of Mother Russia were the new buzzwords. 'When a Russian feels any foreign pressure, he will never give up his leader,' Russian Deputy Prime Minister Igor Shuvalov said as the sanctions began to bite. 'Never. We will survive any hardship in the country – eat less food, use less electricity.'[29] Despite the absurdity of one of the richest men in the Russian government, with a family fortune estimated at

$220 million, spouting a message of austerity to spite the West, this and other similar appeals to Russians to unite around Putin worked: the president's approval ratings continued to climb, even after the euphoria of the annexation of Crimea had worn off. 'It's no longer just about the economy,' said Maria Lipman, a Moscow-based political analyst. 'Many Russians feel like they are living in a besieged fortress, and they believe that Putin is the only one who knows how to protect them. Accordingly, they are prepared to make sacrifices for him.'[30]

'I fuck your sanctions,' read a T-shirt on sale in central Moscow that spring, the image of the Russian flag penetrating the Stars-and-Stripes from behind leaving no room for ambiguity. In such an atmosphere, there could be no room for dissent. As fighting raged in eastern Ukraine, Putin lashed out at those who questioned the Kremlin's actions, dubbing them 'a fifth column' and 'national traitors', who were seeking to stir up unrest in Russia for the benefit of their Western masters. Ironically, the latter insult, an unusual expression in Russian political discourse, was a direct translation of *'nationalverräter'*, the term that Adolf Hitler had used to describe his enemies in his autobiography, *Mein Kampf*. It seems improbable that Putin, a fluent German speaker from his days as a KGB officer in Soviet-controlled East Germany, would have been unaware of this.

Even support for Putin's actions in Ukraine would not be enough to save opposition leaders. In June 2014, Udaltsov and Razvozzhayev were sentenced to four and a half years each in penal colonies for their part in organizing what the authorities said were the 'mass riots' ahead of Putin's May 2012 return to the Kremlin. Although Udaltsov's enthusiasm for the pro-Russian 'people's republics' that had sprung up in eastern Ukraine had largely severed his ties with the liberal wing of the opposition, Boris Nemtsov, despite being on the opposing side of the anti-Putin movement, was one of the two dozen or so protesters who gathered outside Moscow city court that afternoon. But despite the presence of machine-gun-toting riot police, there was little of the sense of drama that had accompanied either Navalny's or Pussy Riot's trial. 'This case has not been under the jurisdiction of genuine legality for even a second,' said Anton Orekh, a commentator for the Echo of Moscow radio station. 'The court's decision was not taken due to any facts or evidence that may have existed, but out of a sense of political necessity.'[31] By far the best description of the situation, however, was the mock coffins for 'the law, honour and rights' that activists left behind them that afternoon on the courthouse lawn.

FRIENDS OF THE JUNTA

The war against the opposition was in full swing. Taking its cue from the president, state media stepped up its already hyper-intensive campaign against dissent, overfulfilling hatred quotas to achieve dangerous new levels of vitriol. In the autumn of 2014, the Kremlin-controlled NTV channel aired two hour-long programmes that 'named and shamed' thirty high-profile figures (all Russian citizens, with the bizarre exception of Sasha Grey, a US porn star turned film actress) who had dared to speak out over the war in Ukraine. The prime-time programmes were entitled '13 Friends of the Junta' and '17 More Friends of the Junta',[32] their titles inspired by Russian state media's wildly inappropriate name for the new, non-military government in Ukraine. ('I know what a junta is!' a red-faced Kremlin supporter screamed at me one afternoon in Moscow, when I attempted to explain that, whatever its faults, the post-Maidan Ukrainian government was not by any stretch of the imagination a 'junta'.)

The most high profile of the celebrities featured in the programmes was Andrei Makarevich, a Soviet-era rock star whose group, Mashina Vremeni (Time Machine), is popular with top government officials. A one-time Putin voter, Makarevich had gone over to the opposition during the 2011–12 protests. On the eve of the Kremlin's seizure of Crimea, he attended a peace rally in Moscow, and signed an open letter condemning Putin's aggression.

Makarevich's acts of rebellion would be neither forgotten nor forgiven. Seizing upon video footage of a concert he had given for children displaced by the conflict in eastern Ukraine, NTV misled viewers into believing that the rock star had entertained Ukrainian government forces, which the channel accused of wiping 'entire villages from the face of the earth'. Makarevich's defiant response was to compose a new song. Its title? 'My Country has Lost its Mind'.[33]

Within a month of the second 'Friends of the Junta' broadcast, NTV went straight for the jugular and aired an obscenity-littered death threat against Olga Romanova, a well-known opposition journalist and head of the prisoners-rights group Russia Behind Bars. In an October 2014 documentary, NTV accused Romanova of siphoning off the group's donations and diverting them to Right Sector, the Ukrainian national-ist movement. The evidence for her 'crime' was flimsy, and Romanova denied the allegations. But during its 'exposé' NTV aired an interview with Oleg Protasov, a tough-looking former convict who spoke about what would happen if prisoners discovered that Romanova had been 'funnelling' money – that was supposed to improve their lives – to the Ukrainian far right. 'No matter who you are with, no matter who [exple-tive beeped out by channel] is protecting you, no matter where you are, you will be found and ripped apart,' Protasov said, staring menacingly into the camera.[34]

'This is the first time a national television channel has aired a cold-blooded pledge to violently take revenge on a Russian citizen,' wrote opposition journalist Stanislav Kucher.[35] 'We are used to seeing lies, black PR and fairy tales about "fascists" when we watch Putin TV,' said Nemtsov. 'We are used to hearing "war is peace," and "the truth is a lie." But what NTV has aired, we've never seen before.'[36]

That wasn't quite true. In another programme aired by NTV just eight days earlier, a masked insurgent in eastern Ukraine said pro-Russia rebels were planning to target the owners of the liberal radio station Echo of Moscow because of the 'lies' it had been spreading about the conflict. In an expletive-ridden rant, the rebel vowed that the station's journalists would 'see death'. 'And death will look like this!' he shouted, poking his fingers towards his eyes.[37]

For older dissidents who had come of age during the Soviet Union, such aggressive media tactics were eerily familiar. 'The Kremlin is again pumping out Soviet-style propaganda,' Lyudmila Alekseyeva, a veteran Soviet-era dissident, told me. 'And the aim is the same: to unite the people behind their leaders and set us in opposition to the whole world. However, the level of public hatred that has been whipped up towards those who criticize the authorities is probably even greater right now than during Brezhnev's rule. At that time, there was tiredness in society, and there wasn't so much anger.'[38]

There is certainly no shortage of anger in Putin's Russia. Huge banners decrying Russia's 'fifth column' and 'national traitors' started to go up on buildings along the New Arbat, the road in central Moscow that Kremlin officials, including Putin, speed through on their way to work. A shadowy 'art collective' called Glavplakat took responsibility for some of the banners, which included opposition figures such as Navalny, Nemtsov and Makarevich, the rock musician. But it is unlikely that the banners could have been unfurled without the approval of Kremlin security agents.[39]

Aggressive anti-Western rhetoric, including a reminder on state TV that Russia is the 'only country in the world realistically capable of transforming the United States into radioactive ash',[40] became the new norm. The Russian Foreign Ministry repeatedly warned its citizens against travelling abroad, where US special services were, it alleged, 'hunting' for them.[41] A leading United Russia lawmaker, Irina Yarovaya, spoke out against the study of foreign languages, claiming it hurt 'Russia's traditions',[42] while a pro-Kremlin youth group laser-beamed a racist image of US President Barack Obama eating a banana onto a building opposite the American embassy. 'Putin believes that the United States organized and orchestrated the Maidan uprising as part of a plot to bring about his downfall,' Gleb Pavlovsky, the former Kremlin adviser, told me. 'The toppling of Yanukovych hardened further his attitudes against opposition figures, whom he considers to be agents of the West.'[43]

It wasn't only Putin who was seeing Western spies everywhere. In June 2015, a middle-aged man near Yaroslavl, a city some 160 miles north-east of Moscow, beat to death an acquaintance who had made the fatal mistake of revealing that he often travelled abroad. The killer then called the police to inform them that he had uncovered and neutralized an 'American spy'.[44] Predictably, vodka was involved, mixed and shaken with a splash of Russia's by now all-pervasive atmosphere of hatred.

This rocketing hostility towards the West was something I would experience for myself, when I travelled once more to the Black Earth region to report on the arrests of two of the anti-nickel activists there on what their supporters said were trumped-up blackmail charges. After my visit, local FSB officers questioned every single person I had interviewed. 'Who brought the American spy here?' they demanded to know, a source later told me. Of greater concern, however, was that the FSB officers were able to convince a number of the activists that I really was an agent of the US State Department, and part of a grand plot by the West to enslave Russia.[45]

The time was ripe for men like Yevgeny Fyodorov, the United Russia lawmaker with his wild conspiracy theories. In late 2014, Fyodorov's National Liberation Movement (NOD) entered into the Anti-Maidan coalition, whose bellicose ranks also included pro-Kremlin Cossacks and the Night Wolves, a gang of leather-clad bikers loyal to Putin. While he would not openly call for violence against the opposition, Fyodorov told me on numerous occasions that he 'understood' if people felt they had no choice but to launch physical attacks against the 'Western-funded fifth column'. Other NOD members were more expressive. 'You British are all scum!' yelled a burly NOD activist, his face red with rage, when I tried to interview members of the movement on the streets of Moscow. 'You and the Yankees want to destroy Russia!' He thrust a meaty finger in my direction. 'I'll tear you and your fifth column apart!' A senior NOD member, who gave his name as Alexei Pisarev, told me in calmer tones, but no less vicious terms, that 'fifth columnists are worse than cockroaches. They may be Russians, but they are our enemies. We have to drive them out.' The Kremlin's new shock troops made *Nashi*, the pro-Putin youth organization of the 2000s, seem like wishy-washy liberals in comparison. 'NOD members often assault us on the streets. Once, they even threw bags of excrement as us,' Mark Galperin, an opposition activist, told me, wrinkling his nose in disgust.

It was quickly becoming clear the Maidan revolution was far from being the catalyst that would trigger a similar uprising in Russia. In fact, it was quite possibly the worst thing that could have happened to the anti-Putin movement.

As the pressure built, Russia's protest art grew darker. Gone were the exuberant, carnival-like performances of Pussy Riot. In their place, a gaunt, shaven-headed artist called Petr Pavlensky arrived on the scene, whose speciality was 'living pain'. As 2014 drew to a close, Pavlensky stripped naked and clambered onto the roof of Moscow's Serbsky psychiatric centre and – to the horror of onlookers in the street below – casually sawed off his earlobe with a massive kitchen knife. As blood trickled down his neck and onto his chest, Pavlensky, apparently indifferent to the pain and the near-freezing temperatures, remained on the edge of the roof for some two hours, before armed police eventually dragged him away. His act of self-mutilation was a reaction to what opposition activists alleged was the Kremlin's renewed use of punitive psychiatry to stifle dissent. Other performances by Pavlensky included wrapping himself naked in barbed wire outside St Petersburg's legislature (the birthplace of Russia's infamous 'gay propaganda' law) and, most notoriously, hammering a long, sharpened nail through his scrotum to pin himself to Red Square's famous cobblestones in order to draw attention to political apathy. In November 2015, he set alight to the doors of the FSB's headquarters in Moscow, in what he called a challenge to state 'terrorism.' 'Pavlensky is an artist for this period of disillusionment. He is grim, disciplined, focused, and ready for pain,' wrote Pussy Riot's Tolokonnikova.[46] It seemed like a recipe for survival in Putin's new Russia.

MEETING ON MANEZHKA

As Russia descended into the maelstrom, Navalny was almost entirely out of the picture, under house arrest as he awaited trial on yet more corruption charges. But his supporters were determined to make as much noise as possible in his absence. In October 2014, I joined a group of activists from Navalny's anti-corruption organization as they attempted to gain access to the grounds of a sprawling villa reportedly belonging to Vladimir Yakunin, the powerful Putin ally and head of the Russian Railways company. The vast property, estimated to be worth some $75 million, was one of a number of similarly impressive constructions at the elite Akulinino gated community near Moscow. Dozens of private security guards manned the entrance, and tall green fences, topped with barbed wire, surrounded the premises. Yakunin's reported neighbours at this oasis of affluence included a number of other heads of state-owned companies, as well as high-ranking officials from Russia's domestic intelligence service.

As police blocked access to what was in theory a public road leading to Akulinino, activists whooped with delight as a fellow anti-corruption campaigner armed with a handheld video camera paraglided low over the opulent mansions. For anti-corruption campaigners, it was unclear how Yakunin could afford such a magnificent property on an annual salary of around $2 million. 'A person can't spend more than he earns, right?' said Nikolai Lyaskin, the pro-Navalny activist. 'We'd just like to know where all these state officials get all this extra money from.' It was a line of investigation that had great potential for the opposition. Putin's ratings may have been sky-high, but corruption remained his Achilles heel: pollsters working for Navalny reported that autumn that 87% of Russians wanted to see criminal charges brought against corrupt officials.

Within months of that unscheduled visit to Yakunin's country home, Navalny was back in front of a judge. On 19 December 2014, state prosecutors asked a Moscow court to jail the opposition leader for ten years on fraud charges. 'At least it's easy to count,' Navalny sighed. Prosecutors also asked for eight years for his younger brother, Oleg. The charges related to the following convoluted scheme: Oleg had undercut his employer, the Russian Post Office, by arranging cheaper delivery prices for the Russian branch of the French cosmetics company Yves Rocher through a company set up by his brother Alexei. The elder Navalny had then outsourced the actual work to a third company. It was not, perhaps, entirely ethical, but, under Russian law, there was nothing criminal about it. Oleg's contract with the Post Office also did not prevent him from doing business on the side. Yves Rocher employees testified that no crime was committed.

For Navalny and his supporters, the state prosecutor's enthusiasm in pursuing the charges was clear evidence of a fresh plot to put the opposition figurehead behind bars. But Putin had already appeared to back down once. What had changed now? Was Russia's long-time leader seeking to dispose of one of his bitterest critics ahead of a possible economic meltdown? The national currency was already reeling: just days before the court hearing, the rouble had briefly crashed to just below 80 to a dollar, completing a 49% slump for the year. In theory, there should have been no better time for the opposition to challenge Putin. In reality, however, the war in Ukraine and the rise in ultra-nationalism that it inspired had marginalized the Kremlin's critics. But would Putin take the chance of leaving Navalny at liberty?

A Facebook group calling for a 'discussion of the verdict', well-known opposition code for a protest rally, on central Moscow's Manezhnaya Square (colloquially known as Manezhka) was quickly set up: some 15,000 people indicated in the first twenty-four hours that they would attend. As the numbers began to rocket, eventually reaching some 33,000, an unlikely optimism swept through the opposition. 'This is going to be one of the biggest demos ever,' declared Roman Dobrokhotov, the opposition activist who had shouted down Medvedev on Constitution Day.[47] 'There is a feeling of change. Don't miss it – this is history.' Navalny supporters began to dream about Moscow's very own Maidan.

But the omens ahead of the court session were ominous. The date for the verdict was 30 December, the fifth anniversary of the conviction of Khodorkovsky, the oil tycoon, on a second set of hotly disputed charges. Was history about to repeat itself?

In what was by now becoming something of a ritual, Navalny supporters and pro-Kremlin activists faced off outside the courtroom in central Moscow where the opposition leader and his younger brother's fate would be decided. 'Navalny is an agent of the United States,' a young NOD activist told me, as police pushed back the crowds in freezing temperatures. 'I want to see him jailed.'

Inside the courthouse, things were chaotic. 'Put the journalists up against the wall!' shouted Navalny, with grim humour, as press scrambled to make it inside the tiny courtroom for what was expected to be another marathon verdict-reading session. Instead, in a twist that had even lawyers confused, the judge, Yelena Korobchenko, simply read out the verdicts – both guilty – then swiftly handed Navalny a three-and-a-half-year suspended sentence, while jailing his younger brother, Oleg, for the same period. Alexei Navalny was also ordered to remain under house arrest, although no one quite understood on what grounds. There was a second or two of stunned silence. This was an outcome that no one had predicted. Putin, it seemed, had outwitted everyone again. 'Why are you jailing him? To punish me even more?' shouted Navalny, with tears in his eyes.

Outside the courthouse, which riot police had by now cordoned off, pro-Putin youth and opposition supporters traded insults and the occasional blow. Few in the opposition had any doubts that the decision to imprison Oleg Navalny had been taken at the highest level. 'This is called taking hostages,' said Grigory Alburov, a member of Navalny's anti-corruption organization. 'They are putting pressure on Alexei's family.'[48]

When he finally made it out of the courthouse, after a long and tearful parting scene with his brother, Navalny was in no mood for compromise. Gone was his talk of peaceful dissent that had so disappointed radicals at the onset of the 2011–12 protests. 'The authorities are deliberately torturing the relatives of their political opponents,' a furious Navalny announced, speaking on the snowy steps of the courthouse. 'Authorities like these have no right to exist. They must be destroyed. I call on everyone to take to the streets today and stay there until they are removed from power.'

The decision to imprison Oleg Navalny realized one of the opposition's worst fears: Putin had shed his previous reluctance to go after the relatives of his bitterest critics. It was a long-standing practice – even Mikhail Khodorkovsky's family had been left in peace following the former oligarch's jailing. Now, the rulebook had been torn up. That same month, Russian investigators also charged Alexandrina Markvo, the wife of Navalny's ex-top banker ally, Vladimir Ashurkov, with what opposition figures alleged were politically motivated fraud charges connected to her organization of literary festivals in Moscow.[49]

As news that Oleg Navalny would not be seeing his wife or two small children for the next few years spread via the opposition's digital grapevine, police began cordoning off Manezhnaya Square, forcing protesters to congregate on the narrow streets around the State Duma. The mood was confrontational: 'What shall we bring? Tyres, white ribbons, axes?' asked one opposition activist in an inflammatory tweet. 'Stalin also loved to jail wives and relatives,' said another.[50] Police took no chances, ordering even small groups of people to disperse. 'Disperse?' asked one astonished woman, standing on her own some way from the main protest, after being approached by a riot cop with a megaphone. 'I'm just here to meet some friends. Is this North Korea, or what?'

No one had considered whether disaffected Muscovites would turn out in numbers for Oleg Navalny, and it soon became clear that attendance at the rally was way down on that ecstatic afternoon in the summer of 2013. It was at times hard to distinguish between those who were protesting, and those who were simply out for a spot of festive shopping. Not that riot police seemed to care, pushing everyone – demonstrators and shoppers – up the central Tverskaya Street. Those who were too slow to comply were snatched and hauled off to waiting police trucks. Some 200 protesters, and a few bemused shoppers, would end up in police custody before the evening was out. Those protesters who remained on the streets were confronted by belligerent activists from the Anti-Maidan movement, including a contingent of pro-Putin Cossacks. Across town, wary police ordered a theatre that had dared to stage a play based on events at the Maidan protest camp to close up for the night.

Even the unexpected arrival of a furious Navalny – who broke house arrest to ride the metro to the protest, where he was immediately seized by police and driven back home – was unable to do more than briefly lift spirits. As arrests mounted, the most stubborn protesters gathered around a huge, glittery New Year's decoration. But by 9.30 p.m. local time, the area was almost clear, with only a small hardcore remaining.

Online chat before the demonstration had been of Molotov cocktails and tent cities, but protesters made no serious effort to resist riot-police snatch squads, with the majority simply content to film arrests on their smartphones. Their reluctance to risk arrest was understandable: Putin had recently signed off on a new law that stipulated five years behind bars for repeated protest-related violations. 'No Maidan in Moscow!' read a slogan beamed onto a wall near the Kremlin by pro-Putin supporters. On that night's evidence, it was hard to argue. 'Three years ago, we were an opposition,' lamented Nemtsov, in the wake of the failed rally. 'Now we are no more than dissidents. The task is to organize a real opposition again.'[51] It was an undertaking that would require Herculean efforts.

18

MURDER AT THE KREMLIN WALLS

The war in Ukraine damaged the opposition movement, but it also provided many activists with a new purpose, and a potential means of striking back at the Kremlin. As the death toll in the conflict rose, some in the opposition redirected their efforts towards proving the presence of Russian troops in the former Soviet republic. Putin denied they were there, and said any Russians fighting on the side of pro-Moscow separatists in Ukraine were 'volunteers'. He maintained that there was nothing Russia could do to stop these people – often heavily armed, and equipped with top-of-the-range combat gear – crossing the border into Ukraine. As for any serving Russian soldiers involved in military action in eastern Ukraine, the Kremlin insisted they had travelled to the conflict zone on their own initiatives during sabbaticals from military service.[1] There were, of course, bona fide volunteers who had journeyed to Ukraine in the belief that, as billboards in the separatist-controlled city of Donetsk declared, they would have the chance to 'fulfil a historic duty' to fight Nazism, but it was inconceivable that rebel forces could have stood up to the Ukrainian army and pro-government militia for so long without the assistance of the well-equipped and well-trained Russian army.

The Kremlin's denials often stretched credibility to breaking point and beyond. When ten paratroopers were captured in Ukraine, Russia said they had got lost and 'mistakenly' wandered over the border.[2] When apparent Russian soldiers cheerfully admitted to journalists that they had been sent to eastern Ukraine by army chiefs,[3] the Kremlin either refused to comment or rubbished the reports. Still, the evidence mounted, from video footage of huge colonies of what seemed to be Russian military hardware moving deep inside Ukraine,[4] to satellite images that NATO said showed Russian tanks fighting on the side of separatist forces. Western journalists also witnessed Russian armoured vehicles driving into Ukraine.[5]

Additionally, there were sporadic opposition media interviews with the relatives of Russian soldiers reportedly killed in eastern Ukraine, including one with the mother of a sapper whose son had told her, 'I'm going to war.'[6] Opposition activists set up a website called Cargo 200 – military slang for the zinc coffins of dead servicemen – to monitor the increasing number of Russian army casualties in eastern Ukraine.[7] But most bereaved relatives were coerced into silence through a combination of threats and financial rewards.

Attempts to reveal the truth were often met with violence. When Lev Shlosberg, an opposition politician in Pskov, a Russian town near the border with Estonia, interviewed soldiers whose comrades-in-arms had been killed in Ukraine, and also drew attention to the fresh graves of paratroopers from the region, he was beaten unconscious by unidentified assailants. All too often the troops being deployed to Ukraine were young conscripts – exempt from foreign service under Russian law – rather than well-trained contact soldiers. 'This is all criminal, this is all against the law – against Russia's own law,' raged Valentina Melnikova, head of the Russian Union of Committees of Soldiers' Mothers pressure group.[8]

'[Putin] is a cunning person. He tells the whole world there are no troops there. But then he says to us "come on, come on",' a Russian solider named Dorjhi Batomunkuyev told the opposition *Novaya Gazeta* newspaper during an interview in the Moscow hospital where he was undergoing treatment for horrific injuries suffered in eastern Ukraine. 'We all knew we were crossing the [Ukrainian] border. What else could we do? We couldn't stop then. We had to follow orders.'[9] (When a newspaper from Batomunkuyev's home region of Buryatia, in Russia's south, printed a follow-up story about the soldier's injuries, a 'public outcry' – most likely a euphemism for political pressure – forced the editor into a drastic move: he not only ordered the article to be removed from the paper's website, but also handed his staff scissors so that they could help him in cutting out the offending piece from 50,000 print copies of the newspaper that were awaiting distribution.[10])

Despite the growing evidence of Russian military involvement in Ukraine, opposition figures were all but helpless in the face of the Kremlin's control over state media, the main source of news for some 90% of Russians. Their investigations simply weren't getting through the deafening white noise of disinformation. The difficulties faced by the opposition were illustrated perfectly in a satirical cartoon by Russia's finest political cartoonist, Sergey Elkin, which depicted a figure slouched in front of a television set, both the screen and the anonymous viewer's brain filled with identical swirls of bewildering electronic static.[11]

Public opinion surveys by the independent Moscow-based Levada Centre pollster indicated that the majority of Russians believed the Kremlin's denials. 'They are all volunteers,' an elderly woman told me in central Moscow in late 2014, as we both watched a small group of opposition activists protest the war. 'They've just gone to protect relatives from the fascists. Wouldn't you do the same in their shoes?'

This willingness to believe the Kremlin's line wasn't merely the result of propaganda, suggested Lev Shlosberg, the opposition politician who had been assaulted after his investigation into the deaths of Russian soldiers in Ukraine. 'People want to believe that Russia is innocent, and that it is not spilling blood,' he told me. 'This belief is a form of psychological defence. A realization of the scale of the deceit involved will only come later, when a critical mass of Russian society has woken up. But this will not be for a long time.'[12]

Not everyone was prepared to wait.

'This is what we need to do,' said Nemtsov, when he entered the Moscow headquarters of his RPR-Parnas party early one morning in 2015. 'We need to write up a report, "Putin: War", publish huge numbers of it, and hand it out on the streets,' the opposition politician told his fellow activists. 'We'll tell people how Putin unleashed this conflict.'[13]

It was an ambitious plan, but one that had no guarantee of success. For starters, it would be a near impossible task to print any such report in sufficient enough numbers to reach even 10% of the population. And, secondly, it was far from certain that even a well-presented report with incontrovertible proof of Russian military involvement in Ukraine would be powerful enough to penetrate the wall of non-stop Kremlin propaganda. It was also unclear what exactly it would take to combat the widespread willingness to turn a blind eye to Putin's sins that Shlosberg had highlighted. But Nemtsov was determined to go through with the project. 'He infected us all with his enthusiasm, like always,' said Ilya Yashin, the opposition figure's political ally and long-time friend.[14]

Some two months later, Nemtsov scribbled a note to his assistant, Olga Shorina, in which he revealed that he had been contacted by a group of disgruntled paratroopers who had fought in Ukraine. 'But for now they are afraid to talk,' Nemtsov wrote. Shorina kept the scrap of paper and later showed it to Reuters.[15]

The day after writing the note, Nemtsov appeared on air on the Echo of Moscow radio station to appeal to Russians to attend a 1 March 2015 protest rally against the war in Ukraine and the growing economic crisis. Public interest in the rally was low: the authorities had given permission, but insisted it take place in a residential area far from central Moscow. For many opposition activists, the decision to agree to demonstrate in what some scathingly dubbed a 'reservation' was indicative of the protest movement's passiveness. Navalny was, however, in favour of the rally, saying it would bring the opposition 'closer to the people'. But the anti-Putin movement's figurehead would not be attending: finally released from house arrest on 18 February, he was jailed a mere fifty-five hours later for fifteen days on charges of handing out opposition leaflets in the

Moscow metro. In Navalny's enforced absence, Nemtsov seized the role of main agitator for the rally.

'Let's just imagine a public debate between me and Putin,' said a furious Nemtsov, glasses perched on the end of his nose, as he spoke at the Echo of Moscow studio. 'I would start with a very simple question, for example, "Why are Russian soldiers being killed while you, Mr Putin, disown these soldiers and lie, saying that they are not involved in fighting? How can you, as commander-in-chief, disown them? How dare you remain commander-in-chief after that?"'[16]

It was to be his final public appearance.

'WE ARE ALL IN A DARK FOREST NOW'

After the radio interview, Nemtsov went to meet his Ukrainian girlfriend, a twenty-three-year-old model named Anna Durytska. The two ate a late meal at Bosco, a chic Red Square restaurant that overlooks the Kremlin, and then walked towards Nemtsov's nearby apartment in a light drizzle. As they crossed the Bolshoi Moskvoretsky Bridge, a concrete walkway over the Moskva River that was completed in 1937 – the height of Stalin's Great Terror – a man overtook the couple, turned around swiftly, and fired several shots. Four bullets stuck Nemtsov, hitting him in the head, heart, liver and stomach. He died almost instantly. Durytska was unharmed, but did not see the assassin's face. The killer then leapt over a barrier into the road, and got into a waiting car with no number plates, which sped off unhindered into a stream of late-night traffic. It was, activists would later note with grim irony, 27 February, the date that Putin had recently declared a new national holiday – Special Forces Day – in honour of the Kremlin's seizure of Crimea.

Reports of Nemtsov's murder shook late-night Moscow. Yashin was the first opposition figure to make it to the bridge. Gazing at the stark sight of Nemtsov lying in a black body bag, he fired off a chilling message on Twitter. 'Nemtsov has been shot. He's dead.'[17] Activists who rushed to the bridge in response were dismayed to find police already hosing down the murder scene, apparently washing away any vital evidence. Others counted at least a dozen security cameras in the immediate vicinity, with at least one pointed directly at the exact stretch of bridge where Nemtsov had been gunned down. How, they wondered, had the killer been able to flee so easily? After all, on the rare occasions that anti-Putin activists attempted to protest on nearby Red Square – one of Russia's most heavily guarded public spaces – they were invariably nabbed within seconds. It was later reported, in what seemed like a suspiciously convenient coincidence for the assassin, that the cameras on the bridge had been 'turned off for maintenance' that very evening.[18]

By morning, Nemtsov's murder was the talk of Russia. Of course, there had been other political murders in the country's violent post-Soviet history, but none of the victims had enjoyed anything like Nemtsov's fame. One of the 'young reformers' who had overseen a disastrous economic restructuring during the late 1990s, Nemtsov had even been briefly considered for the presidency, before the ailing Yeltsin eventually decided on Putin. Even two decades on, despite being banned from appearing on state-run television, he remained a household name. I had visited Nemtsov at his central Moscow headquarters in the spring of 2013. Gregarious to the point of coarseness, he had addressed me, as he did everyone, as '*ty*', the informal Russian form of 'you', which is considered rude when not speaking to anyone who is not friend, family or close acquaintance. Curious to see how he had charmed US Congressmen into adopting the Magnitsky Act, I asked if we could switch to English. The transformation was instant. Gone was the rather rude Russian politician, and in his place was a perfect gentleman. 'Yes, of course,' he purred, acquiescing to my request. You could say what you liked about Nemtsov, but he never failed to make an impression. And now he was dead, murdered by an assassin's bullets within sight of the Kremlin's illuminated walls. He was just fifty-five years old.

The Investigative Committee, the powerful law-enforcement organization answerable only to Putin, quickly announced what it considered
to be the most probable motives for the murder. Unsurprisingly, none
of these included the possibility that Nemtsov was killed for his tireless
opposition to the Kremlin. Instead, the Investigative Committee's list of
possible motives included a violent row linked to Nemtsov's famously
colourful private life, a business dispute, or an attempt to destabilize
Russia. 'Nemtsov could have been a kind of sacrifice for those who stop
at nothing to attain their political ends,' said Investigative Committee
spokesman Vladimir Markin.[19] He also suggested that the killing may
have been ordered by 'radical figures' involved in the fighting in Ukraine.
An unnamed law-enforcement source later told Russian media that
Nemtsov had been killed by Adam Osmayev, the Chechen commander
of a pro-Ukrainian volunteer battalion, in a bid to destabilize Russia.
Osmayev rubbished the allegations, and described Nemtsov as a 'true
hero'.[20]

Yet the most unexpected of the possible motives put forward by investigators was that the bitter Kremlin critic had been murdered by religious
extremists in revenge for his stance on the January 2015 attack by Islamist
gunmen on the offices of the *Charlie Hebdo* satirical magazine in Paris.[21]
This was a deeply flawed theory for one simple reason – Nemtsov had
written only one short text about the shootings and the caricatures of the
Prophet Mohammed that had provoked them. In the piece, entitled 'The
Islamic Inquisition' and posted on the website of the Echo of Moscow
radio station, he had said that Islam was a 'young religion' that had yet
to 'mature'. He also said there could be no justification whatever for the
violence in Paris.[22] His comments stirred up exactly zero controversy,
and there was not a single report of any Muslims being offended by the
text. Given the far more explosive statements being made by Russia's
far right, it was also highly unlikely that Islamist militants would have
felt it necessary to scour the website of a liberal Moscow radio station in
search of 'offensive' texts.

'Suggestions that Boris [Nemtsov] had in some way insulted Islam
are just ridiculous,' raged his former ally Yashin. 'Investigators need

to ask, "Who benefited?" And the answer to that is Vladimir Putin,' the opposition activist told me. 'We have long been used to smear campaigns, criminal charges and even beatings, but this has taken things to a new level. We are all in a dark forest now, and anyone who opposes Putin is in danger.'[23] It was an accusation that gained further credibility when it was revealed that police officers had removed documents and computer drives from Nemtsov's apartment in the hours after his assassination.

Nemtsov, of course, had known that his opposition to Putin and his not-so-secret war in Ukraine meant he was a target. He often received death threats, including one that he reported to the authorities just weeks before he was killed. (No action was taken over his complaint.) As political repression increased in the backdrop to the war in Ukraine, Nemtsov had feared arrest – reportedly hiding out for months in Israel in mid-2014 – and, to a lesser extent, assassination. 'Every time I call her [my mother], she says, "When are you going to stop having a go at Putin? He'll kill you!" And she's totally serious about this,' he told a Russian opposition journalist just two weeks before he was murdered. When asked by the reporter if he shared her fears, he responded: 'A little. Not so much as Mum, but still… But I'm not that afraid of him [Putin]. If I was that afraid, I wouldn't head an opposition party, and I wouldn't do what I'm doing.'[24]

'He knew he was in danger,' Nemtsov's assistant, Olga Shorina, told me. 'But he didn't think the situation in the country had reached the stage where the Kremlin's political opponents could be killed in assassinations designed to send a signal to the whole country.'[25] Despite the hazards involved in political opposition to Putin, Nemtsov had not employed bodyguards. Indeed, I had seen him the day before his murder, walking along a street in central Moscow with a woman I didn't recognize. People turned their heads to stare at him. 'He always insisted that, if they wanted to kill him, they would, and it didn't matter how many bodyguards he had,' said Yashin.

Nemtsov's eldest daughter, Zhanna, a journalist with the Moscow-based business channel RBC, also accused the authorities of complicity in her father's death. 'I believe the murder was politically motivated, and because of this it will not be completely solved, and far from everyone who is guilty will be punished. At least while Putin is Russia's president,' she told me in an email from Europe, after fleeing Russia over concerns for her safety.[26]

When pressed to comment on allegations that the Kremlin was involved in Nemtsov's shooting, Putin's spokesman, Dmitry Peskov, sighed and suggested that the opposition figure was not worth the Kremlin's bullets. 'In political terms he did not pose any threat to the current Russian leadership or Vladimir Putin,' he said. 'If we compare popularity levels, Putin's and the government's ratings and so on, in general Boris Nemtsov was just a little bit more than an average citizen.'[27] It was a scathing assessment of the opposition figure's role, and one that brought back memories of Putin's infamous statement that Anna Politkovskaya, the investigative journalist murdered in Moscow in 2006, had done 'greater damage' to the Kremlin through her death than with any of her publications. Nemtsov's murder, Peskov added, bore 'all the hallmarks of a provocation'. It was a message that was picked up on and amplified by state-run TV, whose top attack dog, Dmitry Kiselyov, insinuated during his weekly news show that the West had ordered Nemtsov's assassination to provoke a Maidan-type protest in Moscow. He also spent an indecently long time highlighting the results of opinion polls that proved Nemtsov did not enjoy widespread political support among Russians.[28] Other pro-Kremlin media promoted the theory heavily. 'Shooting Nemtsov, aiming at Putin', was the headline on the website of the best-selling *Komsomolskaya Pravda* newspaper, which suggested to its millions of readers across Russia that the CIA had killed Nemtsov in a false-flag operation to discredit Putin.[29]

Although state media exaggerated and distorted the facts, for many neutral observers it was hard to see why the Kremlin would have ordered Nemtsov's murder at a time when the anti-Putin opposition was struggling to remain a viable political force. Nemtsov's association with Yeltsin's catastrophic presidency meant he would always be distrusted by large numbers of voters. His RPR-Parnas party, which he co-founded with Mikhail Kasyanov, the former prime minister known as Misha 2% for his alleged fondness for bribes while in office, had largely failed to capture the imagination of disaffected Russians. 'Of course, anyone who was in Yeltsin's government is forever associated with the image of the 1990s,' Nemtsov had once admitted to me. Suggestions that he had been shot in order to prevent the release of his report on Putin's secret war in Ukraine, which he had barely had time to begin work on before his murder, also appeared far-fetched. There already existed plenty of evidence of Russian military involvement in eastern Ukraine: what exactly could Nemtsov have uncovered that would have spooked Putin enough for him to have the veteran opposition politician killed?

Yet while Nemtsov was unlikely to have toppled Putin, at the ballot box or otherwise, his activities, from his no-holds-barred reports on top-level graft to his campaigning for the imposition of foreign asset freezes against corrupt officials, had undoubtedly caused serious headaches for influential figures close to the Kremlin. There was little question that he had plenty of powerful enemies. But the nagging question remained: if the authorities had taken to murdering opposition figures on the streets of Moscow, then why was Navalny – by far the most serious threat to Putin's kleptocracy – still alive?

'PROPAGANDA KILLS'

Just days before Nemtsov's assassination, some 40,000 people had marched through the centre of Moscow to denounce Russia's 'fifth column'. The rally was attended by NOD activists, Cossacks and the pro-Putin motorcycle club, the Night Wolves. One prominent banner accused Nemtsov of being an 'organizer of Maidan'. Although many at the rally, which was covered extensively by state television, had been bussed in for the event, there were also plenty of true believers. 'The fifth column must be destroyed. It threatens Russia's very existence,' said an excited twenty-something NOD member, who gave his name only as Alexei. On stage, a worker from a Urals-based tank factory hammered home the message. 'These traitors are an insignificant few, but we must remember that they are arrogant and cynical people who will stop at nothing to destroy our country,' he shouted. 'Motherland! Freedom! Putin!' chanted some in the crowd in response.

'I do not want the United States to do to my country what it has done to other countries,' Alexander Zaladantsov, the heavily tattooed, middle-aged leader of the Night Wolves motorbike gang, told me after the rally.[30] 'We will defend Putin and Russia by any means necessary.' It was a remarkable turnaround for a man who had helped defend Gorbachev's reforms against a KGB-backed coup in 1991. 'I was a naive youngster in those days,' he explained, before launching into an impassioned, if somewhat incoherent speech about the 'eternal greatness' of Stalin. 'You in the West will never understand. Even now he frightens you,' he told me.

It wasn't only Zaladantsov whose opinions had undergone a radical rethink. The attitudes of ordinary Russians towards state-sponsored political terror also appeared to be shifting rapidly. According to the results of a public opinion survey published in early 2015 by the independent, Moscow-based Levada Centre pollster, some 45% of Russians – a figure that had almost doubled in just two years – said they believed the millions of victims of Stalin's gulags and purges could be 'justified' by historical circumstances.[31]

The atmosphere was explosive. News of Nemtsov's grisly demise came as a shock for his fellow activists, but there should have been little surprise. Less than twenty-four hours before his murder, shots were fired at the windows of an apartment owned by Anna Stepanova, the head of Nemtsov's RPR-Parnas party in the central Russian city of Nizhny Novgorod.

'If, just a few days ago, people in our city were carrying signs that said, "Let's kill off the fifth column," and today they kill Nemtsov, then what will happen tomorrow?' asked Anatoly Chubais, who served in Yeltsin's government alongside Nemtsov, after visiting the murder scene.

For opposition activists like Ksenia Sobchak, the socialite turned Kremlin critic, Nemtsov's murder seemed to signal that this state-encouraged hatred of political dissent had taken on a life of its own, inspiring rogue elements to take bloody revenge against opposition figures that they – and Putin – believed were Russia's enemies.

'It would be in some way less disturbing, if Putin had ordered Nemtsov's murder,' she wrote in a much-discussed article. 'This would be an awful system, but at least it would still be a system. A manageable system. But there is no Putin who gave the order for the murder. There is only Putin who has created a hellish terminator that he has now lost control of. There is no one controlling the process any more. There is chaotic hatred. A hatred that is fuelled every day by the national media.'[32]

✱

In the aftermath of Nemtsov's assassination, the rally that he had been promoting on the night of his death was scrapped, and – after hours of tough negotiations – the opposition was permitted to gather instead in central Moscow for a march of remembrance. Ironically, this would be the closest to the Kremlin that Putin's opponents had been allowed since the birth of the white ribbon protest movement in 2011.

The mood ahead of the rally was a potent mixture of despair and defiance. 'I know who killed Boris Nemtsov,' wrote one Russian émigré Facebook user,[33] in a post that went viral among opposition supporters. 'He was killed by the hatred poured into the air… He was killed by those who draw Obama with fangs… He was killed by those who hate darkies, yids, Ukrainians, and, especially their neighbours. But physical death is not so important. We all die sooner or later. But take your children away from Russia, so that they do not become infected.'

Others were possessed of a quiet determination. Nemtsov's assassination had raised the stakes to unthinkable heights, and the only way out now was forward. 'The morning after Nemtsov's murder, we all came to work convinced more than ever that we have to continue our political activities, to push on further,' Georgy Alburov, one of Navalny's key activists, told me ahead of the rally. 'What else can we do?'

The march in honour of Nemtsov took place on 1 March, officially the first day of spring on the Russian calendar. From morning onwards, long lines of people clutching flowers and photographs of the veteran opposition figure streamed through central Moscow. Nemtsov's murder had stirred something in the Russian capital. 'Enough is enough,' Artyom, a middle-aged man with a bushy beard, told me as we queued to gain entry to the start of the march. 'It's time for Moscow's decent, intelligent people to reclaim the streets from the thugs and the killers.'

And they came that afternoon in the tens of thousands, many holding aloft the Russian tricolour, marching through the heart of Moscow, past Red Square and the psychedelic domes of St Basil's Cathedral, until they filed, slowly, onto the landmark bridge where Nemtsov had been gunned down in cold blood. 'No War!' chanted the crowd, as it marched towards the murder scene, where a growing pile of flowers lay in the slow, constant drizzle. A police helicopter buzzed low above the mourners. Just feet from where Nemtsov had been shot dead, a protester held up a sign: 'Propaganda kills.'

It was hard to escape the feeling that afternoon that Nemtsov's death marked a turning point. Who would triumph in the vicious battle for Russia's soul? The self-styled 'patriots' fed a steady diet of hate speech by national TV? Or these tens of thousands of Muscovites alarmed by Russia's increasing international isolation? 'I am not afraid,' read another popular banner. Others held up placards with a play on Nemtsov's first name so that it read, simply, 'Fight!' It was a noble sentiment. But the struggle was getting harder, and much more dangerous.

Two days after the march, thousands queued in the snow and ice to pay their last respects to the slain opposition leader, whose open coffin lay on view in the Sakharov human-rights centre. Nemtsov then was laid to rest at Troyekurovskoye Cemetery, a sprawling graveyard on the edge of western Moscow that also contains the graves of journalists Anna Politkovskaya and Dmitry Kholodov, who was murdered in 1994 after investigating military corruption. Neither Putin nor any other high-ranking Russian politician was in attendance.

'Nemtsov's murder could be the start of a wave of killings, if the Kremlin continues to set people against one another,' opposition politician Gennady Gudkov said as he stood in line to pay his respects. 'This could lead to civil war.' The sense of impending violence was almost tangible.

As Ksenia Sobchak left the funeral, a stranger whispered to her, 'Keep in mind, Ksenia, you're next.' If Putin's rumoured goddaughter was now a target, then no one in the opposition was safe.

Two days later, an anti-Putin activist named Alexei Semenov was savagely beaten in Moscow by assailants wielding baseball bats. His attackers were never found.

For Navalny, talk of a pro-Kremlin 'rogue element' inspired by state television to murder Nemtsov was a ludicrous and dangerous illusion. 'I believe that Nemtsov was murdered by members of a government (the special services) or pro-government organization on the order of the country's political leadership (including Vladimir Putin),' he said in a statement from jail on the morning of the funeral.

'Let's stop repeating this nonsense that "Boris was killed by an atmosphere of hatred,"' he went on. 'What atmosphere of hatred are you on about? We have had an atmosphere of hatred since 2007, but in the past few months we have seen the organized creation of pro-government extremist-terrorist organizations, who openly declare that their aim is to fight the opposition in ways the police can't.'

Navalny also tore into the popular view that Nemtsov possessed insufficient political clout to warrant a Kremlin-ordered hit, highlighting the politician's ceaseless endeavours to bring together disparate groups within the opposition movement, as well as his fearless anti-corruption work. 'He did things, rather than waiting for the regime to fall. This is why he was both relevant and dangerous.'

Navalny drew historical parallels between Putin and some of the world's most infamous dictators. 'Those who say Nemtsov's death was of "no benefit to Putin" can join in the corner those who say "[ex-Haitian dictator François] Duvalier had no need of killings, Stalin had nothing to gain from the Red Terror, or Augusto Pinochet gathered everyone in the stadium for a game of football",' he wrote. 'This was beneficial for Putin. Open up your history books – it's all written there.'[34]

Less than three months after Nemtsov's murder, the report that the opposition politician had been working on before his death finally saw the light of day. Completed by fellow activists and some of Russia's finest opposition journalists, it was entitled, as Nemtsov had planned, 'Putin: War'.[35] Along with dozens of other journalists, I attended its 12 May 2015 presentation at the central Moscow headquarters of Nemtsov's RPR-Parnas party. Expectations were high. But, although it was well presented and written in an accessible style, the report failed to live up to the hype. It relied on open source material and there were, as its authors freely admitted, 'no sensations' within its glossy pages.

However, as a vivid chronicle of the escalation and consequences of Putin's aggression in Ukraine, which the report's authors estimated had cost the lives of at least 220 Russians soldiers, 'Putin: War' was unheralded. 'It's everything that Boris wanted it to be,' said Yashin.

Predictably, activists had struggled to find printers willing to handle such overtly anti-Putin material. As a result, they had managed to produce only some 3,000 copies. The report was, of course, available online, but its limited availability in print meant it had more in common with Soviet-era dissident literature than a powerful weapon in the battle to bring down Putin. 'It's unlikely to change public opinion,' confessed opposition journalist Oleg Kashin, who had worked on the report. In truth, Nemtsov's posthumous report was little more than a potshot at Putin. But by this stage, the opposition's depleted armoury was capable of little else.

THE CHECHEN LINK?

Early on 7 March 2015, eight days after Nemtsov had been gunned down, Zaur Dadayev, a senior Chechen police officer, was detained by armed investigators while driving to visit relatives in Magas, the capital of the

North Caucasus republic of Ingushetia. His cousin, Anzor Gubashev, a security guard at a hypermarket near Moscow, was also arrested the same morning. Like Dadayev, he was seized while driving to visit family in Ingushetia. Both men were charged with Nemtsov's murder.

Dadayev's arrest raised eyebrows. A member of the powerful Chechen interior ministry battalion, Sever, he was rumoured to be close to Ramzan Kadyrov, the ruthless Chechen leader given free rein by Putin to run the volatile mountainous republic as a generously funded personal fiefdom in return for suppressing separatist and Islamist forces. De facto ruler of the republic since the death of his father, Chechen President Akhmad Kadyrov, in a bomb attack in 2004, he had recently formed an unholy alliance with Vladislav Surkov, the half-Chechen architect of Putin's 'sovereign democracy'. The arrest of one of Kadyrov's trusted officers in Moscow on charges of carrying out modern Russia's most high-profile murder was a development that was as unexpected as it was ominous.

'Dadayev is a deeply religious person and like all Muslims he was very shocked by the actions of Charlie [Hebdo] and by comments supporting the printing of the caricatures of the [Prophet Mohammed],' said Kadyrov in an Instagram post, his preferred means of communication with the world. Given that the Chechen leader had organized a 500,000-strong rally in Grozny against the caricatures just days after the killings in Paris, his comment was widely viewed as a thinly disguised justification of Nemtsov's murder. Yet it was still hard to believe that the assassination had a religious angle. In other comments, Kadyrov also described Dadayev as 'a genuine Russian patriot'.[36]

Later that week, Putin awarded Kadyrov the Order of Merit, the first of three state awards that the former rebel fighter would receive over the next nine days. If little else was clear, it was obvious that Putin had no qualms about honouring a man who had just praised the main suspect in the cold-blooded killing of one of his most outspoken critics.

Some forty-eight hours after their arrests, both Dadayev and Gubashev were dragged handcuffed into a Moscow court by masked police officers clutching automatic weapons. The judge informed the court that Dadayev, the alleged gunman and ringleader, had confessed to the shooting. The Chechen police officer made no comment other than to raise his index finger and say, 'I love the Prophet Mohammed.' Three other Chechen men were also ordered by the court to remain in custody pending further investigation, although they were not charged. Russian media reports said another suspect, Beslan Shavanov, had blown himself up with a hand grenade when police came for him in Grozny. Dadayev later said he suspected Shavanov had been murdered.

Investigators were under immense pressure to close the case as swiftly as possible, and they appeared to be taking no chances. Almost inevitably, when Andrei Babushkin, a member of Russia's human-rights council, visited Dadayev in jail, the Chechen told him that he had been tortured into confessing. Dadayev also claimed he had admitted to the murder only after investigators had agreed to free an officer colleague also being held in connection with the killing. 'I thought that I would be able to tell the court the full truth. That I am innocent,' he told Babushkin. He also said he believed that his confession would save his life.[37]

Someone also appeared to have been putting pressure on Dadayev's relatives. Less than twenty-four hours after he had confessed to Nemtsov's murder, his family members abruptly annulled the contracts for legal advice that they had signed with both his Moscow-based lawyer, Zaurbek Sadakhanov, and Kheda Saratova, a well-known human-rights worker based in Grozny. 'The family were either afraid, or they hoped that Kadyrov would be able to get Dadayev out with a mere wave of his hand,' Saratova told me. 'But they were badly mistaken.'[38]

The arrests set off alarm bells among opposition activists. Chechens have frequently been fingered as 'trigger men' in high-profile killings in Russia, but critics say those who order the murders are never brought to justice. 'Two Chechens somehow appointed guilty. So predictable, there's not even anything to say,' commented Vladimir Milov, an opposition figure who had co-authored with Nemtsov a 2010 report on Kremlin corruption.[39] 'Our worst fears are coming true: the hitman has been arrested but the commander will remain free,' said Yashin.[40]

That Kadyrov had been ill-disposed towards Nemtsov was not in doubt. In his autobiography, *Confessions of a Rebel*, Nemtsov related how the future Chechen leader had threatened him in 2002, after he proposed changes to the North Caucasus republic's constitution that would have greatly reduced the powers of the president. 'When I came out of the hall, a person came up to me and said that I should be killed for my speech. I asked "Who are you?" and he pulled out FSB identification. It was Ramzan Kadyrov,' wrote Nemtsov. 'I can't say that I was very scared, as the Chechens around me said he was joking. But I didn't see any sign of a joke in his eyes. I saw only hatred.'[41]

Kadyrov had also called for Nemtsov to be imprisoned over his role in the mass anti-Putin protests that broke out in Moscow in December 2011.[42] 'Kadyrov has serious psychological problems,' Nemtsov responded, speaking to journalists on the streets of Moscow. 'He needs to be treated, and urgently. He should be hospitalized and treated for schizophrenia.'[43] Despite the death threat, and the well-documented history of mutual animosity between the two men, Kadyrov was not summoned to Moscow for questioning. 'Putin is afraid to have Kadyrov questioned,' Vadim Prokhanov, a lawyer for the Nemtsov family, told me. 'He is afraid of discrediting him, and the consequences of a Chechnya without Kadyrov in charge.'

Kadyrov's enemies frequently meet grisly ends. 'He acts like a medieval tyrant. If someone tells the truth about what is going on, it's like signing one's own death warrant,' said Movladi Baisarov, a former Chechen special forces officer, in a Russian newspaper interview in 2006.[44] A month after that interview, Baisarov was shot dead in Moscow while 'resisting arrest'. Eyewitnesses claimed he had been executed by Chechen police officers while their Moscow counterparts stood by and watched. His murder was just the beginning of a trail of blood that critics say leads straight to Kadyrov. 'You don't survive long once Kadyrov names you as his personal enemy,' said Russian journalist Sergei Darenko.[45]

In January 2009, Umar Israilov, a former bodyguard for Kadyrov, was gunned down as he walked out of a grocery store in Vienna. Israilov had accused Kadyrov of abductions and torture, and had reportedly been warned to withdraw the allegations. Three Chechen men were later jailed by a Viennese court over his death. Kadyrov denied any link to the shooting. 'If I had wanted him dead I could have killed him in Chechnya and no one would have known about it,' I later witnessed him tell astonished fellow journalists at a late-night news conference in Grozny.[46]

In the aftermath of Nemtsov's murder, opposition figures recalled a huge rally that Kadyrov had overseen in a stadium in Grozny in late 2014. Addressing some 20,000 heavily armed members of the Chechen elite guard, including members of the black-clad Kadyrovtsy, his much-feared private army, Kadyrov asked Putin to consider the assembled fighters 'a special volunteer unit of the commander-in-chief'. He also instructed his forces to be ready to fulfil any order from Putin anywhere in the world. 'We recognize that Russia has a regular army, an air force and nuclear weapons, yet there are some tasks that can only be carried out by volunteers,' he declared, before shouting: 'Long live our great motherland, Russia! Long live our national leader, Vladimir Putin! Allahu Akbar!'[47]

Kadyrov may have professed loyalty to the Kremlin, but opposition figures – including Nemtsov – questioned how long that loyalty would last as funding for the republic dried up amid Russia's growing economic problems. 'The unspoken contract between Kadyrov and Putin – money in exchange for loyalty – is coming to an end,' Nemtsov wrote. 'Where will these 20,000 Kadyrovtsy go? What will they demand? How will they behave? When will they come to Moscow?'[48]

PUTIN GOES AWOL

The already portentous atmosphere in Moscow was heightened when, just six days after Nemtsov's murder, Putin appeared to go missing. At first, nobody noticed anything untoward. That is until the *RBC* business newspaper reported on 12 March 2015 that Putin had not been seen in public for a week, and that there had also been no new television footage of the president during the same period.[49] This was an unthinkable amount of time for a man whose words and actions usually dominate national television broadcasts. Speculation that something was amiss increased when a government official in Kazakhstan told Russian media that a visit by Putin to the Central Asian republic had been cancelled because he had fallen ill.[50] Another visit, this time by South Ossetian officials to Moscow, had also been put off for the same reason, reports said.[51]

When questioned, Putin's spokesman, Dmitry Peskov, insisted that the 'national leader' was in fine health, and that he would soon appear in public. However, he could not say when. But if Putin was not ill, then where was he? In a bid to calm the situation, the Kremlin posted old images of Putin online, but the deceit was quickly discovered by bloggers and opposition media. State TV then aired a bizarre news item in which Putin's impending meeting with his Kyrgyz counterpart, Almazbek Atambayev, was reported in the past tense.[52] A spokesperson for the channel said the report had been an error, but, when a line of mysterious trucks was spotted outside the Kremlin's walls that very same evening, speculation reached fever pitch.[53] Putin had been deposed in a palace coup. He was visiting his alleged lover, the 'extremely flexible gymnast', Alina Kabaeva, who had reportedly given birth to a baby Putin in Switzerland. Or was he dead? (Someone quickly spliced together footage of Putin saying 'and snuffed it', over a grimy hip-hop beat, and uploaded the clip to YouTube.[54]) Russians with long memories started to wonder how long it would be before their television channels started to air nothing but looped performances of *Swan Lake*, the Tchaikovsky ballet that had been broadcast by state media during the unsuccessful 1991 coup by KGB hardliners, as well as ahead of the announcements of the deaths in quick succession of Soviet leaders Leonid Brezhnev, Yury Andropov and Konstantin Chernenko.

Amid the cacophony of conspiracy theories, there soon emerged one dominant version of events. That Putin had retreated from public view in order to resolve a vicious behind-the-scenes conflict between the FSB and Kadyrov. For the many analysts and journalists who supported this theory, the only issue in doubt was the final outcome: whose side would the president take? Would Putin risk losing the support of the Moscow-based state security service, or would he abandon his merciless Chechen ally?

The tangled web of alleged plots and possible motives around Nemtsov's murder had been complicated even further by widespread speculation that the FSB was exploiting the brazen assassination to put pressure on Kadyrov, a bitter foe and rival for influence. The history of enmity between the FSB and the Chechen leader dated back almost a decade. In May 2007, just months after Kadyrov had become president of Chechnya, formalizing his already de facto rule of the republic, local FSB officers had refused to allow armed men from Kadyrov's personal guard into their headquarters. Kadyrov's response? He ordered his men to weld shut all the building's entrances and exits.[55] A violent escalation of the situation was only averted by the intervention of Nikolai Patrushev, the then head of the FSB. Four years later, when Chechen security personnel were arrested in Moscow on abduction and torture charges, but then subsequently allowed to walk free, furious FSB officers leaked information and gave anonymous interviews to opposition newspapers.[56]

'The FSB hate Ramzan [Kadyrov] because they are unable to control him,' Alexey Malashenko, an expert on the Caucasus region at the Carnegie Moscow Center, told *The New York Times*. 'He does whatever he wants, including in Moscow. Nobody can arrest members of his team if there is no agreement with Putin.'[57]

The FSB was also rumoured to be nervous about Kadyrov's growing political ambitions. 'There are only two politicians in Russia, Putin and Kadyrov,' said analyst Andrei Okara. 'The rest are bureaucrats, propaganda agents or clowns.'[58] It was an evaluation that rang true. Aside from Putin, Kadyrov was the only high-level official in Russia both willing and able to force his own agenda on the national stage. Despite his frequent declarations of devotion to Putin, his actions demonstrated a genuine independence, something no other member of the Russian political elite could boast. This independence was highlighted dramatically later that year when Kadyrov, enraged by the killing of a Chechen man in Grozny by police from the neighbouring Stavropol region, ordered his security forces to open fire on law-enforcement officers from other Russian regions. 'I am officially stating, if any [security officer], whether from Moscow or Stavropol, appears on your territory without your knowledge, shoot to kill. They have to take us into account,' he said in a statement aired on Grozny TV. Kadyrov later said his comments had been the result of 'emotions', but the incident was another reminder of the Chechen leader's seemingly insatiable appetite for confrontation.[59]

For much of his blood-soaked reign, Kadyrov had been content to concern himself with events in Chechnya and the neighbouring North Caucasus republics. But with the start of the war in Ukraine, and the dramatic deterioration of Russia's relations with the West, Kadyrov increasingly sought to influence Kremlin policy. From an offer by the Chechen parliament to provide weapons to 'separatist movements' in Texas to the flow of Chechen fighters to eastern Ukraine, Kadyrov was flexing his muscles like never before. It was likewise no secret that he coveted a high post in Moscow, and that he wished to install his cousin, Adam Delimkhanov, as his successor in Chechnya. There was even talk that Kadyrov, this former rebel fighter with only a rudimentary formal education, had his eye on the Russian presidency. All of which would have made the FSB extremely uncomfortable.

Accordingly, a series of security services leaks to Russian media followed Nemtsov's murder, including a report that suggested the killing had been orchestrated by one Major Ruslan Geremeyev, a Chechen security officer and close Kadyrov ally. Another security services source told the opposition-friendly Rosbalt news agency that at least one of the suspects in the murder had used a government ticket-booking service to reserve his seat on the plane that took him to Moscow from Grozny.[60] Rumours of a vicious behind-the-scenes power struggle gripped Moscow's chattering classes.

'For the first time in his 15-year rule Putin has encountered a really serious problem: a virtually open conflict between the two pillars of his power, the federal security establishment and Ramzan Kadyrov,' wrote Stanislav Belkovsky, a well-connected former Kremlin insider. 'As far as I know, the FSB is almost directly accusing Ramzan Kadyrov of involvement in Boris Nemtsov's murder, and is demanding that Kadyrov be jailed. Putin can't give up Kadyrov, but he can't humiliate the federal security force either.'[61]

If anything was to happen to Kadyrov, a new war in Chechnya would be almost inevitable – would Putin back out on the Faustian agreement he had concluded with the former rebel fighter? It seemed unlikely. War in Ukraine was one thing, but a new brutal conflict in the Caucasus would pose a direct threat to Putin.

Ten days after he had first gone missing, Putin resurfaced. He looked and sounded in good health. But his reappearance had coincided with reports that investigators were about to reclassify the Nemtsov murder from a contract killing to a hate crime. This would mean that the investigation would end with Dadayev and his alleged accomplices. In these circumstances, Kadyrov would be safe from any possible prosecution. Had Putin made his choice?

'Putin appeared, live and legitimate, at exactly the same moment when Interfax reported that the Nemtsov assassination wasn't a contract hit,' said Leonid Volkov, a leading activist and analyst with Navalny's anti-corruption movement. 'Putin had to make a decision. Either feed Kadyrov to the FSB-men, or give up the FSB to Kadyrov. It's a difficult and unpleasant choice… And he chose the one and only thing he could choose: Kadyrov.'[62]

If analysts like Belkovsky and Volkov were right, then Nemtsov's murder had exposed dangerous fault lines within Putin's system. Yet there could be no cause for celebration for opposition activists. Putin's foes were in more danger than ever. Just weeks after Nemtsov's assassination, one of his fellow party members, an activist named Vladimir Kara-Murza, fell into a coma with acute kidney failure after becoming ill at the offices of a state news agency in Moscow. Just days before, Kara-Murza and his colleagues at the Open Russia pressure group had released a documentary film detailing torture, murder and corruption allegations in Chechnya. The activist's family suspected poisoning, but tests were inconclusive. A week after he had lost consciousness, Kara-Murza emerged from his coma. Unsurprisingly, he did not feel safe in a Moscow hospital, and fled Russia to seek continued medical treatment abroad. 'I am certain that this was not an accident, but I cannot say anything definitively,' he told me, from a hospital in Europe. 'What is certain is that over these past fifteen years political opponents of Vladimir Putin have had a very unfortunate track record.'[63] His father, also an opposition journalist named Vladimir, echoed his son's thoughts. 'Maybe they've thought up some new poison,' he said. 'If someone wanted to scare us, then they have done so.'[64]

EXODUS

The Kara-Murzas were not the only ones frightened. Even before Nemtsov's murder, as the crackdown on dissent gained pace, there had been a fresh wave of emigration from Putin's Russia. The official statistics were startling: the number of disenchanted Russians who left their country for foreign shores in the two years following Putin's 2012 return to the Kremlin was some five times higher than in the two before he began a new presidential term. Experts said the real number may have been much higher.[65]

Those leaving were some of Russia's best and brightest. In an opinion poll published in mid-2014 by Moscow's Levada Centre pollster, one in every four Russians with a higher education indicated they were seeking to emigrate. The figure rose to nearly one in three among those who described themselves as 'well-off'. Of those respondents planning to move abroad, 31% said they wanted to provide a 'worthy and hopeful future' for their children.[66] But unlike past brain drains in modern Russia, which were more about economics, the reasons behind this exodus had more to do with politics than money.

The list of talented Russians who have fled their country since Putin returned to the Kremlin makes for lengthy and depressing reading. One of the most high profile of those to book their tickets on the modern-day version of 'the philosophers' steamboat' – the name given to the exodus of educated Russians after the Bolshevik Revolution – was Yevgenia Chirikova, the housewife turned eco-activist who had played a major role in the 2011–12 protests. 'I decided to remove my greatest vulnerability from Russia – my children,' she explained, after settling in Estonia.[67]

Another to have turned his back on Russia is Pavel Durov, the founder of the successful VKontakte social network website, often described as Russia's Facebook. In a statement explaining his departure, Durov said he had been forced out of the company over his refusal to co-operate with the security services, and that his company was now under the 'full control' of Kremlin-friendly figures. Leonid Bershidsky, a well-known journalist who was the founding editor of Russia's top business daily, *Vedomosti*, as well as the first publisher of the Russian edition of *Forbes*, is another who has cut his losses. 'The Kremlin doesn't care because it doesn't consider the likes of me Russia's best and brightest,' he told me by email after his departure to Germany. 'To them, we're the traitors, the fifth column.'[68]

While the exit of opposition-friendly activists and journalists was unlikely to cost Putin too many sleepless nights, there were others leaving with them whom Russia could ill afford to lose, from scientists to economists to talented young graduates. 'The brain drain is significant and symptomatic,' said Andrei Kolesnikov, a Moscow-based political analyst.[69]

'[I] try to count how many friends and colleagues have left Russia already, and stop counting when I run out of fingers on both hands,' wrote Moscow-based human-rights worker Tanya Lokshina in May 2015, in an article that read as an obituary for the brief flowering of Russian civil society that had occurred in 2011 and 2012. 'Some left because they could no longer do their work. Some feared for their lives or the lives of their loved ones. This exodus is a loss for Russia. These people were in fact Russia's future, the future stolen from the Russian society by the powers that be.'[70]

For many of those in the anti-Putin movement who have dared remain in Russia, their struggle has taken on an undisguised moral element. Modern-day examples of the Communist-era *inakomyslyashchie* – literally, 'those who think differently' – these men and women are no longer simply pushing political programmes: many are unaffiliated with any of Russia's beleaguered and often outlawed opposition parties. Instead, by their willingness to speak out, to risk dismissal from their workplaces, or arrest, or beatings, or worse, they are simply refusing, in the famous words of the Soviet dissident Alexander Solzhenitsyn, to 'live a lie'. Their bravery rarely makes the news, either in Russia or the West. They are Russia's near-anonymous, modern-day dissidents, possessed of a quiet resolve to build a fairer future for their troubled homeland.

They are people like Mark Galperin, a forty-seven-year-old anti-Putin activist who is facing up to five years behind bars after being one of the first to be charged under Putin's new draconian laws on public protest. 'We are engaged in a struggle. It's our task to bring about regime change,' he told me, when we met in a central Moscow café one afternoon in the spring of 2015. 'It is the minority who always make history.' Aside from criminal charges, Galperin and his fellow activists face frequent harassment, and even assault, from state-sponsored activists emboldened by Putin's attacks on the opposition. 'These pro-Kremlin groups will not stick their necks out for Putin when push comes to shove,' Galperin said. 'But opposition activists risk their freedom, their lives every day.'[71]

They are people like Ruslan Leviyev, a former police investigator from the Siberian city of Surgut, who left the force after becoming disgusted by the 'culture of corruption' he had witnessed, and moved to Moscow in 2009. Inspired, like so many others, by the anti-Putin protests of 2011–12, Leviyev, a tattooed twenty-nine-year-old, is now one of the country's top 'social media dissidents'. Armed only with a computer, and aided by a team of five anonymous internet assistants, Leviyev scours social media in search of evidence of Russian military involvement in eastern Ukraine. His quest frequently takes him offline: Leviyev has travelled to towns and villages across Russia in search of graves of soldiers killed in eastern Ukraine. 'Sometimes when I explain to the family members of dead soldiers that it's wrong that we are sending young men to die in an illegal war, and that Putin disowns them when they perish, I can make a connection. They start to understand,' he told me, when I questioned him as to his motives for his arduous and dangerous work. Under a new law signed into force by Putin in May 2015 that makes all deaths of Russian soldiers during 'special operations' a state secret, Leviyev and his fellow

activists now face up to seven years behind bars. But the activist refuses
to be frightened off. 'I'm determined to carry on. I'm ready for prison.
I'll get through it, if it comes to it,' he told me, as we spoke opposite
a freshly painted portrait of the Soviet military commander Marshal
Zhukov in central Moscow. 'All this hysterical propaganda has resulted
in a degradation of society. We have to put an end to this as soon as possible. Otherwise things will only get a lot worse.'[72]

They are people like Denis Bakholdin, a thirty-three-year-old financial expert, whom I first met ahead of the anti-war protest in Moscow
in March 2014. He was standing near Red Square, in his hands a sign
urging people to attend the upcoming rally. It was rush-hour, and it
didn't take long before he attracted the attention of passers-by. 'Only a
bastard would go on that!' yelled a middle-aged man, his face flushed
with rage, after reading the sign, which was painted in the colours of both
the Russian and Ukrainian flags. 'We don't need a Maidan here!' Shortly
after, a swarm of pro-Kremlin youth activists surrounded Bakholdin and
his dozen or so fellow protesters. 'Traitors!' they chanted, before police
officers moved in to break up the gathering.

Bakholdin is a rank-and-file protester who says he has no interest in
a career in politics. A quietly spoken, studious man, he has paid a high
price for his public opposition to Putin's rule. Shortly before that afternoon's protest, he had been dismissed from his well-paid job at a privately
owned Moscow bank. The reason? His refusal to promise he would cease
his frequent attendance at opposition rallies. The vice-president of the
bank, it turned out, was a member of Putin's United Russia party, and
had ordered management to 'tame' Bakholdin, or get rid of him. 'I told
them straight out that I was opposed to Putin, and that what I do in my
own time is my own business,' Bakholdin told me. His defiance means
he is unlikely to find work any time soon: bank management wrote in
his work book – the document that all Russians are obliged by law to
present to employers – that he had 'violated work discipline on multiple
occasions'. He is now surviving on his rapidly dwindling savings.

I suggested that Bakholdin would perhaps be wise to consider following the well-beaten path out of Russia for a few years. If not until

Putin leaves office, then at least until the searing hatred for those who dare to dissent has cooled. He smiled, as if humouring me. 'I've thought a lot about leaving Russia, and trying to start a new life in Europe,' he shrugged. 'I've seen how much better things are there. But, look, if your neighbour has better wallpaper and nicer furniture, you don't just move into their apartment. You try to improve your own home, right?' He paused. 'So that's exactly what I plan to do here.'[73]

EPILOGUE

SACRED POWER AND RUINED LIVES

Vladimir Putin has now ruled Russia for longer than anyone else except Soviet leaders Joseph Stalin and Leonid Brezhnev. By the end of his current six-year term, in 2018, he will have drawn level with Brezhnev. According to Russia's constitution, he can remain president until 2024, the year that he will turn seventy-two.

Today's Putin barely resembles the little-known security services chief to whom Yeltsin entrusted Russia on the cusp of the new millennium. The sorcerers of state television and their shadowy Kremlin controllers have transformed him into the living embodiment of Russia's sovereignty. 'There is no Russia today, if there is no Putin,' says Vyacheslav Volodin, the Kremlin's hardline political adviser.[1] It is an opinion shared by millions of Russians.

Surrounded by an ever-narrower circle of confidants and advisers, it is unsurprising that Putin has come to believe his own propaganda. That he is the sole figure who can guarantee his country's immediate future in the face of what he believes is a Western plot to first weaken and then enslave Russia. That Mother Russia will perish without his iron fist.

'Anyone would change, after more than fifteen years in power,' said Marat Guelman, the one-time political consultant, who managed state television for Putin in the early days of his rule. 'But especially in Russia, in the chambers of the Kremlin, where power is not only absolute, but sacred. When Putin first came to power in 2000, he was concerned with resolving concrete issues. Now, he believes he is writing history. And the lives of individual people have no meaning when you are a historical figure, rather than a mere president.'[2]

Yet, while Putin has all but crushed the opposition movement and seen his domestic approval ratings soar to unprecedented heights, there remain very real threats to his long rule.

By the summer of 2015, a combination of low global oil prices and Western sanctions over the Kremlin's actions in Ukraine had pushed Russia's economy into recession for only the second time since 2000. Olga Golodets, the deputy prime minister responsible for social affairs, warned of a 'critical' rise in the number of Russians living below the poverty line. There were, she said, 23 million Russians – 16% of the total population – living on less than $170 a month. This was an increase of three million people in just twelve months, and one that would have been far greater had Russia not raised the official poverty level ahead of the announcement.[3]

As Russia sinks deeper into the quagmire of negative economic growth, and living standards decline, Putin will require more than war in Ukraine to distract Russians from growing domestic woes. If Moscow's relatively wealthy protesters were fighting for what Navalny called 'abstract ideas, like freedom and a sense of worthiness', then the next wave of demonstrations may be sparked by far more tangible issues. Hunger defeats blind patriotism, hands down. 'Hysteria can't last long,' said Vladimir Sorokin, one of modern Russia's most famous writers. 'A person screams and screams, and then he gets tired. He wants to eat, for example. He looks around and sees he has nothing to eat. And asks "why was I shouting?"'[4]

The country's poorest voters are not the only ones Putin will have to keep distracted. The fortunes of Russia's richest twenty-one people declined by $61 billion in 2014, a quarter of their combined wealth, while Putin's inner circle of businessmen friends have lost millions of dollars in assets due to international sanctions. Thus far, there is little indication that these powerful businessmen intend to turn against Putin – the majority of them, after all, only gained their fortunes after he came to power. 'It would be naive to think that such methods would scare us,' said Gennady Timchenko, the ultra-wealthy businessman and Putin's former judo buddie. 'Don't try to pressure Russia. Blackmail is counterproductive. We will endure everything and find a way out.'[5]

But the Kremlin is clearly nervous. Putin has reacted to dwindling funds by awarding even more state contracts to his closest business allies, namely Timchenko and Arkady Rotenberg, his boyhood friend. While this generosity is likely to keep his inner circle on his side, it means that there is less and less of the cake left for the rest of the business elite. In September 2014, Vladimir Yevtushenkov, chairman of the Sistema holding company, and Russia's fifteenth richest man with an estimated fortune of $6.8 billion, was arrested on money-laundering charges. While there was no suggestion that Yevtushenkov had been plotting against Putin, analysts suggested that his arrest was a timely signal to the business elite not to even consider rocking the boat. The message appears to have been understood. But how long will it be obeyed?

And then there is the war in Ukraine. In unleashing this fratricidal conflict, Putin also uncorked violent passions at home. So far, the hatred inspired by the Kremlin's skilful manipulators of public consciousness has been directed against the 'junta' in Kiev or the 'fifth column'. But what will happen when the war is finally over? Once summoned, the spirits of loathing cannot be so easily exorcized.

As I wound down my research for this book in the autumn of 2015, Putin's solution to these problems appeared to be – more war. On 30 September 2015, the very day that pro-Russian rebels in eastern Ukraine announced the end of the conflict in the former Soviet republic, the Kremlin ordered airstrikes to support its sole Middle East ally: Syrian President Bashar al-Assad. Ukraine was all but forgotten, as attention switched instantly to the Middle East. Pro-Kremlin experts dutifully appeared on national television to describe Syria as a 'holy land',[6] while the Russian Orthodox Church praised the airstrikes as part of a 'blessed battle'.[7] Even state television weather forecasts helped whip up enthusiasm for the new conflict, describing 'meteorological conditions' in Russia's new battlefield as ideal for 'effective strikes on ground targets'.[8] Putin's approval ratings remained sky-high. But this was a dangerous game the ex-KGB man was playing. 'Putin thinks that what he does in Ukraine and in Russia is the same as what he is doing in Syria,' former Kremlin spin doctor Gleb Pavlovsky told me. 'He does not see that he is playing on different boards, and at different games.'[9]

As Russians gear up to vote in parliamentary elections in 2016, followed by presidential polls in 2018, there will be no let-up in the Kremlin's crackdown on dissent. At local elections in the autumn of 2015, a coalition of opposition forces involving Navalny and Nemtsov's RPR-Parnas party was kept off the ballot in every region it attempted to run, except one. In the sole region where it was allowed to compete, central Russia's sleepy Kostroma, the opposition faced a swathe of dirty tricks, from the arrest of its election campaign head, Andrei Pivovarov, to an inevitable smear campaign that portrayed the coalition of democrats as 'treacherous' pawns of the US State Department.

For Putin, remaining in power is a matter of survival. The risks of criminal charges over Chechnya and Ukraine, and allegations of massive corruption, are simply too great for him to stand down.

'Putin understands far too well that, when he steps down, for real, I mean, not just by handing over to Medvedev, then, within six months, a year, he will be prosecuted,' Navalny has predicted. 'He has no political – or physical – future.'

Putin acted as guarantor of Yeltsin's future safety, but who can he trust to ensure his own? Who, in other words, will play Putin to his Yeltsin?

Yet the prospect of a desperate Putin is dangerous not only for Russia's beleaguered opposition, but also for the world. Putin has already waged war in Ukraine to tighten his grip on the keys to the Kremlin. We have no way of knowing just how many more lives he is willing to ruin to ensure they do not slip out of his grasp.

NOTES

PROLOGUE: ONE DAY IN DECEMBER

1   http://www.transparency.org/cpi2011/press
2   http://navalny.livejournal.com/2011/12/10
3   Interview with author, October 2012.
4   http://www.youtube.com/watch?v=mWUxcGCfdiI
5   http://www.mk.ru/politics/news/2012/06/28/719977-yashin-utverzhdaet-chto-putin-poobeschal-quotisportit-zhiznquot-oppozitsioneram.html

CHAPTER ONE: PUTIN'S PACT

1   http://news.bbc.co.uk/2/hi/world/monitoring/584845.stm
2   http://www.youtube.com/watch?v=EXiQpEzZhPQ
3   Interview with author, May 2012.
4   http://www.youtube.com/watch?v=VP0R_xzLIL8
5   http://www.novayagazeta.ru/society/54824.html
6   http://www.youtube.com/watch?v=zgKazTrhXmI
7   http://www.spiegel.de/international/world/spiegel-interview-with-alexander-solzhenitsyn-i-am-not-afraid-of-death-a-496003-3.html
8   http://www.youtube.com/watch?v=Iopmpe5g50g

CHAPTER TWO: PUTIN AND HIS 'SOVEREIGN DEMOCRACY'

1   Vladimir Putin, *First Person: An Astonishingly Frank Self-Portrait by Russia's President* (New York: PublicAffairs, 2000), p. 19.

2   Putin made this comment in the documentary *I, Putin*, Director: Hubert Seipel, 2012.

3   Oleg Blotskiy, *Vladimir Putin: Doroga k vlasti* [Vladimir Putin: The Road to Power] (Moscow: OSMOS-PRESS, 2002).

4   Putin, *First Person*, p. 42.

5   As told to the author by a former neighbour who wished to remain anonymous.

6   Leon Aron, *Roads to the Temple: Truth, Memory, Ideas, and Ideals in the Making of the Russian Revolution, 1987–1991* (New Haven: Yale University Press, 2012; Kindle edition).

7   http://www.theatlantic.com/international/archive/2013/02/how-the-1980s-explains-vladimir-putin/273135

8   Ibid.

9   http://www.youtube.com/watch?v=fWYvLx_Z_Pc

10 Daniel Treisman, *The Return: Russia's Journey from Gorbachev to Medvedev* (New York: Free Press, 2011; Kindle edition).

11 Peter Baker and Susan Glasser, *Kremlin Rising* (New York: Scribner, 2005; Kindle edition).

12 http://www.youtube.com/watch?v=DkUUAsZx-oo

13 Masha Gessen, *The Man without a Face: The Unlikely Rise of Vladimir Putin* (New York: Riverhead Books, 2012; Kindle edition).

14 http://www.youtube.com/watch?v=RHeWMA6Ocqc

15 Angus Roxburgh, *The Strongman: Vladimir Putin and the Struggle for Russia* (London: I.B.Tauris, 2012), p. 16.

16 This description of Putin's duties as deputy chief of staff is from a February 2013 interview by the author with Andrei Soldatov, a respected investigative journalist and author, who is considered Russia's leading expert on the FSB.

17 http://www.kommersant.ru/doc/15816

18 http://www.osce.org/odihr/elections/russia/16275

19 http://news.bbc.co.uk/2/hi/world/monitoring/media_reports/739432.stm

20 http://polit.ru/news/2000/04/14/547021/. Interestingly, the Kremlin removed its reference to 'any other citizens' from the English-language transcript of the text.

21 http://www.kommersant.ru/doc/145511?isSearch=True

22 The story of the Moscow apartment bombings and the mysterious incident in Ryazan has been covered in a number of books. Among them are David Satter, *Darkness at Dawn: The Rise of the Russian Criminal State* (New Haven:

Yale University Press, 2004) and John B. Dunlop, *The Moscow Bombings of September 1999: Examinations of Russian Terrorist Attacks at the Onset of Vladimir Putin's Rule* (Stuttgart: Ibidem, 2012). A number of Russian journalists, such as Masha Gessen, believe the FSB and Putin were responsible. Andrei Soldatov, the security services expert, is sceptical that the spy agency was involved. 'It was, in fact, part of a vigilance exercise,' he told me. 'The FSB was not very skilful at explaining all this and they were crazy to try to silence critics, but they were not guilty.' The jury, however, is still out.

23 http://www.rferl.org/content/Ten_Years_On_Troubling_Questions_Linger_Over_Russian_Apartment_Bombings/1818652.html

24 http://www.pressarchive.ru/moskovskaya-pravda/1999/07/22/102104.html

25 Vladimir Putin, *Ot pervogo litsa* (Moscow: Vagrius, 2000), p. 137.

26 Interview with author, January 2013.

27 Ivan Zassoursky, *Media and Power in Post-Soviet Russia* (New York: M.E. Sharpe Inc., 2003), p. 239.

28 http://newtimes.ru/articles/detail/64376

29 http://www.osce.org/odihr

30 Interview with author, July 2013.

31 http://www.youtube.com/watch?v=vXd6mECndYs

32 Interview with author, April 2013.

33 Treisman, *The Return*, p. 121.

34 http://online.wsj.com/article/SB119820263246543973.html

35 Photographs of Surkov's Kremlin office can be seen at http://zyalt.livejournal.com/347515.html

36 http://www.lrb.co.uk/v33/n20/peter-pomerantsev/putins-rasputin

37 David E. Hoffman, *The Oligarchs: Wealth and Power in the New Russia* (New York: PublicAffairs, 2002), p. 123.

38 http://expert.ru/russian_reporter/2012/04/surkov

39 http://www.theamericanconservative.com/articles/putins-philosophy

CHAPTER THREE: THE 'ORANGE THREAT' AND THE EARLY DISSENTERS

1 http://content.time.com/time/world/article/0,8599,1900838,00.html

2 Roxburgh, *The Strongman*, p. 138.

3 Interview with author, April 2013.

4   Ibid., and all other comments from Kozlovsky.

5   http://www.spiegel.de/international/spiegel/spiegel-interview-with-kremlin-boss-vladislav-surkov-the-west-doesn-t-have-to-love-us-a-361236.html

6   Andrei Sinyavsky, *Soviet Civilization: A Cultural History* (New York: Arcade, 1990), p. 261.

7   Roxburgh, *The Strongman*, p. 145.

8   Interview with author, September 2013.

9   http://www.newsru.com/russia/29nov2010/yakemenko.html

10   http://2005.novayagazeta.ru/nomer/2005/46n/n46n-s09.shtml

11   http://www.rferl.org/content/article/1057762.html

12   http://www.bbc.co.uk/blogs/adamcurtis/posts/the_years_of_stagnation_and_th/. The Surkov interview can be found in the embedded video on Adam Curtis' excellent blog post on Limonov, Siberian punks, and more.

13   http://www.kp.ru/daily/23370/32473

14   Valery Panyushkin, *12 Nesoglasnykh* (Moscow: Zakharov, 2009).

15   http://www.youtube.com/watch?v=zjKpvEVwKIs

16   http://www.independent.co.uk/news/people/profiles/garry-kasparov-the-master-who-wont-be-putins-pawn-1020501.html

17   http://lenta.ru/lib/14159606/full.htm

18   http://www.nytimes.com/2007/12/22/world/europe/Minaev-sidebar.html?pagewanted=all&_r=0

19   http://www.nytimes.com/2008/03/02/magazine/02limonov-t.html?pagewanted=print

20   http://www.theguardian.com/world/2010/dec/12/eduard-limonov-interview-putin-nightmare/. Limonov seems to admit firing at the city in his *Book of the Dead* (*Kniga mertvykh*).

21   http://www.youtube.com/watch?v=yp7BVcl78s0

22   http://nbp-perm.narod.ru/Molitva.htm/;   http://www.youtube.com/watch?v=VmeVkyNfa4o

23   Interview with author, May 2013.

24   http://www.kasparov.ru/material.php?id=47E0ECF312151/;   http://www.kasparov.ru/material.php?id=4848C9109184D

25   http://exiledonline.com/adam-curtis-on-edward-limonov-kremlin-politics-russian-punk-rock-the-exile

CHAPTER FOUR: MEDVEDEV AND THE SCENT OF CHANGE

1   http://www.heritage.org/research/commentary/2007/12/medvedevs-challenge
2   Treisman, *The Return*.
3   http://www.washingtonpost.com/wp-dyn/content/article/2007/12/10/
    AR2007121000330.html
4   http://www.cbc.ca/news/world/putin-chooses-a-successor-1.669535
5   http://www.kp.ru/daily/24016/87560
6   N. Svanidze and M. Svanidze, *Medvedev* (St Petersburg: Amfora, 2008). I have also
    drawn on Treisman, *The Return*, for my portrait of Medvedev's early days, as well
    as the following articles: http://online.wsj.com/article/SB119820263246543973.
    html/; http://www.thedailybeast.com/newsweek/2008/02/16/russia-s-mighty-
    mouse.html
7   http://sptimes.ru/story/24510?page=2
8   http://www.theguardian.com/world/2008/mar/03/russia.eu
9   http://en.rian.ru/russia/20071210/91721798.html
10 http://www.bloomberg.com/apps/news?pid=newsarchive&sid=au1xAx6fOwls
11 http://www.newsru.com/russia/24jul2006/medvedev.html
12 http://archive.kremlin.ru/eng/speeches/2009/04/13/2258_type82916_215119.shtml
13 http://eng.kremlin.ru/news/298
14 Interview with author, December 2012.
15 http://www.youtube.com/watch?v=S6Ksc7R6jhc
16 http://en.rian.ru/russia/20110914/166848594.html
17 http://slon.ru/russia/pavlovskiy_surkovu_ob_itogakh_raboty_politika_eto_
    tekst_slava_ne_vyshlo_teksta-943743.xhtml
18 http://in.reuters.com/article/2012/03/05/russia-medvedev-khodorkovsky-
    idINDEE82405120120305/; http://edition.cnn.com/2011/OPINION/01/07/
    treisman.medvedev.putin/index.html
19 http://kashin.livejournal.com/2897301.html
20 http://www.foreignpolicy.com/articles/2011/11/08/oleg_kashin_investigation_
    russia_journalist_beating
21 http://www.theguardian.com/world/2011/jul/06/russian-lawyer-death-jail-kremlin
22 http://www.reuters.com/article/2013/07/11/us-russia-magnitsky-
    idUSBRE96A09V20130711
23 Alena V. Ledeneva, *Can Russia Modernise?: Sistema, Power Networks and Informal
    Governance* (Cambridge: Cambridge University Press, 2013), p. 3.

24   Interview with author, April 2012.

25   http://www.youtube.com/watch?v=BCukOkS5Lbw

26   http://en.rian.ru/russia/20101021/161035520.html

27   http://www.youtube.com/watch?v=EkhEmvMEIhY

28   http://www.theguardian.com/commentisfree/2010/aug/11/wildfires-moscow-smog-russia-putin

29   http://www.youtube.com/watch?v=2U_SJCMa1oI

30   http://www.youtube.com/watch?v=O9nvQhUBA0k

31   http://www.thetimes.co.uk/tto/life/celebrity/article2978933.ece

32   Stanislav Belkovsky, *Chernaya metka oppozitsii* (Moscow: Algoritm, 2013).

33   http://www.novayagazeta.ru/news/57118.html/; http://www.newsru.com/russia/31may2012/tzepovyaz.html

34   http://www.newyorker.com/reporting/2011/04/04/110404fa_fact_ioffe

35   http://www.vedomosti.ru/newspaper/article/259142/

36   http://www.levada.ru/indeksy

37   http://www.itu.int/en/ITU-D/Statistics/Pages/stat/default.aspx

38   Interviews with author, 2012 and 2013.

39   http://bankwatch.org/news-media/for-journalists/press-releases/baseball-bat-attack-hospitalises-khimki-forest-activist-la

CHAPTER FIVE: NAVALNY AND THE 'CROOKS AND THIEVES'

1   http://www.youtube.com/watch?v=leHWbcmd74E

2   http://www.youtube.com/watch?v=dmx_8jo0eqE

3   Konstantin Voronkov, *Alexei Navalny: Groza zhulikov i vorov* (Moscow: EKSMO, 2011).

4   http://www.youtube.com/watch?v=swI3s_q04mg

5   http://www.newyorker.com/reporting/2011/04/04/110404fa_fact_ioffe

6   INDEM foundation study, cited by opposition politicians Vladimir Milov and Boris Nemtsov in their *Putin. Korruptsiya* report / Karen Dawisha, *Putin's Kleptocracy: Who Owns Russia?* (London: Simon & Schuster, 2014).

7   http://www.theguardian.com/world/2006/nov/08/russia.tomparfitt

8   http://www.foreignaffairs.com/articles/139169/joshua-yaffa/alexei-navalnys-day-in-court

9   Voronkov, *Alexei Navalny*.

10 Ibid.

11 http://navalny.livejournal.com/526563.html#cutid1; http://www.bbc.co.uk/news/world-europe-11779154

12 http://www.youtube.com/watch?v=sVobecY5DFY

13 http://uk.reuters.com/article/2011/01/14/transneft-shareholder-idUKLDE70C1PF20110114

14 Voronkov, *Alexei Navalny*.

15 http://www.newyorker.com/reporting/2011/04/04/110404fa_fact_ioffe

16 Ibid.

17 http://rospil.info/; http://www.newyorker.com/reporting/2011/04/04/110404fa_fact_ioffe

18 http://www.levada.ru/06-05-2011/alekseya-navalnogo-znayut-6-rossiyan

19 http://www.reuters.com/article/2011/02/15/us-russia-rich-idUSTRE71E1QN20110215

20 http://www.theguardian.com/world/2009/jul/30/russian-billionaire-timchenko-libel-economist

21 http://www.reuters.com/article/2013/07/31/us-timchenko-loans-idUSBRE96U0R720130731

22 http://www.ft.com/intl/cms/s/0/9ed1d460-279a-11dd-b7cb-000077b07658.html#axzz2fw4SQbcZ

23 http://www.bbc.co.uk/news/magazine-17730959/; http://www.putin-itogi.ru/rab-na-galerah/#palace

24 http://www.themoscowtimes.com/news/article/activists-who-reported-putins-palace-put-in-jail/484104.html

25 http://izvestia.ru/news/375014

26 Voronkov, *Alexei Navalny*.

27 http://worldfellows.yale.edu/about/who-we-are

28 Interview with author, June 2013.

29 http://newtimes.ru/articles/detail/64376

30 http://www.youtube.com/watch?v=Eg2qZCyyt2g

31 Voronkov, *Alexei Navalny*.

32 Ibid.

33 http://mobile.reuters.com/article/worldNews/idUSTRE7AT0U320111130?irpc=932

34 Voronkov, *Alexei Navalny*.

35 Ibid.

36 http://www.kasparov.ru/material.php?id=47287115AE769

37 http://navalny.livejournal.com/242897.html

38 Voronkov, *Alexei Navalny*.

39 http://www.youtube.com/watch?v=CZCxh46BB4M

40 http://www.newyorker.com/online/blogs/ask/2011/03/alexey-navalny-julia-ioffe. html

41 http://navalny.livejournal.com/204377.html

42 http://navalny.livejournal.com/139478.html

43 http://www.afisha.ru/article/new-politics-navalny/page2

44 http://www.youtube.com/watch?v=Y2ZdqukGkpU

45 Satter, *Darkness at Dawn*.

46 http://www.levada.ru/11-06-2013/izvestnost-i-populyarnost-lozungov-oppozitsii

47 http://www.theguardian.com/world/2010/dec/13/two-dead-football-racist-riot-moscow

48 http://www.telegraph.co.uk/news/worldnews/europe/russia/8809581/Chechen-warlord-Ramzan-Kadyrov-enjoys-a-quiet-multi-million-pound-birthday.html

49 Ibid.

50 http://mag.newsweek.com/2010/10/24/ramzan-kadyrov-talks-about-chechnya-s-future.html

51 Interview with author, November 2012.

52 http://navalny.livejournal.com/204377.html

53 http://navalny.livejournal.com/282477.html

54 Voronkov, *Alexei Navalny*.

55 http://www.youtube.com/watch?v=gEGxNveNB38

56 Voronkov, *Alexei Navalny*.

57 http://www.youtube.com/watch?v=jVrAPFBSKnk

58 Ben Judah, *Fragile Empire: How Russia Fell in and out of Love with Vladimir Putin* (New Haven: Yale University Press, 2013), p. 206.

59 http://www.youtube.com/watch?v=1OQGs5gpUhc

60 Telephone interview with author, February 2012.

61 https://www.facebook.com/vera.krichevskaya/, 5 July 2013.

62 Interview with author, January 2013.

63 http://www.youtube.com/watch?v=Eg2qZCyyt2g

64 http://newtimes.ru/articles/detail/38107

65 Ibid.

CHAPTER SIX: CASTLING AT THE KREMLIN

1   http://www.telegraph.co.uk/news/worldnews/europe/russia/8451710/Is-Russias-
     puppet-president-ready-to-stand-up-to-his-master
2   http://www.youtube.com/watch?v=v1hLtFn4CLU
3   http://www.reuters.com/article/2011/03/21/us-libya-russia-idUSTRE72K
     2J220110321
4   Roxburgh, *The Strongman*, p. 308.
5   http://www.ft.com/cms/s/0/4bfa1f38-9a90-11e0-bab2-00144feab49a.
     html#axzz2fw4SQbcZ
6   http://www.youtube.com/watch?v=8QfmKNZNW4M
7   Interview with author, January 2013.
8   Interview with author, May 2013.
9   http://www.youtube.com/watch?v=kjoxCG3Ls8s
10   http://www.youtube.com/watch?v=1OQGs5gpUhc
11   http://www.youtube.com/watch?v=VIfwyql7Syo
12   http://articles.washingtonpost.com/2011-11-21/world/35281872_1_nascar-fans-
     alexei-navalny-martial-arts

CHAPTER SEVEN: POLLS AND PROTESTS

1   Interview with author, December 2011.
2   Interview with author, December 2011.
3   http://www.youtube.com/watch?v=vXrR2alb9p8
4   http://en.rian.ru/russia/20111127/169086652.html
5   http://www.svoboda.org/content/blog/24411689.html
6   http://hro.rightsinrussia.info/archive/elections/2011/observer
7   Interview with author, March 2013.
8   http://www.electoralgeography.com/en/countries/r/russia/2000-president-
     elections-russia.html
9   http://www.youtube.com/watch?v=u0xNrJ3qPFE
10   http://www.economist.com/node/21541455
11   http://navalny.livejournal.com/2012/12/05
12   Telephone interview with author, December 2012.
13   http://www.nytimes.com/2013/04/17/world/europe/trial-of-russian-activist-
     aleksei-navalny-to-begin.html?pagewanted=all

14 http://www.youtube.com/watch?v=WkgEonmQ34k

15 http://www.theguardian.com/world/2011/dec/08/vladimir-putin-hillary-clinton-russia

16 Interview with author, January 2012.

17 http://en.rian.ru/society/20111208/169480989.html

18 I didn't see this with my own eyes, but a friend swore it was true.

19 Interview with author, December 2012.

20 http://www.nytimes.com/2011/12/11/world/europe/thousands-protest-in-moscow-russia-in-defiance-of-putin.html?pagewanted=all

21 Gessen, *The Man without a Face*.

22 http://www.telegraph.co.uk/news/worldnews/europe/russia/8947840/Russian-protests-live.html

23 Interview with author, December 2012.

24 http://en.rian.ru/russia/20081217/118898625.html

25 http://www.foreignpolicy.com/articles/2011/12/15/the_condomnation_of_vladimir_putin?page=full

26 http://www.novayagazeta.ru/politics/55288.html

27 http://www.theguardian.com/world/2011/dec/22/dmitry-medvedev-proposes-electoral-reforms

28 http://izvestia.ru/news/510564

29 http://www.nytimes.com/2011/12/28/world/europe/putin-takes-another-swipe-at-russian-protesters.html

30 http://www.youtube.com/watch?v=eWqJuQLLMVk

31 http://www.bloomberg.com/visual-data/best-and-worst/most-heavily-policed-countries

32 http://www.youtube.com/watch?v=PSINIEcAUxM

33 http://www.levada.ru/17-06-2013/opros-na-mitinge-oppozitsii-12-iyunya

34 Interview with author, February 2012.

35 Judah, *Fragile Empire*.

36 Interview with author, July 2013.

37 Ryszard Kapuściński, *Shah of Shahs* (London: Penguin, 1982).

CHAPTER EIGHT: UDALTSOV AND THE NEW LEFT

1 http://www.levada.ru/17-06-2013/opros-na-mitinge-oppozitsii-12-iyunya

2 Telephone interview with author, January 2012.

3   Ibid.

4   http://www.leftfront.ru

5   Telephone interview with author, March 2012.

6   Oleg Kharkhordin, *The Collective and the Individual in Russia: A Study of Practices* (Studies on the History of Society and Culture) (Berkeley: University of California Press, 1999), p. 269.

7   http://www.youtube.com/watch?v=mqRYM43211g

8   http://www.youtube.com/watch?v=oO6Pn3n4UzM

9   http://www.levada.ru/08-02-2013/rossiyane-o-politicheskoi-i-ekonomicheskoi-sisteme-strany

10 http://en.rian.ru/politics/20130314/180000297.html

11 https://publications.credit-suisse.com/tasks/render/file/?fileID=BCDB1364-A105-0560-1332EC9100FF5C83

12 http://www.poisknews.ru/theme/publications/6620/; http://www.newsru.com/finance/13apr2011/minimum.html

13 http://www.eia.gov/countries/country-data.cfm?fips=RS

14 http://en.rian.ru/russia/20120117/170806801.html

15 http://www.vesti.ru/doc.html?id=941171

16 http://www.rferl.org/content/article/1095282.html

17 Telephone interview with author, March 2012.

18 http://www.newsru.com/russia/24sep2012/uznali.html

19 Interview with author, February 2013.

CHAPTER NINE: PUSSY RIOT VS THE KREMLIN

1   http://www.washingtontimes.com/news/2012/aug/13/putin-russia-little-separation-church-state/?page=all

2   http://www.nytimes.com/2011/12/30/world/europe/russian-orthodox-church-turns-from-kremlin-ally-to-critic.html?_r=0&gwh=6990A8CE40FD4CB5C786B61FB0D42F24

3   Ibid.

4   http://piter.tv/event/patriarh_kirill_verit_ne/; http://uk.reuters.com/article/2012/02/08/uk-russia-putin-religion-idUKTRE81722Y20120208

5   Oliver Bullough, *The Last Man in Russia and the Struggle to Save a Dying Nation* (London: Allen Lane, 2013), p. 45.

6   http://online.wsj.com/article/SB119792074745834591.html?mod=hpp_us_inside_

today; http://www.sedmitza.ru/lib/text/429346/. See also Bullough, *The Last Man in Russia* for a more complete account of KGB agents in the Orthodox Church and Gleb Yakunin's story.

7   http://www.nytimes.com/2012/04/06/world/europe/in-russia-a-watch-vanishes-up-orthodox-leaders-sleeve.html?pagewanted=all&gwh=F5D1A81E3CF3879 E54F9D0BCEF2EBB32

8   http://www.youtube.com/watch?v=GCasuaAczKY

9   http://www.youtube.com/watch?v=FoJqzGG7u_k

10 Tolokonnikova's husband, Pyotr Verzilov, told me this when I spoke to him in the autumn of 2012.

11 Interview with author, June 2013.

12 Daniil Kharms, *The Plummeting Old Women* (Essays & Texts in Cultural History) (Dublin: The Lilliput Press, 2011; Kindle edition).

13 Pussy Riot, *Pussy Riot!: A Punk Prayer for Freedom* (Kindle edition, 2013).

14 http://plucer.livejournal.com/61945.html#cutid1

15 http://en.rian.ru/society/20120419/172921607.html

16 http://nplusonemag.com/pussy-riot-closing-statements

17 http://en.rian.ru/russia/20120327/172417090.html

18 Ibid.

19 http://www.youtube.com/watch?v=bX_s1ZVbKJY

20 Interview with author, August 2012.

21 http://www.youtube.com/watch?v=p-6KNpz-Axo

22 http://en.rian.ru/russia/20120912/175920501.html

23 http://www.thestar.com/news/world/2012/08/19/husband_of_pussy_riot_member_says_theyll_revisit_canada.html#

24 Interview with author, August 2012.

25 http://expertmus.livejournal.com/92361.html

26 Interview with author, July 2012.

27 Anna Dickinson, 'Quantifying Religious Oppression: Russian Orthodox Church Closures and Repression of Priests 1917–41', *Religion, State and Society*, 28(4), 2000.

28 http://www.youtube.com/watch?v=ek6TiJHky2Q

29 http://www.neva24.ru/a/2012/04/16/Alla_Pugacheva_zastupilas

30 http://www.neva24.ru/a/2012/04/16/Alla_Pugacheva_zastupilas

CHAPTER TEN: PUTIN'S RETURN

1   Navalny made this comment to journalists ahead of a protest in Moscow the weekend after the Pushkin Square rally.

2   From the film *Winter Go Away* (*Zima Ukhodi*). See Further Reading/Watching for more details.

3   http://www.youtube.com/watch?v=hAqqJ-uQRZQ

4   From *Winter Go Away*.

5   http://www.bbc.co.uk/news/world-europe-17254548

6   http://en.rian.ru/analysis/20120824/175417856.html

7   http://www.youtube.com/watch?v=GFzm6QAZYpM

8   Interview with author, May 2013.

9   Interview with author, September 2012.

10 Interview with author, December 2012.

11 http://er.ru/news/2012/3/19/isaev-dvizhenie-belyh-lent-prevrashaetsya-v-politicheskuyu-sektu

12 http://www.youtube.com/watch?v=BjHK3oUL9s8

13 http://www.youtube.com/watch?v=PN0PUd2b2nE

14 http://www.youtube.com/watch?v=RupZW2Zcfwg

15 http://tvrain.ru/articles/aleksej_navalnyj_ja_hochu_byt_prezidentom-340365

16 http://www.nytimes.com/2013/06/09/world/europe/trial-sends-warning-to-rank-and-file-putin-foes.html?pagewanted=all&gwh=781FC029D6596C2628E25F50E2B256BA

17 http://www.colta.ru/articles/media/575

18 For more information on the fates of the 6 May detainees, see http://6may.org/en

19 http://top.rbc.ru/society/11/05/2012/649923.shtml

20 http://www.newrepublic.com/article/113581/moscows-may-6-protesters-perfect-show-trial-putin-era/; http://en.rian.ru/analysis/20130611/181620847/Moscow-Riots-Go-to-Court-7-Arguments-for-the-Jury.html

21 http://grani.ru/Events/Crime/m.197585.html

22 Interview with author, January 2013.

23 http://www.vedomosti.ru/politics/news/1736387/sociologi_vyyasnili_kto

24 You can listen to the song at http://www.youtube.com/watch?v=x2VGBNjxDgk

25 http://en.rian.ru/russia/20120513/173424491.html

26 http://grani.ru/Politics/Russia/activism/m.197638.html

27 http://www.youtube.com/watch?v=GzC2P-cXQJQ

CHAPTER ELEVEN: TIGHTENING THE SCREWS

1   http://www.gazeta.ru/news/lenta/2012/03/07/n_2232833.shtml
2   http://www.rosbalt.ru/moscow/2012/05/12/980164.html
3   http://en.ria.ru/russia/20120712/174570350.html
4   Interview with author, January 2013.
5   Interview with author, January 2013.
6   http://www.youtube.com/watch?v=hlkHcFpQCmw
7   Interview with author, July 2012.
8   http://echo.msk.ru/news/915894-echo.html
9   http://www.newyorker.com/online/blogs/newsdesk/2012/06/search-and-destroy-navalny-sobchak.html
10 http://rus.delfi.ee/daily/abroad/sobchak-mne-skazali-chto-esli-b-vyshla-zamuzh-za-chekista-problem-by-ne-bylo.d?id=64528026
11 http://ksenia-sobchak.com/kseniya-sobchak-ya-mogu-xranit-svoi-dengi-dazhe-v-unitaze
12 http://www.youtube.com/watch?v=ebJgbtYl77E
13 http://www.nytimes.com/2012/07/27/world/europe/in-russia-aleksei-navalny-accuses-chief-investigator-of-secret-european-holdings.html?gwh=52CAFB2EA49CF6027680AC922E3800DB
14 http://rospravosudie.com/society/opravdaem
15 http://navalny.livejournal.com/758143.html
16 http://www.rferl.org/content/advantage-navalny/24906984.html
17 http://navalny.livejournal.com/2012/10/23
18 http://www.smh.com.au/articles/2003/12/08/1070732146155.html
19 http://ria.ru/politics/20120427/636540215.html
20 http://newtimes.ru/articles/detail/53551
21 https://twitter.com/Kasparov63/status/332127672102699010
22 http://www.themoscowtimes.com/news/article/sentence-overturned-in-osipova-case/453162.html
23 http://www.independent.co.uk/news/world/europe/activist-taisiya-osipovas-prison-sentence-is-called-terrifying-revenge-8084737.html
24 http://www.telegraph.co.uk/news/worldnews/europe/russia/11632983/Russian-officials-daughter-with-ties-to-Putin-spared-jail-due-to-Nazi-amnesty.html

CHAPTER TWELVE: PUSSY RIOT – THE VERDICT

1 http://www.newrepublic.com/article/politics/105846/how-punk-rock-show-trial-became-russias-greatest-gonzo-artwork

2 Pussy Riot, *Pussy Riot!: A Punk Prayer for Freedom* (New York: The Feminist Press at CUNY, 2012).

3 http://www.telegraph.co.uk/news/worldnews/europe/russia/9479937/Sir-Paul-McCartney-supports-Pussy-Riot.html

4 http://www.telegraph.co.uk/news/worldnews/vladimir-putin/9448370/Vladimir-Putin-says-Pussy-Riot-should-not-be-treated-too-harshly.html

5 http://www.mk.ru/social/article/2012/07/30/731253-dopros-poterpevshey-po-delu-pussy-riot-sprovotsiroval-skandal.html

6 http://www.newrepublic.com/article/politics/105846/how-punk-rock-show-trial-became-russias-greatest-gonzo-artwork

7 Pussy Riot, *Pussy Riot!*

8 http://www.newyorker.com/online/blogs/newsdesk/2012/08/the-absurd-and-outrageous-trial-of-pussy-riot.html

9 Interview with author, October 2012.

10 Pussy Riot, *Pussy Riot!*

11 Ibid.

12 http://www.novayagazeta.ru/politics/59955.html

13 http://www.bbc.co.uk/russian/russia/2012/09/120925_razan_dalny_verdict.shtml

14 Interview with author, June 2013.

15 http://www.gq.ru/blogs/politblog/18876_rossiya_osenyu.php

16 http://en.ria.ru/analysis/20120830/175525037-print/Vitaly-Milonov-Laying-Down-Gods-Law-in-Russia.html

17 http://en.ria.ru/analysis/20120830/175525037-print/Vitaly-Milonov-Laying-Down-Gods-Law-in-Russia.html

18 http://www.gazeta.ru/comments/2012/06/18_a_4630085.shtml

19 http://www.theguardian.com/world/2012/sep/12/medvedev-says-free-pussy-riot

20 Interview with author October 2012. http://en.ria.ru/analysis/20121017/176700893/Pussy-Riots-Samutsevich-For-Me-Russia-Is-Like-A-Big-Prison.html

CHAPTER THIRTEEN: DARK DAYS

1 http://www.youtube.com/watch?v=WPGHtMW-u0g

2   http://www.youtube.com/watch?v=8V3khrqYD4c

3   http://www.youtube.com/watch?v=kSxiSet4a8k

4   Interview with author, March 2013.

5   Interview with author, February 2013.

6   Interview with author, February 2013.

7   http://www.nytimes.com/2013/02/14/world/europe/russian-ethics-official-steps-aside-over-property-disclosures.html?_r=0

8   http://uk.reuters.com/article/2012/12/20/uk-russia-putin-usa-idUKBRE8BJ0AQ20121220

9   http://www.ft.com/cms/s/0/6f540560-3fdb-11e2-9f71-00144feabdc0.html#axzz2fw4SQbcZ

10 http://tvrain.ru/articles/amerikantsy_o_spiske_buta_on_razrushil_nashu_zhizn_osoznaet_li_eto_putin-333286/

11 http://www.youtube.com/watch?v=fiWGM4KXNNc

12 http://www.ft.com/cms/s/0/9abc9eb2-5032-11e2-a231-00144feab49a.html

13 http://en.rian.ru/crime/20110329/163260677.html

14 http://www.themoscowtimes.com/opinion/article/child-abuse-in-russia-is-routine/473633.html

15 https://twitter.com/tvrain/status/290403008024571905

16 http://en.rian.ru/russia/20130114/178771708.html

17 http://www.telegraph.co.uk/news/worldnews/europe/russia/9877843/Kremlin-accuses-Texas-mother-of-killing-adopted-Russian-son-in-new-row-with-US.html

18 http://www.youtube.com/watch?v=TMM9KNUAIjY

19 http://www.kommersant.ru/doc/2132256?fp=21

20 http://www.vedomosti.ru/politics/news/8110671/vciom_76_naseleniya_podderzhivayut_zapret_na_usynovlenie_v

21 http://nadkin-muzh.livejournal.com/45563.html

22 http://valdaiclub.com/valdai_club/62642.html; http://www.ft.com/cms/s/0/cdedfd64-214f-11e3-a92a-00144feab7de.html#axzz2fw4SQbcZ

23 Interview with author, January 2013.

24 http://www.colta.ru/docs/9285 – Sorokin interview.

25 Interview with author, May 2013.

26 http://en.novayagazeta.ru/politics/57847.html

CHAPTER FOURTEEN: NEXT TARGET – THE NEW LEFT

1   http://www.ntv.ru/peredacha/proisschestvie/m4001/o113556

2   Ibid.

3   http://www.nytimes.com/2012/10/23/world/europe/leonid-razvozzhayev-
    russian-opposition-figure-says-he-was-kidnapped-and-tortured.html?gwh=B
    1B172F4768A57E56EBF6D49D23FDBCB

4   Interview with author, February 2013.

5   http://www.gazeta.ru/politics/news/2012/10/18/n_2577069.shtml

6   http://www.theguardian.com/world/2012/oct/17/russia-opposition-leader-
    detained-udaltsov

7   Interview with author, October 2012.

8   http://lokomotiv.livejournal.com/2012/10/19

9   Ibid.

10 http://www.csmonitor.com/World/Europe/2012/1022/Russian-rendition-
    Kremlin-grabs-opposition-figure-from-Ukraine-streets

11 http://m.forbes.ru/article.php?id=232952

12 http://www.youtube.com/watch?v=3xkLMzS-mSg

13 http://www.csmonitor.com/World/Europe/2012/1022/Russian-rendition-
    Kremlin-grabs-opposition-figure-from-Ukraine-streets/(page)/2

14 http://newtimes.ru/articles/detail/58712 and all Razvozzhayev quotes about
    torture

15 http://gorod.afisha.ru/archive/navalny_ks

16 http://en.ria.ru/russia/20121026/176933872.html

17 Telephone interview with author, January 2013.

18 http://www.gazeta.ru/politics/2013/03/29_a_5121781.shtml

19 http://www.kommersant.ru/doc/2181515

20 http://www.newsru.com/russia/14may2013/navalnyrbc.html

21 http://www.buzzfeed.com/maxseddon/che-guevara-in-the-caucasus

22 http://mobile.reuters.com/article/worldNews/idUSBRE9620SF20130703

23 http://news.yahoo.com/russian-mayor-arrested-suspected-corruption-072333583.
    html

24 http://www.colta.ru/docs/26473

25 http://www.youtube.com/watch?v=nnt6GHUY5sc

26 Interview with author, June 2013.

CHAPTER FIFTEEN: THE PEOPLE'S WRATH

1   http://savekhoper.ru/?page_id=2
2   http://news.bbc.co.uk/2/hi/europe/6528853.stm
3   http://www.worstpolluted.org/projects_reports/display/43
4   Interviews with author, 2013.
5   Interviews with author, April 2013.
6   Interviews with author, April 2013.
7   For two thorough and thoughtful examinations of the 'Primorsky Partisans' story, please see Lucy Ash's BBC article: http://www.bbc.co.uk/news/world-europe-11829793; and Judah, *Fragile Empire*.
8   http://www.youtube.com/watch?v=7sNN6jfLwyw
9   Parts of this chapter originally appeared in my article 'Nickels and Dimes' for OpenDemocracy Russia. http://www.opendemocracy.net/od-russia/marc-bennetts/nickel-and-dimes

CHAPTER SIXTEEN: END OF THE LINE FOR NAVALNY?

1   http://www.youtube.com/watch?v=wEKBcxs2kj0
2   Telephone interview with author, May 2013.
3   http://www.nytimes.com/2013/03/28/world/europe/with-case-reopened-the-russian-activist-aleksei-navalny-expects-the-worst.html?_r=0
4   http://navalny.livejournal.com/2012/12/13
5   http://mobile.reuters.com/article/idUSBRE9450C920130506?irpc=932
6   http://www.nytimes.com/2013/04/17/world/europe/trial-of-russian-activist-aleksei-navalny-to-begin.html?pagewanted=all
7   http://www.newyorker.com/online/blogs/newsdesk/2013/06/russia-putin-losing-sergei-guriev.html
8   Interview with author, June 2013.
9   http://www.globalpost.com/dispatch/news/afp/130405/i-want-be-president-russian-opposition-leader-navalny
10 http://www.theguardian.com/world/2013/apr/16/alexey-navalny-putin-critic-trial-embezzle
11 Interview with author, April 2013.
12 Interview with author, February 2013.
13 http://izvestia.ru/news/548376

14 http://en.ria.ru/russia/20131128/185094229/Russia-Opens-Criminal-Case-into-Former-Defense-Minister.html

15 http://lenta.ru/news/2013/06/18/navanly

16 http://www.youtube.com/watch?v=VQGpcEjezqQ

17 Ibid.

18 http://www.youtube.com/watch?v=o1Q3QnOIwiM

19 http://www.rferl.org/content/navalny-news-analysis/25051220.html

20 http://www.youtube.com/watch?v=075fnZ9x9Xc

21 http://www.youtube.com/watch?v=3nQ9bxARF-8

22 http://www.therecord.com/opinion-story/3905780-putin-foe-s-reprieve-puzzles-russians

23 http://www.economist.com/news/europe/21585043-charismatic-dissident-runs-american-style-campaign-inspired-wire

24 http://www.youtube.com/watch?v=s862YkKBt10&feature=youtu.be&t=36m46s

25 http://www.levada.ru/04-10-2013/rossiyane-ob-anavalnom-i-eroizmane-kirovlese

26 http://www.forbes.com/sites/markadomanis/2013/07/15/did-russian-opposition-leader-alexey-navalny-just-endorse-a-race-riot/; http://democratia2.ru/group/a47e81dc-97e8-48e0-9697-16fa4afb2875/content

27 http://www.echomsk.spb.ru/blogs/chirikova/15689.php

28 http://www.youtube.com/watch?v=3nQ9bxARF-8

29 http://www.mk.ru/specprojects/free-theme/article/2013/09/11/913755-svideteli-navalnogo.html

30 https://twitter.com/xenia_sobchak/status/376831797549891584

31 http://slon.ru/russia/kashin_vybory-988444.xhtml

32 http://www.themoscowtimes.com/news/article/putin-finally-says-navalnys-name-journalist-tweets/486380.html

33 http://slon.ru/fast/russia/adnya-navalnyy-eltsin-vova-ya-vernulsya-969644.xhtml

34 http://navalny.livejournal.com/866661.html

35 http://navalny.livejournal.com/2013/10/16

CHAPTER SEVENTEEN: 'NATIONAL TRAITORS'

1 http://www.theguardian.com/world/2013/dec/23/pussy-riot-nadezhda-tolokonnikova-freed-russian-prison

2 http://www.theguardian.com/world/2013/dec/19/vladimir-putin-mikhail-khodorkovsky

3　http://www.bbc.com/news/world-europe-25485746

4　http://www.theguardian.com/world/2014/dec/18/rouble-collapse-putin-russia-president-economy-crisis

5　http://www.bbc.co.uk/news/world-europe-22720228

6　http://www.telegraph.co.uk/news/worldnews/europe/russia/7902905/Russian-corruption-means-foie-gras-roads-would-be-cheaper.html

7　http://www.theguardian.com/sport/blog/2013/oct/09/sochi-2014-olympics-money-corruption

8　http://www.putin-itogi.ru/zimnyaya-olimpiada-v-subtropikax/

9　Interview with author, February 2014.

10　http://www.reuters.com/article/2011/02/15/us-russia-rich-idUSTRE71E1QN20110215

11　http://www.theguardian.com/world/2013/sep/22/ukraine-european-union-trade-russia

12　http://www.spiegel.de/international/europe/how-the-eu-lost-to-russia-in-negotiations-over-ukraine-trade-deal-a-935476.html

13　http://charter97.org/ru/news/2014/2/21/87584/

14　Interview with author, February 2014.

15　Interview with author, February 2014.

16　https://www.youtube.com/watch?v=BfeYhbKrSts; http://www.1tv.ru/sprojects_edition/si5905/fi30118

17　http://www.putin-itogi.ru/putin-voina/

18　http://www.timesofisrael.com/ukraines-jewish-leaders-celebrate-electoral-defeat-of-far-right

19　http://www.rferl.org/content/russian-tv-announces-right-sector-leader-yarosh-led-ukraine-polls/25398882.html

20　https://www.youtube.com/watch?v=rQdSWWP4Puc

21　http://www.themoscowtimes.com/news/article/putin-says-plan-to-take-crimea-hatched-before-referendum/517169.html

22　http://izvestia.ru/news/586703

23　http://www.themoscowtimes.com/article/509561.html

24　https://www.youtube.com/watch?v=eUq7Sds_9bI

25　http://www.bbc.co.uk/monitoring/how-russian-tv-uses-psychology-over-ukraine

26　http://www.theguardian.com/commentisfree/2014/jul/31/vladimir-putin-western-sanctions-russia-flight-mh17-state-propaganda

27 http://www.bloombergview.com/articles/2014-07-17/flight-mh17-and-the-role-of-ukraine-s-rebels/; http://lifenews.ru/news/136801

28 Interview with author, April 2014.

29 http://bigstory.ap.org/article/81c9b47d7d3c42d9a32b74bbf29e2dee/russia-country-must-prepare-deeper-longer-crisis

30 Telephone interview with author, August 2015.

31 http://www.newsru.com/russia/25jul2014/sudnyi_den.html

32 http://www.ntv.ru/peredacha/professiya_reportyor/m720/o290376/; https://www.youtube.com/watch?v=NZjB6vVD6xo

33 https://www.youtube.com/watch?v=b2FjeVVftAo

34 http://www.vocativ.com/world/russia/next-russian-state-tv-death-threats-kremlin-critics/

35 http://snob.ru/profile/28436/blog/78030

36 https://www.facebook.com/boris.nemtsov/posts/651319564937647

37 http://www.ntv.ru/novosti/1058436/

38 Interview with author, April 2014.

39 http://www.themoscowtimes.com/news/article/art-groups-giant-banner-labels-kremlin-opponents-5th-column/497929.html

40 https://www.youtube.com/watch?v=EkMT_oLempE

41 http://www.themoscowtimes.com/article/497922.html

42 http://www.newsru.com/russia/30jan2015/yarovaya.html

43 Interview with author, June 2014.

44 http://www.yar.kp.ru/online/news/2088830/

45 http://www.politico.eu/article/russia-environmental-protest-cossacks/

46 http://calvertjournal.com/articles/show/3373/pavlensky-performance-art-protest

47 https://twitter.com/Dobrokhotov/status/546034900265345024

48 Interview with author, December 2014.

49 http://www.newsweek.com/2015/03/27/exclusive-opposition-leaders-london-are-putins-next-target-314743.html

50 http://www.vocativ.com/world/russia/alexei-navalny-arrested-protests/

51 http://www.ft.com/intl/cms/s/2/4ecd1a04-bd1d-11e4-b523-00144feab7de.html#axzz3gN6D7IF2

CHAPTER EIGHTEEN: MURDER AT THE KREMLIN WALLS

1 http://www.theguardian.com/world/2015/jan/19/russia-official-silence-for-families-troops-killed-in-ukraine

2 http://www.bbc.com/news/world-europe-28934213

3 http://www.ft.com/intl/cms/s/2/76bac354-59c2-11e4-9787-00144feab7de.html

4 https://www.youtube.com/watch?v=l7Q6MBVpDZ8

5 http://www.telegraph.co.uk/news/worldnews/europe/ukraine/11035401/Russian-armoured-vehicles-and-military-trucks-cross-border-into-Ukraine.html

6 http://www.theguardian.com/world/2014/sep/03/ukraine-soldier-youre-better-clueless-because-truth-horrible-moscow-ilovaysk

7 http://gruz200.net/

8 http://www.newsweek.com/2014/09/12/russian-mothers-waiting-news-their-missing-sons-267909.html

9 http://en.novayagazeta.ru/politics/67620.html

10 https://meduza.io/feature/2015/04/08/byvaet-i-takoe

11 http://www.themoscowtimes.com/upload/iblock/ae8/5421-02-tv_zomb10.jpg

12 Interview with author, July 2015.

13 http://www.putin-itogi.ru/putin-voina/

14 Interview with author, May 2015.

15 http://uk.reuters.com/article/2015/03/05/uk-russia-nemtsov-ukraine-idUKKBN0M120620150305

16 https://www.youtube.com/watch?v=B9oVvGcLWeo

17 https://twitter.com/ilyayashin/status/571421500949041153

18 http://www.telegraph.co.uk/news/worldnews/europe/russia/11444367/Boris-Nemtsov-murder-security-cameras-turned-off-for-maintenance.html

19 https://www.washingtonpost.com/world/russian-opposition-leaders-see-kremlin-links-to-nemtsov-murderrussian-opposition-leaders-see-kremlin-links-to-nemtsov-murder/2015/02/28/1626f9b2-bed6-11e4-9dfb-03366e719af8_story.html

20 http://news.yahoo.com/chechen-commander-ukraine-drawn-russian-intrigue-084530080.html

21 http://www.theguardian.com/world/2015/mar/09/boris-nemtsov-speculation-about-islamist-link-useful-for-kremlin

22 http://echo.msk.ru/blog/nemtsov_boris/1470712-echo/

23 Interview with author, February 2015.

24 http://sobesednik.ru/politika/20150210-boris-nemcov-boyus-togo-chto-putin-menya-ubet

25 Interview with author, July 2015.

26 Interview with author, June 2015.

27 http://www.theguardian.com/world/2015/feb/28/was-boris-nemtsov-killed-russia-opposition-traitors

28 http://www.vesti.ru/doc.html?id=2391788

29 http://www.kp.ru/daily/26348.7/3230418/

30 Interview with author, May 2015.

31 http://www.wsj.com/articles/russia-hedges-over-stalins-legacy-1431077407; http://khpg.org/en/index.php?id=1427808703

32 http://snob.ru/profile/24691/blog/88680

33 https://www.facebook.com/bakushinskaya/posts/931432850224960

34 https://navalny.com/p/4156/

35 http://www.putin-itogi.ru/putin-voina/

36 http://www.theguardian.com/world/2015/mar/08/boris-nemtsov-five-suspects-appear-in-court-over-opposition-leaders-killing

37 http://www.bbc.com/news/world-europe-31829723

38 Interview with author, July 2015.

39 http://www.ft.com/intl/cms/s/0/781e9acc-c4bb-11e4-a2e0-00144feab7de.html

40 http://www.rferl.org/content/russia-nemtsov-ally-skeptical-of-arrests/26889849.html

41 http://theins.ru/news/4264

42 https://www.youtube.com/watch?v=J0-RRSGXzKs

43 https://www.youtube.com/watch?v=xJDJM0ZVAM8

44 http://www.washingtonpost.com/wp-dyn/content/article/2007/02/15/AR2007021501940.html

45 http://foreignpolicy.com/2015/03/16/a-showdown-in-moscows-power-putin-nemtsov-kadyrov-elite/

46 http://www.thetimes.co.uk/tto/sport/football/international/article2940189.ece

47 https://www.youtube.com/watch?v=-UqfPoED0QM; http://www.bbc.com/russian/russia/2014/12/141229_chechnya_kadyrov_volunteers_stadium_speech

48 https://www.facebook.com/photo.php?fbid=739535322782737&set=a.289618704441070.64195.100001788291627&type=1&permPage=1

49 http://top.rbc.ru/politics/11/03/2015/550069bb9a7947fd834cec7e

50 http://uk.reuters.com/article/2015/03/11/kazakhstan-putin-idUKL5N0WD22420150311

51 http://www.reuters.com/article/2015/03/12/us-russia-crisis-putin-health-idUSKBN0M816620150312

52 http://www.businessinsider.com.au/russian-state-media-published-putin-in-the-future-2015-3

53 https://twitter.com/sranysovok/status/576476703654039552

54 https://www.youtube.com/watch?v=3-yxHhW4P3Y&feature=youtu.be

55 http://www.kommersant.ru/doc/884022

56 http://www.novayagazeta.ru/inquests/57374.html

57 http://www.nytimes.com/2015/03/20/world/europe/chechens-ties-to-putin-are-questioned-amid-nemtsov-murder-case.html?_r=0

58 http://glavred.info/politika/okara-v-rossii-dva-politika-putin-i-kadyrov-ostalnye-byurokraty-ili-klouny-297627.html

59 http://www.rferl.org/content/kadyrov-authorizes-shooting-of-security-oustide-chechnya/26974169.html

60 http://www.rosbalt.ru/moscow/2015/07/09/1416813.html

61 http://foreignpolicy.com/2015/03/16/a-showdown-in-moscows-power-putin-nemtsov-kadyrov-elite/

62 https://www.facebook.com/leonid.m.volkov/posts/880783811944253

63 Interview with author, July 2015.

64 http://www.bbc.com/news/world-europe-33009049

65 http://www.reuters.com/article/2014/07/24/russia-putin-emigration-idUSL6N0PI4TH20140724

66 http://www.levada.ru/05-06-2014/emigratsionnye-nastroeniya

67 http://www.novayagazeta.ru/news/1693251.html

68 http://www.vocativ.com/world/russia/russias-new-brain-drain/

69 http://carnegie.ru/2015/05/26/russia-s-brain-drain-why-economists-are-leaving/i92o

70 https://www.hrw.org/news/2015/05/01/russias-stolen-future

71 Interview with author, March 2015.

72 Interview with author, June 2015.

73 Interview with author, March 2014.

EPILOGUE: SACRED POWER AND RUINED LIVES

1 http://www.themoscowtimes.com/news/article/no-putin-no-russia-says-kremlin-deputy-chief-of-staff/509981.html
2 Interview with author, May 2015.
3 http://www.business-gazeta.ru/article/136567/
4 http://www.radiopolsha.pl/6/249/Artykul/211307
5 http://tass.ru/opinions/top-officials/1353227?page=3
6 http://www.youtube.com/watch?v=ckIYkaO-EWg
7 http://vz.ru/news/2015/9/30/769701.html
8 http://www.theguardian.com/world/video/2015/oct/05/russian-forecaster-says-weather-is-excellent-for-bombing-syria-video
9 Interview with author, October 2015.

All hyperlinks were valid at the time of first publication.

INDEX

ACKNOWLEDGEMENTS

Greetings and love to: my wife, Tanya Nevinskaya, who put up with nine months of my worrying while I tried to write the first edition of this book. (Then let me sleep in after my late nights completing the update chapters.) Masha Bennetts, our excellent daughter, who can now astound me with her wit and wisdom in two languages. Mum (aka Jo Bennetts) for teaching me to read (and not only!). Dad (aka Bill Bennetts) for buying me *2000AD*, once I'd learned how. (And for many other things, as well!) My sister, Siobhan Parker, as well as Mike and Sam. All my aunts, uncles, and cousins. Tamara Nikolaevna and Murka the cat. Vitya the cat.

Even more greetings to: the Tulovskys (Stas, Masha, Zhenya, Katya, Liza, and Styopa the cat). Dmitry and Marina Dudenkov. Daniel Humphries and family. Peter van Dyk, Natasha Doff and Andrew Roth for keeping me company at so many cold protests. Dan Peleschuk. Tom Balmforth. Mikhail Trofimenko, Vera, Ulyana, and Aglaya. Yulia Vainzof. Alex Mitchell, Jessica Adams, and Elvis. The Petukhovs (Gregory, Kati, and Lily). Alexei Korolyov. Maria Kuchma. Chris Boian for sending me to North Korea (and Chechnya and Iran!). Anastasia Markitan. Diana Markosian.

Many thanks to everyone at Oneworld Publications, but especially Mike Harpley for taking on the book in the first place. And even more thanks for his excellent suggestions to improve its structure, etc. Any shortcomings in the final version are mine alone. Many thanks also to Chris Wellbelove, my agent at Greene & Heaton, for his initial interest in the idea.

Thanks also to Jabeen Bhatti. Mary Tobin for a great copyedit. Gaya Marina Garbaruk for transcribing interviews for me.

Caroline Antonyuk née Handforth (1970–2015) – RIP.

Contacts:

marcbennetts@yahoo.com

@marcbennetts1

marcbennetts.com

Свобода лучше, чем несвобода...

BEATRIX THE BOLD

and the CURSE of the WOBBLERS

Simon Mockler

Piccadilly
PRESS

First published in Great Britain in 2019 by
PICCADILLY PRESS
80–81 Wimpole St, London W1G 9RE
www.piccadillypress.co.uk

A CIP catalogue record for this book is available from the British
Library.

ISBN: 978-1-84812-765-4
also available as an ebook

1
Printed and bound in Great Britain by Clays Ltd, Elcograf S.p.A.

Piccadilly Press is an imprint of Bonnier Books UK
www.bonnierbooks.co.uk

For Louis and Penelope

1

The Small Girl
and the Big Secret

In a faraway palace in the Kingdom of Morden lived a small girl, with a big secret. The secret and the girl, whose name was Beatrix, lived side by side but never met. The secret was big, but the palace was bigger, and there were plenty of dark places for it to hide.

When I say the palace was far away, I mean far by coach and horses, which didn't have comfy seats and bouncy tyres like a modern car, but wooden wheels and itchy straw on the seats. They gave you a considerable pain in the bottom, so any journey, even if it was just to your friend's hut in the next village, seemed *bottom-achingly* far away.

To get to the palace, you had to go over the hills, through the woods, along the bumpy track, down Sore Bottom Alley, left on Red Rump Road and then straight down Numb Butt Lane.

If you did make it all that way, and didn't decide to give up halfway, you would have seen one of the strangest looking palaces in the world. It was at least twice as big as Buckingham Palace, but instead of being neat and orderly like a palace usually is, it was a very higgledy-piggledy sight. There were towers and turrets that reached as high as the sky. There were statues of kings and queens on the roof that looked like they might topple forward if a pigeon pooped on their head. And there were rooms built on rooms with stairs

on the outside because they'd forgotten to build them inside.

The whole thing looked like it had been built by a giant out of different sized cereal boxes and loo rolls and egg cartons, all stuck together and covered with gold paint.

The first word every visitor said when they saw it was...

'Ow! My bottom hurts.'

No, they didn't. (Well some of them did.) The first thing they said was:

'What an enormous palace! The queen who lives here must be very rich.'

As everybody knows, kings and queens are usually very rich. In the olden days you could tell they were rich because instead of wearing the same pair of pants for a year like everyone else, they'd change them at least once a month. Sometimes even twice.

What you might not know is that as well as

rich kings and queens, there are super rich kings and queens. They have even more money and more underpants than the rich ones. In fact, they probably have more pairs of underpants than a mega-rich footballer like Cristiano Ronaldo.

Now, *hold onto your hats*. What I'm about to say will sound crazy. Super rich kings and queens are rich, but they're not the richest. There are kings and queens so rich they've forgotten what money is. They know they have a lot of it, but they think of it like you or I think about air. And you don't really think about air. It's just there.

You might think that a queen who lived in a golden palace was that kind of rich, and had at least two pairs of pants to wear every month. Maybe even three. You might be thinking that she could buy whatever she liked. But you'd be wrong.

Firstly, this story happened a long time ago and the kind of things you or I might buy hadn't been invented yet. There were no roller skates, no iPads, no apps and no Pokémon. You couldn't even buy a football. The village blacksmith had a very attractive range of horseshoes, and the grocer could make a lovely sprout soup which he'd deliver

 to your house, but that was about it. Most things were either made of mud or wood. You can have a lot of fun playing around with mud and wood, but you can't make an Xbox.

Secondly, the queen was only ten years old, and although she was the queen, no one had told her so.

I'll say that again, because it's important and you're probably still thinking about how to make an Xbox out of mud and wood. No one had told her she was the queen.

Being a queen might seem like a very obvious thing to you and me. You're either a queen or you're not, and most of us are not. But Queen Beatrix didn't know she was a queen, she was just Beatrix.

This was the secret, the very big secret, that lived with her in the palace. It hid in the dark corners, away from the light. For a secret this big to stay hidden, it had to be helped by a lot of people, and there was a whole army of servants in the palace who were ready to cover it up, ready to throw a blanket over it, to distract Beatrix by pointing in the wrong direction or by telling her a joke. It wasn't an easy job, this − it was a bit like trying to hide an elephant. But with a big enough blanket, and a big enough palace, even an elephant can be made to disappear.

2

Ivan the Vicious
and Esmerelda the Terrible

The chief keeper of the secret was the young girl's aunt, whose name was Esmerelda. Her full title was *Esmerelda the Terrible*, but no one called her that to her face apart from people who wanted to get their head chopped off. And there aren't many people like that.

She didn't like having her niece in the palace, but she liked the fact that she had been given lots of gold to look after her. Aunt Esmerelda loved

gold more than anything else. She loved it more
than blackbirds love worms, more than policemen
love catching robbers and more than teachers love
the school holidays. She loved it so much she had
pots full of paint made from *real*
gold all over the palace.

Whenever she met
someone she thought
looked a bit ugly or
dirty she'd splash
some gold paint on
them. (And it was
best not to complain,
otherwise she might
cut off your head.)

Her husband was
Ivan the Vicious.
People did call him
'Vicious' to his face,
but Ivan didn't mind.

When you're in charge of an army, it's best to be a bit scary, otherwise it's very hard to make the soldiers do what you want. Ivan had five thousand soldiers in his army. That's a lot of people to boss around, but being known as Ivan the Vicious, (or occasionally 'Mr Vicious') made it a lot easier.

Beatrix didn't find her aunt particularly terrible, or her uncle terribly vicious, but she did find them both rather *strange*. Aunt Esmerelda laughed at things that definitely weren't funny, like 'Shall we have kippers for breakfast? Yes, I think we shall, a ha ha ha,' or 'Do hurry up and get dressed, otherwise you'll die of the cold, a ha ha ha ha.' Beatrix didn't think there was anything funny about having kippers for breakfast, or about dying of the cold, but her aunt laughed away in a sing-song voice that sounded like someone tapping a goldfish bowl with a tea spoon.

Uncle Ivan hardly ever laughed, even when Beatrix tried out her best jokes on him. He didn't like children, and he didn't like jokes. And he especially didn't like children who told jokes. Still, every now and then Beatrix would try out a joke on him, just to see if he changed his mind:

'What's a duck's favourite food?' she said. 'Quackers!'

Her uncle grunted, as if there was food caught at the back of his throat. Beatrix tried another one:

'What do you call a man with a spade on his head? ...Doug!' she said, giggling. Her uncle drew a breath through clenched teeth. His body tensed. His hand was hovering over his dagger. Beatrix carried on, a little bit afraid but keen to see what he'd do next.

'What do you call a fly with no wings...?' This time Beatrix didn't even have time to give the punch line. Her uncle took his dagger out of its sheath and in one smooth movement threw it hard against the wall, pinning a tiny bluebottle to the wood panelling.

'A walk,' she said, almost in a whisper.

'I call it... dead,' Ivan said. He said the word 'dead' as if it had three 'd's at the end. Then he pulled the knife from the fly and wiped it on his leg.

Sometimes at breakfast, as they sat and ate their kippers, she would ask him about her parents. Poor Beatrix didn't even know if they were alive or dead. But Ivan would just shrug and grunt and say 'Best not to ask.' If anyone else had said that Beatrix would have kept asking them until they gave her an answer, but when her uncle said the words in his quiet voice,

not wanting to look at her, his knife skilfully removing the tiny bones from the kipper, she knew she shouldn't ask. In the end she stopped asking.

The other question she'd stopped asking was:

'Can I go outside and play?'

Every time she asked this question her aunt came up with a different excuse. Although she'd decided to stop asking this question, one day Beatrix just couldn't resist trying it *one more time*.

3

The Outside World

It was breakfast time, Uncle Ivan had stomped off after finishing his kippers and she and Aunt Esmerelda were alone.

'Can I go outside and play?' she asked.

Just as she always did, Aunt Esmerelda came up with an excuse.

'Why ever would you want to go outside? You have everything you need right here. And there's nothing to see outside the walls of the palace.

Just a lake and the Dark, Dark Woods, then a *very* steep drop and after that nothing.'

'What do you mean, *nothing?*'

'I mean…' And here her aunt paused. 'You know the feeling you get just before you fall asleep, when you're falling and falling then suddenly you wake with a jolt?'

'I think so,' Beatrix replied.

'Well it's like that, only you don't wake up. You go around the lake through the Dark, Dark Woods then you step off the edge. After that you just keep falling. It's not something I'd recommend. And even if you managed to avoid falling off the edge of the woods into a bottomless pit, you'd be gobbled up in a moment by the **Wobblers**.'

Esmerelda chewed on her kipper, staring ahead.

Beatrix frowned. She didn't believe her aunt. It sounded like one of those things your mum and dad say just to stop you doing something you want, like telling you you can't have an ice-cream because you won't have room for dinner. As if an ice-cream would ever get in the way of dinner — it just melts in your tummy! And the Wobblers! Everyone in the palace was *terrified* of Wobblers. And no one had ever even seen one.

A **Wobbler** was like a cross between a goblin and a weasel, with a very large belly and sharp teeth. It was said they lived in the woods and liked to gobble up children for their tea. They were called 'Wobblers' because when they ran their bellies wobbled about like enormous plates of jelly.

Although this sounds funny, it was actually very dangerous — all children love jelly, and you'd be tempted to hang about if you saw a large wobbly jelly running towards you through the woods. Hang around much longer though and you'd be wondering why that jelly has a long nose, teeth, extremely bad breath and is about to eat you whole.

Beatrix pushed aside her breakfast. She didn't believe in Wobblers. She didn't believe in bottomless pits. She believed her aunt was hiding something from her.

'It's not fair,' Beatrix said.

Esmerelda smiled a funny, twisted smile.

'Is it fair that I have to look after you, and keep you safe? Believe me, I would happily let you play outside, see you fall off the edge of the world or get eaten by Wobblers. But that wouldn't be fair, would it? So what would you prefer – the kind of fair that lets you get eaten by a vicious Wobbler, or the kind of fair that keeps you safe?'

Beatrix shrugged. She didn't think it sounded like a very fair question.

'Safe, I suppose,' she said eventually, although

she didn't really mean it. Beatrix liked danger. She liked climbing high walls and throwing knives.

'Good,' her aunt said. She put down her knife and fork and picked up a paintbrush. Then she dipped it in a pot of gold paint and splashed it all over the face of the servant standing next to her. All the while she stared at Beatrix, a horrible smile fixed on her face, as if she had tried to eat a banana sideways and it had got stuck. It was obvious she wished it was Beatrix's face she was splattering with paint.

Esmerelda put the brush down. Then she got up from the breakfast table, turned and walked away as if she was a completely normal human being.

'Sorry,' Beatrix said, passing a handkerchief to the servant.

'At least she didn't chop my head off,' he said, wiping his eyes.

'And at least you now have a gold handkerchief,'

Beatrix said. She had a habit of seeing the best in bad situations.

The servant smiled at her. Beatrix suddenly had a thought. 'Have you been *outside* of the palace?' she asked.

The servant jumped back as if he'd just trodden on a bee. He looked terrified at the question. He glanced over his right shoulder, then he glanced over his left, as if he might be in trouble just for hearing what Beatrix said. Then he leant forward, and waved his fingers up and down, as if he wanted to show rain. He pointed down the corridor, then he drew a square with his fingers in the air. He did all this in a couple of seconds.

Rain, corridor, square. Beatrix was puzzled. They

played a game at Christmas where they tried to guess what song, book or battle someone was talking about without using any words. But it wasn't Christmas and she wasn't in the mood for a game.

'Never mind, thank you.' She sighed, thinking she would be kept in the dark forever.

The servant picked up the empty plates from the table, turned and carried them off. When she looked up, he'd disappeared. That was another thing Beatrix didn't understand; how servants were always appearing and disappearing, as if by magic. Beatrix didn't believe in magic.

The thing is, although Beatrix was being kept in the dark, even if someone had told her she was a queen she wouldn't have believed them. (Well, you wouldn't believe me if I told you there was an elephant hidden in your house, would you?)

When she looked in the mirror, she didn't see a queen. She saw someone who was quite good at telling jokes, not very good at dancing, very good at throwing knives, very good at standing on her head and whose hair was so curly it looked like a bird had made a nest in it. So far, that hadn't happened, although Beatrix sometimes left her window open at night and placed a trail of breadcrumbs from the sill to her bed in the hope that a sparrow might make its home there.

In this way, Beatrix, her aunt and her uncle and the very big secret lived together in the palace. It was a strange world, a bubble of a world, and like all bubbles there would come a time for it to burst. And because this was a very big bubble, a bubble the *size of an elephant*, that would mean a great deal of mess.

4

The Ten Rooms

The palace was the only home Beatrix had ever known. As you know, she was not allowed to leave it. She had never ordered sprout soup in the village, bought new shoes for the horses she didn't know she had, or ridden the golden carriage along Numb Butt Lane. (Lucky her.) Beatrix's world was very strange when seen from the outside, but it was *even stranger* for her, stuck on the inside. And it wasn't just because everyone was keeping an elephant-sized secret from her.

Beatrix lived in ten rooms in the east wing of the palace. She wasn't allowed anywhere else. Each year, on her birthday, she would be allowed into a new room. There were all the usual rooms you have in your house, like a bedroom and a toilet and a dining room. (Although because this was the olden days, some of those rooms were not quite the same as they are now – the toilet was just a seat with a hole in it over the lake!) But there were also some very unusual rooms. A war room, for instance, so Beatrix could practise fighting battles, and a story room, with a stage and seats just like a mini-theatre.

This was Beatrix's favourite room. It was opened on her ninth birthday. It wasn't just the best room in the palace, it was also the best present Beatrix had ever been given. In fact, it was probably the best present ANYONE has ever been given.

In the world. EVER. It had a big wooden wheel for choosing stories. It looked like the kind of wheel they use to steer ships, but it had pictures all over it. You spun the wheel and the Wobblers and moons and dragons and battles would *whirl* round in a big blur, and when it stopped a storyteller would jump out of a trap door in the floor, all dressed up and ready to go, acting out a fantastic tale about the picture at the top of the wheel.

But it wasn't just the stories Beatrix loved — there was an endless supply of popcorn, too. Not the kind of popcorn we eat today. That hadn't been invented yet. This was olden-days popcorn. They made it by frying up chicken skin in honey then chopping the skin into small, crunchy pieces. Sounds gross, but it was actually very tasty. A bit like having KFC for pudding.

Unusually for a really good present, the story room was from Esmerelda. For Beatrix, this was the *strangest* thing about Aunt Esmerelda. She could go from being mean as a Wobbler to doing a very good imitation of someone who was actually quite nice in no time at all.

As well as a war room and a story room, there was also a classroom so Beatrix didn't have to leave the palace to go to school, and a garden room so she *never* had to go outside.

The garden room had an open roof and high walls that were covered in vines and creeping plants, and there were fruit trees planted in huge pots made of gold. It even had a waterfall at one end, which needed ten servants to pump the water up from the lake to make it work. Because the lake was so stinky, they didn't use the waterfall much, but it still looked very impressive. It was made from huge stones stacked on top of each other, and when it wasn't all wet it was a pretty perfect climbing wall for Beatrix.

Behind the waterfall there was a mysterious and **very dark** cave. Beatrix's aunt, her uncle and all the servants told her that she must never go in the cave, for (of course) Wobblers lived inside, and a Wobbler would gobble her up as soon as she entered.

When Beatrix wanted to go into a different room, she had to ring a bell and ask a servant to unlock the door for her. And so that's what she did now.

'Please, Mrs Fartinpants,' (that was the name of

her nanny – I know this name sounds a bit rude to us now, but in those days a 'fartinpant' was a small round cake baked over the fire. It tasted a bit like a pancake and the batter bubbled up as it cooked. Mrs Fartinpants came from a big family of bakers who specialised in bubbling fartinpants).

'Mrs Fartinpants, please could you unlock the door to the war room and please could you fetch Uncle Ivan so I can practise throwing knives and winning battles?'

'All right, but only if you promise to put on a jumper. It's always cold in there and I don't want you catching a chill while you're knife throwing.'

Mrs Fartinpants was always worried about her catching a chill, but never seemed to worry about her *knife throwing*. When Beatrix stood against the wall and her uncle threw knives into the wood panelling around her, Mrs Fartinpants worried she might be standing in a draught.

Ivan wasn't worried about Beatrix's knife throwing either. After all, learning about war from the age of two hadn't done him any harm – that's if you didn't count the broken leg, cracked head, four broken ribs, bump on his head that made him speak Japanese for a week, and the fact that his little toe now just sort of hung off the side of his left foot as if all the bones had fallen out.

5

Battle Practice

Beatrix enjoyed her lessons with Uncle Ivan. He let her move tiny metal soldiers across a big battlefield on a table, and he always got *very excited* when she used the mini-catapults to knock down the baddies.

'You must always lead from the front. That way you will have the respect of your army,' he would say. 'You ride at the front of all your soldiers, showing them you are not afraid.'

'Isn't that dangerous?'

'Of course. That's why they respect you. You put yourself in the same danger as your army. Also, if a king or queen has to lead the army into war, they'll always think twice about whether they want to start a war,' Uncle Ivan said. 'And starting a war is something that should be thought about at least twice.'

'Because you might die?'

'Because everyone might die.'

'Mmm. OK,' Beatrix said, looking over the battlefield. It didn't feel much like a game any more. 'But I'm only ten and a half. And I'm not in charge. So I think for now you should carry on leading the real army, agreed?' Beatrix said. Uncle Ivan frowned, his eyebrows coming together like two big furry caterpillars about to start a fight.

'Yes, well, for now obviously it would be me. But if you *were* the leader of the army, and I'm definitely not saying you are, because if you were that would make you the queen, which is ridiculous. Ha ha ha.'

Uncle Ivan's laugh didn't sound much like a real laugh, it sounded more like an echo.

'Anyway, if you were the leader of the army, then you would have to lead from the front. Look, you see this?' He pointed at the battlefield and the toy soldiers on it. The red army had surrounded the grey army. The king was about to be captured. 'How does the grey king get out of this one?'

Beatrix shrugged. 'I don't know.'

'Think about it. What would you do?'

She looked at the scene. There was really no way for the grey king to escape.

'OK,' said Beatrix. 'Well, has it been raining on the battlefield?'

'No, no more than usual,' said Uncle Ivan. 'Actually it's summer. No rain. Everyone is hot and sweaty under their armour and in a hurry to finish the battle and have some fartinpants.' Uncle Ivan was feeling hungry. It was almost an hour since he'd eaten.

'All right then. How about the archers tie dried grass from the field to the end of their arrows, set fire to it and fire at the enemy army's horses who are all bunched up on this side. The grass will catch fire around the horses and make them panic. They'll charge through their own army, opening a gap here…' Beatrix pushed aside some of the toy soldiers. 'The king's soldiers run through the gap, force half the enemy army into this river, surround the remaining troops and capture their king. Done,' Beatrix said, standing back. She folded her arms and *puffed out her chest* like her uncle.

'Hmmm,' said Ivan. 'How do you make this fire?'

'Two stones knocked together. Special stones. They spark. My teacher Wilfred the Wise can do it.'

'Is it magic? You can't rely on magic to win a battle. Better to rely on your fighting skills.' As he said 'fighting skills' he withdrew his knife from his belt and flung it against the wall, pinning a spider to the wood panelling. 'You're sure it's not magic, this fire of yours?'

'It's not magic magic. It's not fly-off-the-roof-of-the-palace magic, or become-invisible magic, but it is a *sort of magic*. It's the kind anyone can do with the right tools. Like changing blue and yellow paint into green by mixing them up.'

'OK.' Ivan's caterpillar eyebrows twitched, rose upwards, then came down again and met in the middle. 'I like it. I do. It's a good idea. Very brave. Very bold, Beatrix, very bold. Actually, it's the kind

of move your father would have made,' Ivan said.
'He always said that the most important weapon
was…' Uncle Ivan tapped the side of his head, 'the
brain.'

Beatrix looked up.

'My *father?*' she said, quick as a flash. 'Was he in
charge of an army?'

Uncle Ivan bit his lip and shook his head. He
got up and pulled the knife from the wall, wiping
the blade on his leg.

'No,' he said. 'No, he wasn't in charge of an army.'

'Why did you say he was?'

'Doesn't matter.'

'Doesn't matter? Doesn't matter?!' Beatrix's
hand swept across the table, knocking all the
knights over. 'This stupid game doesn't matter!'
she said.

Uncle Ivan grabbed Beatrix, his big hands
pressing her thin arms to her chest like iron clamps.

'Listen, Beatrix. It is to keep you safe. I have

sworn to keep you safe. We all have. So please, no questions. No questions because I can't tell you the answers. OK?'

His voice was serious and quiet, his grip strong. All Beatrix said was 'OK.'

'Oh and *promise me* you won't tell your aunt what I said about your father. She'll be really cross.' When he said this he actually looked afraid, and he hardly ever looked afraid.

On that day, Beatrix caught her first glimpse of the elephant hiding in the corner of the room. Her uncle had tripped up and accidentally caught the cloth that was covering it with his toe and pulled it away to reveal... Something. Something strange, something *not quite right*. Something hidden. Her aunt and uncle were keeping a secret from her. She knew it. It wasn't just about what was outside, or who her parents were... it was also about keeping her 'safe'. What did they mean, *keeping her safe?* Who did they need to keep her safe from?

6

The Classroom

Beatrix was thinking about what her uncle had said as she sat in the classroom waiting for lessons to begin. The classroom looked very much like an ordinary classroom. There were examples of good work on the walls and tall windows that made it very hot in summer and very cold in winter. It smelt the same as any other classroom too, having a whiff of old PE kits and polish. There was one big difference though. There was only *one* desk, right in the centre of the room. And there was only *one* student, and that was Beatrix.

It's very hard to mess about or chat to your friends when it's only you and the teacher. In fact, it's pretty much impossible. You're always top of the class, but you're always bottom of the class too, because it's just you. Also, Beatrix didn't really feel a very big sense of achievement when her teacher decided to put her latest drawing of a Wobbler on the wall, even if it was the best drawing of a Wobbler anyone in her class had ever done.

Today, Beatrix was going to see if she could get her teacher, Wilfred the Wise, to tell her more about her father. She knew her uncle and aunt would never tell her anything (at least not on purpose). But if there was anyone who might tell her a bit more about her parents, it was Wilfred.

Wilfred the Wise had *always* wanted to be a magician rather than a teacher, but he'd failed the magic exams so had decided to teach instead. It wasn't his fault he failed the magic exams – one of the tricks he had to perform was flying. It required actual magic, and Wilfred the Wise was wise enough to know that he couldn't do actual magic. Sometimes he doubted whether such a thing even existed, especially when he fell from the roof of the palace into the stinky lake whilst flapping his arms like a crazy pigeon. But Wilfred the Wise had found he quite enjoyed teaching.

He was kind, he liked telling stories, and he liked Beatrix.

'Mr Wise, Mr Wise?' Beatrix said, her hand in the air. 'Today I wondered if we could do something a bit different. Today I thought it would be good if we could find out **more** about our families.'

Wilfred looked surprised. 'I was going to teach maths today. We still haven't done all the numbers. As everybody knows, there are five hundred numbers and we've only done up to two hundred.'

'I think it would be better to do history,' Beatrix said. 'And we could learn about history by drawing a family tree and finding out what our parents and grandparents did.'

Wilfred looked at Beatrix. He could see a very determined expression in her eyes. He couldn't tell her the truth – if he did Esmerelda would chop his head off faster than you could say *Please put my head back on, it's really gross to see my body from the other side of the room*. He decided to do what all grown-ups do in this situation. He decided to distract her by suggesting they do something completely different.

'Sounds like a very interesting project. And I do love history. How about we do something completely different, and a lot more fun? Why don't I tell you about the magic tricks I had to perform when I sat the magic exams instead?'

'I'd really rather learn about my family,' Beatrix said.

'Of course you would. And it's very interesting. But I need time to prepare that lesson. Why don't we do your family tree project another day, after I've had a chance to look everything up? It's very complicated,' he said to Beatrix.

Beatrix folded her arms and shook her head, feeling very cross. Wilfred had answers, she knew it, but just like everyone else he didn't want to tell her.

Beatrix was right in thinking that Wilfred knew

the secret, but unlike most of the people who knew the secret, Wilfred also knew why the secret had to be kept. And when he stood in the classroom with four of the finest knights in the kingdom standing in each corner, locked doors made of heavy oak reinforced with iron and Ivan the Vicious and his five thousand soldiers guarding the rest of the palace, he wondered if it would be enough to keep the young queen safe.

It should be enough, if you were dealing with a normal-sized army of normal-sized soldiers. But there was a force much bigger and more powerful out there. An army that wanted to kill Queen Beatrix the Bold. The Evil Army from Beyond the Woods.

This army was made up of the most brutal, *vicious* soldiers ever to walk this earth. If they were insects they'd be Killer Wasps, if they were fish they'd be Great White Sharks and if they were Jelly Babies, they'd be the green ones.

They were uglier than Orcs, stronger than smelly cheese and better at fighting than a Roman gladiator trained by a kung fu master with a GCSE in Chinese burns and Grade 8 in giving wedgies. This was an army not to be messed with. This army was raised knowing only one word, and that word was KILL. This made it very difficult when they were trying to talk about normal things like what the weather was going to be like tomorrow (cloudy with a chance of KILL!), or how to make the perfect sprout soup. Freshly-picked sprouts, boiling water, a pinch of salt, a twist of black pepper. Simmer for twenty minutes then KILL KILL KILL!

Wilfred the Wise had heard the stories, some of which he believed, and some of which he didn't. But there was one thing he was sure of. If the Evil Army *ever* found out that Beatrix was in the palace, there would be trouble, **big trouble**, and he wasn't sure if all Ivan's soldiers and all his viciousness would be enough to keep the young queen safe.

7

Hide and Seek

After lunch, Beatrix was allowed to go into the garden room and play hide and seek with Mrs Fartinpants. Today, as usual, Mrs Fartinpants was the seeker, and Beatrix needed somewhere to hide. Hiding from Mrs Fartinpants was very difficult. She seemed to know every single nook and cranny in the palace. It was as if she could walk through walls.

Beatrix glanced at the waterfall, and at the

mysterious, dark cave behind it. If she could just get past the servant guarding the entrance she would have a great hiding place and a chance to explore the cave.

Beatrix approached the servant. He was a very wide man and he almost completely blocked the entrance. Beatrix had an idea. Something to make him get out of the way.

'Hi,' Beatrix said.

'Good afternoon,' said the servant.

'Did you know that Mr McDonald has just made a fresh batch of fartinpants? You know how good a cook he is. They're in the kitchen if you want them. I must say they smell dee-licious,' she said.

The very wide man shifted slightly. Beatrix was sure she saw his nose twitch.

'I don't smell anything,' he said.

'Don't you? I do. You should hurry or you'll miss out,' Beatrix replied.

The man looked at her. His eyes narrowed. He wrinkled his nose.

'Still don't smell anything, and I have a very good sense of smell. Do you know what I think, young lady?' he said. 'I think that you're playing hide and seek, and you've got your eye on my cave.'

'OK,' Beatrix said. 'You're right. But it does look like an exceptionally good hiding place, so how about letting me in?'

'Oh no no no,' the man said, very slowly. 'That would be impossible. You can't go in there. Wobblers live in there.'

Beatrix put her head in her hands. Wobblers. *Always* Wobblers!

'And there are snakes too. And rats. Trust me, you don't want to go in there. And there are some very low ceilings. You could get a nasty bump on the head. Also, there are some uneven floor tiles. So all in all it's far too dangerous for children.' The man placed his hands on his hips. He was even bigger with his elbows pointing out.

Beatrix looked round. There was no getting past him. There was nothing else to do except give up.

Except... She'd never been this close to the cave before. Sometimes she'd heard whispers coming from inside it, and she'd seen what looked like shadows creeping about in there. And now, behind the guard, she could glimpse light. Suddenly, she remembered something. She remembered the mime the servant had done at breakfast, showing water falling down. Did he mean rain… or did he mean waterfall?

Was there a *way out* behind the waterfall?

'You go find another place to hide. One that isn't full of Wobblers,' the guard said.

Beatrix ran back inside to find somewhere else to hide. She ducked down behind a long wooden table in the corridor next to the dining room. From her hiding place, she heard voices. It sounded like Uncle Ivan and Wilfred the Wise. They were in the dining room. Uncle Ivan was doing his best to whisper, but he had such a booming, deep voice that even his whispers sounded like someone banging a drum with a metal pipe.

There is nothing quite like the sound of a grown-up attempting to whisper to make a young child prick up their ears, and Beatrix had more reason than most to listen.

She crept towards the dining room, taking care

not to make a sound on the creaky wooden floor. The door hadn't been locked and was still open. She peered cautiously round it.

Uncle Ivan was sitting at the table with his back to her, his knife in his hand. He loved that knife so much, he probably loved it as much as your mummy and daddy love their mobile phones. It was always close by – in his hand, on his belt or on the table in front of him, ready for him to pick up and fiddle with.

Wilfred the Wise sat opposite him, leaning close to Ivan.

'I have *heard* things,' Ivan said to Wilfred, staring deep into Wilfred's eyes.

'What kind of things?' Wilfred asked. They had just had beans for lunch and he'd been sitting next to Esmerelda the Terrible, so he may well have heard some peculiar things.

'There are stories. Rumours that the Evil Army from Beyond the Woods are closing in,' Ivan said.

'Rumours?' Wilfred said. He didn't like rumours. He preferred facts. 'I don't like rumours. I prefer facts,' he announced, rather importantly. Rumours caused problems. The whole 'Wobbler' thing had started as a rumour, but now people actually believed in them. They even believed they started off with three eyes and then one dropped out when they reached the age of seven. Ridiculous.

'Rumours, facts – call it what you want. I've had reports from the Watch Tower at the end of Numb Butt Lane. Strange things are happening.'

Beatrix leant forward. This was getting interesting.

8

Code Pink

'What *kind* of strange things?' Wilfred said.

'Well, last night a man with an enormous tape measure was seen measuring the width of the lane. The night before, another man was seen making sketches of the palace by candlelight. The night before that another man was seen digging a tunnel near the palace walls.'

Wilfred was shocked. 'This is very worrying.

Very worrying indeed,' he said. 'They're making plans. They're getting ready to strike.'

Making plans, getting ready to strike? Beatrix thought. *Who, why?*

Ivan frowned. 'Do you think so? I thought that at first. Then I thought perhaps it was some building work Esmerelda had ordered – she knows I hate Numb Butt Lane, I can't stand going to the shops and getting a sore bottom. I thought she was planning to have it smoothed over as a birthday treat. A lovely surprise for me.'

Wilfred stared at Ivan in astonishment. 'When has Esmerelda ever got you a surprise birthday present?'

'Never – but that's why it would be a surprise.'

'What did she get you last year?'

'A knife.'

'And the year before?'

'A knife.'

'And the year before?'

'A knife. No, a knife case. And a knife.'

'And when's your birthday?'

'It's in the summer.'

'And what time of year is it now?'

'Winter.'

'So adding up all these facts, do you think it's *likely* that the three men seen at night close to the palace were working on a secret plan to make Numb Butt Lane less numbing, or do you think they might possibly have been working out how to capture and kill the queen?'

The queen?! Beatrix almost said the words out loud. What queen? There was no queen in the palace! At least, no one had ever told her about a queen. And why did the Evil Army want to kidnap this queen?

Ivan the Vicious spun the knife on his fingers. Then he threw it against the wall and slapped Wilfred on the shoulder.

Beatrix jumped, knocking the door shut by

accident. She turned and ducked quickly.

Uncle Ivan's head appeared round the door. He glanced this way and that, eyebrows twitching, then he disappeared back into the dining room.

'No one there,' he said, pulling the door closed behind him and locking it.

Beatrix crept forward again and pressed her ear against the door. She could just about hear what they were saying.

'This is why I like you, Wilfred,' Ivan said. 'You're so wise. I knew I could rely on you for good advice.' He peered out of the window. 'They're planning to kill the queen. I'll double the patrols around the palace,' Ivan went on. 'And put more guards outside her room. If anyone from the Evil Army from Beyond the Woods sets a foot in this place you know what I'll do…' His hand reached out for his knife but he'd already thrown it at the wall. His hand waved about in the air like an odd sock on a washing line.

'You'll carry a spare knife?' Wilfred said.

'Yes. No!' He stormed angrily across the room and pulled the knife out of the wall. 'I'll throw this at them.'

'Maybe also carry a couple of spares,' Wilfred said quietly. 'Will you tell the queen the danger she is in?'

Ivan shook his head.

'I cannot. Nor can Esmerelda. We made a solemn oath to her parents and an oath *can never be broken.*'

'What happens if you break it?' Wilfred said.

Ivan looked confused. 'Erm, I don't know,' he said. 'Oaths cannot be broken.'

'OK,' Wilfred said. He was all for keeping oaths and promises and whatnot, but if an Evil Army was to come for him, he'd quite like to know about it. He decided to make a plan, a plan that would help Beatrix escape if the Evil Army attacked the palace. It was number one on his list of things to do. He also needed to sharpen all the pencils in the classroom, that was number two on the list. Oh, and he needed to buy some more loo paper.

'She must be kept safe at all costs,' Wilfred said. Ivan nodded and got up from the table.

'I'll make sure the Danger Level is raised to Code Red,' he said.

'Is that the most serious code we have?' asked Wilfred.

'No, there's also Code Pink. That's when we've reached the most dangerous situation you could ever imagine.'

'Don't you think this should be Code Pink?' Wilfred said, feeling a little puzzled. 'It sounds like the Evil Army is planning to attack as soon as they can.'

Ivan frowned.

'Thing is, I can't tell my soldiers we have a Code Pink, they don't like the colour. You should have heard the arguments about Code Red. I want it to be Code Blue, that's a boy's colour. Or a Code Black, that would be really cool. That's why I never use a Code Pink.'

Not for the first time, Beatrix found herself thinking that grown-up conversations could be *very strange*. She heard Ivan's heavy footsteps approaching the door and ran back to her hiding place behind the table. Ivan appeared in the doorway, looked to the left and right. Then he walked forward into the wall.

Beatrix blinked. What on earth? Ivan had completely disappeared! She couldn't believe it. It was as if he'd walked straight through a solid stone wall and vanished. Wilfred appeared a moment later, muttering something to himself that might have been a magic spell or possibly just a reminder to buy some more loo roll, then did exactly the same thing. He vanished into thin air!

Beatrix had had enough. If no one inside the palace was prepared to tell her what was going on, then she was sure she could find someone outside the palace who would tell her. Anyone. There *had* to be people who weren't afraid of her uncle and aunt or hadn't made any silly oaths.

She was going to find out *how* they managed to disappear into walls like ghosts. She was going to find out about this mysterious queen and the people who wanted to attack her. She was going to find out *what* was behind the waterfall. And it wouldn't be a **Wobbler**.

9

Beatrix's Plan

In the dead of night, when all was silent and dark, Beatrix slipped out of her bed.

She'd spent the rest of the day in her room, preparing for her escape. She wasn't sure what was at the end of the cave behind the waterfall, but if there was some kind of window, she might need to climb down the palace walls to make her escape. Although she was already a pretty good climber she wanted some extra practice, so she'd tied her bedsheets together and thrown them up so they caught on one of the beams that supported the roof. The bedsheets were made of fine linen and formed a strong rope for her to clamber up.

Next, she thought, *I'll need a disguise. I need the kind of clothes they wear in the villages so I can fit in. I'll need some food too.* Luckily she had a stash of fartinpants in the cupboard of her enormous bedroom, so she took them out and hid them in her bag.

As she looked through the clothes in her cupboard, she realised that all of them were very fancy indeed. Now that she was looking for something simple she could see that most of them looked pretty much like the kind of clothes a queen would wear. Why didn't she have any *normal clothes?* She didn't really have time to think about it now, but still, it was very strange.

Beatrix went over to her bed, pulled off the pillow case and cut holes for her head and arms with her knife. She tried it on. It looked pretty funny, but at least she didn't look like… Beatrix stared at her reflection in the big silver mirror. At least she didn't look like a queen. She stopped for a moment, confused. Then she shook her head. No time. There was no time to think about these things now. She tore a strip off her last bedsheet and used it to make a belt. What she needed now was some sort of hat to cover her curly hair. She looked through her cupboard.

Her hats were much like her dresses, lined with wool or fur and with precious stones sewn into them. They wouldn't do at all. At last she found an old pair of pants in her drawer and put them on her head. They fitted pretty well, which she thought was strange, as she was sure her head was smaller than her bottom. Anyway, it was better than nothing and she could sew the leg holes up so at least they didn't look too much like a pair of pants.

It was *very late* by the time Beatrix made her way down the corridor, bag in hand, towards the garden room.

Even though it was dark and cold, Beatrix wasn't scared. Because, although she didn't know it yet, she was Beatrix the Bold. All the same, she felt a slight tingle on the back of her neck and butterflies in her stomach as she walked along the creaking floorboards in the dark. Doesn't matter, she told herself. They're only very small butterflies and they hardly touch the sides. She crept along another corridor, up the spiral staircase, down the normal staircase, up another spiral staircase, past the statue of a very big soldier riding a very small horse and out into the garden room.

It was exciting to be alone in the garden in the moonlight. She waited to see if there were any knights patrolling the garden, listening for the clank and creak of their armour. Nothing. They must be somewhere else. She'd have to be careful though. The air was very still and all the plants seemed to be holding their breath, as if waiting till morning. At the end of the garden was the waterfall, and next to the waterfall was the cave.

Beatrix walked towards it, careful not to make a sound. She could hear something. From a distance, it sounded like the rustle of sweet wrappers. As she got closer, it sounded more and more like hushed voices.

Was it **Wobblers?** It couldn't be Wobblers – Wobblers didn't speak English, they spoke

Wobblish, which was a cross between English and gibberish, and sounded like Welsh.

Beatrix crept silently forward. She climbed over the big stones at the bottom of the waterfall. No one was pumping water at this time of night, but the stones were still wet and slippery and glistened in the moonlight. She entered the cave – and heard voices.

'I *always* have to clean the floors, it's not fair,' one of the voices said. 'It hurts my back.'

'You're lucky you don't have to clean the chimneys. I got stuck up one the other week.'

Beatrix was as still as an egg in an egg cup. Eventually, the whispering voices grew quieter and disappeared into the darkness.

10

The Secret Passage

Beatrix breathed a sigh of relief and looked around. She wasn't sure where the cave would lead. It was dark and the floor was extremely uneven, but there were no snakes, rats or Wobblers so far.

As she walked forward, the floor became less bumpy. Instead of lots of uneven rocks, there were smooth stones. It started to feel a lot less like a cave, and a lot more like a passageway in the palace.

A secret passageway. Ahead of her, she noticed a window. A square of bluey-grey night sky that was lighter than the black walls. She walked towards it. The window opened onto the lake. But, unlike all the windows in her rooms, there were no bars on this one.

Beatrix looked out over the water in the moonlight, at the stars in the sky. She'd never seen so much open space before. It was breathtaking. So was the drop. She was high above the lake. She'd thought she might need a rope but she hadn't realised quite how long it would need to be.

Beatrix ran back to the garden room. She'd had an idea. There were vines growing close to the wall, and they looked thick and strong. Beatrix pulled at one of them as hard as she could. Slowly the vine came away. Carefully she took one of her throwing knives from her belt and cut through the stem at its base, then she lay it out flat on the ground. *Not long enough*, she thought.

She took hold of another vine, pulled it from the wall and cut the stem as before. *That should do it,* she thought. She tied the vines together then dragged them back along the cave behind the waterfall and attached them to an iron hook. Then she threw the length of vine out of the window so it dangled over the side. It reached all the way to the lake.

The water in the lake bubbled and belched. It smelt disgusting. That's because all the toilets in the palace emptied into it. It was not the kind of lake you'd go fishing in, let alone swim across.

'A little late to be wandering around the palace on your own, isn't it?'

Beatrix jumped. Aunt Esmerelda was standing there. *How* had she crept up so quietly? She was quieter than a cat in a pair of sheepskin slippers. Make that two pairs of sheepskin slippers. Very small ones.

'I was just walking. I couldn't sleep. I thought
I heard something.' Beatrix's heart pounded. She
hid her bag behind her back. If Esmerelda saw it
there was no telling what she'd do.

Aunt Esmerelda looked at Beatrix, and her eyes
grew narrow.

'I do so much for you, don't I?' Esmerelda said.

'Yes. Of course you do,' Beatrix said, trying to think of something her aunt actually did for her, rather than all the things she told the servants to do for her.

'And you like your rooms, and all the lovely toys, and the garden room, and all your lessons, don't you?'

'Very much so,' Beatrix said, thinking that she'd also like to leave the palace once in a while. She stood in front of the hook, praying Esmerelda wouldn't notice the vine she'd tied to it.

'Because just then, it looked like you might be thinking about escaping.' Esmerelda placed her hands on her hips like a dinner lady who's decided you don't deserve any chips. 'And anyway, you know you're not allowed to go behind the waterfall, what with all the Wobblers and other nasty things.'

'Of course I wasn't trying to escape!' Beatrix said. 'I was just looking at the reflection of the moon on the water. It's so lovely. It looks like it's fallen in and gone for a swim.'

Esmerelda snorted. 'I can always arrange to have you taken away, you know. You don't have to live here. There are *other* places. Not as nice of course. But perhaps it might be an awful lot better for me. I wouldn't have to worry about you.'

There was silence. Beatrix didn't have anything to say in reply. She suddenly just felt tired and sad. She didn't have anyone else, she only had Ivan and Esmerelda. She could feel her eyes fill with tears. She brushed them away with her fingers and turned so Esmerelda couldn't see.

Esmerelda sighed, then she held out her hand to Beatrix.

'Come now, there's no need to cry,' she said. 'Don't look so worried. I'm only joking. You know I would always look after you, don't you? I was just upset because I thought you might want to escape. I would hate that. Ivan would hate that too.'

Beatrix looked at Esmerelda's outstretched hand. She didn't want to take it.

'You know what, Beatrix, instead of going to bed, how would you like to go to the story room? We could take blankets and snuggle down and stay up late listening to stories. Would you like that?'

Esmerelda sounded sorry. Proper sorry. The kind of sorry you feel when you do a trick on the trampoline, land on your best friend's foot and the foot ends up pointing the opposite way to their other foot.

Beatrix took her aunt's hand, and with her other hand she dropped her bag silently onto the floor, kicking it with her heel behind a big rock.

'Yes, yes – I think I would like to go to the story room,' Beatrix said. She had to admit it sounded pretty good. She liked staying up late and she liked stories. Also, Esmerelda sounded like she *actually* wanted to do something fun with her, which was very unusual. For a second, Beatrix almost felt bad about the fact that she was trying to escape in the middle of the night. She still wanted to, but she felt guilty. Her aunt and uncle cared about her, and she had a good life in the palace, after all.

And Esmerelda wasn't terrible all the time. She was a bit like a big prickly cactus. On a hot day, when you needed a nice patch of shade, you could sit in her shadow and relax – you just had to be careful you didn't get too comfy and doze off against her or you'd get prickled.

11

Esmerelda's Secret

It was the next morning, and Aunt Esmerelda was far away in the cellar of the palace. The room she was in was her personal treasure store, and it was filled with gold coins and jewels and paintings of her favourite vegetable, the sprout.

Even though she was surrounded by lots of gold, Esmerelda the Terrible was feeling *terribly cross*. She wasn't feeling cross because Ivan had just told her the Evil Army from Beyond the Woods

might attack them soon and try to kill Beatrix –
that didn't bother her at all. It wasn't *even* because
she had caught Beatrix trying to escape last night.
She was feeling cross because she had run out of
things to buy.

So far that week she had bought:

 a pair of underpants *woven*
from golden thread,

 a suit of golden armour
for Ivan that was three
sizes *too small* but had been
on special offer,

a real statue of a gold horse,

a gold statue of a real horse,

five tins of golden syrup and a packet of Frosties that were coated in gold instead of sugar.

There was nothing left for her to buy. Even the three servants she paid to *think* of things to buy had run out of ideas. Anyway, their last idea was pants – I mean it was literally pants, the golden pants that had been delivered that week.

You might be wondering why Esmerelda wasn't worried about the Evil Army from Beyond the Woods. After all, even if she didn't care about Beatrix, there was still a chance that they would break most of the stuff in the palace. They might even destroy the palace. Once they'd done that, they might decide to chop off the heads of Esmerelda and Ivan for fun and play football with them. *Even worse* than chop off her head, they might take Esmerelda's gold.

But Esmerelda was not in the slightest bit worried about all this. Which, I'm sure you'll agree, is rather strange. In fact, she wasn't even surprised when Ivan told her of the danger they were in, which is even stranger. Some might say it was *suspicious*. You didn't need to be a great detective to work out that it smelt fishy. You didn't even need to be a fisherman.

Instead of telling Ivan to reinforce the walls and make sure he had a spare knife in his belt, all she said when he told her about the danger was:

'Oh really? That's a shame. It's been such fun having Beatrix in the palace. A ha ha ha.'

Ivan stared at her. He didn't know what to make of this.

'But, um, they are called the Evil Army because they are quite evil,' he said. 'Quite angry too. They say the Evil Army is meaner than Killer Wasps and Great White Sharks and Green Jelly Babies.'

Esmerelda held up her hand. 'Silence,' she said. 'Stop bothering me with all this gloomy news. Let's look on the bright side for once. If they destroy the palace we can build a new one. If they take Beatrix, we can have those ten rooms back. They would make a lovely cupboard for all my clothes. And we could put a roof on that horrid garden room. Who on earth wants a room where the rain falls and the snow melts and the sun shines?'

'But her mother and father pay us to keep her SAFE,' Ivan said, his eyebrows looking as if they were ready to start a fight. His voice boomed across the room. 'And we took the roof off that room so she could play outside without going to the woods or the lake where she would be in danger,' he said.

'I know all that,' Esmerelda replied crossly. 'And we have worked hard all these years to look after her. And now they've given us *so much* gold to keep her safe that I've run out of things to buy. Do you know how sad that makes me, my dear Ivan? Think about how annoying it is, to be rich and not be able to spend the money.'

Ivan stared at Esmerelda. Sometimes he didn't understand her at all.

'I'll hear no more of this,' Esmerelda said. 'I can't be bothered to listen to moany people – all this doom and gloom. A ha ha ha.'

Ivan frowned. Even though he was a vicious soldier, he was actually a very trusting person, and it didn't even occur to him that Esmerelda might be up to something terrible. (Sometimes he completely forgot she was called Esmerelda the Terrible.)

'Well at least stop painting the servants,' he said. 'They don't like it.' He huffed and puffed and turned, then walked to the armoury to sharpen his knives.

Aunt Esmerelda waited till his footsteps had faded into the distance, then she dismissed her servants and put down the pot of gold paint she held in her hand. When she was sure she was quite alone, she crept along the corridor and down a winding passageway towards the story room.

Esmerelda took a key from her pocket. She opened the door, entered the room and walked to the centre of the stage. She lifted up the trap door and peered through.

Beneath the trap door was a room whose walls were reinforced with iron and were more than a metre thick. There was a comfy looking bed, lots of candles and a huge pile of gold coins. The only thing it didn't have was a toilet, but Esmerelda wasn't planning to stay in there that long. All she really needed was somewhere to be safe when the Evil Army attacked the palace.

It wouldn't take them long to find Beatrix, not with the map she'd given them. She wasn't worried about Ivan's guards either. They wouldn't be able to stop the Evil Army – there weren't enough of them. Besides, the attack was just a distraction so the soldiers could sneak into Beatrix's room and *kidnap* her. In return they'd promised to pay Esmerelda an awful lot of gold and build her a new palace that would be much bigger and much better than the one she currently lived in.

Of course, she'd have to write to her sister and tell her what had happened, but she was sure she could squeeze out a tear or two when the time came. Esmerelda paused, thinking about Beatrix. For a moment, the tiniest of moments, she felt a strange sensation. What was it? Indigestion? Had she eaten too many sprouts for lunch? No, it was something else. Was it guilt? Was it shame? Was it her, what did they call it... her *conscience?* She batted away the feeling as if it was an annoying fly. If Beatrix hadn't been snooping about the palace looking for ways to escape, she wouldn't have needed to do this. She couldn't risk Beatrix running away. If she did, she wouldn't get all that lovely gold from her parents for looking after her. There was no time to waste. She would tell the Evil Army to launch their attack **immediately**.

12

Bang Crash Wallop

Have you ever wondered what it would *sound* like if ten thousand VERY ANGRY soldiers decided they were going to charge into your house with battering rams made from whole tree trunks, break down the windows and doors with axes, rip up all the floors, knock down the walls, throw the tiles from the roof and pull the heads off all your little Lego figures?

Well, that's what it was like when the Evil Army

attacked the palace. The first thing the people inside the palace heard was a distant rumbling. It was a deep rumble, like the sound of a very large and empty belly when it gets a whiff of bacon frying in the pan, or like the sound of thunder during a summer storm. It wasn't a scary sound, but it was a very unusual sound, as the sky was clear and blue, there were no clouds in sight and there was no bacon sizzling in a pan.

After the rumbling came the whistling. It could be heard over the rumble of footsteps and carts and horses' hooves. It was a high-pitched, piercing sound. The Evil Army from Beyond the Woods didn't usually whistle, but when you're charging at full speed along Numb Butt Lane on the back of your horse or inside a cart those bumps come thick and fast and are very painful. The soldiers didn't want to cry, because that would not look good. Instead, they pursed their lips and clenched their fists and whistled.

When they reached the end of Numb Butt Lane there came another sound. A shouty sort of sound. The soldiers shouted and shouted and got more and more angry with every shout. No prizes for guessing what they were shouting. It was their favourite word – 'KILL KILL KILL KILL KIIIILLLLLLLL!'

The man in charge of the Evil Army was General Alfred Burpintime. When you think of a general, you probably picture a tall man, powerfully built, with a deep voice and fierce, fiery eyes (a bit like Uncle Ivan). Perhaps he's sitting on a horse, and he's wearing a suit of armour or an army coat with bright brass buttons.

General Burpintime wasn't a tall man, in fact he was rather small – about the same height as a postbox, but much, much fatter. So fat, he looked like a pregnant postbox about to give birth to a parcel. His voice was not deep, it was high-pitched with a faint lisp. He had no hair on the top of his head but long hair at the sides. He had a very thick moustache above his top lip. The moustache looked a lot like a baby squirrel.

He preferred not to lead his army from the front, unlike Ivan the Vicious. That was far *too dangerous*. It made much more sense to give his army the orders, then wait quietly at the back, at a safe distance, preferably in a tent to keep out of the sun or rain and seated on a comfy chair. He usually took a good book to keep him busy during the battle and a large jar of marshmallows so he didn't get hungry. They were his favourite sweet, all soft and squidgy and safe. No one had *ever* been injured eating a marshmallow. On the other hand, lots of people had been very seriously injured fighting with swords and axes.

General Burpintime was standing on a hill a safe distance away as the soldiers charged at the gates of the palace. When he wanted his soldiers to attack, he blew into a ram's horn, which was an ancient instrument a bit like a trumpet made from (you guessed it) a ram's horn. It was very noisy and not very tuneful. It sounded like an elephant that's got its trunk caught in a teapot.

When he wanted them to stop attacking, he blew into a recorder, which was an ancient instrument a bit like a recorder. It was very quiet. The soldiers hardly ever heard the call to stop attacking, which may explain why everyone thought they were such an evil army.

Although he didn't want to join in the fighting, and didn't actually like talking to his soldiers, General Burpintime was still very good at being a general. He watched the battle unfold from the hill, eating marshmallows one after another. He felt very pleased with himself. The gates were broken and the Evil Army from Beyond the Woods had begun their attack. Young Queen Beatrix would soon be taken from her room. Yes, everything was going well, exceptionally well.

He ate one last marshmallow. It looked as if they would be finished by tea time. Splendid. He returned to his tent and read the next chapter of One Hundred Ways to Eat Marshmallows.

Once Beatrix was caught, he could tell his boss that they didn't need to worry about **the Curse** any more. His boss, the Evil Overlord, was always going on about **the Curse** and how a queen would one day lead an army and take over their kingdom and crush them into the dirt. He wanted Queen Beatrix kidnapped, then killed. Or killed then kidnapped – he didn't mind which way round.

If he had known a little more about Beatrix, General Burpintime might not have been feeling so relaxed. Because a young girl who has already been taught how to throw knives, make fire, command an army and dance the foxtrot is certainly *not* the kind of girl who can be easily kidnapped.

But he didn't know all this. He just thought she was a silly little girl, so he wasn't worried. He was reading about marshmallows and thinking about what to have for tea. Meanwhile, there was chaos and fighting and confusion inside the palace, and Beatrix was about to get all the answers she'd *ever* wanted, and more.

13

Three Very Smelly Soldiers

Beatrix was in bed when the battle started, trying to make sense of everything she'd overheard from Uncle Ivan and Wilfred the Wise and everything she'd seen beyond the waterfall. She was also thinking about whether she still wanted to escape when, *suddenly*, there were strange noises from outside the palace, and then even stranger noises from inside the palace. There were bangs and thumps and shouting and cries. There were crashes and bashes and bangs and wallops. There were ouches and ooohs and dear-oh-dears. There were splats and sprays and splits and crunches. There were snaps and crackles and pop-pop-pops.

It was not a nice thing to hear. Beatrix crept out of bed. Something told her she should stay where she was. It was better not to add herself to the confusion, to become another ingredient in the splattery cake-mix of battle. So she climbed up the bedsheets that were still in place from the day before, and pulled them up after her. She crouched down on the high beam, hidden up in the roof. There she watched, and she listened, and she waited.

The bangs and crashes were getting closer. She could hear footsteps thumping along a corridor. Voices too, voices that were angry but muffled, like dogs barking under a duvet.

'You should have dug a bigger tunnel. I could

hardly fit through. I've got mud in my helmet, mud in my chain mail and mud in my underpants.'

'The tunnel was big enough. You've been eating too many cheese and onion sandwiches. You're *always* eating them. If you spent more time reading the map and less time eating cheese and onion sandwiches we wouldn't have got lost in the cellar.'

'Will you two shut up? We're almost there. There might be guards outside. Now, there's a lever here, if I pull it…'

Beatrix watched as something very strange happened. The large painting on the wall in her room suddenly sprang outwards. The whole thing, including the frame, was actually *a giant door on hinges!* Behind it was a tunnel. Finally she understood how the servants, and her aunt and uncle, and Mrs Fartinpants, mysteriously appeared and disappeared from her room without using the door. How many more secret passages were there in the palace? She knew about the one behind the waterfall that looked like a cave, and she was sure there were others. But why did they all lead to her rooms? Did that make her the secret? And if she was a secret, what sort of a secret was she?

More worrying than the tunnel and the idea that she was some sort of secret, were the three very large soldiers standing in her room. They had stopped arguing. They stood in the doorway. Their sharp swords glinted in the light.

They didn't *look* like Uncle Ivan's soldiers. Instead of normal, shiny metal armour they wore black and red armour with paintings of skulls and snakes on it. On their heads they wore helmets that looked like metal buckets. There were two holes cut out for the eyes and a semi-circle cut out for the mouth. Beatrix couldn't decide if the bucket was funny or scary. On the one hand, it looked a bit like a child had drawn a smiley face on the helmet, which was quite a funny thing to do to a very mean-looking soldier. On the other hand, even with a funny face on the helmet, it was pretty clear that the people wearing the helmets were not there to tell jokes. This was a shame, Beatrix thought. She was sure they could have made a joke out of the fact that they had buckets on their heads, even if it was just to ask if anyone had seen their friend Doug, who had a spade on his head.

Once they were sure there were no guards in the room the three soldiers put their swords away and took their helmets off. Beatrix immediately wished they hadn't. The bits of their faces that were not covered in itchy-looking beard were all red and hot and puffy from wearing the helmets. But that wasn't the worst thing. There was a very strange pong, like a cheese and onion sandwich left on a radiator for a couple of hours with the heating turned up to the max.

'You're *not* going to eat that now, are you?' one of the soldiers said, as he saw his friend reaching into his helmet and pulling out bits of yellowy-white bready stuff.

'Umph corpse I yam,' the man replied through a mouthful of cheesy bread. He swallowed. 'It's always better after a bit of a battle. It warms it up nicely. Makes it taste like a toasted sandwich.'

'You're disgusting.'

'No, you're disgusting.'

'Am not. You're disgusting.'

'You're disgusting.'

'No. You're disgusting.'

'You're disgusting.'

'You're the most disgusting. Look, that sandwich has got bits of hair stuck to it. It is the most disgusting sandwich you've ever eaten, apart from when you tried to eat a tadpole sandwich.'

Beatrix watched these big, burly soldiers in wonder. Had they really come all this way just to have an argument about how to eat a cheese and onion sandwich? For a moment, she forgot to be afraid. It was all she could do not to laugh out loud. Although she did feel a bit sick at the thought of a tadpole sandwich.

'Stop it. You're both disgusting. Where's the map?' said the third soldier.

The biggest of the three held a piece of paper that looked like a map, but he kept turning it round and round whilst scratching his head.

'She'll be in one of these ten rooms. That's what her aunt said.'

Beatrix *almost stopped breathing* when she heard this. Her aunt Esmerelda was behind this?

'Well let's find her then. Do you have the sack?' one of the soldiers said.

'Yes. It's quite small. We may have to chop her into little pieces to get her into it.'

Beatrix felt sick and dizzy. Her breaths were getting faster and her heart was beating hard against her chest. All they had to do was look up, and they'd see her. She held onto the beam to steady herself.

The three soldiers didn't look up. Instead, they started opening cupboards and chests and pulling out whatever was inside. They pulled off her bed cover and threw the mattress on the floor. They tore it to pieces with their swords. They chopped the head off the rocking horse for no reason at all, and when one of them sneezed he grabbed a curtain and wiped his nose on it.

Ugh, Beatrix thought. *What disgusting soldiers.*

The knives she used for knife throwing were hidden under her bed, which was a shame, because they might have come in handy. Beatrix watched and waited. She didn't know what to do. The soldiers were a lot bigger than her. She couldn't fight them and she couldn't out-run them. Besides, where would she go? She only knew the ten rooms. The doors were locked and she had to ask Mrs Fartinpants to open them for her. That was no good. She could take her chances in the tunnel behind the painting. It had to lead somewhere. If the three soldiers left the room she could swing down and slip into it. But the soldiers didn't leave the room. They paced up and down, trying to work out which way up to hold the map.

Then, as if by magic, Wilfred the Wise appeared beside her on the beam.

14

On the Roof

'How on *earth* did you get here?' Beatrix said in her quietest whisper.

'By magic,' he whispered back.

'I don't believe you.'

'Well it's true. Kind of. I'll tell you how I did it later. But right now I need to tell you something. You're in a great deal of danger.'

Beatrix rolled her eyes.

'I guessed that from the three men down there

who said they want to chop me into small pieces and put me in a sack. What are we going to do?'

'Oh, don't worry. I have a plan,' Wilfred the Wise said. He stood there, nodding his head, as if that was all he needed to do to make everything OK. Beatrix stared at him.

'While they were destroying all your toys I dropped a large amount of glue into each of their helmets.' He pointed down at the helmets, which the soldiers had left on the floor. 'As soon as they put them on again, they'll stick fast to their heads. That's when we make our escape.'

Beatrix frowned. She thought Wilfred was going to say something else, but he didn't.

'How does that help?' she said. 'They'll just be wearing their helmets. If anything, they'll be better protected than if they didn't have their helmets on, and their helmets won't even come off.'

'Yes I know, but when they do take them off it'll really hurt…' Wilfred paused. 'But I see your point.

It doesn't really help us at the moment. Maybe we should just creep out silently through the secret door in the ceiling. That's how I got in.'

'Yes, I think that would be best.' Beatrix gave Wilfred a little shove to hurry him up as she followed him along the beam. There was a special panel in the ceiling which was hidden, but Wilfred knew exactly where to press so that it would spring back. He pressed it, and a square of sky appeared in the ceiling. He pulled himself through, then helped Beatrix through after him.

Beatrix stood on the steeply sloping roof. She could see further than she had ever seen. She could see the Dark, Dark Woods and the lake, and she could see that the world didn't end once you got to the edge of the lake. She could see the hills and trees and mountains in the distance. There was snow on the hills and a river that wound its way down the mountain like a silver ribbon. Things she had never seen before, a whole world

she'd only glimpsed through the windows of the palace. Now she saw the final jigsaw with all the pieces put together. It was wide open and wonderful.

Beatrix breathed deeply. For the first time in her life she felt free. She knew *immediately* that whatever lay ahead, it would be bigger and better than living in a world made up of ten rooms. No more locked doors. No more having to ask someone every time she wanted to go into a different room.

Wilfred reached out to put the special panel back in place, but as he did so he knocked a large roof tile out of place with his foot. He tried to grab hold of it but it fell through the gap, bounced off the mattress, then hit the floor with a crash.

The three soldiers stopped breaking whatever it was they were breaking and looked at the pieces of broken tile. For a moment they were confused. Then they looked up, catching sight of Wilfred as he replaced the panel in the ceiling. In less time than it takes to squash a fly they had thrown their helmets on and were climbing up onto Beatrix's bed. They threw ropes over the beam, then pulled themselves up onto it. They moved quickly – surprisingly quickly. In the meantime, Wilfred scrambled up the steep roof with Beatrix.

From this height, the world below looked very small. They were standing on a narrow ledge.

'So what's your plan?' Beatrix said.

Wilfred looked down. It was a long way to the ground.

'I know a very good flying spell,' he said. 'It's *almost* guaranteed to work.'

'I have a better idea. I know a way out. Behind the waterfall there's a secret passage. I tied a vine to a hook on the wall. It should be strong enough for me to use to escape.'

Wilfred shrugged. 'Well, if you're sure you don't want to try the flying spell...'

Beatrix ran along the rooftop with Wilfred following behind her. There were statues in the way that they had to clamber round. Kings holding swords, knights on horseback – as if someone had cast a spell and turned them to stone. There were steps that joined the roof of her room to another part of the palace. Beatrix ran up them.

'If we've just run along the roof of my room, then the garden room must be this way,' she said, her breaths coming thick and fast. 'We can climb down the waterfall.'

Wilfred stopped, out of breath. He turned and glanced over his shoulder. The three soldiers who had been in Beatrix's room were now running up the roof. They were not far behind them. He was pleased to see they'd put on their helmets. They would be wearing those helmets for quite a while, and when they finally got them off, they'd be bald!

He turned and helped Beatrix climb onto the stones at the top of the waterfall. Not that she needed any help. And then he stopped for a moment, and held Beatrix's hand a little tighter.

'Those soldiers…' he said, as Beatrix got ready to climb down. 'They have come for you. They want to kidnap you – or even worse, to **kill** you. You must get far away from here.'

'I know that, I'm not a *complete* idiot!' Beatrix replied as she climbed down the rocks. 'But what I don't understand is WHY they want to kidnap or kill me?'

Then she remembered the conversation she had heard between Wilfred and Ivan when she was playing hide and seek. She remembered they'd said the Evil Army wanted to attack the castle, that they wanted to kidnap the queen.

Beatrix stopped climbing, clinging onto the rock. A thought had just struck her. A giant, inflatable hammer of a thought, banging on her head.

'Keep moving!' Wilfred shouted. 'Why have you stopped?'

'Am I...' Beatrix said, climbing down the last few rocks. She knew what she wanted to say, but she didn't know if she wanted to say it out loud. *Am I the queen?* The wardrobes full of fancy clothes, the secret passages that led to her room... The locked doors, the knights and the servants... It was all starting to make sense.

They reached the bottom of the waterfall. The soldiers from the Evil Army were running along the top of the wall – they would be at the waterfall in a matter of seconds.

'Am I...?' she said again, slowly.

'Are you what?' Wilfred replied.

'Am I the queen?' She said the word slowly, as if it was from a foreign language and was difficult to pronounce, like the word croissant or xurros. She felt strange when she said it. It was not a nice feeling. It was the feeling of being completely unprepared. She wasn't prepared for whatever being queen meant. Especially not if it meant three soldiers from the Evil Army from Beyond the Woods were going to chop her into pieces.

'I thought this day might come,' Wilfred said. 'There is no time to tell you everything now. For now all that matters is that you escape. I should have planned it. I was going to, it was at the top of my list of things to do. Plan your escape, that was number one. Sharpen my pencils, that was number two. Buy more toilet paper was number three.' He took a pencil from his pocket. 'Nice and sharp, see? One out of three isn't bad.'

'Don't worry about it,' Beatrix said. 'I've made plans. I've got a bag of fartinpants and a change of clothes in the cave behind the waterfall. I'll climb down the palace wall and swim across the lake. Where shall I go when I get to the other side? How do I get to the village?'

'There's a field on the other side of the lake.

In the middle of it is a large stone that looks like your uncle Ivan's nose.'

'Uncle Ivan's nose?'

'Yes. You can't miss it. It even has a bump in the middle and some tufts of grass growing out of it. A path leads from there to the village. Once you get there you can buy a horse and get away. You need to get as far from here as you can. Here,' he handed Beatrix a small bag of gold, 'you'll need this.'

Beatrix took it. 'But... but what about you? *They might kill you.*'

'Don't worry about me, I can do magic to protect myself.' He glanced nervously at the waterfall.

'No you can't. I mean, not real magic. You said so yourself. And I don't think one sharpened pencil will stop their swords,' Beatrix said.

'I don't have to fight them. I just have to block the eyeholes on their helmets. I don't need a spell for that. I just need some turnips.'

'Turnips?'

'To push in the eyeholes.'

'How will you get them in the eyeholes?'

'With this.' Wilfred's hands waved in front of her face like a curtain in the wind. All of a sudden he was holding a catapult. 'Now, make sure you don't swallow any of the water from the lake when you swim across or you'll get a terrible tummy ache. Go. Hurry. You must get away.' His hands were pushing her into the secret passage.

Beatrix threw her arms around him and gave him a hug. She turned.

'Do you actually have some turnips on you?' she said. Wilfred held up his hands. As if by magic, there were three turnips in each one.

'You see? Trust in the magic,' he said.

'Trust in the turnips you had hidden up your sleeve, you mean,' Beatrix said.

Wilfred was already aiming a turnip at one of the soldiers. He fired. Splat!

Beatrix ran into the darkness of the passageway like a rabbit down a rabbit hole.

15

The Great Escape

The passageway was pitch black. Beatrix held one hand out in front of her and one on the wall, feeling her way. She almost tripped on the uneven floor, but managed to stop herself tumbling forward.

In front of her she saw a small rectangle of light. The light grew bigger. It was the window. She could see the lake and the trees through it. Underneath the window was the large stone.

She bent down anxiously to see if her bag was still there. It was! She grabbed it and slung it over her shoulder. She *squeezed* through the narrow gap of window and carefully lowered herself onto the ledge on the outside wall. This time, no one stopped her.

The daylight was bright after the darkness of the tunnel. The water beneath her was a murky brown colour. Occasionally bubbles would break through the surface, a bit like they do when you're sitting in the bath relaxing. Even though she was a long way up she could still smell the whiffy whiff of boiled cabbage each time a bubble popped on the surface of the lake.

She gripped the vine with her hands then climbed down as quickly as she could.

Her hands slipped and she felt the vine burn against her skin as she slid down. Her heart skipped a beat. She gripped more tightly. Made it to the bottom.

The hardest part was lowering herself into the water.

Ugh. It was cold and slimy and *disgusting*. It felt like it was sticking to her skin, coating her in a layer of grease. She could feel things brushing past her under water and it made her shiver. Were they reeds or fish or… something else? Keep your head up, just keep your head up, she kept telling

herself. This was not the time to do front crawl.
Or butterfly. (Generally speaking, butterfly is *always*
a bad idea. What's the point of it? It's like walking
on your hands. Fine if you want to show off but a
lot more effort than just walking on your feet.)

Beatrix swam as fast as she could. There was
mist on the surface of the water. Behind her she
could still hear the sound of the battle from within
the palace walls, echoing over the calm water of
the lake, growing quieter as she swam towards the
shore.

Finally, she felt her feet touch solid-ish ground.
The bottom of the lake. The suck and squelch of
the mud. There were reeds around her. She pulled
herself forward then climbed out onto the grass.

Yuck. Yuck. Yuck. She felt as if she had been
for a swim in the bottom of a greasy cauldron.

Beatrix looked back at the palace. She had
never seen it from the outside. It was enormous.
She could see where the garden room was,

116

and the windows for her bedroom. But they only took up a tiny part of the huge building.

Even though the building was big, it still looked helpless and a little bit sad. The Evil Army had set fire to the gates and smoke was billowing into the sky. They'd destroyed part of the wall. The palace looked as if it was about to give up.

Beatrix didn't know how she felt about being a queen, but she knew how she felt about someone destroying her home and attacking the people who lived inside it. She could feel her blood get hot, her teeth grind together. She wanted to shout. She wanted to scream a command that would make them stop, make them all run away and leave the palace alone.

She couldn't. She mustn't. She had to stay calm, and she had to do what Wilfred had told her. Find the stone shaped like Uncle Ivan's nose and change out of the clothes she was wearing. She had to get somewhere safe. Once she was safe, she could work out what she needed to do. And she had already decided she wasn't going to run away. Not when Wilfred and Ivan were having to fight the Evil Army. Not when poor Mrs Fartinpants was stuck in the palace, and certainly not when Aunt Esmerelda had given the Evil Army a map and told them where to find her. Esmerelda was not going to get away with that. Beatrix would make sure of it.

The stone was in the middle of the field, as plain as day. *What a peculiar thing,* she thought. It was a large stone, triangular in shape, with tufts of grass growing out of two holes on top of it.

It was certainly shaped like Uncle Ivan's nose.

She ran over to it and ducked down behind it. She quickly changed out of her dress, which was woven from golden thread and had diamonds attached to it, and put on the clothes that were in the bag. The pillow case dress didn't look too bad but she decided *not* to wear the pant hat until she got to the village.

She stuffed her dress under the stone to hide it, ate one of the fartinpants and looked around. The palace was behind her. The woods were in front of her, and ten metres away a small boy with a funny little dog stood and stared at her.

16

A Boy Called Oi
and a Dog Called Dog

'Hello,' Beatrix said. The small boy frowned fiercely at her. His face was *very* dirty and his hair was long and thick and fair. It was all stuck together like school-dinner spaghetti. His eyes were fierce and green, the colour of dragon scales in picture books.

'Come any closer and my dog will bite you,' he said. Beatrix looked at the dog. Its tongue was hanging out and it was panting. It only had a couple of teeth left in its mouth. She couldn't imagine it would hurt much if it did bite. One ear was up and one was down. She wasn't sure what kind of dog it was but it looked happy. It didn't look like it was a *bitey* kind of dog.

'What's his name?' she asked.

'Dog,' the boy said.

'Dog?'

'That's right. Dog. What you doing here? This is my field. Me and Dog look after it.'

Beatrix looked at the field. It was mostly mud with a few stones.

'You shouldn't be in it. It's for growing stuff like beans and such,' he said.

Beatrix took another fartinpant out of her bag. 'Are you hungry? My cook makes a wonderful fartinpant,' she said. The little boy didn't look too sure whether to take it, but Dog trotted over to her and held up his paw. Beatrix shook Dog's paw then broke off a bit for him to eat.

'He's a very clever dog,' she said. She gave the rest to the boy and he stuffed it in his mouth faster than Esmerelda with a spoonful of golden syrup.

'What's your name?' she said.

'Oi,' he said, through a mouthful of cake.

'Oi? That's a funny name. Does it have a special meaning?'

Oi shrugged.

'Don't know. But it ain't funny. If it was, people would laugh when they said it – but no one laughs when they say it, they just look angry. Oi, don't do that. Oi, why aren't you watching the field? Oi, bring me a nice cup of bean beer.'

'Well, Mr Oi, I need somewhere to sleep and I need somewhere to make plans. I have a very important war I need to win. My name is –' Beatrix paused – 'my name is Queen Beatrix.' It felt funny calling herself Queen Beatrix, but she decided she might as well get used to it. 'Do you have a bedroom or a playroom I could share? Even a garden room would do. I'd be quite happy to sleep under the stars beside a nice warm fire.'

Oi looked at her like she was a Wobbler whose third eye had just fallen out.

'We got a hut made of mud where my ma and pa and brothers and sisters sleep,' he said. 'Don't think there's much room though, as we got to let the animals in at night. Keep 'em safe from the Wobblers.'

'Wobblers? I wouldn't worry about them. They're not real, you know. At least, I don't know anyone who's actually seen one in real life. How many animals sleep in your house?'

'Just a couple of pigs. And a cow. And two chickens. And two sheep. And a horse. And Nelly the goat. And there's mice, but they're not invited. And then there's Dog. And of course Cat.'

'You have a cat too? Doesn't Dog chase it?'

'Cat's not a cat. She's a dog. We called her Cat so we wouldn't get her mixed up with Dog. Obviously,' Oi said. 'You can't have two dogs called Dog, that would be ridiculous.'

'I see,' said Beatrix. But she didn't really see. Still, she thought it was best not to say anything about it in case she sounded rude.

'So you have two dogs, one called Cat and one called Dog. And lots of other animals that are *pretty smelly* and they all sleep in your house in the same room as you and the rest of your family?'

'Yep,' said Oi.

Beatrix had just escaped from the Evil Army, climbed down a very high wall and swum across a stinky lake. She didn't want to lie down on the floor in a house made from mud with mice running in and out of her hair and cows making the kind of smell cows make when they've been chewing grass all day.

'I'd really rather stay somewhere secret,' she said. 'I won't be here for long. I just need somewhere to make plans. I was going to leave but I don't want to go whilst the palace is under attack. Is there a cave or a barn I could sleep in?'

Oi scratched his head.

'There's a cave in the woods. I sometimes stay there. It's cold and a bit damp but you can make a fire. Just make sure you don't disturb the bears.'

'Bears?' Beatrix said. 'You sleep in a cave with real live bears? Isn't that *dangerous?*'

Oi shrugged. 'Only if they wake up,' he said. 'And they don't wake up till the spring. It's a special sort of sleep. Lasts for months. And to be honest, it's not really the bears you want to worry about at this time of year. It's the spiders. They get awful hungry and creep out of their webs. They can give you a nasty nip. Bring you out in a rash and spots and all sorts. I squashed one the other night that was at least as big as three fartinpants.'

'This cave sounds even worse than your house,' she said. Oi frowned and looked a bit hurt.

'I mean, not that your house sounds bad,' Beatrix added quickly. 'I'm sure it's lovely during the day once all the animals have gone and the mess has been cleaned up. But there must be somewhere else?' Beatrix said. 'Another cave? A cabin?'

Oi shrugged. 'There's a hunting lodge up in the woods that the soldiers from the palace use. It's got proper beds and a big stone fireplace, but if Ivan the Vicious catches you there, then there's no telling what he'll do to you,' Oi said. 'Probably bury you in the ground so only your head sticks out, put golden syrup in your hair and let ants crawl all over you. You're better off with the spiders and bears. Oh, and the snakes. Did I mention snakes?'

'Snakes?!' Beatrix said. 'No you didn't. Anyway, it's fine. Ivan won't do anything,' she went on. 'He's my uncle. Take me to the hunting lodge at once. I have very important plans to make. A war has been started. My aunt Esmerelda has betrayed me. The palace I live in is under attack. My friends are in grave danger and the Evil Army wants to chop me into tiny pieces and take me away.'

'Sounds like you are not having a good day,' said Oi, nodding his head slowly and shrugging his shoulders. 'Probably *even worse* than my day.'

'Why, what's happened to you today?' Beatrix said, sounding surprised. She suddenly realised she had been so full of her own worries she hadn't even asked about Oi.

'Same thing as happens every day,' said Oi.

'Which is what?'

'Nothing,' Oi said, looking sad. 'Nothing happens to me every day. Over and over again it happens. All I do is watch this field full of mud, just in case someone comes along and tries to steal it.'

'Who would *steal* mud?'

'The mud thieves,' Oi said. Beatrix looked at Oi and Oi looked at Beatrix.

'Mud thieves?' she said.

'I dunno. My older brothers tell me I have to stay in the field all day because of the mud thieves. Especially around Christmas. People love to give a nice box of mud as a present, and our mud is the best you'll find. But to be honest you're the first person I've seen turn up here,' Oi said.

She took a gold coin out of her purse and gave it to him. 'I'm buying your mud. You work for me now. I'll need a general to command my army. From this day forward you shall be Sir General Oi.'

Oi looked back at her. His eyes were full of wonder, and a considerable amount of surprise.

'All right,' he said. 'But don't you want me to find someone else to guard your mud?' he said.

Beatrix laughed. 'No. Forget the mud. What I'd really like to know is why a war has been started. Why on earth the Evil Army wants to chop me into tiny pieces and take me away,' she said. 'And you know what? Not one person – not one single person – not my uncle or Mrs Fartinpants or Wilfred the Wise or anyone else, ever told me that this might happen.'

'Oh, I know why,' said Oi. 'If you're Queen Beatrix, then it's because of the Curse of the Wobblers. It's one of the most famous stories there is – **Queen Beatrix and the Curse of the Wobblers.**'

17

The Curse of the Wobblers

'The Curse of the Wobblers?' Beatrix said. They had begun walking through the forest. Sir General Oi was leading the way along a narrow path with Dog beside him. Beatrix was feeling quite annoyed that a very messy boy whose clothes were mostly made of mud seemed to know so much about this curse when she didn't know *anything at all.*

'Aah well, it's one of those stories they tell

around the fire on winter nights,' Oi said. 'A tale of danger and witches and –'

Oi stopped suddenly, got down on his hands and knees and placed his ear flat against the root of an ancient oak tree. Beatrix tripped over his bottom and came crashing to the ground.

'Why did you do that?' she asked, pulling some leaves and grass from her hair and rubbing her knee, which was grazed.

'Shhhhh,' said Oi, his head still on the root of the tree.

'Shhh?' Beatrix replied. *'Shhh?* I won't shush, you just tripped me up.'

He placed a finger over his lips and stared at her. His face told her this was not a game. Dog sat next to him, his ears pricked up as if he was listening too.

Oi stood up. 'Pack of wolves over that way.' He pointed. 'About two minutes away. At least seven of them. I can hear the sound through the ground. Also, one of them keeps howling.'

Beatrix got to her feet.

'Wolves in the woods, bears and spiders in the caves, snakes in the grass. This must be the most dangerous forest in the world,' she said.

Oi shrugged. 'Don't know. Never been to any other forests. Anyway, danger's not dangerous till it's standing in front of you.'

'Won't they be able to smell us?' Beatrix said.

'Well, I don't think they'd be able to smell you. You smell like a stinky fish lake – no offence – not a tasty snack.' Oi looked at the plants growing by the tree root. He picked leaves and rubbed them onto his clothes.

'They won't want to eat me now either,' he said. The leaves had a funny, musty smell, like old socks. 'As long as we stay on this path, we should be OK.' He marched off. 'Best to go a *bit quicker* though,' he called out over his shoulder.

Beatrix hurried after him. She was beginning to realise that General Oi was a very useful general indeed. In fact, she wasn't sure she would be able to survive in the forest without him.

'About this curse,' she said, jogging along behind him. 'You were going to tell me about one of the stories they tell around the campfire in winter.'

'Oh yeah. Well, let me see if I can remember it. Curse stories can be complicated. They usually begin a long time ago with a witch who's very cross at someone. Now, with the Curse of the Wobblers, I think the witch was *very* cross with the Evil Army. So she said that a child would be born under a falling star who would have special powers over Wobblers. And the child would be super clever and magic. Then one day the child would become queen and lead an army of Wobblers to take over all the Evil Army's land, and crush them into the dirt, like, er...'

'Like dirt?'

'Yes. Like dirt. And that's the curse,' Oi said, nodding. 'Although when we tell it around the campfire we do it with music and I play a solo on the recorder when we get to the bit about the falling star.' He tapped his pockets with his hands, as if he was looking for a recorder. 'Don't have it with me now, but I can whistle the tune if you like,' he said.

Beatrix was silent for a moment. Then she said,

'What a lot of nonsense. I told you – there's no such thing as **Wobblers**. And as for *me* having power over them, or any kind of magic power – it's ridiculous!'

Oi shrugged.

'Ridiculous or not, that's what they say. Look, the hunting lodge is through the trees. We're just in time – it's getting dark.' As he spoke they heard the howl of a wolf, and both of them felt a shiver run down their spine. Even Dog let out a whimper.

18

The Hunting Lodge

From the outside, the hunting lodge looked like a little castle. It had turrets on the roof and a heavy wooden door. Beatrix pushed it, thinking it might be locked. It was stiff and creaky but it opened when she gave it a shove with her shoulder.

Oi waited behind her. He looked nervous.

'Are you sure Ivan the Vicious won't be here?' he whispered.

'Poor Uncle Ivan is risking his life fighting the

Evil Army – but even if he was here, he wouldn't mind.' She paused. 'Well, he'd mind *a little bit*, as he doesn't like children and we both smell terrible. But he'd probably just throw a couple of knives into the wall, stop talking and play with his toy soldiers,' she said. For a moment, Beatrix felt very sad. She already missed her uncle and she had only been gone a few hours.

Inside the lodge it smelt damp and dusty. It was very gloomy, but there was just enough light left in the day for them to see. On the walls there were paintings in heavy wooden frames. They showed Uncle Ivan and his knights hunting stags and wild boar. (A boar is a wild pig – it's hairy and a very fast runner.) One of them showed the knights using an eagle to hunt rabbits.

Weapons were hung on the wall next to the paintings and around the top of the room there were stuffed animal heads mounted on wood. Oi and Beatrix thought they looked creepy. There were deer heads with enormous antlers and eyes made of green glass, and some very angry looking boars with curved tusks and snarling mouths.

Beatrix didn't like the look of these stuffed

animals one little bit. It was as if someone had tried to perform a magic trick and it had gone wrong, leaving animals stuck halfway through a wall. If Goldilocks had walked into this house, she definitely wouldn't have stuck around to try a bowl of porridge. It felt as if the room was watching you.

'What's that?' Beatrix said, standing very still. It looked like there was a tall man standing silently in the corner of the room.

'Hello?' she called out, stepping back. Her voice echoed around the room. The man in the shadows didn't reply.

'Tell me who you are at once,' she said. Her voice was strong but her hands were shaking. Oi pushed past her.

'Take that!' he said, throwing a stone at the man with a quick flick of his wrist. The stone hit the man on the head. The head fell clean off the body, hitting the ground with a clatter and rolling over the floor. They'd either just destroyed the first ever human-sized robot – or, it was a suit of armour and they'd knocked the helmet off.

'Phew,' Oi said, picking up the helmet. He walked over to the suit of armour and put it back onto the body.

'Phew indeed,' Beatrix replied. 'I'm going to start a fire. Then we can light a few candles and cheer this place up. It's awfully dreary. Why don't you see if there's any food?'

Oi found some biscuits to eat and some eggs in a store room. There was a shield hanging on the wall with two swords crossed beneath it. He climbed up onto the fireplace and took the shield down. It was made of metal and would make a perfect frying pan. He cracked the eggs onto it and fried them over the fire. There were blankets in a wooden chest that they wrapped around themselves as they ate the fried eggs and biscuits.

It was one of the tastiest meals Beatrix had ever eaten, but it was very strange to eat in the flickery light of the fire. It made the shadows jump around on the walls, and some of the stuffed animal heads almost looked as if they were moving.

'What are you going to do?' Oi said, as he scooped up the last bits of egg with his biscuit.

'About what?' Beatrix replied.

'How will you get rid of the Evil Army?'

She scratched her head. What she really wanted

to do was go home and have a bath. It was hard to think of anything else.

'I don't know,' she said.

'Are you sure you can't do magic?' Oi asked. 'According to the curse, the queen who will defeat the Evil Army can do magic.' He stared into the fire, looking thoughtful. 'Maybe that's why they're so scared of you and want to chop you up. They think you can do magic!'

'Well that's just silly. I can't. No one can. Not even a great magician like Wilfred the Wise. Don't tell me you believe in magic?' Beatrix said.

Oi shrugged. 'I didn't before,' he said.

'Before what?'

'Well, every day I had to sit in a field of mud, watching the mud. Just me and Dog, guarding mud. Mud mud mud. If anything will make you stop believing in magic, it's guarding mud. Mud and magic go together like smelly socks and soup.' He stopped, and turned to look at Beatrix.

'But then you turned up in a dress made of jewels as bright as sunshine, with a bag of gold, right out of a stinky lake. Now, don't try and tell me that's not a little bit magic.'

Beatrix sat up suddenly.

'What is it?' Oi said.

'It's not magic. But you have just given me an idea,' she said. 'I have a plan. I know how we can get rid of the Evil Army. We don't need magic, we just need to do something they think is magic.' She looked up at the shadows on the walls. The antlers of the deer looked like they were moving, and they were twice as big in shadow as they were in real life.

'Like what?'

'Like summon up an army of Wobblers to run through the Evil Army's camp. Those soldiers will run back to their woods as fast as a rabbit with its tail on fire if we do that.'

'Good idea,' Oi said. He nodded his head slowly. 'They hate Wobblers more than anything else. More than having a bath, more than saying please and thank you, more than brushing their teeth... But where are we going to get Wobblers from? I've never even seen one. And they're very dangerous.'

'We're not going to get any Wobblers. We're going to make them *think* we've got some.'

'Oh right,' said Oi. 'How do we do that?'

Beatrix smiled and stood up. 'With lanterns, antlers, shadows – and some dressing up.'

At that moment there was a sudden bang and the front door flew wide open. Dog began barking furiously and Oi jumped up, reaching for one of the *enormous* swords that hung from the walls. The wind blew leaves and twigs into the room and all the candles went out. The only light was the flickering flames of the fire.

'Who's there?' Beatrix shouted.

In the doorway stood a tall man in a long cape and a hood.

'I thought I might find you here,' Wilfred the Wise said. '*So* glad you escaped. What's for tea?'

19

How to Defeat an Evil Army

'**W**ilfred!' Beatrix shouted, running up to greet him. 'You got away! That's brilliant. How did you find us?'

'Oh you know – I might be a failed magician, but I still know some magic,' he replied *mysteriously*, tapping the side of his nose with a long, bony finger.

'You mean you followed our muddy footprints through the field and into the woods all the way to the hunting lodge?' Beatrix said.

'Well, yes. And it worked like magic, because I found you. You should be more careful – it's dangerous out there. There's an Evil Army out to get you.'

Wilfred had a bag over his shoulder. He took it off and opened it. Inside was a fresh batch of fartinpants. He took them out and shared them with Beatrix and Oi.

As they started to eat, he told them how he'd managed to blind the Evil Army soldiers with turnips, and how he'd found Uncle Ivan and told him that Beatrix had escaped.

'Your uncle told me I had to find you, to make sure you were safe. He said I should take you somewhere far away until the danger has passed.'

Beatrix almost choked on her fartinpant. '*No way.* I'm not going anywhere. Not while there's an Evil Army attacking my palace. We'll defeat them. I've already worked out a plan, but before I explain it, I want you to tell me more about this business of me being a queen. I can't believe you knew the secret and you didn't tell me!'

'Ah yes. Well, all I was told by your uncle was that you were the queen of a distant land and I needed to teach you everything I knew and keep you safe from the Evil Army. I didn't ask any questions. You know how cross Ivan can get if you ask questions,' Wilfred said.

Beatrix frowned. 'All right. But Uncle Ivan has got a lot of explaining to do when I get back home. Now you're here, you can tell me about the soldiers attacking the palace,' she said. 'How many of them are there? Where's their camp? Who's their leader? And how afraid of Wobblers are they, on a scale of one to one hundred?'

Wilfred sat down. 'General Alfred Burpintime is their leader,' he said. 'He's a strange man, but he's actually a very good general. His soldiers will do whatever he tells them.'

'So if we can scare him, get him to run away, will the rest of his army follow?' Beatrix said.

'Quite possibly,' Wilfred replied.

'And is he scary and vicious like Uncle Ivan? Does he like to smash things and lead the army from the front?'

'Not really. I've heard that he's quite happy for his army to get on with the business of being evil and breaking things and chopping heads off and whatever else they do while he stays in his tent. He doesn't like to join in the battle. He usually has a good book to keep him busy during the fighting and he likes to write songs on the recorder.'

'He certainly doesn't sound like Uncle Ivan,' Beatrix said.

'No, he isn't. But although he doesn't join in the fighting, General Burpintime is still *very good* at being a general. He was the one who told his soldiers to measure Numb Butt Lane so he could work out how long it would take his army to run along it and break down the palace gates. And he planned your kidnap, making sure his soldiers dug a secret tunnel under the palace walls whilst keeping Ivan's army busy with an attack on the front gates.'

'That *is* pretty clever,' Beatrix said. 'Although the three soldiers he sent to try and kidnap me were definitely *not* very clever.'

Wilfred smiled. 'No, they were not very clever. I wish I could be there when they try and take off their helmets.' He looked at the notes Beatrix had made. 'I'll try and draw their camp – it was on top of the hill at the end of Numb Butt Lane. You could see it from the palace. Hundreds of tents. There must be thousands of soldiers. We're going to have our work cut out. Now, tell me about this plan of yours.'

20

Wilfred, Beatrix, Oi the Boy and Dog the Dog Practise Their Plan

As you may already be aware, the adult Wobbler has two eyes, whilst the baby Wobbler is born with three eyes. One eye falls out when it reaches the age of seven. Some people say they look like a weasel crossed with a goblin, whilst others say they look more like a goblin crossed with a weasel. Whatever the case, they are not nice to look at.

Their hair falls out in summer and grows back in a different place in winter, so you might see a Wobbler with no eyebrows but a hairy tongue, or with a bald head but hairy palms. The Evil Army from Beyond the Woods knew this. Esmerelda the Terrible and Uncle Ivan the Vicious knew this. The school teachers who taught Wobbler Studies in schools everywhere knew this. The artists who painted knights fighting Wobblers in the Dark, Dark Woods and mountains of the Kingdom of Morden knew this.

It was accepted and understood by everyone, but the funny thing about Wobblers is that *no one had ever actually seen one*. Not a baby Wobbler with three eyes, not a fully grown Wobbler with two eyes and not an elderly Wobbler with a pair of reading glasses perched on the end of its nose and a copy of the *Daily Mail* under its evil arm.

Everybody knew someone who'd seen a Wobbler, or at least they knew someone who remembered talking to someone who thought they'd seen a Wobbler, but no one had ever *actually* seen a Wobbler. Wobblers were a bit like the Tooth Fairy or the Easter Bunny, but with a lot more anger and a funny hole in their head from where the third eye had fallen out.

Now, this is all very interesting if you are studying the history of the Wobbler at school, but that's not why I'm telling it to you. I'm telling you this because, in the hunting lodge, Queen Beatrix, Wilfred the Wise and Oi the Boy were discussing the matter at length as part of their planning.

Because no one knew what Wobblers really looked like, all they had to do was make a few scary puppets people would think were Wobblers, and they should be able to deliver a massive scare bomb to the whole of the Evil Army camp.

'How about we use the head of the deer that's on the wall?' Beatrix said.

'And the suit of armour!' Oi said.

'And some squidgy balls of mud we can throw and pretend are their eyes!' Wilfred said.

'Ugh. That's *disgusting*,' Beatrix replied. 'I like it! Mud balls for the baby Wobblers' eyes, to make a splat when we throw them. Antlers and armour for the grown-ups.'

They were all very excited at this plan, but having played around for a few minutes, dressing up as Wobblers and practising throwing mud, they were worried that the disguises might not be convincing enough. And that they would only be able to pretend to be four Wobblers (and that was including Dog, who didn't much like being told to walk on his back legs whilst wearing a funny-looking helmet).

'Hmm,' said Beatrix, looking at Oi in his armour with antlers on his head.

She was worried the Evil Army might just think he was a funny-looking boy who'd found some armour and stuck antlers on his head. And if they thought that, they wouldn't be running away, they'd be removing the antlers and then removing Oi's head. Or removing his head and then removing the antlers.

'We need something else,' she said. 'Something to make us look like we're actually, you know, scary.' She looked around the room. Once again, she noticed the shadows flickering on the wall.

'You see that?' Beatrix said, pointing at the shadow Oi cast on the wall in the candlelight. 'You see how it moves and is so much bigger and scarier than Oi?'

Wilfred and Oi looked at the shadow. It *was* pretty scary – that's if you ignored Oi doing his funny Wobbler dance.

'Wilfred, if you make a fire when we get there we can light torches and cast huge shadows inside General Burpintime's tent!'

They all agreed this was a good idea.

'And I'll add some smoke too – I know a trick for that. They won't be able to see what's going on,' Wilfred said.

'Won't there already be smoke from the fire?' Beatrix said.

'Yes, but I can make more smoke. It's really very easy. I use chalk dust and soot.'

'And Dog can make the most *horrible* howling noises – can't you, Dog?' Oi said.

Dog made a horrible howling noise.

They spent the next hour rehearsing their plan. It was a bit like practising a play. And when they were certain of every last detail they packed all their disguises and equipment on their backs and set off to find the Evil Army's camp.

21

The Dark, Dark Woods

Wilfred the Wise, Oi the boy, Dog the dog and Queen Beatrix made their way through the Dark, Dark Woods. (The Dark, Dark Woods were right in front of the Tall, Tall Mountain. People liked to use the same word twice in those days, because there weren't as many words to describe things as there are now.)

'Are we nearly there yet?' said Wilfred the Wise. He was terribly impatient when it came to journeys. That's why he had three packets of sweets with him. Eating them helped to pass the time. He'd already eaten one packet, and completely forgotten to share them with Oi and Beatrix. This was because he was a little bit scared about walking in the woods at night. The shadows were *extremely shadowy* and there were thin clouds that reached across the moon, like spindly skeleton hands. He shivered whenever he looked up at them.

'It's not far,' Oi said. 'There are two paths we can take to the hill at the end of Numb Butt Lane. It'll be two hours' walk if we take the Path of Pain and Sorrow, and four hours' walk if we take the Path of Joy and Happiness.'

Wilfred chewed on a chewy sweet and thought about this for a moment.

'Well, sounds like it will take a lot longer if we follow the Path of Joy and Happiness. We should probably take the other one. We need time to set up so we can unleash the Wobblers before dawn. If we take the other path we'll get there as the sun's rising and our trick won't work,' he said.

'Right you are,' said Oi, 'we'll take the Path of Pain and Sorrow.'

'Just out of interest,' Beatrix said, following close behind him, '*why* is it called the Path of Pain and Sorrow?'

'Oh, mostly because of the brambles – they catch on your socks and knees and give you awful scratches,' Oi said.

'Mostly because of the *brambles?*' Beatrix said. 'Is there something else along the path that might cause pain and sorrow?'

'Not really,' Oi said. He turned around and carried on walking. The path in front of him separated. There were wooden signs beside each path. One sign said PAIN AND SORROW. The other said JOY AND HAPPINESS. They looked like they'd been carved into the wood a very long time ago. The PAIN AND SORROW sign was cracked, with moss growing on it and spider webs all over it. The JOY AND HAPPINESS sign was also cracked, with moss and spider webs all over it, but someone had carved a little flower into the wood to make it look a bit more happy and joyful.

'Right, the Path of Pain and Sorrow it is then,' said Oi, leading the way. 'We don't want to be late. As Wilfred says, we need plenty of time to get ready.'

They walked on in silence. Wilfred remembered to offer his third bag of sweets to the two children.

They had a lot of things to carry and needed the energy. After they'd been walking for a few minutes Oi said:

'There is one thing you should know about the path of Pain and Sorrow.'

'What's that?' Beatrix said.

'It's probably just a made-up story. Only I'd feel bad if I didn't tell you,' he said.

Wilfred the Wise stopped chewing on his chewy sweet. 'What kind of a story is it?' he said, his voice quiet. He felt as if the forest was listening to him, even though he knew that wasn't possible. Trees don't have ears.

Something caught the light. A *flash* of animal eyes in the dark. A wobble of jelly. The forest wasn't just listening to him, it was watching him too. What was it? What wobbled like jelly in the woods at night? Surely it couldn't be a plate of jelly. He stared for a moment longer. Whatever it was had gone.

'It's one of those silly stories they tell around the fire,' Oi said. 'Like the Curse of the Wobblers or the fact that Queen Beatrix can do magic.' Just then an owl hooted overhead and the three of them jumped. 'If I remember rightly... You know when you have a nightmare and you wake up all of a sudden?'

'Yes,' said Beatrix, trying not to think about nightmares. It was scary enough in the forest without thinking about bad dreams.

'Well, they say that when you wake up during a nightmare, all the scary characters are freed from your head. They fly through the air and gather together in a great swirling whirlpool cloud of nightmares in the middle of the Dark, Dark Forest.' Oi scratched his head, as if this might help him remember more. 'And if you enter the whirlpool, which looks a bit like mist or fog, then all these shapes fly at you, and there are so many baddies, so many terrible things, that your brain just *melts*,' Oi said.

'Hmm,' said Beatrix.

'Hmm,' said Wilfred the Wise.

'Grrrr,' said Dog the dog.

'And I'm guessing,' Beatrix said after a moment, 'that the Path of Pain and Sorrow goes through this swirling whirlpool cloud?'

'Yes,' Oi said. 'Come to think of it, that's why it's called the Path of Pain and Sorrow. It's nothing to do with brambles. Although there are still a lot of brambles, so you should be careful.'

They carried on walking in silence.

'What a lot of nonsense,' Wilfred said loudly. 'As someone who has spent many a year trying to perform magic and has met the greatest magicians of our age, I can confirm that the scary monsters from all our nightmares are not waiting for us in a swirling whirlpool cloud, ready to melt our brains with fear. I mean, you're just not going to see a dog with three heads or a dragon-witch or a skeleton wearing your mum's pyjamas or –'

'A skeleton wearing your mum's pyjamas?' Beatrix interrupted.

'Whatever. You're not going to see it. There is absolutely **no chance** of your brain melting. Now, although the path is bumpy, I suggest we run as fast as we can till we get through the woods. This has absolutely nothing to do with the swirling whirlpool of nightmares, because that *doesn't exist*. But I do think we should hurry up. Come along now.'

With that, Wilfred sprinted off along the path, running as fast as Usain Bolt chased by a hungry cheetah, with Beatrix and Oi close behind him. They ran and they ran and they ran, and when the mist appeared mysteriously in the middle of the forest they ran *even* faster.

22

The Evil Army's Camp

At last they arrived at the edge of the forest and found themselves on top of the hill at the end of Numb Butt Lane. They were running so fast, they almost ran right into the Evil Army's camp. They stopped, ducking down in the bushes to get a better look.

Fires were burning and the air smelt of wood smoke and the bean stew the Evil Amy had eaten for dinner. It made them all feel very hungry.

There were five huge, round tents in front of them and behind them were more rows of tents. Between each tent a fearsome-looking soldier stood guard.

Beatrix and Oi climbed up a tall oak tree to get a good look at the camp. In the moonlight, the rows of tents looked like enormous mushrooms sprouting on the forest floor.

'Must be about a hundred soldiers in each tent,' Oi said. There were ten rows of tents and ten tents in each row.

'All in all, about ten thousand soldiers,' Beatrix said (she was good at mental maths). She looked at the guards who stood around the edge of the camp. They stamped their feet to try and keep warm and sang strange songs in low voices. They were not good singers. Imagine a boy band with an elephant as the lead singer and three whoopee cushions on backing vocals – that was pretty much the sound they made.

They were a lot bigger than the toy soldiers

Beatrix had practised with in the war room. Their armour glinted in the moonlight like the black shell of a beetle and their faces were in shadow, as if they were ghosts. For a moment, Beatrix wanted to climb down the tree, run back through the woods and get as far away from the camp as she could, but she forced herself to stay and watch them.

They were stamping their feet because they were cold, she thought. No one likes being cold. They don't like it here. They want it to be morning.

Why were they singing? They were singing so they could hear each others' voices in the night. It helped them feel like they weren't alone. It made them feel less scared.

Which meant, Beatrix realised, that some of them must be scared.

Why were they scared? Because they were camping

on the edge of the Dark, Dark Woods. And it was dark. And they believed in **Wobblers**.

Perfect, Beatrix thought. Her plan was so devilishly dastardly, so disgustingly disgusting, so *terribly terrible*, that it would have the soldiers running back home in their pyjamas without even pausing to pick up their teddy bears.

'What's going on over there?' Oi whispered. He was pointing at the large tent in the middle of the camp with silver stars painted all over it and a flag flying from the top. Four brightly burning torches stood outside it. 'Who's that funny-looking little man outside, and why is he shouting?'

In front of the tent was a little round ball of a man in a smart black and red army uniform. He was stomping backwards and forwards, shouting at three of his soldiers. Beatrix could tell he was angry, even from a distance. You could almost see the steam coming out of his ears. He was shaking his fist and shaking his head – he was shaking all over. Every few seconds his hand would dive into his pocket, grab a handful of what looked like marshmallows and shove them into his mouth.

'That must be General Burpintime,' she said.

'What's he doing?' Oi whispered.

'He looks like he's telling those soldiers off,' Beatrix replied, staring at the three men who stood in front of General Burpintime. 'I think they're the ones who tried to kidnap me.'

23

General Burpintime
Loses His Temper

General Burpintime was indeed extremely angry. He may have been a small man but he had a very big temper. He stamped and he stomped and he huffed and he puffed and if there had been a straw house, a wooden house and a brick house nearby he would have blown them all down with one blast of his angry breath (complete with sticky little bits of half-chewed marshmallow).

'Where's the girl? The queen — where's Beatrix?' he shouted. If there was one thing Burpintime definitely didn't want to do, it was tell the Evil Overlord that he'd failed to kidnap Beatrix. He didn't understand how this silly little girl had managed to escape from three of his best soldiers. Perhaps there was something to this curse after all. No normal child would have been able to get away. That thought made him nervous, and when he became nervous he did two things. One was eat marshmallows. The other was get very, very angry!

'We don't know where she is!' the soldiers wailed. 'She ran up onto the roof and then down a waterfall that had no water then she *disappeared* somewhere and a magician blinded us with terrible magic that smelt like turnips. Then he cast a spell that made our helmets stick to our heads. We couldn't see and we fell into a lake which was quite the most horrible thing you could ever fall into.'

'Did the magician have a sword?' General Burpintime asked. His voice was soft and menacing. Beatrix and Oi didn't like the sound of it. It slithered through the cool night air like a snake. It was the kind of voice head teachers use when they want to find out which pupil did the really, really BAD THING. It was the kind of voice that could make a big, vicious dog back into a corner. It was the kind of voice that is quiet because anger has squashed almost all of the sound out of it.

'No, no – he didn't have a sword,' the soldiers replied.

'And did the little girl have a sword?' General Burpintime said. This time his voice was even softer, as if it was being squeezed between two big fluffy pillows. It was softer, but somehow *more* menacing.

'No. Course not. That would be dangerous.'

'And did you have swords?' General Burpintime said. Beatrix and Oi could barely hear him now.

'Yes, yes of course we did. We always have swords. We're the Evil Army!' the soldiers replied.

'THEN WHY DIDN'T YOU USE THEM TO KILL THE MAGICIAN AND BRING BACK THE GIRL?!' General Burpintime shouted so loudly that Beatrix almost fell out of the tree.

The soldiers didn't answer.

'We tried using the swords, but we couldn't because of the magic,' one of the soldiers said at last. 'Who ever heard of a spell that would stick your helmet to your head? And a spell that could make turnips fly into your eyes? It's evil. It shouldn't be allowed. There should be a law against using magic on poor soldiers like us.'

'Magic?' General Burpintime said. 'MAGIC?!' he said again. He didn't believe in magic any more than Beatrix or Wilfred the Wise believed in magic.

'Allow me to perform some of my own magic

and remove the helmet from your head,' he said. 'I know a very good spell that I'm sure will work. If one of you will be so kind as to bend forward so your head is the same height as my hands, I will demonstrate.'

'Of course, general.' The biggest of the three soldiers leant forward. General Burpintime reached up and took hold of the soldier's helmet. He pulled it with all his strength. The soldier let out a gasp of pain. Although General Burpintime was a very small man who enjoyed playing the recorder and eating marshmallows, he was extremely strong. He was *even stronger* when he was angry, and at that moment he was angrier than a wasp that has got stuck inside a jam jar.

He pulled and he twisted and he yanked and he turned. He twisted and he pulled and he heaved and after a final couple of strong yanks and a whack on the side the helmet came off. Then General Burpintime smelt the helmet. He could smell two things, and neither was the smell of magic. The first was the very strong smell of a warm cheese and onion sandwich, the second was the smell of glue. In amongst the glue he thought he saw a very furry gerbil, before realising it was hair from the soldier's head.

'Glue,' he said. 'Not magic.'

He turned his attention to the other two soldiers and repeated his technique for removing the helmets. When he'd finished he looked at the three of them and shook his head.

Oi was shaking with silent laughter. He nudged Beatrix.

'They look like their mum's just cut their hair,' he whispered.

'Now, just so I've got this straight. Just so I've understood what you're saying. You're telling me

that a little girl with no training in Chinese burns
or giving wedgies and no sword and no spear,
simply *ran away* and you couldn't stop her?'

The three knights looked at one another
awkwardly. When General Burpintime said it, it
sounded so much worse.

'Where did she go?' he asked.

The three knights shuffled uneasily on the
spot. What they really wanted to do was to go

and have a nice lie-down, eat some sausages and beans, then go home.

'*Well?*' General Burpintime said. 'Don't you have any answers?'

'I think she went somewhere in the palace. Probably,' one of them said.

'She'll be in a cupboard somewhere. You know how kids like finding hiding places,' said another.

'She'll be easy to find. We'll go back tomorrow.'

'You're absolutely right you're going back tomorrow,' General Burpintime said. 'We're going to destroy that palace. We're going to take it apart stone by stone until we find that girl. Then once we've found her, we're going to set fire to the place and throw every last one of them into that disgusting lake.'

'Hurrah!'

'Hooray!'

'Splendid!' the three soldiers called out.

'Now get off to bed. It's way beyond your

bedtime. We'll rest tonight and then tomorrow, at dawn, we'll completely destroy the palace.'

No, you won't, Beatrix thought as she climbed down from the tree. The Evil Army was going to be extremely disappointed. This was a night they would remember for the rest of their lives. For this was the night the **Wobblers** would break free from the stories and fairy tales told about them and come to life. And they were bigger, and scarier and angrier in real life than they were in any story. This was the night the **Wobblers** would tear apart the camp belonging to the Evil Army and scare the soldiers so much that half of them would wish they'd brought a spare pair of underpants.

24

Wobblers Attack!

'You were up there a long time. Did you see which tent belongs to General Burpintime?' Wilfred asked as Queen Beatrix climbed down the tree. He was talking very quickly and, even though it was dark, she could see his hands were shaking. He looked *very* nervous.

'Yes, it's right in the middle. It has silver stars all over it and a big flag on top. We'll have to wait a bit though, they're only just going to bed.'

'Were there any soldiers guarding it?'

'A couple, same as the other tents. But they're guarding the entrance. If we can find a way to sneak behind it, we can cut a hole at the back and climb through.'

'Very well. Let's get ready. Oi – can you put the outfit on Dog?'

'Will do,' Oi replied. Dog didn't look very happy about wearing a helmet with a couple of forks stuck into the top of it, but he remembered the game they had all played back in the hunting lodge and seemed to understand that he had to stay quiet and not bark or growl until they told him to.

'There we go,' Oi said. Dog looked very much like a dog wearing a helmet with forks stuck in it, and not very much like a *terrifying* creature that roamed the woods at night looking for children to gobble up. He stood up on his hind legs, which was the trick he always did when he wanted to get another fartinpant or biscuit.

As he stood the light from a campfire cast his shadow on a tree trunk. It was tall and crooked and seemed to have little stumpy arms and huge ears.

'Look,' Beatrix said, pointing at the shadow. They all stared as the spooky shape flickered and danced on the tree trunk.

'You know what?' Wilfred said. 'If we can get the shadows right, this *might* just work.'

'Good – I think we're ready,' Beatrix said. 'Let me just climb up the tree to check Burpintime has gone to bed.' She clambered up the tree and looked out over the camp. There were fewer fires now and the soldiers standing guard kept shifting about and looking over their shoulders. They looked nervous. They looked as if they didn't want to be guarding a camp on the edge of a forest full of Wobblers in the middle of the night.

Beatrix climbed down the tree. 'Everyone follow me,' she said. She crept forward slowly, lying flat on her belly, then waited behind a rock close to the camp. She threw a stone into the woods. It made a rustling sound.

'Who's there?' the nearest guard called out, walking towards where the sound had come from. He had taken out his sword. Beatrix, Oi and Wilfred slipped past him into the camp.

General Burpintime was fast asleep on a large camp bed in the middle of the tent. His uniform was folded neatly on a chair ready for the next day, with a fresh pair of socks and a very large pair of underpants next to them. His comfy slippers were under the chair and his boots were next to them. He had laid out his medals on a little bedside table in order of importance.

The medals were similar to Boy-Scout badges. There was a green one he'd been given for learning how to tie different knots. There was an orange one he'd been given for lighting a fire,

and there was a red one he'd been given for using
that fire to burn down people's houses (that one
was not like a Boy-Scout badge).

There was a black one with a skull and cross
bones that he'd been given for scaring small
children, a blue one he'd been given for swimming
ten metres (he could only do doggy paddle) and
a pink and white one he'd been awarded because

he could fit more marshmallows in his mouth than anyone else in the entire army.

Tomorrow morning his captain would pin them to his jacket so that once his army had finished destroying the palace and thrown everyone into the lake, he could walk around the ruins and show everyone what a brave soldier he was.

For now though, General Burpintime was fast asleep. His pillow was soft and fluffy and he dreamt he was sleeping on a giant marshmallow. His arms gripped it protectively, because in his dream **Wobblers** kept creeping into the tent to try and steal it. He tossed and he turned and he snored so loudly it sounded like he was playing the tuba.

'At least the noise of him snoring will cover up the sound of us creeping into the tent,' Beatrix whispered to Oi and Wilfred. She cut a hole in the canvas, then scrambled through the gap.

Oi, Dog and Wilfred followed quickly after her. They crouched behind General Burpintime's bed.

'OK,' Beatrix said, in a low voice. 'Wilfred, get some sparks flying and we'll light the torches. Oi and Dog, if you stand here the shadow will fall over there.' She pointed at the wall of the tent. 'Wilfred, are you ready?'

Wilfred nodded. He had moved a wooden crate behind General Burpintime's bed and was standing on it. The crate was covered by his long cape. Wilfred was already tall, and because of the crate he appeared even taller. As tall as a giant. The hood of his cape was pulled up but instead of his head underneath it, you could just about make out the stuffed head of a wild boar. The mouth was locked in a ferocious roar with sharp teeth glinting in the low light. It was extremely heavy and Wilfred had to stay very still to make sure it didn't fall off, but it was a truly terrifying sight.

If anything would convince General Burpintime that a Wobbler was in his tent, ready to eat him, it was Wilfred's disguise.

'Ready, Wilfred?' Beatrix whispered. He gave a thumbs up. 'Ready, Oi?' Beatrix said. Oi nodded. 'Ready, Dog?' Beatrix said. Dog wagged his tail. 'Excellent. Let's do this!'

What happened next happened *very quickly* indeed. Firstly, Beatrix leant over the general and whispered into his ear in a horrible, spooky voice:

'Wake up wake up – the **Wobblers** are here! Time to gobble you up, my dear!'

Then Wilfred blew a cloud of chalky soot into the general's eyes – just as he was waking up – at the same time waving a flaming torch in front of his face.

General Burpintime coughed and cried and looked more than a little horrified. On the wall of the tent were three silhouettes that moved jerkily in a strange dance, with hungry jaws that were snapping open and shut. One of them was howling in a most horrible way, a bloodcurdling howl, worse than a wolf that's trodden on a drawing pin.

'We are the **Wobblers** from deep in the Dark, Dark Woods,' Wilfred announced in his deepest voice.

'You are *not* welcome here. Leave this place before we chop you and your army into tiny pieces and make pies from your insides...' He pulled out a sword and flashed it this way and that in the way that he had seen soldiers do when they were practising for battle.

Meanwhile Oi and Dog and Beatrix kept up their funny dance and hoped General Burpintime would hurry up and leave. The disguises were extremely heavy and they weren't sure how long they could keep moving. Beatrix put her hand to her forehead as if plucking out an eye then threw a ball of mud across the room. It landed with a splat in the middle of General Burpintime's army uniform.

General Burpintime didn't move. Even the sight of the shadowy eyeball trick didn't wake him out of his trance. He was completely frozen with fear.

'Well?' Wilfred said. 'Can't you hear me? I command you and your army to leave.'

Burpintime still didn't move. 'If you don't leave I shall –' Wilfred looked around the room – he needed inspiration – 'I shall destroy all your medals. Including this one, for… swimming ten metres. Doggy paddle? That's not much of a medal.' He couldn't help saying this, even though he wasn't sure it was something the Chief Wobbler would really say. He picked up the medal with his sword and flicked it onto the floor.

At that moment, two guards burst into the tent.

'Are you all right, general? You're not having one of your nightmares again are you?' they said.

The tent was full of smoke. It was hard to see what was going on. The general looked at his two guards, and seeing them seemed to unfreeze him.

He jumped up, shouted,

'RUUUUUUUUUUUNNNNNNNNN!'

and ran out of the tent without even pausing to put on his slippers. As he ran he shouted, *'Wobblers! Wobblers! Run for your lives – they want to make you into pies!'*

The two guards looked at the strange figure of Wilfred the Wise, almost as tall as the tent was high, swaying to and fro, his glassy eyes and hungry mouth looking even more glassy and hungry in the flickering light. They looked at the shadows that danced around him, then they took one look at each other and ran out of the tent as fast as they could.

25

The Evil Army Runs Away

Beatrix hid behind the general's bed. Wilfred, Oi and Dog did the same. From outside the tent came all sorts of sounds. The sound of soldiers shouting in confusion, the sound of bumps and knocks and scrapes, trips and falls and fear. Soon the whole army was awake and running in a hundred different directions at once. Soldiers tripped over the ropes holding up the tents, tents fell on fires, fires grew bigger and their flickering flames escaped upwards into the trees.

Then, in a matter of minutes, all was silent. All that could be heard was the crackle of fire and the rush of the wind through the empty tents. Beatrix poked her head out of the tent to see what was going on. All the enemy soldiers had run away. The camp was deserted. Fires were burning and the air was heavy with smoke.

Wow, she thought. Did we really do all this?

She slipped back inside. 'They're gone,' she said. 'They've all run away – it worked!'

Wilfred took off his mask, gasping for air.

'Fantastic. I must say it was getting hard to breathe in there.' He opened the tent and looked outside. 'Wait a minute,' he muttered, as he caught sight of something – a strange shape moving behind one of the tents. The shape moved so quickly he wasn't sure if he'd seen anything at all. It definitely wasn't a soldier – it was too small. It looked like a weasel crossed with a goblin, or maybe even a goblin crossed with a weasel. Wilfred shook his head. Wobblers didn't exist... *did they?*

'We need to get back to the palace,' Beatrix said. 'I want to tell Uncle Ivan that the Evil Army has gone. It looks like they left in such a hurry that they didn't take any of their weapons! Uncle Ivan will want to chase them through the woods and make sure they don't come back.' She pushed past Wilfred and ran out of the tent, with Oi and Dog following behind her.

It wasn't long before Beatrix, Oi, Dog and Wilfred were standing outside the gates of the palace. Beatrix banged impatiently on the doors and called out for them to be opened.

'Let me in! Let me in! It's me, Beatrix!'

The guards looked down from the two towers on either side of the gates at the little girl and the boy and the dog and Wilfred. They were still half-disguised as Wobblers, with bits of armour and twigs and leaves stuck to their clothes.

'We spent all day yesterday fighting those Evil Soldiers, and only just managed to keep them out of the palace. I'm not about to let in a bunch of hungry-looking Wobblers,' called out one of the guards.

'But we're not Wobblers!' Beatrix replied.

'How do I know you're not a Wobbler? You look like a Wobbler,' said another guard.

'You know I'm not a Wobbler because Wobblers don't exist!' she shouted back, a little more angrily than she'd meant.

'That's what you'd say if you were a Wobbler,' the guard said, as if he'd caught her in a clever trick.

'Oh for goodness' sake,' Beatrix said. 'Just send for my uncle, Ivan the Vicious. Or you'll find out why he's called Vicious.'

The guards looked at one another. If the girl really was Ivan's niece, then they would be in serious, Ivan-shaped trouble if they didn't do what she asked.

'All right. Wait there. And don't do no Wobbler magic on us,' the guard said.

Beatrix wished she had some Wobbler magic to open the gates and make the man hurry up. Oi looked up at the palace, which loomed high above the gates.

'Nice house,' he said. 'Looks big. Must be able to fit a lot of cows and sheep inside.'

'It's mainly people. And I've only actually been in ten rooms. They never let me see the rest of the place.'

'That's strange.'

'It was to keep me safe,' Beatrix said.

'Didn't work very well, did it?'

'Not when you have an evil aunt who's quite happy to betray you so she can buy another pair of golden underpants,' Beatrix said.

Oi laughed. 'You mean all this happened because she wanted a new pair of pants?'

'I think it was the gold she wanted. She's not that fussy what shape it comes in.'

The gates of the palace swung open. Uncle Ivan was charging down the great stone steps of the palace into the courtyard. He picked Beatrix up and gave her the biggest hug he'd ever given her. (In fact, this was the *first* hug he had ever given her.)

'You're back! I'm so glad you're safe,' he said, his gruff voice sounding even more gruff than usual.

'We dressed as **Wobblers** and scared off the army,' Wilfred said. 'It was all Beatrix's idea. *A brilliant plan.*'

'General Burpintime ran faster than I've ever seen anyone run in my life,' Beatrix said. 'And his army followed him into the woods. You must hurry. Chase them far away and bring back their weapons.'

'Brilliant,' Ivan said, 'quite brilliant. I always knew you'd make a fantastic general – you were always so good at playing with my toy soldiers.'

'Toy soldiers?' Beatrix said.

Ivan smiled. 'Model soldiers for extremely important war gaming,' he said, as he put her down.

'Where's Esmerelda? I overheard soldiers from the Evil Army when they were in my room trying to find me. They said she'd told them where I was and given them a map and everything.'

Ivan stared at her. He looked shocked.

'Which soldiers? What do you mean? I know Esmerelda can be strict, and perhaps she is a little quick to splash gold paint in people's eyes and chop off heads, and she is called "Terrible", but she wouldn't do that. She couldn't. You're her niece. She *swore* to look after you!'

'That's what they said. She gave them a map. She told them where I was. I promise, Uncle Ivan. I wouldn't make it up. Hurry after them and you can ask them.'

Uncle Ivan's eyebrows drew close together. He looked *very* upset and confused.

'I can't believe it. I thought she must have left with you, to look after you and make sure you were OK.' He ran a heavy hand through his hair. 'If she's not with you then I don't know where she is. She must've hidden somewhere. I just can't believe she would have betrayed you to the Evil Army.'

'No, but sometimes people do things you don't expect, don't they? Like not telling me I'm *actually* Queen Beatrix?' Beatrix said, accusingly.

'Ah yes – I was going to tell you soon... soonish. When you were older. We'll discuss later, I promise. First I'm going to chase the Evil Army far from the Kingdom of Morden with one hundred of my best men!' he said.

Ivan climbed up onto his horse and it reared up dramatically on its hind legs and let out a terrific '*Neeeeiiiggghhhhhh!*' He charged out of the palace gates, the horse's hooves clattering on the stones as if a giant had dropped a box of boulders.

'Impressive,' Oi said. 'Does he know he's still in his pyjamas?'

'I doubt it,' Beatrix said. 'I'm not sure if he even remembered his sword. Or knives. Anyway, it's almost sunrise and it's been a very long night. How about we see if the cooks can rustle up some breakfast?'

26

The Great Feast

In Beatrix's dining room a great feast was underway. Everyone from soldiers to servants was helping themselves to the food, including Mrs Fartinpants, who gave Beatrix an enormous and *very* squashy hug. (For once, the food wasn't too bad. No nettle jelly, no cauliflower soup with old socks and no sprouts – just lots and lots of fartinpants, tasty bean stew and, as a special treat, meat balls squashed flat so they would fit perfectly

into bread rolls. The cook, Mr McDonald, called these 'squashed-meat-ball-and-bread-rolls'. It was to be at least a thousand years before they were renamed 'hamburgers'.)

Oi had *never* seen such a magnificent meal. The food he ate in his field always seemed to taste of mud. It looked a bit like mud too. Sometimes it probably was mud, but he was usually so hungry he didn't care. None of the food here tasted like mud, and Oi was eating even faster than Dog, who could eat three fartinpants in one mouthful, and almost as fast as Wilfred. Wilfred might as well have been performing a magic trick, the way he made everything on his plate disappear into his belly.

Ivan the Vicious had returned in time for the feast. They'd captured all the weapons the Evil Army had left and brought them back to the castle, and chased away all the Evil Soldiers that were lost in the woods, with a special weapon known as the Tumbler. It looked a bit like a paddle with a very long handle. You raced your horse up to the Evil Soldier and as you sped past you swung the paddle to give them a terrific *thwack* on the bottom. The soldier tumbled forward and you got extra points if they did a somersault.

Before he sat down to eat, he wanted to find Esmerelda, so he and Beatrix looked high and low for her all around the palace. Beatrix was astonished at the size of the place. It was very strange seeing all the rooms she'd never seen before. There were endless corridors and towers and staircases. There were rooms within rooms and secret passages all over the place. Most of the walls were covered in shiny gold paint and all the mirrors made it seem as if every turning turned in four different directions at once. It felt like an enormous maze. Beatrix had to run to keep up with Uncle Ivan just so she didn't get lost.

They tried all seventeen of the enormous dressing rooms where Esmerelda stored her collection of golden robes, but she wasn't in *any* of them. They tried the counting room, where Esmerelda counted her gold, and they tried her personal treasure store, but there was no Esmerelda and there wasn't much treasure left in there either.

'It's no use,' Ivan said. 'She must have escaped.'

'What about the story room? Esmerelda loved that room. Sometimes I'd find her sitting there, listening to stories without me. Let's try it. We've looked *everywhere* else.'

Beatrix led the way down the sloping passageway and Ivan kicked the door open with a heavy boot. The room was empty. The chairs were arranged in a semi-circle in front of the stage, with the big, spinning story wheel on one side. The stage was set up to look like a forest at night, with a painting of the moon on the far wall, spindly trees in the centre and leaves all over the floor.

'What's that?' Ivan said, pointing at the floor. A shiny shape had caught the light.

Beatrix reached down and picked it up.

'A gold coin,' she said, holding it up to the light. 'Unusual for Esmerelda to leave a gold coin lying around.'

'Unless she was in a hurry,' Ivan replied.

'Let's try the trap door the storytellers use. Maybe she's down there, hiding under the stage.'

Beatrix brushed away the leaves from the centre of the stage to reveal the trap door. Ivan pulled hard but it wouldn't open. He **stamped** his feet – but it still wouldn't give way.

'Are you in there, Esmerelda? If you are, you better come out now!' he shouted. There was no answer. He stormed out of the room and came back a few moments later with an enormous axe.

'Last chance!' he shouted.

Beatrix stepped back as Uncle Ivan swung the heavy axe into the wooden floor. The wood splintered and split beneath the weight of it. He swung it again and the wood cracked, a hole opening up. Beatrix peered through the gap.

'What's down there?' Ivan said. 'Can you see anything?'

Beatrix crouched low. 'Nope. Can't see anything. It's too dark. I can *smell* something though. Goodness. It's pretty whiffy down there.'

Beatrix backed away as Ivan swung the axe once more and the trap door gave way. He climbed down. Beatrix lit a candle and passed it to him, then climbed down herself.

The trap door had been hiding a rather smelly

room with lots of pots of gold paint, no toilet and a huge pile of gold coins. There was no sign of Esmerelda.

'She must have been hiding here during the battle,' Ivan said. 'And now she's escaped.' He gritted his teeth and threw a knife at the wall, making a funny 'Nnrrggghhhh' sort of noise. 'I'll find her. She *must* be punished. I still can't believe she would be so mean. Maybe all the gold poisoned her brain like, like...'

'Like poison?'

'Yes, exactly like poison,' he said.

Beatrix pulled the knife out of the wall and passed it back to him, handle first.

'You know what?' Beatrix said. 'I'm not sure we *need* to do anything to punish her. She loves gold so much that having so much of it is almost like a punishment anyway. It certainly doesn't make her happy. In a way, I feel sorry for her.' Beatrix thought about that for a moment, then

thought about the Evil Army attacking the castle.
'Sorry – and INCREDIBLY ANGRY,' she said.
'But anyway, today is a time for partying and
feasting and eating lots of yummy squashed-meat-
ball-and-bread-rolls, so let's go and join Oi and
Wilfred before they eat everything themselves.'

27

Later That Night

The party continued into the afternoon, the evening and on into the night. Oi and Beatrix stayed up well past their bedtime – in fact, no one told them to go to bed at all that night.

When darkness fell and it was very late, Wilfred the Wise, Beatrix, Oi, Dog and Ivan left the party and went to sit around the fire in the garden room, toasting marshmallows. Beatrix told Ivan all about her adventures – how she'd escaped from the castle with Wilfred's help, how Oi had shown her the way to the hunting lodge and explained about the curse and how they'd scared the socks off General Burpintime with their Wobbler dance.

'But there are *still* some questions I'd like answers to,' Beatrix said, looking up at the stars. 'Wilfred told me I was a queen and that the Evil Army attacked the palace because they wanted to kidnap me. Oi told me that there's some sort of curse, which explains why the Evil Army is afraid of me. But I still don't know the whole story,' she added, softly.

Ivan rubbed his eyes and sighed. He leant forward, looking deep into the fire. 'These are good questions, but I'm not sure I will be able to answer them all. I'll tell you what I know,' he said. In his hand he held his knife – he twisted the blade between his fingers then put it down. He took a pipe from his pocket, pressed some tobacco into it and lit it.

'It was a bleak winter day, almost two and a half horse years ago…' He took a long puff on his pipe and blew a thick cloud of smoke out into the night sky.

'What's a horse year?' Beatrix asked.

'It's four human years. This happened almost ten years ago, so it's about two and a half horse years,' Ivan replied.

'Well let's just say it's ten years ago then,' Beatrix said. 'I've never heard of a horse year.'

'It's like a dog year, but shorter,' Oi said. 'There are seven dog years for every human year – ain't that right, Dog?'

Dog looked up and wagged his tail.

'Can we just get on with the story?' Wilfred said. 'You were saying that it was a bleak winter day ten years ago…'

'That's right,' Ivan said. 'One of the coldest winters we've ever had – the ground was frozen hard as stone. The lake was frozen hard as stone too. Everyone was frozen hard as…' He scratched his head, trying to think of a good way of describing how cold everyone felt. He didn't have much practice telling stories. Hard as a diamond? No, too shiny. Hard as a nail? No, too small. Hard as a coconut? Definitely not, they hadn't even been discovered yet. 'Everyone was frozen hard as stone,' he said at last. 'It was *freezing*. Freezing cold. I was in the north tower.'

'Sitting on the loo?' Beatrix said.

'No!' Ivan replied. 'I was practising throwing my new knife. Esmerelda had given me it for Christmas. It was such a *wonderful* surprise.'

Wilfred was about to say something about how Esmerelda always gave Ivan a knife for Christmas, but he thought better of it. They'd never get to the end of the story.

'What did you see?' Oi said.

'On the horizon was a carriage being driven fast over the icy ground with four riders racing

alongside it. They wore blue and
gold armour that shone like
jewels against the white snow.
The rider at the front carried
a flag with your family crest
on it,' Ivan said, pointing his pipe at Beatrix.
'They sped down the hill – half sliding, half
galloping – and raced all the way up to the gates,
as if an army of Wobblers was behind them.'

'*Was* there an army of Wobblers behind
them?' Wilfred asked.

'No. Course not,' Ivan said. 'No one's ever *seen*
a Wobbler, have they? They arrived at the palace
gates, we let them in and they drove across the
courtyard right up to the entrance to the palace.'

'What was in the carriage?' Beatrix asked. 'Was
it my father and mother?'

Ivan shook his head. 'No. They weren't in the
carriage. Inside the carriage were two very big
soldiers, a big box of toys and a very small nurse

holding tightly onto a tiny baby. That baby was you. The nurse wouldn't come out of the carriage until we'd made sure no one was in the courtyard. They didn't want anyone to see you. You were *a secret.*'

'So my mother and father weren't in the carriage?' Beatrix said, feeling a little sad.

'No, they weren't. But one of the soldiers gave us a letter with the seal of the House of Beluga stamped across it, which is where your family comes from. Your father and mother rule the lands between the Very High Volcanoes and the Sea of Sinking Ships.'

'That sounds like quite a dangerous place to live,' Beatrix said.

'It is, but the walls of their castle are high and strong, and there's lots of gold in the mountains.'

'What did the letter say?' Beatrix asked.

'The letter said that they were sending you to live with your aunt Esmerelda, in secret, for twenty years.'

'Twenty years?' Beatrix said. She couldn't believe her mother and father, whoever they were, would have just given her away like that.

'Yes. Twenty years,' Ivan said.

'Why?' Oi said. 'Seems like a very funny thing to do. She'd be all grown up by the time they saw her again.'

'Well, your parents told you to guard a field of mud,' Beatrix said, a little defensively. She didn't want anyone saying anything bad about her parents without knowing the full story.

'Do you want me to continue?' Ivan asked. For a moment he sounded more like an angry teacher than a fierce general (although sometimes there isn't much difference).

'Of course,' Beatrix said. 'What was in the letter?'

'The letter came with strict instructions – we had to memorise it, then burn it. I was only allowed to reveal what it said to you and Aunt Esmerelda. Now, if I remember, the letter said…' Ivan frowned, looked up at the stars, searching for wherever he'd put the memory. He cleared his throat. He spoke slowly and carefully.

28

The Letter

'Dear Esmerelda and Ivan,

We write to you on a matter of great importance.

We have made the hardest decision we have ever had to make, a decision that has brought great sadness upon us, and upon our kingdom.

Our daughter, Queen Beatrix, was born eight weeks ago. On the night of her birth a shooting star crashed into the mountainside that surrounds the castle. It opened up a huge hole in the mountain; earth and rocks were thrown about; trees crushed as if they were no more than twigs.

The Wise Men and the Wizards said that the falling star was a sign. There were ancient stories of a child born on a winter's night as a great star fell. They said this child would have special powers, the secret powers of the stars themselves. They said she would be in danger, terrible danger, as long as she lived in our castle, from all who were jealous of her power.

Of course we didn't believe them, but news of the shooting star and the birth of the child travelled fast. Soon people arrived at the castle, asking if it was true, asking if a child had been born who had the power of the stars, who could control the seas, who could command the beasts and creatures of the forests. They crowded outside the gates of the castle. More and more of them, every day, demanding to see the baby.

Soldiers from the Evil Army were seen amongst them. There were spies in the castle. We had no choice. We had to get Beatrix to safety and so we took the decision to send her away and tell everyone the child had died.

My darling Beatrix, if and when you have the chance to read this letter, or hear its contents, you were sent away in the middle of the night as if you'd never been born, with six of my best soldiers to keep you safe, to be looked after by your aunt Esmerelda and your uncle Ivan, the bravest soldier I have ever known...'

Ivan stopped and frowned. Wilfred, Oi and Beatrix stared at him, waiting for him to continue.

'There wasn't anything else. Just blurry marks on the page,' he said. 'From the tears.'

'Did they ever come and see me? In secret?' Beatrix asked. 'I would, if I was them I would have made sure I did.'

'Your mother came on your second birthday. It was a long and dangerous journey. She had to wear a disguise. She was very happy to see you but it almost broke her heart. She didn't want to leave, but she never came again. The pain was *too much*.'

Beatrix felt tears well up and roll down her cheeks like big salty raindrops.

'What's she like, my mother?' she said.

'Very beautiful,' Ivan said. 'Tall and strong with long dark hair. Curly, like yours. Kind to the people she rules over and generous with gold. Not a bit like her sister, Esmerelda.'

'And my father?'

Ivan frowned. 'He's small, but fierce. And he's very funny – he's always telling jokes. What's that one he told me… I'll remember it in a minute, hang on…' Ivan cleared his throat. 'Why did the beach wee? Because the sea blushed!'

Everyone looked very confused, including Dog.

'No, that's not it,' Ivan said. 'That doesn't make any sense. Why was there seaweed on the beach, because… Aargh. No. Anyway. He was very funny. Trust me.'

'Do you mean, why did the beach blush? Because the sea weed?' Beatrix said.

'Yes! That's it,' Ivan said. 'You're just like him. Always telling jokes. He's funnier, though.'

'He's had more practice than me!' Beatrix replied.

The four of them stared into the fire.

'I think I shall go and see them,' Beatrix said. 'I want to tell them what's happened. The Evil Army know I'm alive. Esmerelda betrayed us. I don't need to stay in hiding *any more*. Besides, if I stay at the palace I'm sure they'll attack again. The Evil Army won't give in, not if they think the curse is going to come true.'

Wilfred the Wise looked worried. 'The journey will be very dangerous. They'll try and find you. You need to be careful.'

'But she's got special powers,' Oi said. 'And me to help her.'

'Oh, I don't believe in any of that nonsense about special powers,' Beatrix said. 'That's just stories, made up by people who can't remember something properly. Then it turns into a legend and just because there's a falling star people think something magic has happened, but it hasn't.

Sometimes things just fall down. Like stars – or like Wilfred, when he tried to do a flying spell.' She looked at Oi. 'You're far more help to me than any special power I'm supposed to have. Without you, I'd have been eaten by wolves before we even found the hunting lodge.'

'Well, can't you at least just see if you've got some power over beasts? Try telling Dog to do something,' Oi said.

Beatrix looked at Dog. 'Sit!' she said. Dog sat.

'There you are!' Oi exclaimed. 'He won't sit for anyone.'

'Nonsense,' Beatrix said. 'And I don't have power over the sea either. Right now I'm thinking about a huge wave crashing on a beach and soaking all the fishermen. I guarantee that's *not* happening.'

She yawned. 'I think it's time for sleep. I feel like I could stay in bed for at least a week.'

'If you do travel to Beluga to find your parents I would also like to go with you,' Wilfred said.

'We could travel together in disguise, as a family of magicians. No one would suspect a thing. I'll even teach you a few tricks.'

'Of course you can come,' Beatrix said, yawning again. 'We'll make plans tomorrow. Oi and Dog should come too. We'll need their help. That's if Uncle Ivan doesn't need us here for anything.'

'No. You should go. See your father and mother. We'll be busy fixing the palace.'

Beatrix stood and looked up at the night sky. The clouds had disappeared and the stars seemed to be shining more brightly than usual. Wilfred looked up, following her gaze. So did Oi, and Dog, and Ivan. At that moment a shooting star sped across the sky. It seemed to *pause* and hover above them, as if it was waiting for them, then it raced eastwards.

'Funny,' Ivan said. 'Looks like that star is going to Beluga. That's the way you go. Eastwards. A dangerous journey, and no mistake,' he said.

'We'll pack you an extra set of knives.'

'And some fartinpants,' Oi said.

'And lots of fartinpants,' Ivan replied.

The End
(sort of)

And this is where we shall end the first book in the life of Queen Beatrix. With plans made real, some secrets revealed and a dangerous quest for the young queen to find her mother and father.

Well, almost. You're *probably* wondering what happened to Esmerelda. And, of course, General Burpintime.

As Ivan, Beatrix, Oi and Wilfred looked up at the stars, Esmerelda was crawling along a tunnel deep under the palace, clutching a bag of gold in her hand. The walls were wet and muddy, and so was she. She was shaking with anger and muttering very rude words under her breath. Things had not turned out how she wanted.

'Stupid sister, making me look after her stupid daughter. None of this would have happened if I hadn't been made to look after Beatrix.'

Like most people who bring disaster on themselves, Esmerelda blamed everyone else. She was planning revenge, even though she was the one who had done wrong. She was planning to go to the Land Beyond the Woods. To join the Evil Army. To tell them where her sister kept all her gold – and to help them to steal it.

The thought of all that lovely shiny gold kept her going as she crawled through the dirt and the mud. It kept her going as she swam across the stinky lake, and it kept her going as she stole a horse from the village and raced away into the night.

While Esmerelda was making her escape, General Burpintime was waiting outside the chamber of the Evil Overlord. (Evil was his first name, but generally he preferred to be called Mr Overlord – it's not nice to always be called Evil.) Mr Overlord was the supreme boss, the commander of the Evil Army, the man who had ordered General Burpintime to kidnap Queen Beatrix. The man he had failed. He felt like he'd been sent to see the headmaster. He was so nervous he was eating marshmallows by the handful.

If watches had been invented, he'd have been checking his watch every few seconds.

Finally, the door opened. He was told to enter. What followed wasn't exactly a telling-off, it was more like an earthquake or an explosion or being in the centre of a thunderstorm. It was the *angriest* thing General Burpintime had ever heard, and he was no stranger to anger.

Burpintime tried to explain about the Wobblers, but this just increased the volume of the angry shouting. Somewhere amongst all that anger he thought he heard something about finding Beatrix and bringing her to the Evil Overlord. And something about him being chopped into a hundred pieces if he didn't do this. And something about her power getting stronger and stronger as she grew older.

But the funny thing was, all the time he was being shouted at, all he could think was that the Evil Overlord was actually pretty lazy. After all, it was a lot easier to shout at someone for getting it wrong than to do it right yourself.

That was the problem with Evil Overlords. They liked to shout but they didn't actually do much to help. And if you didn't do what they wanted they'd just tell someone to chop you into a hundred pieces. Not for the first time, General Burpintime wondered if he should have chosen a different job. Playing the recorder, for instance, or making marshmallows. Or maybe he should have just stuck to doing doggy paddle. He was getting quite good at it. Next up was his Twenty Metre badge.

Oh, one final thing. As Esmerelda was crawling through her tunnel and General Burpintime was getting a major telling-off, something *very strange* was happening. In a distant land on a faraway shore, three fishermen were looking out at a perfectly calm sea. All of a sudden, a huge wave appeared on the horizon. It rolled towards the beach, getting bigger and bigger – *so big*, it picked up boats and fishing nets and pieces of driftwood, till finally it crashed over the fishermen, soaking them to the skin.

'Well, I've never seen anything like that before,' one of them was heard to say.

Another scratched his head. '*Very unusual* at this time of year,' he said. '*Very unusual indeed.*'

Quiz

How much can you remember about Beatrix the Bold and her adventures? Test yourself with the quiz below!

1. What does Uncle Ivan call a fly with no legs?

2. Wilfred the Wise teaches Beatrix maths, but how many numbers does he think there are?

3. What did Esmerelda give Ivan for his birthday three years ago?

4. What does Beatrix use for a hat when she's planning her escape from the palace?

5. What is General Burpintime's first name?

6. How old is a Wobbler when its first eye falls out?

7. How does General Burpintime tell his soldiers to stop attacking?

8. What kind of sandwich does the Evil Army soldier store under his helmet?

9. Where was Esmerelda hiding in the palace?

Answers: 1. Dead, 2. 500, 3. A knife and a knife case, 4. A pair of pants, 5. Alfred, 6. Seven years old, 7. He blows into a recorder, 8. A cheese and onion sandwich, 9. Under a trap door in the story room

How to Cook Fartinpants

1. Make a fire. You will need:
A garden, wood, stones, a responsible adult, fire

Go to a nearby forest to collect the wood and stones. Don't go to the woods at night. It's spooky and Wobblers might be about. Place the stones in a circle in your garden. Put the wood in the middle. Ask a grown-up to start the fire. If they say they don't know how, tell them they are not a proper grown-up and get them to Google it.

2. Make the fartinpants. You will need:
A pan, 110 grams of flour, two eggs, a pint of milk, a big bowl for mixing, a responsible adult (you can use the same one who started the fire as long as they're not too burnt).

Mix the eggs, milk and flour in a bowl with a whisk. Tell the grown-up to pour a good dollop of the mixture into a hot pan. Make sure you add a little bit of butter into the pan first. If it burns, the pan's too hot. Flick or toss the fartinpants over once they start bubbling, so that they're cooked on both sides.

3. Eat the fartinpants. You will need:
Golden syrup, a big mouth, your hands

Spoon lots of golden syrup onto the fartinpants, grab with both hands and shove into your mouth. Remember to put some in your pockets for later in case you need supplies for an adventure.

Make Your Own
Pillow-case Dress!

To do this you will need:
1. A pillow case
2. Scissors
3. String
4. A pillow-case shop (optional)

1. If you want to use a new pillow case go to a shop that sells pillow cases, and pick out a plain pillow case. If not, take one off your mum or dad's bed. Don't use your own, or you won't have a pillow case any more!

2. Cut a hole on either side for your arms.

3. Cut a hole at the top big enough for your head to go through. If the hole is too small, your head won't go through, and you'll have made a ghost costume instead.

Note: Scissors can be dangerous. If you think you might end up with less than four fingers after doing this, please ask a grown-up to help. Be warned – they will spend at least an hour looking for a pair of scissors and get very grumpy when they can't find them.

4. Tie the string around your waist to make a belt. If you want the full Beatrix the Bold look, put a pair of pants on your head too!

How to Make an Xbox
(out of mud and wood)

To do this you will need:
1. Mud
2. Wood
3. £300

Take the mud and wood and stick it together in the most imaginative way possible. When the mud dries, write the word 'Picasso' on it in black pen. Go on the *Antiques Roadshow* and tell the expert it's a sculpture your great-great aunt gave you. She was given it by Picasso many years ago. Sell the sculpture for £300. Buy an Xbox.

Acknowledgements

Many thanks to everyone who helped bring Beatrix into the world: my agent Chloe and the team at Northbank Talent, my editor, Georgia and everyone at Piccadilly Press, Cherie Zamazing for her wonderful illustrations and cover design, Louis for listening carefully to each re-draft, remembering tiny details that I'd forgotten and letting me know which pant jokes are funny, Penelope for energy and inspiration and Mary-Anne for bearing with me as I spend a large amount of time fretting over whether I've included too many pant jokes.

Don't miss Beatrix's next adventures!

Beatrix the Bold has already averted her own kidnapping and fought off an Evil Army. Now she needs to find her long-lost parents, and fend off her villainous aunt Esmerelda. She just has to cross a vast kingdom to get there and save a bunch of children from deadly peril while confronting a terrifying dragon... Easy, right? But when you're Beatrix the Bold and you've got Oi the Boy, Dog the Dog and Wilfred the Wise by your side, you can do *anything*...